A HISTORY OF ENGLISH FORESTRY

A HISTORY OF
ENGLISH FORESTRY

N.D.G. JAMES

Basil Blackwell · Oxford

© N.D.G. James 1981

First published in 1981 by
Basil Blackwell Publisher
108 Cowley Road Oxford OX4 1JF England

British Library Cataloguing in Publication Data
James, Noel David Glaves
   A history of English forestry.
   1. Forests and forestry — England — History
   I. Title
   634.9'0942   SD179

   ISBN 0-631-12495-0

Set in 11 on 13 pt Vladimir by Pioneer Associates. Printed in Great Britain

FOREWORD

Sir Marcus Worsley, Bt *President of the Royal Forestry Society of England, Wales and Northern Ireland*

The Society is proud to be associated with this important book. Written by a past President of the Society who has long been one of the country's outstanding foresters, it is certain to be regarded as a reference book and a mine of information about English forestry.

Readers will reflect, I think, that in the politics of forestry little changes. One hundred years ago when the Society was founded there were already many people calling for an active forestry policy. The Society provided a focus and forum for them. There were a number of forward looking official reports. Yet no major steps were taken until the nation was shocked out of its apathy by the trauma of the First World War.

Again today there is no lack of information, private and governmental about the shortage of timber to come. Yet again too little is being done. There is lacking a clear and positive Government policy. The cheap imports, which saved us in the last hundred years and more from the consequences of our reckless deforestation over previous centuries, simply will not be there to save us in the future.

Mr James stresses also the debt which English forestry owes to imports, both of species and skills. The Society's primary task is to spread, through its meetings and its journal, knowledge of the best practice and of new ideas. Much of this work takes place on a local level but much also consists of foreign study and travel. This book shows how much we have learnt, and of course can still learn.

Forestry in England may not be a big industry, but its contribution to the nation's economy is a vital one. As Mr James says in his concluding paragraph: 'Of all the four sources of energy — wood, coal, oil and mineral gas — wood alone can be renewed by man.' That is challenge enough for the foresters of today.

To the
Royal Forestry Society
of
England, Wales and Northern Ireland
in Commemoration of its Centenary
1882-1982

CONTENTS

ILLUSTRATIONS

PREFACE AND ACKNOWLEDGEMENTS

This book covers a period of approximately nine hundred years from the Normans to the present day and, as the title indicates, it is primarily concerned with the development of forestry in England. However, it also includes events which concern Great Britain as a whole and, in a few cases, matters which are Welsh or Scottish in origin. I hope that this book will be found useful, not only as a guide to earlier times but also as a record of the expansion of modern forestry during the twentieth century.

Blakemore House, Kersbrook, Budleigh Salterton, Devon   N.D.G.J.

March 1980

ACKNOWLEDGEMENTS

During the course of writing this book, I have received a considerable amount of assistance and information from many individuals, libraries, publishers and institutions and I wish to thank the following for their invaluable help.

Messrs Edward Arnold (Publishers) Ltd for permission to quote from *English Estate Forestry* by A.C. Forbes; The Trustees of the Bedford Estates for permission to reproduce a map from the Estate Wood Books; Messrs Ernest Benn, Ltd for permission to quote from *Timber at War* by Frank H. House; Mr O.N. Blatchford, Principal Research Communications Officer, Forestry Commission; Mr R. Bryant; Colonel D.A. Campbell, OBE, Mr. J. Campbell, Miss A.V. Child, Mr A.C.T. Cochrane, the County Archivists for Cumbria and Northumberland; the City or County Librarians for Avon, Carlisle, Cumbria, Derbyshire, Exeter, Hereford, Northumberland, North Yorkshire, Salop, Wiltshire and Windsor; Mrs C.W. Collins, Librarian, Forestry Commission; the Editor, *Country Life,* for permission to use material from an article on the Gunby Hall Tree Book which was the first published source of information on the subject; Mr E.F. Craggs; Dr A.M. Davidson; Mr J.W. Davis, MBE; Mrs M. Dick, Secretary of The Institute of Foresters; Messrs Dixon & Sons for permission to photograph a trawler which they were building; Dollar Air Services Ltd, for providing a photograph of a helicopter; Mr C.R. Elrington, General Editor of the Victoria County Histories for permission to quote from them; Messrs Eyre & Spottiswoode (Publishers) Ltd for permission to quote from an article entitled 'The Dialogus de Scaccario' by D.C. Douglas and G.W. Greenaway which appeared in *English Historical Documents,* Vol. II, 1953; The Forestry Commission for permission to quote from a large number of the Commission's publications and to use two photographs; The Friends of Salisbury Cathedral for permission to quote from *The Sarum Magna Carta* by Dr Elsie Smith; Mr D.P. Graham; Mr R.M. Gard; Mr R.S. Glenn; The Hamlyn Publishing Group Ltd for permission to quote from the *War Memoirs of David Lloyd George*; Mr R.H.B. Hammersley, MVO; Mr J. Hardcastle; Mr R.M. Harley; Mr E.H.M. Harris, Director of The Royal Forestry Society of England, Wales and Northern Ireland; Mr Richard Harrison; Mr R.H. Hide; Mrs A.M. Howe; Mr B.N. Howell; The Institute of Agricultural History and Museum of English Rural Life, Reading University, for permission to use three photographs; the Librarian of the Institute of Royal Engineers; Mr P.S. Leathart, MBE, Editor of *The Quarterly Journal of Forestry* for permission to make use of many extracts and quotations; Mr E.R. Lloyd; The Longmans Group Ltd for permission to quote from *English Farming Past and Present* by Lord Ernle; Mrs D.B. Lunt; Mr Russell Meiggs; Mrs A. Millar; The National Trust; Mr P.W.W. Ninnes; Major P.C. Ormrod, M.C; Oxford University Press for permission to quote from *The Concise Oxford Dictionary of English Place-Names* by Eilert Ekwall, *The Shorter Oxford English Dictionary* revised and edited by C.T. Onions and *The Disappearance of the Small Landowner* by A.H. Johnson; The Phaidon Press Ltd for permission to use a photograph of part of the Bayeux Tapestry; Mr R. Phillips; the Editor of *Punch* for permission to reproduce a cartoon entitled *Afforestation's Artful Aid*; Mr A.G. Pyman, MBE; Mr A. Qvist; Mr A.O. Reardon, Editor of *Forestry and British Timber*; Major-General T.A. Richardson, CB, MBE, Editor of *Timber Grower*; The Royal Agricultural Society of England; The Royal Bath and West and Southern Counties Society; The Royal Society of Arts; Her Majesty's Stationery Office for permission to quote from *Home Timber Production 1939-1945* by Russell Meiggs; The Selden Society for permission to quote from *Select Pleas of the Forest* by G.J. Turner; Mr Jonathan Smith for permission to use a photograph of a traction engine and timber carriage; Mrs S.M. Stirling, Librarian of The Devon and Exeter Institution; Mr M.J.S. Turner; Lieutenant-Colonel P.R. Thomas; Mr Bruce Urquhart; The Victoria and Albert Museum; Professor J.M. Wallace-Hadrill, FBA; Messrs Frederick Warne (Publishers) Ltd for permission to quote from *Deer, Hare and Otter Hunting* being Vol. XXII of The Lonsdale Library; Mr E.R. Wheatley-Hubbard; Lieutenant-Commander P.C. Whitlock, MBE, RN, formerly Commanding Officer HMS *Victory*; Mr W.O. Wittering for permission to use an old print; and Lieutenant-Colonel J.L. Yeatman, DL.

PART ONE

THE MEDIEVAL FORESTS

EARLY DEVELOPMENT
AND LAWS   1

INTRODUCTION

In some respects, history can be compared to a river following a winding course which, instead of finding its ultimate outlet in the sea, flows on interminably towards the distant future. It is made up of a perpetually moving stream of events and, like a river, it cannot be divided into clear-cut sections since the changes and developments which make up history do not exist as single moments of time but flow on so that they overlap and merge one into another. Nevertheless, when considering the course of events it is convenient and helpful to adopt some division of time whether it is a king's reign, a major war, the span of a century or some other period of a convenient duration.

The length of time covered by the first three chapters of this book extends from the Norman Conquest to the beginning of the reign of Elizabeth I. The end of the sixteenth century can be regarded as the close of a span of nearly 500 years, during which the forests as created by the Normans and early Plantagenets, together with their code of administration, were in existence. Some features of the old forests still remained for another 100 years or so until the process of their disintegration was ultimately completed.

During the 900 years between the Norman invasion and the middle of the twentieth century, some words acquired a different or a changed meaning and this is particularly so in the case of the word 'forest'. In early times a forest was an area or district reserved to the king for hunting and the fact that trees may have been growing in some parts of it was largely incidental. At the demise of the medieval forests the idea of growing trees for timber production gradually took root, hastened to a large extent by the need for timber for the Navy. When in the middle of the nineteenth century, iron and steel replaced timber for ship building one of the main objects in growing trees for timber ceased to exist in a matter of months.

The forests of the Middle Ages which are described in the opening chapters, are chiefly those that were established or extended by individual kings and for this reason they are often referred to as 'royal' forests. However, if a forest was conveyed by the king to one of his subjects, it ceased to be a royal forest and although its character and extent might remain virtually unchanged it then assumed the status of a chase which was no longer subject to forest law. As several chases are included, the title of 'medieval forests' has been used in preference to 'royal forests'.

Although the Danes and the Saxons had reserved for hunting, areas of land that were subsequently incorporated into the medieval forests, it was the Normans who increased and enlarged these reserves and who drew up the code of forest laws which were to remain in force for several hundred years.

The Function of the Medieval Forest

The creation of the medieval forests by the Normans has always been attributed to their great love of hunting and in support of this, William I is said to have loved the deer as if he had been their father. This may have been the case in the early years of the Normans but as time passed the forests provided succeeding kings with other valuable assets in addition to their sport. The establishment of these forests, which were controlled directly by the sovereign and were subject to special laws, gave the king a singular degree of authority over large areas of land. Within the bounds of a forest, he retained all the rights of hunting, he could prohibit or restrict the felling of trees and he exercised considerable powers over certain industries within a forest, particularly in respect of forges and tanneries. In effect he had powers to deal with any matters which might adversely affect the beasts of the forest or interfere with the pursuit of hunting.

Consequently the king was in a very advantageous position to bestow gifts on, or grant concessions to, those whom he wished to reward for their services. Such favours included qualified permission to hunt and take deer, grants of venison or timber, warrants to create assarts, that is to say, to convert forest land on which trees were growing into agricultural land, and liberty to erect and work forges. Such gifts or concessions were of considerable value and frequently they provided the king with a not insignificant means of raising money from those who were prepared to pay for these privileges. On the other hand, those who were unwilling or unable to obtain such concessions and took the law into their own hands were subject to fines for trespass against the vert and venison of the forest. Thus, what the king did not get with his right hand he might well obtain with his left.

There is another aspect of the economic value of the medieval forests which should not be overlooked: so long as the royal forests were well stocked with deer — and it was the purpose of the forest laws to see that this was so — they provided a constant source of fresh meat. Lord Ernle[1] observes that under the manorial system; 'Cattle were seldom fatted even for the tables of the rich; oxen were valued for their power of draught; cows for their milk. It may, indeed, be said that fresh butcher's meat was rarely eaten.' Sheep were valued for their wool but not for their meat. Without beef or mutton the main source of meat lay in the forests where deer existed in considerable numbers and wild boar were to be found in more restricted areas. Pickering Forest in the north east of Yorkshire had a great reputation for wild boar at the beginning of the thirteenth century.[2] Boars were to be found in many forests throughout the country during the Middle Ages, the last wild boar being killed in the middle of the seventeenth century. Boar hunting was said to be the favourite sport of Henry I and was greatly enjoyed by King John who also had a great liking for the flesh of the wild boar.

Not only did the forests provide a constant supply of meat but their widespread distribution throughout the country ensured that the king and his court could draw on fresh supplies whenever they travelled to different parts of the realm. Since transport was difficult and refrigeration was non-existent, there were very considerable advantages in this. Thus the medieval forests had considerable material value as well as providing sport and entertainment for the king and his friends.

THE LANDSCAPE OF THE MEDIEVAL FOREST

In trying to create a picture of a medieval forest it is as well to bear the following points in mind. In the first place a forest was an area of unenclosed land, the boundaries of which were marked by such features as streams, tracks, bridges, roads, valleys and other conspicuous features of the country-side. The land which lay within the forest boundaries was invariably owned partly by the king — as demesne land — and partly by his subjects. This privately owned property might consist of agricultural land, woods, houses or villages. Thus within a forest there could be two categories of land; that which belonged to the king and that which belonged to members of the realm. The words 'forest' and 'woodland' did not mean the same thing, since a forest included some land which was neither wooded nor waste.[3] All those who lived within the bounds of a forest were subject to forest law as well as common law,[4] and in some respects this affected the land owned by a subject. For example a man was not allowed to fell trees on his own land or to erect a high fence which might prevent deer from having free access.

Those areas within a forest that belonged to the king and that formed his demesne were to a large extent made up of waste land, that is to say, uncultivated ground on which grew the natural vegetation of the district, whether it happened to be heather, willows, grass, gorse, reeds, blackthorn or trees. Some forests, like Dartmoor and Exmoor, were areas of moorland which were devoid of woods and only contained scattered trees or small spinneys in the most sheltered parts. Some, like Hatfield Chase near Doncaster, were for the most part 'one great morass'[5] while others like the Forest of Dean and Sherwood Forest, contained a fair proportion of trees.

Where site and soil conditions were acceptable, some natural regeneration of tree species would have taken place. At the same time, this would be considerably reduced where deer browsed on young trees and where pigs fed on oak and beech mast at the time of pannage. When the unrestricted growth of trees takes place, colonization of the adjacent marginal areas soon occurs, as can be seen today on the site of old railway tracks and on ungrazed common land. Sometimes nature took a hand in controlling the situation, as occurred in the year 1222 when a great storm blew down so many trees in the royal forests that special orders were issued by Henry III to his forest officers, with regard to the disposal of the timber. A high proportion of large trees must have suffered and this would have created gaps in the tree canopy which, subject to the restricting activities of deer and pigs, would be filled with young self-sown seedlings. The course of a stream flowing through waste or woodland could be changed by the process of erosion or by a large tree falling across it and so obstructing the flow. Where this happened, the adjoining land could be flooded and become waterlogged which in course of time would create completely new conditions.

Land which belonged to a subject within a forest, presented a different appearance since it would be used for raising crops and, to a limited extent, for stock although the woods which formed part of a subject's property were probably similar to those in the king's demesne. The forests of the Middle Ages were thus very different to those of the twentieth century. Today it is reasonable to assume that a forest is an area of land covered with trees but in medieval times this was not the case.

Two of the earliest definitions of a forest are to be found in the *Dialogus de Scaccario* of Richard fitz Nigel[6] which was written about 1179 and in *A Treatise of the Laws of the Forest*[7] by John Manwood, the first edition of which appeared in 1598. The definition of a forest as given by fitz Nigel is that:

> *the king's forest is a safe refuge for wild beasts; not every kind of beast, but those that live in woods; not in any kind of place, but in selected spots, suitable for the purpose.*

He added that such places were to be found in well-wooded counties 'where there are hiding places and rich pasture for wild beasts'.

Manwood provides a more graphic definition. He says:

> *A forest is a certain territory of woody grounds and fruitful pastures, priviledged for wild beasts and fowls of forest, chase and warren, to rest and abide in, in the safe protection of the king, for his princely delight and pleasure, which territory of ground, so priviledged is meered and bounded with unremovable marks, meers and boundaries, either known by matter of record, or else by prescription: And also replenished with wild beasts of venery or chase, and with great coverts of vert, for the succour of the said wildbeasts, to have their abode in: For the preservation and continuance of which said place, together with the vert and venison, there are certain laws, priviledges and officers, belonging to the same, meet for that purpose, that are only proper unto a forest and not to any other place.*

He goes on to say:

> *And therefore a forest doth chiefly consist of these four things, that is to say, of vert, venison, particulars and priviledges, and of certain meet officers appointed for that purpose, to the end that the same may be the better preserved and kept for a place of recreation and pastime meet for the royal dignity of a prince.*

THE FRAMEWORK OF THE FOREST

A forest was thus an extensive area which included waste land, woods and, in some cases, farm land, houses, buildings and villages. The forest was unenclosed but its limits were defined by recognized metes and bounds and while some of the land might belong to the king much of it belonged to his subjects. The king held the exclusive right to hunt over all the land within the forest and arising out of this, the whole area and those who lived in it were subject to a code of forest laws, enforced by specially appointed justices and officers.

A chase was similar to a forest inasmuch as it was unenclosed and defined by metes and bounds, but it differed from a forest in two main respects: it could be held by someone other than the king and it was not subject to forest law. In some cases, however, a chase might be acquired by the crown or a royal forest might be granted to a subject and in such circumstances the position would be reversed. When this happened, some of the less important facets of forest law were sometimes transferred to a chase as for example cheminage in Cranbourne Chase or the fence month or the lawing of dogs.[8] An explanation of these terms will be found in later chapters.

A park, unlike a forest or a chase, was enclosed by a fence or wall. Parks were to be found both within the bounds of the forest and beyond them. When a subject wished to make a park within the metes and bounds of a forest or in the immediate vicinity of one, it was usually necessary to obtain a licence from the king to do so. Where the proposed park was not so situated, it was unnecessary during the times of the Plantagenets to obtain a licence provided that nothing was done to interfere with the king's rights of hunting.[9]

Having made a park, the next step was to stock it with deer and in some cases the king might make a grant of live deer to a subject for this purpose. In 1225, William de Cantilupe was granted two bucks and twenty does from Rockingham Forest in order to stock his park at Ashton, and in 1280, six does from Wychwood Forest were given to the Earl of Lincoln towards stocking his park at Middleton.[10]

Where a park was made outside the bounds of a forest some owners endeavoured to add to their stock of deer by building deer leaps or *saltatoria* which were also known as salteries or deer lopes. These were constructed in the boundary fence of the park and their basic design comprised a length of fence, 10 or 12 feet long, which was lower than the rest of the fence. The object of this was to facilitate the entry of deer into the park from outside. At the same time a wide deep ditch or pit was dug on the landing or park side of the fence which would make it more difficult for a deer to negotiate in the reverse direction, if it wished to leave the park. If a deer leap was built too close to a forest, the owner could be required to remove it, the acceptable degree of closeness being a minimum of about two miles. Enclosing land for a park was known as imparking and the fence that was erected around a park was generally built of pales, the work of constructing it being known as empaling. Those in charge of maintaining the fence were known as palers, palesters or palifers and were under the authority of the keeper or parker.

A warren provided another aspect of the royal prerogative. In the Middle Ages the general public had a right to hunt wild animals on any unenclosed land, provided that such land was not under forest law or under any other restriction as regards hunting, consequent upon a grant by the king. The term 'warren' was used either to denote the actual right to hunt and take certain wild animals or in reference to the land over which such a right was exercised. From time to time the king granted rights of free-warren to both monasteries and individuals subject to the following limitations: that the right was only granted in respect of land which belonged to the grantee; that the land was not in a royal forest and that no other person was allowed to hunt over the land without permission of the grantee. Rights of free-warren were only exercisable by the grantee and his heirs and not by his assigns. Furthermore, he was required to keep a warrener or warden to ensure that no one hunted in the warren without his express permission.

To ensure that the laws of the forest were properly observed, inspections known as regards were carried out. When first instituted it was intended that these inspections should be made every three years by 12 knights who were known as regarders. However, in course of time the interlude between each regard increased until ultimately they only took place at very infrequent intervals. The regarders were required to provide answers to a number of questions contained in the chapters of the regard, details of which are given under the section entitled 'The Officers of the Forest' in Chapter 2.

Another form of inspection was the perambulation which was a scrutiny of the metes and bounds in order to ensure that the limits of the forest had not been extended and, if they had been, to take steps to restore the *status quo.* Although a forest was not enclosed, its boundaries were carefully recorded and in so doing any features such as streams, valleys, roads, bridges, hills, buildings or special trees which were known as border trees were carefully noted in the perambulation. The following extract from the commencement of the perambulation of Selwood Forest in Somerset in 1297, illustrates the method adopted.[11]

> *A Perambulation of the Forest of Selwode in the County of Somerset by the view of Malcolinus de Harleigh and Johannes de Wrotesleghe, appointed by the Lord King to view the said perambulation . . . . Was made there on the 13th day of March, in the 26th year of the reign of King Edward by the oath of the aforesaid jury who say that the Bounds of the Forest begin at the bridge of South Bruham which is the last water of the Brue: and thence by a via to La Barwe: and thence by a certain via as far as the house called Bruke: and thence by keeping the said house on the right as far as the gate of the hall of the Lord King (which was there) when the Park of Wycham was inclosed: and thence by Hayham as far as the water of Frome: and thence by the said water, keeping it on the right as far as the bridge of Waleditch: and from thence along the edge of the Boscus of Selewode . . . .*

Perambulations were not carried out at regular intervals in the way in which the regards were intended to be, but only when for some reason, the occasion demanded action. For instance, when the Norman and Plantagenet kings extended the forest areas, widespread unrest resulted from their action. Although some land was disafforested by Henry II, under the terms of the Magna Carta in 1215 John agreed to further extensive disafforestation: a translation of the Sarum Magna Carta reads: 'All forests that have been made in our time shall immediately be disafforested.'[12] The next year John died and he was succeeded by Henry III who was nine years old when he came to the throne. In the following year — 1217 — the Charter of the Forest was issued, ostensibly by the young king. This charter laid down that any land which Henry II had afforested should be inspected and, with the exception of the king's own demesne land, should be disafforested immediately. In order to accomplish this task, special inspections or perambulations were ordered to be carried out by 12 knights especially selected for the purpose. Although this undertaking should have been finished in 1224, some perambulations, including those of the Lancashire forests, were not completed until after that date. In 1225 a second Charter of the Forest was issued and, in accordance with its provisions, further perambulations were made. Subsequently, perambulations were initiated on the orders of the monarch as may be noted from the extract from the perambulation of Selwood Forest which has already been quoted. Although records do not show any definite pattern of dates after 1230, a large number of perambulations were made from 1298 to 1300, while very few were held after the middle of the seventeenth century.

Land which had been forest in the days of Henry II, Richard I or John and later disafforested in accordance with the Charters of the Forest, was termed purlieu and this word is still to be found on present day maps as, for example, Dibden Purlieu on the eastern boundary of the New Forest, between Beaulieu and Hythe. The occupier of purlieu land enjoyed certain rights in the adjoining forest but these were of far less value than the rights of his neighbour who lived within the forest. At the same time, he was subject to considerably less stringent forest laws, the most important of which was an undertaking not to disturb deer which came onto his land. The word purlieu also occurs in the forms purlew, purley and pourallee.

The fact that those who occupied purlieu land enjoyed a more advantageous position than those who lived within the forest, apparently led to a feeling of contempt, probably emanating from jealousy. This was especially so in Sherwood Forest where to call a man 'a purley' was regarded as a derogatory remark. Manwood[13] calls those who had free land within the purlieu to the yearly value of 40 shillings 'pourallee men'. On the boundaries of Galtres Forest and Duffield Frith occupiers of purlieu land were known as 'bounderers' while in some forests the word 'purlieu' was replaced by a local name as in the inlodges and outlodges of Clarendon Forest; the inbounds and outbounds of Cranbourne Chase: the wynlands or wydelands of the Peak Forest and the venville lands or venlands of Dartmoor.[14] Some of these names or variations of them are still to be found on the map and where they occur it is a fair indication that the site was originally in close proximity to a medieval forest.

The forests of the Middle Ages were distributed over a large part of England with the exception of Kent, East Anglia and Lincolnshire, and most of them were treated as separate entities for the purposes of administration. In a few cases some of the smallest forests formed a single administrative unit. In Oxfordshire, the two diminutive forests of Shotover and Stowood were generally regarded as one and were sometimes considered to be part of the not far distant Forest of Bernwood which lay in the adjoining county of Buckinghamshire. It was usual for a forest of any reasonable size to be divided into sections which were known variously as bailiwicks, walks or wards although in some forests other names were used. The New Forest was divided into nine bailiwicks, Bere Forest into two walks, Duffield Frith into four wards, Dartmoor Forest into four quarters, Kinver Forest into three hays and Clarendon Forest into five parts. In the Forest of Essex, subdivisions were referred to as bailiwicks in 1489 but by 1582 they had become known as walks.[15] These divisions were formed in the interests of administration and decentralization. When investigating medieval forests some confusion can arise over their names and locations by reason of the fact that occasionally a bailiwick or other comparable subdivision is treated as a separate forest and the name of the bailiwick transposed into the name of a forest. In other cases, a large wood is sometimes referred to as a forest when in fact it is nothing of the sort.

Earlier in this chapter, it was pointed out that although the medieval forests were not wholly covered with trees as are the forests of the present day, many of them contained areas of trees and undergrowth. In course of time, these trees tended to encroach onto the adjoining land and so increase the extent of these wooded sites. Within these woodlands were to be found open grass-covered glades known as launds or lawns which were much used by deer and were tended by a launder. The word is derived from the Old French *launde* but by the eighteenth century it had come to mean a level area of grass which was kept mown and which is now known as a lawn. Forbidden launds were those on which domestic animals were not allowed to graze when agisted in the forest.

THE ESSENCE OF FOREST LAW

After the Battle of Hastings, William I lost no time in taking such steps as were necessary to establish, extend and safeguard those areas which were designated as forest. However, he was not only operating in a foreign country but in one which he had only recently conquered and it was clear that the need to protect these forest areas and the deer which they harboured was a matter of paramount importance to him. Since it was from the English that any trouble might be expected, William decided on two courses of action. The first was an attempt to reduce any resentment at the establishment of new forests or the extension of existing ones, by producing a set of forest laws known as the *Constitutiones de Foresta* or *Charter of the Forest* and which was alleged to have been drawn up by Canute at Winchester in 1016. Although some writers have accepted this as being genuine, the great majority have questioned its authenticity and have condemned it as a forgery, deliberately prepared by the Norman lawyers so as to undermine any resistance to the new regime. This document purported to show that the Normans were only putting into practice a code of forest laws which Canute had drawn up some 50 years earlier.

Some historians consider that this document was drawn up in the reign of Henry I (1100-1135) and not by William the Conqueror. If this was so, one cannot but question the purpose of producing an instrument of this kind, some 40 or 50 years after the work of creating and extending forests had begun. Although Domesday Book only mentions a few forests by name, such as the New Forest, the Dean, Windsor, Wychwood and Gravelinges (Groveley),[16] there is no doubt that many others were in existence in 1086.[17] Additional forests were formed by William II to whom are also attributed the brutal forest laws of the time. Mutilation or death were not unusual punishments for offences relating to the forests although, without condoning such action, it should be borne in mind that the Normans had conquered the country and doubtless regarded the pleasures of the chase as the justifiable fruits of victory. Furthermore they were faced with considerable problems in maintaining control of their newly acquired possessions while some of their own kinsfolk were not averse to questioning the king's authority. Consequently they probably had little hesitation in resorting to savage methods of control. After the death of William Rufus while hunting in the New Forest in 1100, Henry I agreed to relax the forest laws but his action was purely of a temporary nature. However in 1184 a statute commonly known as the Assize of Woodstock[18] was enacted and this provided the first code of forest law that applied to the kingdom as a whole. It also established the principle that the laws of the forest were independent of, and distinct from, the common law of the land. Common law continued to apply to those offences that were unconnected with the forests and outside the scope of forest law.[19] Five years later Henry II died and was succeeded by Richard I who was too deeply involved in crusades to be concerned with his forests, spending less than one year of his ten year reign, in England. In 1199, John came to the throne and it was not long before he began to pursue a policy of renewed afforestation and to enforce the forest laws to their fullest extent. The situation deteriorated to such a degree that when the Magna Carta was drawn up in 1215, it included four references to forests in what are generally referred to as clauses 44, 47, 48 and 53. Of these, clauses 47 and 48 were especially important and read as follows:[20]

> *Clause 47   All forests that have been made in our time, shall immediately be disafforested . . . .*
> *Clause 48   All evil customs connected with forests and warrens, foresters, warroners, sheriffs and their officers, or river-banks and their wardens are at once to be investigated in every county by twelve sworn knights of the same county chosen by upright men of the same county.*

In the same year after Magna Carta, the king died and Henry III, a boy of nine, succeeded to the throne. Little time was lost in preparing legislation that aimed at settling many of the grievances that emanated from the royal forests and the operation of the forest laws, and in November 1217 the Charter of the Forest[21] was issued in the king's name by the regent, the Earl of Pembroke. Consequent upon this action, all forests created by Henry II were ordered to be viewed or inspected by 'good and lawful men'. On 11th February 1225 the Charter was issued again without any alterations to its provisions,[22] and this was followed by further perambulations.

Turner[23] makes the following comments on the Charter:

> *The language of the Charter is notable. A forest was a district which might include both woods and open country; yet it was only woods that were to be disafforested. Perhaps in some cases the kings had afforested woods in the neighbourhood of their forests but had allowed the open country which surrounded them to remain exempt or partially exempt from the forest laws. It is probable, however, that the word 'boscus' was not intended to be construed literally, but was used loosely of districts which were assumed to be for the most part wooded. Again, the woods which Henry II had afforested were only to be disafforested when they had been afforested to the damage of their owners. A qualification so vague as this was open to very different interpretations by the King and the owners of the woods. But more significant than the language of the Charter were the actual conditions under which the disafforestments were to be made. The woods which King Henry II had afforested were to be viewed by good and loyal men, and there was to be no disafforestment until they had been viewed; but the woods which King Richard or King John had afforested were to be forthwith disafforested and no view of them was necessary.*

The Charter of the Forest was not only an important landmark in the history of medieval forests but at the same time it served to emphasize the continuing efforts of the king to extend his forests and the counter efforts of the barons to limit them. With the accession of Edward I this struggle was renewed and in 1277 The Custom and Assize of the Forest,[24] which was also known as The Articles of Attachments of the Forest was passed. This was chiefly concerned with safeguarding the king's rights in his forests. At the same time the king's efforts at reafforestation continued and, presumably in an attempt to exert upon him some measure of control, A Confirmation of the Great Charter and the Charter of the Forest was enacted in 1297. This included the words '. . . that the Charter of Liberties, and the Charter of the Forest, which were made by common Assent of all the Realm, in the Time of King Henry our Father, shall be kept in every point without Breach', and laid down that those who broke these Charters would be excommunicated.[25]

This was followed by a new series of perambulations which the king was required to confirm. In 1305, he obtained the Pope's absolution from his previous undertakings but in the same year, under further pressure from the barons, another *Ordinatio Forestae* or Ordinance of the Forest was passed.[26]

In 1307, Edward I died and was succeeded by Edward II who reigned for 20 years, during which period no new forest legislation was enacted. On the accession of Edward III the situation changed dramatically and in 1327, the first year of his reign, three important statutes were passed. The first[27] stated that these two charters should 'be observed and kept in every article' and that:

> the Perambulation of the Forest in the time of King Edward, grandfather to the King that now is, be from henceforth holden in the like Form as it was then ridden and bounded; and thereupon a Charter to be made to every Shire where it was ridden and bounded. And in such Places where it was not bounded, the King will that it shall be bounded by good men and that a Charter be thereupon made as afore is said.

The second statute[28] dealt with the rights and treatment of those charged with an offence under forest law and the third[29] set out the rights of a subject to take timber for the repair of houses, hedges and fences from his own woods which were situated within a forest.

It would seem evident that the king's intentions as regards his forests were viewed with considerable mistrust and suspicion, since the formal confirmation of the Great Charter and the Charter of the Forest was re-enacted on many occasions during his reign including 1327, 1328, 1331, 1336, 1340, 1357, 1362, 1363, 1371 and 1376. When Richard II came to the throne these confirmations continued although to a lesser extent, as in 1377, 1381, 1383, 1384 and 1388, with two in the reign of Henry IV and one in the time of Henry V.

THE LAWS OF THE FOREST

In considering the whole body of forest law, the courts and their officers, it should not be forgotten that the ultimate object was to protect and secure the king's interest in his forests and also his enjoyment of the chase. The action that was taken to achieve this object followed two logical courses. The first was to protect the forest itself, known as the vert, that is to say the trees and undergrowth which grew within the bounds of the forest. The second was to protect the beasts of the forest, namely the red deer, the fallow deer, the roe deer and wild boar which were collectively known as venison. The meaning of the word venison thus differed from the modern definition which is restricted to the flesh of a deer.

The vert which was also known as green hue, hew or hugh comprised both the larger trees and the smaller species such as hazel, elder and sallow and also their foliage and produce on which the deer might feed. The produce included acorns, beech mast and berries and was termed deer fruit. The word vert is derived from the French *vert* meaning green which in turn comes from the Latin *viridis* which has a similar meaning. Manwood[30] described vert as 'every plant that doth grow within the Forest and bear green leafe which may hide or cover a deer under it' and defines a plant as 'trees, woods, bushes or such like'. He also divided vert into two classes, over vert or hault boys (from the French *haut bois*) and nether vert or south boys (from the French *sous bois*). Over vert consisted of large trees or great wood and Manwood observes that 'Old ashes and holly trees, they are accompted over vert'. 'Nether vert', he adds, 'is properly all manner of underwood, and also bushes, thornes, gorse and such like'. He further sets out three reasons why vert was carefully preserved: first, to provide cover, shelter and seclusion for the beasts of the forest; second, on account of the deer fruit and browsewood that it produced and third 'for the comliness and beauty of the same in a forest' and 'for the very great sight and beholding of the goodly green and pleasant woods in forests'. In addition to over vert and nether vert there was a further category known as special vert which could be of two kinds. In the first place special vert was applied to any tree or bush which bore fruit on which deer could feed and Manwood specifically mentions 'Pear trees, crabtrees, hawthorns, blackbush and the like'. Although he does not mention acorns and mast these were undoubtedly included since they were classed as deer fruit. The reason for the designation of 'special vert' was that the punishment for destroying this vert was far more stringent than for the destruction of other vert. Both over vert and nether vert could be classified as special vert if they bore fruit. In the second place the term special vert applied to every tree which grew in the king's demesne woods within a forest whether it was great wood or underwood or whether it bore fruit or not.

During the winter months when the deer found it difficult to obtain sufficient food, foliage and small branches which were known variously as browse, browsewood, clear browse or shrowdes were cut down by the foresters so that the deer could feed on them. Browse was usually cut from the branches of oak but ash, maple, hazel, holly and even ivy were used when the need arose, the branchlets being not more than an inch thick. Browse was frequently gathered in the late autumn and put on one side until it was needed when the hard weather came, but sometimes freshly-cut material was fed. Quite apart from the browse and deer fruit, it was the vert which formed the actual forest and this was a fact which was readily recognized in the Middle Ages. Consequently three of the most serious offences that could be committed against the forest itself were those of purpresture, waste and assart.

Purpresture was an encroachment upon the forest and might entail the enclosure of a parcel of land or the erection, without warrant, of a new house or building where there had been none before. Manwood[31] indicates the gravity of this offence in the following description of it:

> *Purpresture in a forest is a trespasse so hurtful and offensive to the*
> *Vert and Venison of the same, that if there were not certain sharp*
> *Laws to inhibit it, and also to punish the offenders therein, for*
> *example sake, forests would in short time decay, and be no forests,*
> *by reason of Purprestures only.*

He adds that purpresture is a 'special means to decay a forest, by building and new erecting of houses and other inclosures therein'. The word purpresture is derived from the Old French *pourprendre* meaning to take or seize.

Waste has been defined as any action which destroyed the covert and was basically the unauthorized felling of trees or underwood within a forest irrespective of whether they were growing in woods that were the king's demesne or whether they were in woodlands belonging to one of the king's subjects. If an owner wished to fell any trees that belonged to him and that were growing within the bounds of a forest, it was necessary for him to obtain a licence to do so from a justice-in-eyre and for the felling to be done 'in the view' of a forester. Failure to do so could result in the woodland being forfeited to the king. The test for deciding whether a particular case constituted waste was dependent on whether a man, standing against the stump of a felled tree, was able to see the stumps of five other felled trees. If he was able to do so, it was held to be waste.[32]

However in 1327 a statute[33] was passed which set out the rights of an owner of a wood that lay within the bounds of a forest and laid down that 'Every Man that hath any Wood within the Forest may take Houseboot and Heyboot in his said Wood, without being attached for the same by any Ministers of the Forest, so that he do the same by the View of the Foresters'. Houseboot or house-bote was timber required for the repair of buildings and heyboot or hay-bote was timber needed for the upkeep of gates and fences. The subject of attachment is dealt with in Chapter 2.

In 1482 an Act[34] was passed which allowed owners of land within a forest, who had felled their woods (after obtaining the necessary licence to do so) to enclose the felled area with a hedge, for a period of seven years after felling, in order to protect the young coppice growth from 'all manner of beasts and cattle'. The main object of this statute was to preserve the vert and so ensure the provision of cover for the beasts of the forest in years to come. At the same time, protection was given to any young trees or seedlings that were growing on the site and this in turn contributed to the future stock of timber.

An assart was the most serious offence against the forest since it not only entailed the unauthorized felling of trees or undergrowth, as occurred in the case of waste, but it also included the removal of the actual stumps and roots. The area was thus permanently cleared of trees and the land used for agriculture. In such cases, not only was the person who created the assart fined but also the occupier of the land which formed the assart, even if he had not created it.[35] The origin of the word assart lies in the French *essarter* which means to grub up or clear, but in parts of Lancashire it was sometimes known as 'ridding' presumably from the verb to rid, the old meaning of which was to clear away or abolish and, thus, to get rid of.

The complement to vert was venison and, as stated earlier in this chapter, it was a term which was used to refer to the beasts of the forest, that is to say red, fallow and roe deer and wild boar and did not simply mean the flesh of a deer as it does in modern usage. The greatest offence against venison was that of killing a deer and in Norman and early Plantagenet times the punishment for this crime was often savage, sometimes entailing the loss of a member or even of life. However, such severe punishments came to an end with the passing of The Charter of the Forest of 1217, section 10 of which laid down that 'No man from henceforth shall lose neither life or member for killing our deer.' In 1327 a further Act[36] provided 'That from henceforth no man shall be taken nor imprisoned for vert or venison unless he be taken with the maner.' In effect this meant being caught in the act of committing the offence and this point is considered at greater length in Chapter 2 under the section entitled 'The Operation of the Courts'.

Apart from the actions of the forest officers to protect the vert and venison, there were certain forest laws which were specifically concerned with safeguarding the deer. These were related to three matters, namely, the fence month, the heyning and the expeditation or lawing of dogs. The fence month, defence month or close month was the period of time during which it was considered that the female deer (hinds or does) gave birth to their young (calves or fawns) and that consequently they needed a special period of quietness and protection during which they would not be disturbed. The fence month extended from 15 days before Midsummer (June 24th) until 15 days after and was thus from 9th June until 9th July. In order to minimize any disturbance to the deer, those who wished to pass through a forest with carriages, carts or pack horses during the fence month were subjected to a tax or levy known as cheminage or chiminage. This matter is considered in rather more detail in Chapter 3. The agistment of stock was also prohibited in most forests during the fence month and although it was permitted in a few cases, the agistment fee was greatly increased during this period.

The heyning which was also referred to as the winter heyning, was a period during the winter months when the agistment of stock in the forest was forbidden so that more food would be available for the deer. In 1668 an Act affecting the Forest of Dean[37] defined the winter heyning as extending from 11th November (Martinmas) to 23rd April (St George's Day).

The third law that directly concerned the protection of deer was that relating to the expeditation or laming of large dogs, so as to ensure that they were unable to chase deer and consequently could not be used for hunting them. There are many references to the illegal use of dogs in the accounts of forest inquisitions or inquiries and Turner[38] has recorded several, of which the following is an example. This account refers to an inquisition on the venison in the Forest of Rockingham in 1246.

> *It happened on the Thursday next before the feast of Saint Margaret, in the thirtieth year of the reign of king Henry (19th July 1246), that, when William, the walking forester in the park of Brigstock, entered his bailiwick of the park, he found Hugh Swartgar, the reaper of the town of Brigstock, leading two mastiffs — to wit, one white and the other red — against the prohibition of the foresters. And a certain man of Brigstock, who was called Henry Tuke, went with the reaper. And when he saw them, the said William wished to attach them, on account of the dogs which they led so late in the park of the lord king. And they refused to allow him to attach them. And the said William the forester went into the town of Brigstock stealthily, and again returned to the place where he had seen them before; and he saw them a second time in the same place. But when the aforesaid Hugh and the aforesaid Henry Tuke saw the forester coming towards them, they forthwith turned and fled, and he could not take them.*

The practice of mutilating dogs which could be used for hunting and taking deer, is thought to have originated in the reign of Edward the Confessor (1042-1066).[39] At first, this consisted of cutting the back sinews of the hind legs and was known as hock sinewing, hoxing, hombling or hambling. Subsequently this form of mutilation was replaced by expedition or the removal of three claws of the forefoot and this operation was commonly referred to as the lawing of dogs. Turner[40] uses the word hombling to indicate expedition rather than hock sinewing but it is probable that, with the passage of time, this word came to be used as a general term for lawing, without differentiating between the two methods. Large dogs that had not been expeditated were consequently known as unlawed dogs and their owners, if they lived within the bounds of a forest, were guilty of an offence under the forest laws. At the same time, the right to own an unlawed dog was sometimes granted by the king to those of his subjects who held positions of importance.

Under the Assize of the Forest[41], lawing was only carried out on mastiffs but this name was used in respect of a type of dog rather than the breed which exists today and this matter is considered in greater detail in chapter 3 in the section entitled 'Hounds and Huntsmen'. In course of time, lawing was applied to all large dogs that were kept within the bounds of a forest whether they were classed as mastiffs or not.

Article 6 of the Charter of the Forest[42] included several rules and directions regarding expedition which may be summarized as follows. Inquiries into the matter of lawing were to be held every third year when the detailed inspection of the forest, known as the regard, was carried out and any person whose dog was then found to be unlawed was subject to a fine of three shillings. Expeditation was to be carried out so that 'three clawes of the forefoot shall be cut off by the skin', the operation only being performed in those places or locations where it had been the custom to do so since the coronation of Henry II (1154-1189). Manwood[43] gives the following description of the procedure:

> The mastive being brought to set one of his fore-feet upon a piece of wood, eight inches thick and a foot square, then one with a mallet, setting a chisel of two inches broad upon the three claws of his fore-feet, at one blow doth smite them clean off.

Cox[44] refers to the fact that in some forests, notably Pickering, outlying communities were permitted to pay a sum of money known as houndgeld or hungill which exempted them from the law regarding expeditation.

Although the lawing of dogs was initially applied to mastiffs, in due course all large dogs whose owners lived within the metes and bounds of a forest were included. As already stated, the object of this mutilation was to reduce the speed of a dog which might be used to hunt deer and it was for this reason that lawing was only applicable to mastiffs. The fact that this practice was extended to include other dogs is an indication that not only mastiffs could be used successfully in hunting deer. However the question doubtless arose as to which dogs should be lawed and which should not, since it was clear that really small dogs could hardly be regarded as a danger to venison. There are two examples of the criterion of size that was adopted. The first is an iron stirrup which may be seen in the Verderers Hall at Lyndhurst in the New Forest. It is said that any dog which could crawl through the stirrup was considered to be too small to need lawing. The second example is taken from Malvern Chase and is described by Turner[45] who stated that all dogs 'that could not or would not be drawn through a strap eighteen inches and one barley corn in length and breadth' were expeditated. As there were three barley corns to an inch, the dimensions were 1 foot 6¼ inches and since the length and breadth were the same, it would seem that the leather 'strap' was in fact a leather slieve or tube, 1 foot 6¼ inches in circumference or approximately 5¾ inches in diameter, through which the dog had to pass. A modern full size stirrup is about 5¼ inches wide and 5 inches deep and if the stirrups of the Middle Ages, as exemplified by the one at Lyndhurst, were of similar dimensions, there would not be a great deal of difference in size between the Malvern Chase strap and the New Forest stirrup. However it is unlikely that any dog larger than a small terrier could pass through either of them.

ADMINISTRATION OF THE LAWS   2

The Courts of the Forest

The organization which lay behind the enforcement of forest law consisted of the attachment courts, inquisitions and the forest eyre which was the ultimate court. Although the names swanimote or swainmote and, in a few cases, woodmote were in course of time applied to attachment courts and, as Cox[1] observes were 'used interchangeably in various local forest proceedings', the true swanimote was a meeting of certain officers of the forest which Turner[2] describes as a forest assembly and not a court in the accepted sense. Article 8 of the Forest Charter[3] stated that swanimotes should only be held three times a year. First, 15 days before Michaelmas (29th September) when the agisters met to deal with the agistment of stock in the demesne woods; second about the time of St Martin's Day (11th November) when the agisters collected pannage dues and third, at the beginning of the 15 days before the feast of St John the Baptist (24th June) which was the beginning of the fence month, when the hinds or the does were expected to begin fawning. The attachment court was the basic forest court and was also known as the forty-day court on account of the fact that the Charter of the Forest directed that it should be held every 40 days. Turner[4] however states they were always held on the same day of the week in a particular bailiwick of the forest. If there were four bailiwicks in a forest, the attachment court would always be held in the first bailiwick on, for example, a Tuesday, in the second bailiwick on a Wednesday and so on. It is clear from such an arrangement that the interval between the courts was therefore 42 days and not 40. The court of attachment, which was held by the verderers, was so called because it received the attachments of the foresters and woodwards which were entered in the verderer's rolls. These attachments are referred to later in this chapter in the section entitled 'The Operation of the

Courts'. The Charter of the Forest[5] further refers to attachment courts as follows:

> Moreover, every forty days through the year, our foresters and verderers shall meet to see the attachments of the forest, as well for green-hue as for hunting by the presentments of the same foresters, and before them attached.

The Custom and Assize of the Forest[6] contains a considerable amount of information regarding attachments, inquisitions and offences against vert and venison. The attachment court had few powers and could not try or inquire into any cases which were concerned with venison and was only able to deal with the less important cases relating to vert; all matters of any consequence were referred to the forest eyre. At the same time, despite the very limited jurisdiction of the attachment court, it was the only forest court that sat at regular intervals and that had any powers of jurisdiction during the interim period when the forest eyre was not in session. Manwood[7] sets out 45 questions or points that the verderers were charged to ask or raise at the attachment court. These covered many aspects of forest law and administration and included such matters as interference with forest boundary stones, oppressive acts by the foresters, burning ground cover in the forest, felling and removing trees or browse, taking the eggs of certain birds, honey, wax and swarms of bees, poaching deer, building salteries, keeping hounds and matters concerning purlieus.

Since the courts of attachment were not empowered to deal with offences against venison, it was necessary to provide some means by which such matters could be investigated and recorded, in order that the facts could be ascertained and placed before the next forest eyre. This was achieved by means of forest inquisitions or inquiries which may be compared to military courts of inquiry of the present day. Turner[8] has divided these inquiries into two classes: special inquisitions and general inquisitions. The special inquisition was convened in order to investigate any unusual occurrence relating to the beasts of the forest as, for example, the finding of a dead deer in the forest. The Custom and Assise of the Forest[9] further laid down that if a dead or wounded deer was found, an inquisition should be held immediately by the four neighbouring villages on the matter and the proceedings and findings entered in the rolls. In addition the finder was to be put by six pledges, the flesh was to be sent to a neighbouring spittal house or hospital or given to the poor and lame if there was no spittal house in the vicinity. The head and skin was to be given to the poor of the neighbouring township and the arrow, if it was found, was to be given to a verderer who was to record the fact in his roll. Although the Assise of 1277 did not specifically mention the fact, the arrow was to be produced at the forest eyre when the case was brought up.

Special inquisitions were also held when trespass had been committed in the forest and it may be noted here that trespass could be against either vert or venison. As already stated courts of attachment could not deal with any offences against venison and only minor offences against vert. Special inquisitions were held before the verderers and foresters of the forest concerned, when the representatives of the four neighbouring townships were present. At the end of the thirteenth century, special inquisitions were gradually replaced by general inquisitions.

General inquisitions differed from special inquisitions in that they were not convened in order to inquire into a specific occurrence, but were concerned with the broader and more general aspects of trespass as a whole. Furthermore, they were held at irregular intervals and in different centres and not in the vicinity of an offence, as in the case of special inquisitions. Normally, general inquisitions were held before the justice of the forest or his deputy, by the verderers and foresters and 12 jurors. Article 1 of An Ordnance of 1306[10] states: 'That all trespasses hereafter to be done in our forests of green-hugh and of hunting, the foresters within whose bailiwicks such trespasses shall happen to be committed, shall present the same at the next swanimote before the foresters, verdors, regardors, agistors and other ministers of the same forest'. This is an example of a general inquisition being referred to as a swanimote as was sometimes done, but these swanimotes were not held on the dates that were laid down for swanimotes in the eighth article of the Forest Charter and they should not be confused. After the passing of the Ordnance of 1306, general inquisitions were held far more frequently than had previously been the case.

The forest eyre which was the supreme forest court, could be brought into operation by the king issuing letters patent appointing justices to hear and adjudicate pleas of the forest, either in a single county or in a group of counties. A little time before the eyre was held, instructions by way of letters close were sent to the sheriff. Consequent upon these, the sheriff summoned the following to the eyre: all the nobility and free tenants who held land or tenements within the bounds of the forest; the reeve and four men from each township situated within the forest; all foresters and verderers who held office or who had held office at any time since the last pleas of the forest; all who had been attached since the previous eyre and all regarders and agisters. In order to facilitate the business of the court, foresters and verderers were required to produce their attachments or attachment rolls; regarders their sealed regards and agisters their agistments, all being in respect of the period since the last eyre.

At least 40 days notice of the date and place of the eyre had to be given and when in due course the court met, one of the first steps to be taken was the appointment of a jury which could number 18, 20 or 24 'of the discreetest men'. After the jury had been sworn the Lord Justice in Eyre or his deputy gave the jury a charge which virtually covered the whole field of forest law. Manwood[11] gives no less than 84 points of which the charge was composed.

Some of these were similar to the 45 items which the verderers had to consider at the attachment court but those that constituted the charge covered a wider range of subjects and probed more deeply into each one. These courts were usually held in the county town and were presided over by the justices in eyre for the pleas of the forest, three or four such justices usually being appointed for each eyre. After one eyre had ended they would move on to the next and Turner[12] illustrates how four justices started at Huntingdon on 6th June 1255 and after completing their work on 20th June, proceeded in due course to Northampton. On 15th November they were at Buckingham and on 24th January 1256 they reached Oxford.

The word eyre stems from the Latin *iter* — a journey (cf. English: itinerary) — and is derived from the old French *eire* or *errer,* the modern French word *erre* meaning a way and *errer* to wander. Owing to the need for the justices in eyre to move from one centre to another, they were also referred to as itinerant or travelling justices. The full title of the eyre, according to Manwood,[13] was 'the High Court of the Lord Justice in Eyre of the Forest' which, he adds, 'was commonly called the Justice-seat'. The eyre was also occasionally known as the court of forest pleas; the word pleas which is frequently used in connection with forest law may be defined as 'an action at law'.

It was originally intended that the eyre should be held shortly after the regard of the forest had been completed. The regard, which was an inspection of the whole of the forest, was carried out by 12 knights, known as regarders, who made their inspections at intervals of three years and who were required to report their findings at the eyre next following. Further information concerning the regard will be found in this chapter in the section entitled 'The Officers of the Forest'. In early medieval times the forest eyre was held in every third year which enabled the regard to be considered soon after it had been completed. Manwood[14] states:

> The Eyre, general Sessions of the Forest, or Justice-seat, is to be
> holden and kept every third year; and of necessity before that any
> such Sessions or Justice-seat can be holden, the regarders of the
> Forest must make their regard . . .

and this is confirmed by Coke.[15] Turner[16] records that by the middle of the thirteenth century, forest eyres were being held every seven years and cites those of 1254, 1261 and 1268. This interim of seven years came to be regarded as the normal interval although in some counties the period was longer and in others shorter. However by the beginning of the fourteenth century, the intervals between each eyre became considerably protracted and a period of 47 years (1287-1334) elapsed between the holding of eyres in Sherwood Forest and 54 years (1280-1334) in the Forest of Pickering.

THE OPERATION OF THE COURTS

The transactions of the courts were based on certain rules regarding the interpretation of the forest laws and the procedures to be followed and this section deals with some of the matters which affected the operation of the forest courts.

One of the fundamental features in the fabric of forest law was that of attachment which was the procedure followed by foresters in order to apprehend a man who had committed an offence against the laws of the forest. Unlike arrest, which was only applicable to a man's body or person, a man could be attached in three different ways; first by his goods and chattels, second by his body, pledges and mainprize and third by his body only. As an example of the first method of attachment by goods and chattels, a forester could attach a man's cow or horse or other goods which he had in the forest and after he had done so, inform the owner of the fact and also of the reason for such action. He would then require him to appear at the next court of attachment and to find the necessary pledges. The goods which were attached were kept in the custody of the forester until the court sat and if the accused did not duly appear at the court, his goods were forfeited to the king and sold on his behalf. When this had been done, more of his goods were attached and if he did not then appear, they were sold and the process repeated until he presented himself in court. If however, the offender came to the court in the first place, his goods that had been attached were returned to him. In the case of offences against vert, if the forester testified that the value of the vert in question was less than four pence, the verderers could deal with the matter instead of referring it to the forest eyre.[17]

The second method of attachment, that is by body, pledges and mainprize, was used when a man was actually found by the forester trespassing against the vert which was known as being taken with the manner. The forester would attach him by his body and require him to find two pledges that he would appear at the next attachment court and when he did so, he would be mainprized, that is released on bail, until the next forest eyre was held. If he committed a second offence it would be necessary for him to produce four pledges, for a third offence eight pledges while for a fourth he would be imprisoned until the next eyre. This procedure was first laid down in 1184[18] and subsequently expanded in 1277.[19]

The third method of attachment was to attach the offender by his body only, without any pledges or mainprize in accordance with the statute of 1277. However a later Act of 1327[20] states: 'That from henceforth no man shall be taken nor imprisoned for vert or venison unless he be taken with the maner', that is to say caught in the act. If in fact he was so taken, he would be attached by his body and imprisoned until he had been granted bail by the king or by the justice of the forest but if this was done he would still be required to appear at the next forest eyre.

There are several matters arising out of the above which need further explanation. As regards pledges, these were undertakings given by other individuals that if the accused were released, they would be responsible for ensuring that he appeared at the next court. If he did not do so, those who had given pledges would be amerced or fined. The more pledges that were required, the more people would be involved and the greater the total sum of the fines, if they fell by default. However, when a man who was charged with an offence appeared before the court of attachment and the court was not empowered to deal with the offence, he was mainprized. Mainprize, which may also be spelt mainprise or mainprice, was the term used to describe the action of the court of attachment in setting a man at liberty on bail, after he had appeared before that court and pending his subsequent appearance at the forest eyre. Those who stood bail for the offender were known as mainpernors. As already noted, being taken with the maner was, in effect, being caught in the act and this applied to trespass against both vert and venison. In the case of vert, this would include such acts as being found felling or lopping a tree, cutting underwood or carrying such material away. As regards venison there were four ways in which an offender could be taken, namely dog-draw, stable-stand, back-bear and bloody-hand. Dog-draw was hunting with hounds or using them to recover a wounded deer, stable-stand was lying in wait for a deer when mounted on a horse and armed with a bow whether with hounds or not, back-bear was carrying away the carcase and bloody-hand entailed having blood-stained hands as a result of killing the deer or gralloching it and this term is probably the origin of the phrase 'to be caught red-handed'. The word 'manner' also occurs as the following variations: maner, mainour and manouvre.

When an offender who had been attached was brought before the court, he was said to be presented and the statement made by the forester when bringing the case was known as the presentment. Every presentment made against an offender, whether in vert or venison, had to provide certain essential information in five respects. First, it must state the christian name and surname of the accused and where he lived and second it must set out clearly where the alleged offence was committed and certify that the place in question was within the metes and bounds of the forest. Third, the presentment must relate exactly what the alleged offence was, as for instance killing a buck, and four it must describe the weapons or tools with which the offence was carried out, as for example with a long bow. Fifth it must recount exactly how the act occurred so as to enable the court to decide whether it was a voluntary offence or a negligent offence. Manwood[21] gives the following example of what would constitute a negligent offence, thus:

> . . . as if a man riding thorow the forest, having a greyhound fast in a
> slip by his side, and the greyhound passing thus thorow the forest

doth espy the deer, and with the force and strength of the greyhound
he doth slip the collar, and so against the will of the owner the same
greyhound doth kill a wild beast of the forest, this is but a negligent
offence in the owner of the greyhound.

If a man was found guilty of the offence with which he had been charged he was said to be 'in mercy', the term being derived from the Anglo-French *à merci* or 'at mercy'. He was then usually amerced or fined by the court, the actual fine being known as an amercement. 'To amerce' is to fine arbitrarily and 'to be amerced' is to be at the mercy of anyone as regards the amount of the fine. Thus amercement is the infliction of a penalty, the severity of which is left to the mercy of the inflictor and hence the imposition of an arbitrary fine. Amercing was not only confined to offenders who were found guilty of trespass against vert and venison; those who failed to attend the court when summoned to do so could be amerced and the practice of assembling swanimotes simply to fine those who did not appear was probably one of the reasons for the specific instructions in the Charter of 1225 as to when swanimotes should be held.[22] Those who had pledged themselves to see that a man attended a court were amerced if he did not appear and at an eyre held at Huntingdon in 1225, a verderer who failed to produce the bows and arrows belonging to the accused, which had been entrusted to him, was held to be in mercy.[23]

If a man was unable to answer a summons, his reason or excuse for failing to do so was reported to the court. These excuses, which were known as essoins, were always the first matter to be dealt with at a forest eyre, similar to the way in which, at the present time, apologies for non-attendance at a meeting are usually one of the first matters on the agenda. If a man who had been summonsed to the court died beforehand, he was said to be 'essoined of death' and his pledges would still be amerced unless his death was proved to the satisfaction of the justices, the person providing such proof being known as the essoiner.

An event or act that was likely to damage or destroy the forest, the vert or the venison in any way or to cause a breach of the forest laws, was known as a nusance of the forest. Nusances[24] (or nuisances) were of three kinds; first, common nusances, which caused general inconvenience and annoyance to those who lived in the forest, as well as affecting the beasts of the forest. An example of this would be the failure by those responsible, to repair a bridge across a river so that the users of it were forced to find another way across and in so doing disturbed the deer. Second, special nusances which could especially or directly harm the beasts of the forest. These included acts by those who hunted illegally in the forest or trespassed against the venison whether by day or by night, whether with hounds or not and irrespective of what weapons or methods were used. Third, there were general nusances or actions which caused damage to the forest in a general way and which indirectly affected the deer. This class of nusance included waste, assarts and purprestures which are considered in detail in Chapter 1 in the section entitled 'The Laws of the Forest'.

Under the provisions of The Assize of the Forest[25] every male who reached the age of 12 years and who lived within the bounds of the forest, was required to swear to keep the king's peace. This rule also applied to any clerks who held land in lay fee within the forest. The oath which had to be taken at the forest eyre was in the following form:

> *You shall true liege man be,*
> *Unto the King's Majestie:*
> *Unto the beasts of the Forest you shall no hurt do,*
> *Nor unto anything that doth belong thereto:*
> *The offences of others you shall not conceal,*
> *But to the uttermost of your power, you shall them reveal*
> *Unto the Officers of the Forest,*
> *Or to them that may see the same redrest.*
> *All these things you shall see done,*
> *So help you God at his holy doom.*

If a forester found any persons in the forest committing an act of trespass, he was in duty bound, by his office, to apprehend and attach them by any means at his disposal and failure to do so could lead to the forfeiture of his appointment. However, it was not only the duty of the forester to take action against a trespasser but also of all who lived in the forest. In addition to the provisions of The Assise of 1184 which is referred to above, The Custom and Assise of 1277[26] stated that: 'If any see any misdoers within the bounds of the forest, to take or carry away any deer, he shall do what he may to take them, and if he cannot, he shall levy the hue and cry, and if he do not do so, he shall remain in the king's mercy.' If a forester was unable to arrest those whom he found trespassing it was his duty to raise hue and cry. This he did 'making an outcry' to those living closest at hand in the forest, requiring them in the king's name to help and pursue the trespassers wherever they went within the bounds of the forest, until they were caught. The offenders were then imprisoned until they found sufficient pledges. Hue and cry could only be made for trespass against venison and not against vert, the offence must have been committed in the forest and not on purlieu land and the pursuit of those concerned could only be carried out within the metes and bounds of the forest. Any officer of the forest could make hue and cry although this was usually done by the forester, but it could only be made in cases where the guilt of the offender was without doubt or question. The word 'hue' sometimes occurs in the form 'huy'. A statute made in 1293[27] laid down that if, after hue and cry had been made, the trespassers either refused to stop or defended themselves with force and arms and, in consequence, one of them was killed by a forester or anyone who was aiding him, no action would be taken against him. On the other hand, malicious action by a forester against an innocent person who was only passing through the forest which led to his death, was, upon conviction, punishable by execution.

OTHER MATTERS TOUCHING THE COURTS

In the earliest times foresters were often quartered or billeted on tenants of land within the bounds of the forest and long after the payment of wages had become customary, efforts were still being made to perpetuate these quartering arrangements. This system, which was in fact a method of payment in kind, was not only in respect of the man but was also sometimes claimed for his horse and his dogs and was known as puture or putre. Cox[28] refers to a claim by a forester of Inglewood Forest for food and drink for himself every Friday with the right to take, whenever he saw fit, a flagon of ale, two tallow candles, oats for his horse and blackbread for his dog. Subsequently, puture was converted into a money payment known as 'putre money' or 'forester fee' although during the thirteenth century the foresters of Dartmoor Forest had claimed poutura which was money paid for liquor.

From an early date, a system of extortion had sometimes been operated by unprincipled foresters who set up ale-houses in the forest and then brought pressure to bear on those who lived within its bounds to buy ale from them. This was known as scotale or skotale and the expression 'to go scot free' is possibly derived from this practice. Other forms of extortion were undoubtedly practised and Article 7 of The Charter of 1225[29] laid down that: 'No forester or bedle from henceforth shall make scot-ale, or gather garbe or oates or any corn or lamb or pig nor shall make no gathering but by the sight and upon the oath of the twelve regarders when they shall make their regard.' What effect this had is a matter of conjecture but in 1350 another Act[30] was passed and this stated: 'That no forester, nor keeper of forest or chase, not any other minister, shall make or gather sustenance, nor other gathering of victuals, nor other thing, by colour of their office, against any man's will, within their bailiwick nor without, but that which is due of old right.'

Honey, wax and swarms of wild bees, known in some forests as bykes, which were to be found in the demesne woods in the forest, were the property of the king, and his rights to honey were set out in the fifth chapter of the Regard of 1229. On the other hand, honey found in woods which were not part of the king's demesne, belonged to the owner of the wood concerned in accordance with The Charter of the Forest[31] which stated that: 'Every freeman . . . shall have also the honey that is found in his woods.'

Under this Charter it was agreed that if Henry II '. . . have made forest of his own wood, then it shall remain forest; saving the common of herbage . . .' and this established the right of common within a forest. The effect of this was to ensure that when an area of land was afforested, any common rights that existed continued in respect of animals that were said to be 'commonable within a forest'. An Ordinance of the Forest made in 1305[32] laid down that those who occupied purlieu land could not exercise rights of common in the adjacent forest. However, if any person wished to alter their position and for their land to become part of the forest again, the king was prepared to accept them and they would then be able to enjoy common rights within the forest. The only stock that were not commonable and therefore not allowed on the commons within a forest were goats, sheep, pigs and geese. If a man grazed more animals on a common than he was entitled to do he was known as a surcharger and such action constituted an offence against forest law since by such overstocking the deer would be driven away.

In order to ensure that those who held common rights did not graze more animals on the common than they should, and also to find out whether those who had no rights were making use of the commons, the forest officers conducted a drive of all commonable animals in order to make an inspection and a count of heads. This was known as the drift of the forests and in the Forest of Pickering it was carried out twice a year, first 15 days before midsummer, that is, on the 9th June, which was the beginning of the fence month, and second about the time of Holyrood Day, namely the 14th September, when the agistment of the king's forests began. However, it was the accepted rule that the forests could be driven as often as the officers of the forest might think prudent. In 1540 a statute[33] was enacted which was commonly known as the 'Drift of the Forests', and which laid down that all forests in England should be driven each year at the feast of St Michael, 29th September, or within the 15 days following, that is before 15th October. The Act also provided that forests and chases in England and Wales could be driven at any other season if it was thought expedient to do so.

In medieval times the feast days of the church, of which the majority were saints' days, were used as convenient reference dates throughout the year. Records of events were frequently related to such days and consequently they were of considerable importance in the transactions of the courts. The following are a selection of examples taken from pleas of the forest:[34] 'on the Friday next after the feast of St Barnabas'; 'on the vigil of St Bartholomew'; 'on the Sunday next after the Epiphany'; 'the Saturday next before the Annunciation of the Blessed Mary' and 'the Monday next before the Invention of the Holy Cross'.

THE OFFICERS OF THE FOREST

In 1238, in order to facilitate the administration of forest law, England was divided into two regions or provinces with the river Trent as the boundary between them and the two parts were simply known as 'north of the Trent' and 'south of the Trent'. To appreciate this geographical division of responsibility it is helpful to follow the course of this river. Rising on Biddulph Moor some one and a half miles north-east of the town of Biddulph in Staffordshire and about a mile from the county boundary with Cheshire, this great river flows across England for 170 miles, before it joins the Humber. From its source, it makes its way southwards through Stoke-on-Trent to Stone where it takes a south-easterly course to Rugeley. Some two miles beyond the town the river changes its course and flows in an easterly direction for some eight to ten miles until joined by the river Tame. At this point it turns north-eastwards to Burton-on-Trent and after receiving the river Dove near Newton Solney, it again bears almost due east to the boundary between Derbyshire and Leicestershire. The river then follows a north-easterly course through Nottingham to Newark-on-Trent where it swings northwards and continues to Gainsborough, passing to the west of Scunthorpe until it joins the Ouse at Faxfleet, to form the river Humber. It will be seen that the course of the Trent provides a clearly defined boundary line which, although it does not reach the west coast, only falls short of the Mersey estuary at Runcorn by about 30 miles as the crow flies.

In the same year a justice of the forest who was sometimes referred to as the Lord Chief Justice, was appointed for each of these two regions but their duties were more concerned with the ministerial aspect of the law and its administration, than with dispensing it in the courts. They were chiefly involved with the release of prisoners on bail, the examination of proposed royal grants of liberties, the supervision of the whole system of forest organization and the various aspects of administration which affected the forests.[35] Since it was impossible for one man to deal with so large an area, deputies were normally appointed. Although neither the chief justice nor his deputy was required by his office to be present at any forest court, they were usually included in the king's commission to justices to hear the pleas of the forest.[36] After Edward II came to the throne their title was changed to warden but this reverted to that of justice when Richard II succeeded. Subordinate to the chief justice were the justices in eyre or itinerant justices who travelled from place to place, in order to hold the forest eyres as already described earlier in this chapter in the section on 'The Courts of the Forest'. Three or four justices were usually appointed for each eyre and of these one was generally the chief justice or his deputy. The chief justices of the forest were men of considerable ability, many of whom had already achieved success in spheres other than that of forest law. The justices in eyre were normally fully experienced in judicial and administrative matters and some of them served as itinerant justices for many years.

Below the justices, in order of authority, were the wardens who were also known by several other titles which consequently has resulted in some confusion. These varied according to different forests and also to different periods of time and included the designations of keeper, steward, bailiff, chief forester and master forester. There were two kinds of wardens: first, those who were appointed by letters patent and who held office as long as the king pleased and second, hereditary wardens. It was usual for a warden to be in charge of a single forest but in some cases he would be responsible for a group of forests in a particular area. In 1300 a woman, Sabine Pecche, was warden of the five Somerset forests of Exmoor, Mendip, Nerroche, North Petherton and Selwood.[37] The wardens, who acted as agents for the king, were responsible for many matters of forest administration, not only in connection with forest law but also in carrying out any instructions that the king might issue. Where a castle lay within the bounds of the forest the warden often held the position of keeper of the castle, as was the case in the Peak Forest, the Forest of Dean and Rockingham Forest.

Of parallel, rather than lesser, importance were the verderers who were directly responsible to the king and not to the wardens. They were elected by freeholders in the county court after the sheriff had received a writ giving him the necessary authority. They then held their appointment for life although they could be removed if they were unable to continue on account of ill health, infirmity or failing to fulfil the qualification that they should hold land within the forest. Verderers were men of substance and were usually knights or important land owners who received neither salary nor perquisites for their services although this did not always apply in later years. Normally four verderers were appointed for each forest but this number could vary and where a forest was divided into a number of bailiwicks four verderers would generally be appointed for each one. However there were exceptions to this rule which was doubtless dependant to some extent on the size of the bailiwick. The duties of the verderers were chiefly concerned with the attachment court and they were required to view and enrol all attachments for trespass against vert and venison. In cases of vert they were empowered to deal with offences where the value of the material was four pence or less. They were also required to attend all forest courts. In 1976 verderers were still elected for the New Forest and the Forest of Dean, their courts being held in the Verderers' Hall at the Queen's House in Lyndhurst and in the Speech House near Cinderford respectively.

Next in the hierarchy were foresters, and their duties and functions can be most readily appreciated, if it is borne in mind that the medieval forester was, in effect, a gamekeeper and that he was mainly responsible for dealing with trespassers, poaching and damage. There were two kinds of forester; riding foresters who were mounted on horses and who were also known as general or itinerant foresters and walking foresters who were on foot. In some cases foresters had grooms or pages who accompanied them on their rounds of the forest. Although it was not laid down how many foresters should be employed in a forest, it was usual to have at least one for each bailiwick. However if the justices in eyre formed the opinion that there were too many foresters, they could order that the number should be reduced. Article 7 of the Charter of the Forest[38] contained the statement that: 'So many foresters shall be assigned to the keeping of the forests, as reasonably shall seem sufficient for the keeping of the same.' Foresters were nominated by the wardens and although in some cases they received wages, it was not unusual for a forester to make a payment to the warden in respect of his being appointed and to obtain his remuneration from those who lived in the forest by means of various kinds of extortion which were claimed as customary rights. These included scotale which has already been commented on in this chapter, charging fees for such matters as cheminage when they were not in fact due and collecting young pigs, lambs and corn after the manner of a tithe. This state of affairs was of such great concern to those who lived within the bounds of a forest that the Charter[39] laid down that: 'No forester or bedle from henceforth shall make scotal, or gather garb or oates or any corn or lamb pig nor shall make any gathering but by the sight and upon the view of the twelve Rangers when they shall make their range.' In this context the term ranger should read regarder and range as regard.

In addition to the foresters who have been described in the preceding paragraph, there were in many of the larger forests hereditary foresters who were known as foresters-of-fee. However it is difficult to define their position precisely as it would seem that in some instances they aspired more to a warden than to a forester while some considered that they were subordinate only to the king. Foresters-of-fee were normally in charge of a bailiwick and while some paid a rent or acknowledgement for this, they enjoyed at the same time many privileges and perquisites. The office of forester-of-fee could be held by a woman or by individuals who did not actively carry out the duties of the office themselves and in both such cases it was necessary for them to appoint a deputy who acted on their behalf. However the presence of the actual holder of the office was always required at forest courts.

Next in rank to the foresters were the woodwards who were faced with the difficult task of having to serve two masters. Within the bounds of a forest, the king's demesne lands might only form a comparatively small part of the forest area as a whole and much of the woodland area might belong to individual land owners. Nevertheless, these privately owned woodlands were subject to forest law and the owners were prohibited from doing anything that might adversely affect the welfare of the deer. Felling timber, creating assarts, burning charcoal and erecting buildings are some of the incidents which could only be done after a licence had been obtained from the king. Private landowners were required to employ woodwards whose duties were not only to look after the owners woods but also to protect the vert and venison in those woods on the king's behalf and woodwards were required to swear an oath to this effect before the chief justice of the forest. A woodward was therefore a private forester who was sworn to defend and safeguard the king's interests.

Manwood[40] who deals with the matter at some length, states that the duties of a ranger lay in the purlieus or pourallees of the forest rather than in the forest itself and he divided the duties into three categories. First, to patrol or range through purlieu land in order to note any offences that had been committed. Second, to drive back into the adjacent forest any deer that had strayed onto purlieu land and third, to present all cases of trespass that he found. The oath which a ranger was required to swear covered these three aspects in the following words:

> *You shall truly execute the Office of a Ranger in the pourallees of Waltham upon the borders of the King's Forest of Waltham. You shall rechase and with your hound drive back again the wild beasts of the Forest, as often as they shall range out of the same Forest into your pourallees. You shall truly present all unlawful hunting, and hunters of wild beasts of venery and chase, as well within the pourallees as within the Forest. And those and all other offences, you shall present at the King's next Court of Attachments or Swanimote, which shall first happen, so help you God.*

Lewis[41] observes that a ranger's appointment 'is confined to such forests as have any known and acknowledged purlieus. He is an officer to and of the forest, but not within it.' Rangers were first appointed in the latter part of the fourteenth century.

Every three years an inspection of the forest, which was known as the regard, was carried out by 12 specially chosen knights who were known as regarders, although in the twelfth century they were sometimes referred to as viewers. To assist them in their task and at the same time to ensure that they carried it out correctly, they were provided with a list of questions to which they were required to give the answers. These questions were arranged under 12 headings which were known as the chapters of the regard and covered the following matters: herbage on the king's demesne; nests of hawks and falcons; forges and mines within the forest; harbours from which timber could be exported; honey in the forest; assarts; two different aspects of purprestures; waste; viewing the king's demesne woods; viewing purprestures, assarts and wastes in the king's woods and lastly, as to who possessed bows, arrows, crossbows, braches (similar to a foxhound), greyhounds or any other thing that could endanger the king's deer. Article 5 of the Charter of the Forest[42] laid down that: 'Our regarders shall go through the forest to make their regard, as it hath been accustomed at the time of the first coronation of King Henry our grandfather (that is, Henry II) and not otherwise'. Article 6 of the same charter states that the view or inquiry as to the lawing of dogs 'shall be made henceforth when the regard is made, that is to say every three years'.

In the previous chapter reference was made to the launds or lawns of the forest. These were glades or open spaces in the king's demesne woodlands which provided grazing for those domestic animals that were allowed in the forest, namely cattle, horses and sheep although the last named were not popular while goats were prohibited entirely. Pigs were allowed to enter during the time of pannage, that is when the acorns and beech mast had fallen, and this time extended approximately from mid-September to mid-November. However, no animals of any kind were allowed in the forest during the fence month. This practice of turning animals into demesne lands was known as agisting and a fee was payable in respect of each animal. The amount due was collected by forest officers who were known as agisters, agistators or gistakers of whom there were usually four in each forest.

Thus the established forest officers whose duties have been described in the preceding pages may be summarized as follows: justices of the forest, justices in eyre, wardens, verderers, foresters, foresters-of-fee, woodwards, rangers, regarders and agisters. In addition to these, there were other minor appointments which included sergeants-of-fee who were persons of local standing and importance. They enjoyed certain hereditary rights in respect of holding land within a forest and in return, were required to protect the vert and venison throughout the whole of the forest but they were not in charge of a bailiwick as was a forester-of-fee. Others were the launders who were responsible for the care of the forest launds which are described in Chapter 1 under the section entitled 'The Framework of the Forest' and the palesters, palers or palifers whose duty it was to maintain the pale fences around any parks that lay within the bounds of the forest. There were also parkers or keepers who were responsible for any deer that were kept within these parks. There remains one other appointment to which reference should be made and that is the bedle whom Manwood[43] describes as: 'An officer or servant of the forest that doth make all manner of proclamations as well within the Courts of the Forest as without'. Bedles are specifically mentioned in Article 7 of the Charter of the Forest[44] with reference to scotale and other forms of extortion.

Wardens, verderers, foresters and woodwards each had a symbol of office which was in the nature of a badge of rank. The warden's symbol was a bow and it was for this reason that they were sometimes referred to as bow-bearers. The badge of the verderer was an axe, the forester's a horn and the woodward's a hatchet or billhook which was later referred to as a sealing axe, on account of it being used to mark, seal or blaze trees that were to be felled, in exactly the same way as the present day forester marks his trees with a slasher.

VERT AND VENISON

3

THE BEASTS OF THE FOREST

In medieval times wild animals that were hunted were divided into three categories according to the areas in which they were found. However, unlike the ecological and environmental areas of the present day, those adopted in the middle ages were governed entirely by legal considerations and comprised the forest, the chase and the warren.

Manwood[1] states that there were five beasts of the forest which were also

1.   *A section of the Bayeux Tapestry depicting a Norman hunting party with hounds and a falcon. c.1075.*

known as beasts of venery namely the hart, the hind, the hare, the wild boar and the wolf and in support of this assertion quotes various earlier authorities on the matter. He admits that the hart and the hind are different sexes of the same species but justifies the separate inclusion of each on the grounds that they were hunted at different seasons. He also observes that 'Although there are no wolves in England at this day, yet there have been plenty of them and they have been accompted beasts of venery'. Manwood's views on the subject appear to have been accepted until the publication of Turner's *Select Pleas of the Forest* at the beginning of this century in which the author drew attention to the following errors in Manwood's list of beasts.[2]

Apart from treating the male and female red deer as two separate species, he fails to include fallow deer but no distinction in law was made between these two kinds of deer. His exclusion of roe deer was based on a decision given in a case which was heard in 1338 and to which further reference is made later in this chapter, but prior to this case roe were recognized as beasts of the forest. As regards the wolf, Turner considered its inclusion entirely unwarranted since this animal was seldom mentioned in any public records and, on the few occasions that it was, these records contained nothing to support Manwood's statement. The cause of these inaccuracies was possibly the influence of writers who were more conversant with hunting customs on the continent than those which prevailed in England. Turner's view that there were only four beasts of the forest, namely the red, fallow and roe deer and the wild boar, has now been accepted.

The red deer, *Cervus elaphus* L., which is indigenous to this country, was the largest beast of the forest and still occurs in England on Exmoor, the Quantocks, the Brendon Hills, the Lake District, Thetford Forest, Sherwood Forest, The New Forest and in parts of Surrey, Sussex, Staffordshire, Cheshire and some of the northern counties.[3] The names that have been applied to the male and female red deer of different ages have varied with the passage of time and in Table 1 three sources are quoted. These are first, medieval names taken from *The Book of St Albans*,[4] second, names given by C. P. Collyns in his book *The Chase of the Wild Red Deer*[5] which concerns Exmoor and the Devon and Somerset Staghounds and was first published in 1862; and third, the names as used on Exmoor in 1976 which Mr E. R. Lloyd, Honorary Secretary of the Devon and Somerset Hunt Club has kindly confirmed.

In medieval times, if a hart was hunted by the sovereign and escaped alive, it was named a hart royal. However, if while it was being hunted the hart left the forest and travelled a considerable distance, so that its return to the forest was rather doubtful, the king issued a proclamation. This made it known that no one should hunt or kill the animal, in the hope that it would ultimately return to the forest in which it had been found. It was then known as a hart royal proclaimed. On Exmoor, a barren female deer or one without a calf is termed a yeld or yeld hind.

Table 1

Changes in the names for red deer of different ages

Year	Male deer			Female deer		
	Book of St Albans 1486	Exmoor 1862	Exmoor 1976	Book of St Albans 1486	Exmoor 1862	Exmoor 1976
1st	calf	calf	male calf	calf	calf	hind calf
2nd	broket	broket knobber or knobbler	male deer or pricket	broket's sister	hearst	young hind
3rd	spayard	spire or pricket	young stag	hind	young hind	hind
4th	staggard	staggart	stag	hind	hind	hind
5th	stag	stag or warrantable deer	stag	hind	hind	hind
6th	hart	stag or hart	stag	hind	hind	hind
7th	hart	stag or hart	stag	hind	hind	hind

The fallow deer, *Dama dama*. L., were so called in order to distinguish them from the red deer since the word 'fallow' means a pale brown or reddish-yellow colour. They were introduced into England some time before the Norman Conquest and are second only to the red deer in size, although the Sika deer (*Cervus nippon. Temminck*) which were introduced in the middle of the nineteenth century are nearly as large. Although, in the past, fallow deer have often been confined to parks, a certain number have always existed in a truly wild state and still do in many woodland areas of England notably the New Forest, Epping Forest and Cannock Chase.[6] In the fifteenth century fallow deer greatly outnumbered both red and roe deer in the forests of Dorset, Essex, Hampshire, Northamptonshire and Wiltshire. Table 2 sets out the names applied to male and female fallow deer of different ages according to three authorities: first, those set down by Dame Juliana Barnes,[7] second, those in respect of male deer as issued by the then Deputy Surveyor of the New Forest, the Hon. Gerald Lascelles in about 1880[8] and third those in use in the New

Forest in 1976 as kindly advised by Mrs K. D. Millar, Joint Honorary Secretary of the New Forest Buckhounds.

Table 2

Changes in the names for fallow deer of different ages

Year	Male deer			Female deer	
	Book of St Albans 1486	New Forest c.1880	New Forest 1976	Book of St Albans 1486	New Forest 1976
1st	fawn	fawn	fawn or buck fawn	fawn	fawn
2nd	pricket	pricket	pricket	pricket's sister	doe
3rd	sorel	sorel	three year old	doe	doe
4th	sore	sore	four year old	doe	doe
5th	buck of the first head	bare buck	five year old	doe	doe
6th	buck or great buck	buck	six year old	doe	doe
7th	great buck	great buck	great buck	doe	doe

The term rascall, raskell or raskall is applied to both red and fallow deer and is used to denote male animals which are out of condition and not fit to hunt. In some forests it also referred to female deer and included all animals which were not fit for venison. In 1670, the result of a census relating to red and fallow deer in the New Forest was published and this gave the following information: red male deer, 103; red rascall, 254; fallow male, 1409; fallow rascall, 6,184.[9]

Of the three species of deer that were designated as beasts of the forest, the smallest was the roe, *Capreolus capreolus*. L., and it was probably for this reason that in the Middle Ages, it was regarded as the least important, not so much from the point of view of sport as from the amount of meat it could produce in comparison to the other two species. Although the roe is a native of this country, the population has varied very considerably since the middle ages. In medieval times they were widely distributed throughout England but with the continuous erosion of woodland areas in order to satisfy the demands for agriculture, iron smelting and building work, their numbers began to decrease. This trend continued for a great number of years and it was not until conditions which were more suitable for them had been provided by the newly planted forests of the twentieth century, that roe deer began to establish themselves in any large numbers. In 1338 a case occurred which cast some doubt on the accepted rule that roe deer were beasts of the forest. It arose by reason of a claim by Lord Percy to hunt roe deer on his manor at Seamer although this manor was within the bounds of the Forest of Pickering. It was held that although Lord Percy and his forebears had taken roe in the past, they were nevertheless beasts of the forest but when this point was subsequently referred to the King's Bench, it was decided that the roe was a beast of the warren. This finding was apparently arrived at in the light of rather doubtful evidence that roe deer drove the other species of deer away. It would also seem that this decision was only applied to this particular case since on two later occasions, one in Derbyshire in 1398 and the other in Salisbury in 1492, trespassers were presented for taking roe deer.[10]

Although the wild boar, *Sus scrofa.* L., had become extinct in England by the middle of the seventeenth century, in earlier times it had been held in great esteem as a beast of the forest. It is said that hunting the wild boar was the favourite sport of Henry I (1100-1135) and that John (1199-1216) was equally devoted to the boar whether in the forest or on the table. Wild pigs are recorded in many parts of England during the Middle Ages including the Forest of Dean (1216), Wychwood Forest (1217), Waltham Forest in Essex (1223), the Forest of Pickering (1227), Clarendon Forest and other Wiltshire Forests in the fourteenth century and Cranbourne Chase during the reign of Elizabeth I (1558-1603). In 1455 one Robert Clare was apprehended for killing four wild pigs on Iwerne Hill near the western boundary of Cranbourne Chase while in the following year, the Vicar of Iwerne was found guilty of killing another four pigs with his bow and arrows in Iwerne Wood.

Inevitably, as disafforestation increased and the number of forests diminished, wild pigs found survival more difficult due mainly to the lack of acorns and beech mast which formed much of their food. Even so, they survived in parts of Durham, Lancashire and Staffordshire into the sixteenth century and were thereafter preserved in parks for hunting for some time. In 1617 James I hunted wild boar at Windsor but they did not survive in a truly wild state in England after the reign of Charles II (1660-1685).[11] *The Master of Game*[12] gives the mating season, which was called 'the brimming', as starting at about the feast of St Andrew (30th November) and lasting for about three weeks. The boars remained with the sows until about the middle of

January and farrowing usually took place in March. This book also makes the
following observations:

> *They wind a man as far as any other beast or farther . . . They root in*
> *the ground with the rowel of their snouts which is right hard . . . They*
> *have a hard skin and strong flesh, especially upon their shoulders*
> *which is called the shield. Their season begins from the Holy Cross*
> *day in September to the feast of St Andrew . . . they are in grease*
> *when they be withdrawn from the sows.*

Holy Cross day, which is also known as Holy Rood day, is the 14th September
and the expression 'to be in grease' meant that they were in the right condition
to be hunted and were therefore in season. It would appear from this that
boars could be hunted from 14th September to 30th November and again
about three weeks after the latter date and this is confirmed by Manwood[13]
who gives the season for hunting the boar as being from Christmas
(25th December) to Lady Day (25th March). Reference has already been made
to the fact that in medieval times the word 'venison' was used to denote the
actual beasts of the forest and thus included the wild boar, whereas at the
present time this word is used to refer only to the flesh of a deer.

The Beasts of the Chase

In addition to the beasts of the forest there were, according to Manwood[14] five
beasts of the chase, namely, the buck, the doe, the fox, the martin and the roe
and to endorse his views he refers to the opinions of Hollinshed,[15] Dame
Barnes[16] and others. Nevertheless this allocation of animals to a chase as
opposed to a forest is open to question. When the king granted a forest to one
of his subjects it became a chase but such a grant would include all rights over
the beasts of that forest and consequently there was no legal implication in the
words 'beasts of the chase'. The expression was simply used to indicate those
animals that were to be found in a chase and did not mean that they were of a
different kind to those that were to be found in a forest. Turner[17] goes on to
point out that although there was no distinct difference in law between the
beasts of the forest and those of the chase, they were hunted in different ways.
It is therefore possible that Manwood's classification was based on a tract on
hunting which was written about 1325 by William Twici[18] who, in describing
different methods of hunting, stated that the hart, the boar, the wolf and the
hare were hunted in one way and the buck, the doe, the fox and other vermin in
another. Twici whose name sometimes appears as Twiti or Twety was
huntsman to Edward II.

THE BEASTS AND FOWLS OF THE WARREN

The beasts of the warren were for the most part clearly defined and comprised the hare, the fox, the rabbit (known in the Middle Ages by the name of coney), the wild cat and in some instances the badger, the wolf and even the squirrel. The ruling given in 1338 that the roe deer was a beast of the warren has already been referred to earlier in this chapter. The beasts of the warren were regarded as hurtful or noxious and, although able to provide sport, they were not preserved. Turner[19] describes the difference between beasts of the forest and beasts of the warren as follows:

> The former were strictly preserved by the forest laws, while the latter were in no sense protected by the charters of warren, which merely reserved the right of hunting in them to particular individuals. The beasts of the forest were the king's venison; they were treated as his property and described as his property. On the other hand, the beasts of the warren were not the lord's beasts, nor were they described as such.

The fowls of the warren were the pheasant, the partridge and the woodcock but there were some instances of the plover and the lark also being included.

Two other animals which have been mentioned and about which a little more might be said are the wolf and the wild cat. Over many centuries the wolf was regarded as a common enemy and steps were frequently taken to encourage its control by such means as money payments or the granting of land to those who were prepared to undertake such work. Some of the last areas in England in which wolves remained were the Peak District, the Forest of Blackburnshire and parts of Yorkshire. It is thought that wolves did not become extinct in England until the end of the fifteenth century, while the last wolf in Scotland is said to have been killed in 1743.

According to Turberville,[20] whose book on hunting was published in 1575, the wild cat was often hunted in England during his time although such hunting usually occurred by chance rather than by design. The last wild cat in England is said to have been shot by Lord Ravensworth at Eslington, Northumberland in 1853[21] but wild cats are still found in the Scottish Highlands and their numbers have substantially increased since 1920.

In medieval times reference was frequently made to the murrain, which appears to have been a general term for any serious disease which affected deer. In some cases the disease spread rapidly and seems to have been highly infectious as in 1286 when 350 red and fallow deer died of the murrain in Sherwood Forest, while in Rockingham Forest 1,400 died in the 63 years between 1422 and 1485. The worst fatalities occurred in Clarendon Forest in Wiltshire in 1470 when 2,209 deer succumbed, while some 15 years later 560 deer died in the Forests of Melksham and Pewsham during the first three years of the reign of Henry VII.[22] When dead deer were found in the forest, the foresters were required to record each one and to hang the carcasses up in trees. In later years, it became the practice to burn the carcasses probably on account of the greater number of deaths and in an attempt to prevent the disease from spreading.

HOUNDS AND HUNTSMEN

The hounds that were used in medieval times were types rather than breeds which had been evolved over a period of years for the purpose of hunting a particular animal or group of animals. Some hounds were collectively referred to as 'running hounds' but the precise meaning of this term is not altogether clear. It would appear that running hounds were those which hunted a stag until it was brought to bay, as opposed to the lymers which, after finding a stag, were called off and the running hounds laid on. This is similar in principle to the method which is still used by the Devon and Somerset Staghounds although the lymers have been replaced by the tufters. In the medieval rolls and records, Latin terms were used for various classes of hound according to the quarry which they hunted and examples of these are *damericii canes* or buckhounds used to hunt fallow deer and *porcerecii canes* or hounds for boar hunting.

The alant or alaunt was particularly fierce and is said to have been introduced to western Europe by a Caucasian tribe known as the Alani who not only used these hounds for hunting but also as dogs of war.[23] They were able to hunt by both scent and sight and were normally used for hunting boar and on account of their savageness they were usually kept muzzled. The brache or rache was a small hound which hunted by scent and was somewhat similar in appearance to a foxhound, although rather larger, while the bercelet was of the same type but smaller in size.

The gazehound or greyhound which in Norman times was known as the levrier[24] was variable in size and appearance, some having a smooth coat and some a rough one. They hunted by sight and the larger hounds were frequently used for hunting deer, so much so that by the Assize of the Forest[25] it was forbidden to keep greyhounds within the forest. One of the 12 questions of the regard was whether anyone in the forest owned braches or greyhounds. The lymer or limehound was so called because when hunting it was held on a horse hide line or leash known as a liam which was a fathom and a half in length (nine feet).[26] It hunted by scent and in appearance was somewhat similar to a bloodhound; it was used in the same way as the tufters are used by the Devon and Somerset Staghounds at the present time. The mastiff was large, powerful and comparable to the present day breed of that name and was employed in hunting wolves and red and fallow deer. Velters were originally very fast hounds after the pattern of a greyhound but later the name appears to have been applied to a hound which was similar to an alant but even fiercer which was used for boar hunting. In some districts deer poachers evolved their own type of hound which was best suited to their needs. This was known as a strakur and was probably the medieval equivalent of the lurcher.

The *Book of St. Albans*[27] which was written in 1486 gives the following list of whimsical names of hounds:

> *Theyse be the names of houndes. Fyrste there is Grehoun; a Bastard; a Mengrell; a Mastif; a Lemor; a Spanyel; Raches; Kenettys; Teroures; Butchers houndes; Dunghyll dogges; Tryndeltaylles; and pryckeryd currys; and smalle ladye's popees that bere aways the flees and dyvers small sautes.*

There were three classes of medieval huntsmen: the berner who was in charge of the running hounds which included the braches; the berceletter who was responsible for the bercelets; and the ventrer or fewterer in whose charge were the gazehounds or greyhounds. There was also a lymerer under whose control were the lymers and who was responsible for locating or harbouring a stag as is done by the harbourer of the Devon and Somerset Staghounds today.

The hunting seasons which are given by Manwood[28] were as follows:

Hart and buck	24th June-14th September
Hind and doe	14th September-2nd February
Roe buck	Easter-29th September
Roe doe	29th September-2nd February
Boar	25th December-25th March

Some authorities consider the date on which hind and doe hunting commenced to be Martinmas (11th November) and the beginning of the season for hart and buck to be 3rd May, but on what grounds it is not clear and the latter date must be regarded with some doubt. The season for hunting the hart and buck was known as pinguedo which was the time when these animals were said to be 'in grease' while the season for hind and roe was termed fermisone.

Although deer were usually hunted, there were other methods of taking them and these were sometimes adopted by poachers. Such methods entailed the use of snares which were variously known as buckstalls, buckstakes, toils, tramels, hayes or deer-hays of which there were several patterns. The simplest consisted of ropes or halters slung between trees or stakes in which the antlers of the deer became entwined. Other kinds incorporated bottles, flowers or other articles which, it was hoped, would excite the curiosity of the deer and so entice them into the snare, while another type consisted of nets in which a deer could become entangled.

The Trees of the Forest

This section deals with the trees of the forest from an historical and legal point of view and not from a silvicultural or botanical aspect. The subject of vert has already been dealt with at some length, in Chapter 1 in the section entitled 'The Laws of the Forest', and it is not intended to add anything further.

In medieval times, trees were often referred to by a name which described or indicated their purpose or use in the forest. Examples of this are to be found in border trees, which marked a boundary, more particularly that of the forest; fee trees, which were usually oaks and were supplied each year to certain officers of the forest as perquisites in recognition of the positions which they held; and fox and vermin trees (also known as fox et varmint trees or fox trees) which occurred in Rockingham Forest in the middle of the fifteenth century and were trees which were given to the foresters as a reward for keeping down foxes and vermin. On the other hand lynery trees were simply lime trees.[29]

Trees that were blown down by the wind or lost large branches during gales were carefully recorded, for even if they were not fit for building purposes, they were often of considerable value for fuel. Those which were uprooted by the wind were known as cablish which is the anglicized form of the Latin *cableicium* or *cablicium* and is similar to the Old French *chablis* which had the same meaning. In a few cases *cableicium* was applied to very large branches that had fallen as a result of the wind and were sound enough and large enough to use for building work, but it was never used in reference to fuel wood. Later, the word cablish was replaced by the terms rotefallen or rootefaler for trees which had been blown down by the wind, while small material was known as wyndfallen wood.[30]

Decayed trees, that were only fit for use as firewood and that were later known as dotards, were referred to as wrassells in Rockingham Forest in 1577 while the word stubb or stub was used in reference to a dead or rotten pollarded tree and not to a stump. The word robura was also used to denote a pollarded or possibly a stunted tree of any species and not necessarily an oak.[31] Ramell was a term for coppice or underwood, spires were young, straight, thriving trees and blestro or blettro were young beech and oak saplings, while blatrous spars were those cut from such saplings. Tynsell wood was small material that probably included faggots and was used in bakers ovens.

Privileges, Charges and Rights in the Forest

In addition to the deer and other wild animals that were to be found in a medieval forest, certain domestic animals were permitted to feed on the herbage within the forest at specified times of the year for which privilege the owners of such animals made a payment. The admitting of domestic animals to a forest was known as agisting, while the common of herbage or right to pasture in the forest was called agistment although this word was also used to denote the money that was due in respect of such animals. The animals that were allowed to be agisted in a forest were for the most part cattle although a limited number of horses were permitted. Sheep were disliked on account of the belief that they not only adversely affected the grazing which the deer needed, but also imparted their scent to the deer and so confused the hounds when hunting. Consequently, in some forests, the agistment of sheep was allowed only by special licence. Goats were normally prohibited from entering the forest because they tainted the grass and, if this occurred, the deer left the area. The fact that goats can cause very considerable damage to trees and underwood was probably a further reason for this prohibition. Pigs, which in medieval times were usually referred to as swine, were treated differently from other domestic animals as regards agistment. In the first place, the object in turning swine into woodland areas was so that they could feed on acorns and beech mast which fell in the autumn and not to graze as other animals did. This 'profit of mast' was known as pannage or pawnage and the period during which pigs were allowed in the forest was termed 'the time of pannage'.

The forest officers who were responsible for the agisting of animals in the forest were known as agisters, agistators, gistakers or gest-takers and under the Charter of the Forest,[32] three swanimotes or meetings were to be held each year and these were to be attended by the agisters, the foresters and the verderers. Reference has already been made to swanimotes at the beginning of Chapter 2. The dates on which these swanimotes were to be held under the Charter were, in chronological order, first, fifteen days before the feast of St John the Baptist (24th June), that is to say on 9th June. This day was also the beginning of the fence month or period during which it was considered that the female deer gave birth to their young, when the officers met to ensure that the forest was quiet and the deer received special protection. The fence month ended fifteen days after the feast of St John, that is on 9th July. The second swanimote was held fifteen days before Michaelmas (29th September) on 14th September which was Holy Rood Day, when the agisters 'come together to take agestment in our demesne woods'. The third meeting was 'about the feast of St Martin in the winter when that our gest-takers shall receive our pawnage'. St Martin's Day or Martinmas is on 11th November.

Since the fence month which began on 9th June was designed to ensure that the forest was as quiet as possible at that time, it would be logical to suppose that stock that might disturb the deer were not agisted until after the end of the fence month, that is 9th July, and Turner[33] endorses this view. Manwood[34] on the other hand states categorically that: 'The time of taking of agistment for all manner of beasts and cattel, that are commonable within the forest, in the king's demesne woods, lands and pastures for herbage only, doth always

begin fifteen days before Midsummer-day and doth last until Holy-Rood Day
and then the same doth end.' In several forests agistment was permitted
during the fence month but in such cases the amount payable was increased
very considerably during the period. The time of pannage for pigs extended
from Holy Rood (14th September) to Martinmas (11th November) and on the
latter date the winter heyning began. This continued until St George's Day
(23rd April), during which time the agistment of stock in the forest was
forbidden in order to conserve food for the deer. After-pannage was money
paid for the agistment of pigs in the demesne woods belonging to the king after
the normal season of pannage had ended, that is, after Martinmas.

Any cattle that were agisted in the forest were required to be branded in
order that their owners could be traced. Fisher[35] provides illustrations of 15
brand marks that were in use in the Forest of Essex which in the fourteenth
century became known as the Forest of Waltham, the remnants of which are
now referred to as Epping Forest. In some forests large byres or cowhouses
which were known as vaccaries or net-houses, were built on demesne land for
the use of cattle that were agisted in the area. The word net-house still survives
in the name neats-foot oil. A subject who owned woodland within the metes
and bounds of the forest, had the right to agist his own woods and the Forest
Charter[36] provided that 'Every freeman may agest his own wood within our
forest at his pleasure and shall take his pawnage'. Under the same statute a
freeman was entitled to drive his pigs through the king's demesne in order to
agist them in his own woods or elsewhere. In the time of Henry II (1154-1198)
an owner of land within the forest was not allowed to agist his land before any
demesne land belonging to the king had been agisted. Subsequently it was
established that the owners of any woods or hedgerows adjoining or near the
king's demesne woods could not turn swine into their woods until the king had
agisted his own.

In addition to the various payments made regarding such matters as the
lawing of dogs and the agisting of stock, there were other fees or
acknowledgements paid to the king in respect of special facilities granted to
him. In some cases, the king granted the right to receive such payments to
others. Cheminage, chiminage or chimmage, which was a toll or payment
made in return for permission to pass through a forest with carts, carriages or
packhorses, is an example. It is generally considered to have been payable only
during the fence month but in some forests cheminage was apparently levied
at other times, although the charge was substantially increased for that
month. *The Charter of the Forest*[37] laid down that only a forester-of-fee who
paid ferm or rent for his bailiwick was allowed to take cheminage and
authorized that the rates of payment should be two pence per half year for
goods carried by cart, and one half penny per half year for goods carried by
pack horse. However, only merchants who came from beyond the bounds of
the foresters bailiwick were to be charged. All those who carried bark,

brushwood or charcoal on their backs were exempt from payment, even if they earned their living by such means, unless they had gathered the material in the king's demesne woods.

Another, somewhat similar, payment was that known as thistletake or thistltak which was to be found in some forests in Cheshire, Lancashire and Yorkshire in the fifteenth century. This was payable by drovers who were in charge of animals which were driven through the forest and was levied at the rate of a half penny per beast, if they allowed the animals to graze as they passed through. In the Forest of the High Peak, woodsilver or wodsylver was charged for billets of wood, but this seems to have been a straightforward charge for goods supplied rather than an acknowledgement fee.[38] In about 1410 reference was made in *The Master of Game*[39] to squillectes which was a term used to denote collections of money and which in all probability included charges such as those described above.

Besides these various charges and tolls there were also certain rights to take wood from the forest for recognized purposes. These rights were known as botes or estovers and comprised house-bote or the right to take wood for the repair of buildings, fire-bote for fuel, plough-bote for the repair of waggons and implements and hedge-bote and hay-bote for the repair of gates and fences. In some forests a right to dig peat or turf, which was known as a right of turbary, also existed.

Finally a note regarding an unusual method of deciding the claim of a subject against the king. In 1266, in the Forest of Bernwood, small thorn trees were claimed by the chief forester or warden. In order to determine the matter, an auger known as a restnauegar was used and the smaller trees which could be pierced by this auger were granted to the forester, while the larger ones through which the auger could not pass were reserved to the king.[40]

SOME ENGLISH FORESTS OF THE MIDDLE AGES I

4

This chapter and the one which follows, contain information chiefly of a topographical nature, relating to 129 ancient forests and chases. For convenience these are described as being of the Middle Ages, though some had their origins prior to the Norman Conquest while the majority of them were royal forests.

Details relating to these forests are not always readily available but the following sources may be mentioned. In 1222 practically the whole of England was subject to a great gale which resulted in a large number of trees being blown down. The damage was so extensive that Henry III issued special orders to his forest officers as to the action that they should take regarding this windblown timber, and the names of the forests to which the king's orders were sent provides one of the earliest records of the royal forests of England.[1] The Patent and Close Rolls of the same period also contain references to contemporary forests while some further information is provided by a few individual authorities.

In his *Glossarium Archiaologicum,* the third edition of which appeared in 1687, Spelman[2] stated that there were 68 forests, 13 chases and 781 parks in England. He also set out a list of 86 forests and in all but 14 cases, he also gave the counties in which they were situated. Of these 86 forests, 67 were in England, 8 in Wales while 11 are difficult to identify with certainty. However, Spelman did not mention the New Forest in Hampshire although he included the New Forest which lay some six miles to the west of Richmond in Yorkshire. If the Hampshire New Forest is added, the number of forests would amount to 68. Forty years later, Cowel[3] repeated the totals which were given by Spelman but observed that 'Besides the New Forest there are sixty-eight forests in England, thirteen chases and seven hundred and eighty-one parks'. From this it would appear that he thought that there were 69 forests. Cowel gives the names of 31 forests, all but one of which are to be found in Spelman's list, and at the end adds the words 'besides several others' which means another 38 for which he does not account.

In 1787, St John[4] provided a further catalogue of forests and chases and divided it into two sections. The first, which he described as 'real forests', were those 'which are reputed to have preserved their *jura regalia,* that is the jurisdiction, laws, courts, officers, game and boundaries'. These consisted of 12 forests of which 10 are included by Spelman, the two outstanding being Aylesholt (Alice Holt) and the New Forest in Hampshire. The second section covers 'nominal forests and chases, some of which have been inclosed and are demised as part of the land revenue and in others the rights of the crown have been totally granted away'. These amounted to 59 forests and 9 chases although two forests are referred to as 'or chases' and 29 of the forests are included in Spelman's list. Of these three sources Spelman and St John are the most valuable while Cowel's list may be disregarded for all practical purposes.

The approximate location of each of the forests included in these two chapters is shown on two key maps, by means of a number which corresponds to the serial number shown against the appropriate forest in the text. Thus Dartmoor Forest is shown as number 17 on the map. Each forest is arranged alphabetically in the text, under the county in which it is situated, while the counties themselves are also placed in alphabetical order. When it is not known in which county a forest is located recourse should be had to the index. Where a reference is made to county boundaries, these are the boundaries that were in existence before the recent alterations to county areas. In those cases in which the names of counties have been altered or new names introduced, the original names have been retained as for example, Cumberland and Monmouthshire.

In this chapter and the following one, many of the descriptions of individual forests contain a perambulation or record of the bounds of the forest concerned. However it must be emphasized that these are only abridged accounts which are included in order to provide some indication of the extent and size of the forest.

BERKSHIRE

1 The Forest of Berkshire

This forest, which covered a large part of the county, was the subject of a special inquisition in 1219 and consequently, in 1221, the following bounds were established. From Oxford, the eastern limit followed the course of the Thames southwards to its union with the river Kennet below Reading. The southern boundary then ran beside the Kennet as far as its junction with the river Enborne, a quarter of a mile to the north of Aldermaston, and continued along this river to its source. From that point, the line of the boundary continued to Inkpen where it turned due north to join the Kennet again at a point about half way between Kintbury and Hungerford. It then continued westward along the Kennet until it reached the county boundary between Berkshire and Wiltshire, about one mile west of Hungerford. From there it followed the county boundary northwards, crossing the M4 motorway approximately half way between junctions 14 and 15, and eventually followed the course of the river Cole until it reached the Thames about half a mile south-east of Lechlade. The northern boundary continued along the course of the Thames to Oxford, thus completing the perimeter of the forest. The Forest of Berkshire was disafforested about 1223.

2   Windsor Forest

Windsor Forest was also known as Windlesor, Windeshore, Wokingham, Okingham or Oakingham Forest while the name Collingwood or Colyngrugges was sometimes applied to that part of the forest which lies between Frimley and Pirbright: Norden[5] shows it as Collingleywood.

The bounds of the forest, starting at the Berkshire-Surrey border near Old Windsor on the eastern perimeter, were as follows. From Old Windsor the boundary followed the course of the Thames southwards, until it joined the river Wey and continued along that river in a south-westerly direction to Guildford. From this town the boundary followed the top of the Hog's Back to approximately Tongham where it joined the river Blackwater which at first forms the county boundary between Surrey and Hampshire and subsequently that between Berkshire and Hampshire. It then continued along the Blackwater until that river joined the Loddon near Swallowfield which it followed until it, in turn, joined the Thames. It thus continued along the course of the Thames to Old Windsor, to complete the perimeter.

The forest was divided into 16 walks, wards or bailiwicks, namely: Egham, Cranborne, New Lodge, Swinley, Windlesham, Chertsey, Brookwoode, Purbrighte, Linchford and Ashe, Frimley, Easthamsted, Sandhurst, Bigshot, Bearwood, Warefielde and Binfield.[6] In 1580, 13 acres in Cranbourne Walk were felled and subsequently sown with acorns which, by 1623, had become 'a wood of some thousands of tall young oaks, bearing acorns and giving shelter to cattle and likely to prove as good timber as any in the kingdom' but in 1642 much of the finest timber was felled for the Navy. At the beginning of the nineteenth century the forest area comprised 25,000 acres of open forest land, 5,400 acres of inclosed crown property and 29,000 acres of privately owned forests, the whole totalling 59,000 acres.[7]

The Forest was disafforested in 1813 with the passing of an inclosure act[8] and Lauder gives the following account of subsequent events:

> The people then ignorantly took it into their heads to imagine, that the deer would become common property the moment the enclosure bill should pass; and they immediately began an immense slaughter, which the forest officers found impossible to arrest. Government, thinking it the wisest plan to endeavour to drive the deer into the park, a regiment of horse guards was ordered out, in addition to

which, hundreds of horsemen assembled from all parts of the neighbourhood, and for several days the thickets and coverts of that richly wooded country echoed with the trumpet calls of cavalry giving the order to charge; and in this way some hundreds of deer were saved and enclosed.[9]

In fact, the cavalry were a troop of the Royal Horse Guards assisted by a detachment of the 5th Regiment of the line. Today the Forest of Windsor is traversed by a number of railway lines and two motorways, the M3 and the M4, and it may also be noted that part of the Great Park which lies to the east of the junction of roads A332 and B383 is known as Cranbourne Chase. This should not be confused with the infinitely larger area of the same name in Dorset.

BUCKINGHAMSHIRE

3   Bernwood Forest

Although this forest, which was also known as Birnwood, has been placed under Buckinghamshire, part of it lay in Oxfordshire. Its bounds varied with the passing of time and in the twelfth and thirteenth centuries the Forest of Brill was considered to be a separate forest although it was later considered as part of Bernwood. On occasions the small forests of Stowood and Shotover near Oxford were treated as part of Bernwood Forest but in Chapter 5 they have been placed under Oxfordshire.

Brill, which lies some ten miles north-east of the centre of Oxford may be regarded as being in the middle of the forest. A perambulation was made in 1298 but unfortunately the exact bounds that were then laid down are difficult to interpret in the present day. However, the forest comprised the following parishes: Brill, Boarstall, Oakley, Worminghall, Long Crendon, Ashendon, Chilton, Dorton, Ludgershall and Wotton Underwood.[10] With this information, together with that which can be gathered from the perambulation of 1298, it is possible to form some idea of the bounds of the forest and it is likely that the perimeter followed a course such as the following. Beginning at Lower Arncott about a mile south-east of Ambrosden, the bounds probably followed the course of the river Ray to a point where the river turns sharply to the south, a mile north of Wotton Underwood. From that point the boundary probably continued in a south-easterly direction for about two and a half miles until it met the river Thame. It is likely that it followed the course of the Thame until the county boundary left the river and turned northwards towards Worminghall. The perimeter of the forest probably continued along the line of the county boundary to within a mile of Lower Arncott and then across the fields to that village.

The name of Bernwood Forest has been perpetuated by the Forestry

Commission who have allocated it to a block of the Commission's woodlands comprising Oakley Wood, Shabbington Wood, York's Wood and Hell Coppice. These lie about a mile to the south-west of the village of Oakley and, in all probability, were within the bounds of the medieval forest.

4   Whaddon Chase

Whaddon Chase lies between Buckingham and Bletchley, the village of Whaddon being approximately seven miles from Buckingham and three from Bletchley. Early in the reign of Henry III (1216-72) reference was made to the Forest of Buckinghamshire but this was apparently a general term which was used to cover the Forests of Bernwood, Salcey and Whittlewood, despite the fact that the two last named lay in the county of Northampton. Although, in 1241, Whaddon Chase was regarded as part of the Forest of Buckingham, the bounds of the Chase were surveyed in 1608. This survey showed that the perimeter of the Chase extended from Whaddon Park to Shenley, Tattenhoe, Little Horwood, Great Horwood, Singleborough, Nash and so back to Whaddon Park.[11]

CHESHIRE

5   Delamere Forest

This forest originally consisted of two forests which were known by the names of Mara and Mondrem although the forms Moni and Mondrum and Mara and Moudrem were sometimes used. The Forest of Mara was bounded by the river Mersey on the north and by the Forest of Wirral on the west, while that of Moudrem, which was adjacent to Mara, extended south-eastwards towards Nantwich. These two forests virtually covered the whole of the hundred of Eddisbury and a large part of the hundred of Nantwich.[12] Cowel[13] refers to this forest by the name of Forest de la Mer and this name probably has its origins in the lakes or meres within the forest bounds. Leland[14] observed that 'Betwixt Sandyford and Northwiche I saw divers pooles in the Forest and toward the ende of the Forest I lokid towards Valle Royal on the right hond about which place be divers fair and large pooles'. On a map dated 1801 which Cary[15] included in his atlas two such features are shown in this forest, one of which is named Oak Mere. Disafforestation took place in 1812 but the Forestry Commission has now established a new Delamere Forest on part of the site of the old one.

6   Macclesfield Forest

This forest, which was situated between Macclesfield and Buxton, was originally known as the Forest of Lyme and Lyme Hall which is now the property of the National Trust is situated about six miles to the north of Macclesfield, near New Mills. Ekwall[16] states that the word 'lyme' is an old name for a large forest district and occurs in Newcastle under Lyme, Ashton under Lyme and, in a less obvious form, Burslem.

The bounds of the forest included the town of Macclesfield and 18 other small townships and covered about one-third of the Macclesfield hundred. The forest was under the authority of a chief forester or warden and eight hereditary foresters-of-fee while swainmotes and forest pleas were held in Macclesfield.[17] Many grants were made of parts of this forest at an early date but Ormerod[18] records that despite these 'a large quantity of ground, called by the name of the several forest, was not alienated from the crown till after the restoration'.

7 Wirral Forest

This forest which was also known by the names of Wireall and Wyrhale, covered the hundred of Wirral and Ormerod[19] gives a list of 68 townships, taken from the Harley MSS which lay within the limits of the forest. Virtually all of these can be identified on a present day map and all are located within the Wirral hundred. This was bounded on the east by the river Mersey, on the north by the sea and on the west partly by the river Dee and partly by a line which corresponds to the county boundary between Flint and Cheshire. The southern limit of the forest started at the county boundary and continued along the river Dee to the north of Chester. It then followed a line which was almost the same as that adopted by the Shropshire Union Canal, to a point half a mile to the east of the village of Stoke. From this point it followed the course of the river Gowy until it flowed into the Mersey.

The Forest of Wirral is believed to have been heavily wooded during the Middle Ages and this view is supported by the old saying:

> From Blacon Point to Hilbree
> A squirrel may leap from tree to tree.

Blacon Point is situated at the southern end of the forest some two miles west of Chester while Hilbree Point is at the mouth of the Dee adjacent to Hoylake, some seventeen miles to the north-west as the crow flies. Disafforestation took place in or about 1376 apparently as the result of a petition by the citizens of Chester who alleged that the forest, which lay at the gates of the city, provided cover and protection for robbers and thieves.

CUMBERLAND

Information regarding the forests of Cumberland is not easily ascertained and in some cases the facts are somewhat obscured. Nisbet[20] has expressed the opinion that the Forests of Copeland, Geltsdale, Brierthwaite and Nichol were in fact chases and not forests but he gives no reasons or authority for this view. In some cases areas which were referred to as 'forests' were part of a larger forest and this has also lead to some confusion.

8 Copeland Forest

Later known as Egremont Forest, Copeland or Coupland Forest lay between Buttermere, Ennerdale Water and Wast Water and in the twelfth century the area was referred to as 'The County of Coupland'. The town of Egremont lies about seven miles to the west of the forest area, being some two miles from the coast and five miles from St Bees Head. At the north-eastern end of Wast Water is Wastedalehead which, although sometimes referred to as a forest, was probably a part of Copeland Forest.

9 The King's Forest of Geltsdale

This forest was also known as Geltstone and lay close to the Cumberland-Northumberland border, about 13 miles east of Carlisle as the crow flies. It takes its name from the river Gelt which rises on Geltsdale Middle and after flowing close to Geltsdale House this river ultimately joins the Irthing which in due course unites with the river Eden. Geltsdale also included Brathwaite, Breirthwaite or Tarnhouse Forest which was also known as Tindale Forest and extended from Geltsdale to the main road from Brampton to Knarsdale (A689) about five miles east of Brampton. The name Tinsdale is still to be found in Tindale Fells, Tindale Tarn and the hamlet of Tindale.

10 Gilderdale Forest

Also known by the name of Gildresdale, this forest was close to the Northumberland border being situated to the west of the village of Alston and some 13 miles north-east of Penrith. The forest area lay to the east of Blackfell and Hartside Height in which the Gilderdale Burn rose.

11 Inglewood Forest

Until the end of the thirteenth century Inglewood was referred to as 'The Forest of Cumberland' but in the middle of the sixteenth century, Leland[21] described it as 'The great Forest of Englewood'. It lay between Penrith and Carlisle and in recent years the M6 motorway has divided the site of the forest roughly into two equal parts. In 1301 a perambulation was made of the forest and the following is a synopsis of the translated Latin text which is given by Nicolson and Burn.[22] The present day names and other observations are given in parentheses.

The bounds of the forest ran from the bridge over the river Caldew outside Carlisle along the road to Thoresbie (Thursby) and from there to Waspatrickwath above the stream of Wathempole (the river Wampool) to the place where the Shauke (Chalk Beck) joins the Wathempole; and from there to the head of Rowland Beck down to the stream at Caldbeck and then by that stream to where it joins the river Caldew. Then going up at Gyrwath and so by the road from Sourbye (Sowerby) to Stanewath below the castle of Sourbye (Cary[23] shows Castle Sowerby about one and a half miles north-east of Hegglefoot and about the same distance north-west of Lamonby) to Mabil Cross (Cary shows this as Mable Cross at the extreme north-east corner of Greystock, now Greystoke Park). From there the bounds proceeded to Kenwathen Hill and then descended to Aleynby (Ellonby) and Blencoe (Great Blencow) as far as Palat (Pallethill) and down the road to Amote (Eamont) Bridge. From that bridge the bounds continued along the river Amote (river Eamont) until it joined the river Eden and so down the course of the Eden to its junction with the river Caldew and from there to the bridge at Carlisle where the bounds began.

The forest was divided into three bailiwicks and 12 verderers were appointed for the whole forest. An eyre was held at Carlisle during the reign of Henry III (1216-72) and again in 1285. It is said that the 'last tree of Inglewood Forest' which was growing on Wragmire Moss blew down on 23rd June 1823 and a pencil drawing of this tree by Lady Dunne is now in the Jackson Collection of the County Library at Carlisle. Wragmire House stands about half a mile to the south of the village of Cotehill which is some two miles south-east of junction 42 on the M6 motorway. The Forestry Commission has commemorated the name of Inglewood by adopting it for a new forest that has been established in the area.

12 Nichol Forest

Nichol Forest was situated in the extreme north of the county and ran parallel to the Scottish border from a point a little to the south of the village of Catlowdy, north-eastwards to the junction of the boundary between Cumberland and Northumberland and the border, about a mile from Kershopehead. The site of this medieval forest is now marked on present day maps as Kershope Forest which is a modern forest belonging to the Forestry Commission. Nichol Forest was named after Nicholas de Stutevill (c. 1205).

13 Skiddaw Forest

This forest lay to the north of Keswick and to the east of Bassenthwaite Lake and although marked on both old and modern maps little information is available about it.

14   Thornthwaite Forest

Thornthwaite Forest was situated between the road from Cockermouth to Loweswater (B5292) and Bassenthwaite Lake. This lake thus formed the division between Skiddaw Forest to the east and Thornthwaite to the west. In recent years a new forest has been created in this area by the Forestry Commission and it has been named Thornthwaite Forest, thus continuing the name of its predecessor.

DERBYSHIRE

15   Duffield Frith

Duffield Frith or Forest was situated to the north of Derby and covered a considerable area. There were four wards or bailiwicks, namely: Duffield which was also known by the name of Chevin, Belper, Hulland and Colebrook which was in the parish of Wirksworth. The forest lay within a perimeter the line of which ran from Duffield to Mugginton, then to Hulland and Wirksworth continuing to Alderwasley, Heage and so by the road from Ripley to Derby (A61) to a point about a mile north of Little Eaton and so back to Duffield. It should be noted that the above is not a perambulation of the forest but simply an indication of the district in which the forest was situated. In the reign of Elizabeth I the forest is said to have had a perimeter of over 30 miles and that this was considerably less than its original extent.[24] It did not become a royal forest until the accession of Henry IV in 1399 although it had ranked as one for at least a hundred years prior to that date.

During the reign of Elizabeth I the felling of timber was excessive and a survey of the trees in the forest, carried out in 1560, showed that there were at that time 59,412 large oaks, 32,820 small oaks and 19,736 dottards that is, trees only fit for firewood. When a further survey was made in 1587, these numbers had been reduced to such an extent that there were only 2,764 large oaks and 3,032 small oaks.[25] Thus in 27 years the stock of large oaks had diminished by 56,648 or an average of 2,098 per year and the small oaks at the rate of 1,103 trees per year. The deer in Duffield Frith were entirely fallow and disafforestation took place about 1648.

16   Peak Forest

The Peak Forest or Forest of the High Peak was situated approximately midway between Manchester and Sheffield and extended from Buxton in the south, to Langendale some two miles north of Glossop. In 1286 the bounds of the forest were as follows. From the junction of the county boundaries of

Cheshire, Lancashire and Yorkshire, near the Woodhead Tunnel, the eastern boundary followed the course of the river Derwent through what is now a chain of reservoirs to Mytham Bridge. From there it continued southwards through Bradwell, Little Hucklow and Tideswell, to the river Wye, and from this point the southern boundary continued to Buxton and the river Goyt where it turned northwards to form the western limit of the forest. The boundary followed the Goyt through Whaley Bridge, New Mills and Marple, until it joined the river Etherow. From there it followed the Etherow through Langendale until it reached the junction of the three counties near Woodhead and so completed the perimeter. The forest was divided into three districts which were the equivalent of bailiwicks and these were Longdendale in the north and north-west, Hopedale in the east and Campana, that is in the open country, in the south and south-west. About the year 1225, a chapel was built at Bowden which later became known as the Chapel in the Forest or Chapel-en-le-Frith. Unlike Duffield Frith, the deer of the Peak Forest were exclusively red except for a few strays.[26]

DEVON

17   Dartmoor Forest

The Forest of Dartmoor or Dartmore lies in an area which is circumscribed by the towns of Okehampton on the north, Newton Abbot on the east, Plymouth on the south and Tavistock on the west. However, the ancient forest comprised rather less than one half of the area that is now commonly referred to as Dartmoor. The first perambulation was made in 1240 and since that date there have been a number of surveys of the bounds of the forest. W. Burt in his preface to Carrington's *Dartmoor*[27] states that other perambulations were made in 1301, 1377, 1557 (partial), 1601, 1609 and 1786. As can be appreciated, certain variations occurred in the recorded bounds of the forest over such a long period of time and several writers have dealt with this matter in great detail, particularly A. B. Prowse.[28] However, the following description of the bounds of the forest is based on those given by Rowe in 1896.[29]

From Cawsand Beacon about two miles south of the village of Sticklepath on the main Exeter—Okehampton road (A30), the eastern boundary proceeds southwards to Hound Tor and then continues to a point on the road to Fernworthy Reservoir about a quarter of a mile south-east of the reservoir. From there it continues to a point about a hundred yards east of the Warren House Inn on the Moretonhampstead—Two Bridges road (B3212) and continues over this road following the line of the Walla Brook and the East Dart river to Dartmeet Bridge on the Ashburton—Two Bridges road (A384). The boundary then follows the course of the West Dart river until its junction with

the O Brook which it follows for about a mile and a quarter, before turning
south to Ryders Hill and along the Wellabrook stream until it joins the Avon
and so on to Peter's Cross. At this point it turns west to form the southern
boundary by way of Redlake, the Erme, Erme Head and on to Plymsteps. The
boundary then proceeds northwards along the course of the Plym for some
three-quarters of a mile when it bears to the north-west to Lylesbarrow and
thence to Nun's Cross, South Hessary Tor, Rendlestone (on the Two Bridges—
Tavistock road), Great Mis Tor, Cocks Hill, Lynch Tor, across the Tavy and
along Rattle Brook to its source. From there, it bears to the north-east, across
the West Okement river passing to the east of High Willhays and crosses the
Blackhaven Brook at an obtuse angle. The boundary then continues to Higher
Tor and so back to Cawsand Beacon.

   The forest was divided into four quarters or wards known as the North,
South, East and West Quarters. Two matters which are of special interest in
connection with the Forest of Dartmoor were certain rights which included
those of pasture and turbary known as venville rights, and claims by foresters
during the thirteenth century for money for liquor which was known as
poutura. Both these matters are referred to elsewhere. The Forestry
Commission have established a forest near Postbridge which still perpetuates
the name of Dartmoor Forest.

DORSET

18   Bere Regis Forest

Sometimes referred to as Bere Forest, this area should not be confused with
the Forest of Bere in Hampshire which is situated about six miles north of
Portsmouth. The Dorset village of Bere Regis stands at the junction of the
roads from Dorchester to Wimborne Minster (A31) and Dorchester to
Bournemouth (A35), being some ten miles east of Dorchester in a direct line.

   In 1259 Henry III granted this forest to Simon de Montefort, Earl of
Leicester, who had married his sister in 1238 and it ceased to be a royal forest
from the former date. There is still a considerable area of woodland and open
heath land between Bere Regis and Wareham including Bere Wood, Bere
Heath, Bloxworth Heath and Morden Heath and it is very probable that these
were situated within the bounds of the medieval forest.

19   Blakemore Forest

The Forest of Blakemore, Blackmore or Blackmoor which was also known by
the name of White Hart Forest or, in its earlier form of spelling, Wheight
Harte, lay between Sherborne and Blandford Forum. Originally this forest
covered a large area and Leland[30] states that it 'streachid from Ivelle (Yeovil)

unto the quarters of Shaftesbyri and touchid with Gillingham forest that is nere Shaftesbyri'. Subsequently there were several perambulations, notably in about 1225 and 1300 and the following description of the bounds of the forest, which is a translation of the Latin given by Leland, is taken from Hutchins.[31]

> . . . the aforesaid forest extendeth itself towards the north unto a certain bridge of Shirborne called Westbrugge (West Bridge), and from the same bridge towards the west and south to the town of Yatminster (Yetminster), and from the same town of Yatminster towards the south of the town of Evershutt (Evershot), towards the east of the town of Cerne (Cerne Abbas), and from the same town of Cerne towards the east to the town of Myddleton (Milton Abbas), and from the same town of Myddelton towards the north unto the town of Stourmynstre Newton Castle (Sturminster Newton), and from the same town of Stourmynstre Newton Castle towards the north to the town of Stoure-Prewes (Stour Provost), and from the same town of Stoure-Prewes towards the west unto the town of Hengstredge (Henstridge), and from the same town of Hengstredge towards the west to the town of Caundell Porse (Purse Caundle), and from the same town of Caundell Porse unto the town of Heydon (Haydon) and from the same town of Heydon towards the west unto the aforesaid Westbrugge.

The story that lies behind the name of White Hart Forest has been told by several writers and their accounts were examined and compared by Bath[32] in 1973. He also gives the origin of the sign which was originally outside the old King's Stag Inn but now stands opposite the Green Man Inn in the village of King's Stag one mile and a half north-east of Pulham on road B3143. An early account of the white hart incident was given by Camden[33] in 1607 while slightly different versions were provided by Coker[34] in 1732 and Hutchins[35] in 1870, and of these three Coker's description is given below.

> From Mapowder the Brooke passeth through deepe and dirtie Soyle under Kings Stagge Bridge, which got that Name upon this Occasion: King Henry the Third, haveing disported himselfe in the Forrest of Blackmore, hee spared one beautifull and goodlie White Harte, which afterwards T. De la Linde, a neighbour Gentleman of antient Descent and especiall Note, with his Companions pursueing, killed at this Place; but hee soone founde howe dangerous it was, to bee twitching a Lion by the Eares: For the King tooke soe great Indignation against him, that hee not onlie punished them with Imprisonment and a grievous Fine of Money but for this Fact hee taxed their Lands; the Owners of which ever sithence yearlie until this Daye, paye a rounde summe of Money by waye of Amercement unto the Exchequer, called White Harte Silver: in Memorie of which this C . . (ounty)

*needeth noe better Remembrance than the annuall Payment. The
Posteritie of this Man ever after gave for the Armes, White Hartes
Heads in a red Shields; when as formerlie they gave the Coate of
Hartly, whose Heire they had married: And the Forrest allsoe from
that time beganne to lose its antient Name, and to bee called the
Forrest of Whiteharte.*

According to Hutchins, it was Sir John de la Linde and not Thomas who was
responsible for killing the stag. The present King's Stag Bridge is shown in
illustration 2.

2.   *King's Stag Bridge near Pulham between Sturminster Newton and Cerne
Abbas, Dorset. It is said to mark the place where a white hart which had been
spared by Henry III when hunting in Blakemore Forest was later killed by
Sir John de la Linde. c.1240.*

20   Cranbourne Chase

Cranbourne Chase, which should not be confused with a similarly named area
in Windsor Forest in Berkshire, extended into parts of the counties of Dorset,
Wiltshire and Hampshire but since the largest portion was in Dorset it has
been placed under that county.

From the earliest days the chase has been regarded as two entities: the Out-
bounds and the In-bounds. The Out-bounds or outer chase amounted to some

800,000 acres, the perimeter of which extended for nearly one thousand miles.[36] The bounds of the outer chase, which were sworn at an inquisition in 1245, began at Bulbridge in Wilton near Salisbury and then followed the river Nadder westwards to Tisbury, continuing along the course of the river Sem and so to Shaftesbury. From that town the western limit of the chase followed a stream which flowed from St John's Hill past Hartgrove and West Orchard to Manston where it joined the river Stour. It continued along the Stour through Blandford Forum to Wimborne Minster to its junction with the river Allen. The boundary then turned northwards along the course of the Allen almost to Wimborne St Giles where it turned south-eastwards to Verwood and Ringwood. At Ringwood the line turned northwards along the course of the river Avon to its junction with the Nadder at Salisbury and so along the Nadder to Bulbridge where the bounds began. Within this tract lay the In-bounds which extended for about ten miles from north to south and three miles in width having a perimeter of some 27 miles and an area of about 40,000 acres. Unfortunately the precise location of the In-bounds is not recorded.[37]

The hunting of deer by unauthorized persons in Cranbourne Chase, which had begun during the Civil War, increased considerably by the beginning of the eighteenth century when similar activities were taking place in Waltham Chase (q.v.). By 1730 violence began to occur in the affrays with the keepers and in 1738 two were killed while further major clashes occurred in 1780 and 1791. After the latter occasion, when one poacher had been killed ten others were transported for life and this action seems to have damped the enthusiasm for the deer-stealers sufficiently to bring this problem to an end.[38] In 1960, Gardiner Forest was renamed Cranbourne Chase by the Forestry Commission.

21   Gillingham Forest

Also known as Gyllynham, this was a small forest which 'was heretofore part of Selwood Forest'[39] and was, according to Leland[40] 'four miles in length and a mile or thereabouts in bredth' but this statement is open to doubt since the perambulations of 1300 and 1668 indicate a length of about five and a half miles and a maximum breadth of four miles. The forest was situated between Gillingham, Mere and Shaftesbury and a small part of it lay in Wiltshire.

From Gillingham the bounds extended northwards along Shreen Water to Huntingford Bridge and then to White Hill and Mere Park. The eastern limit followed the line of the Dorset-Wiltshire boundary to Little Down, Shaftesbury and Alcester from where it turned westwards to Duncliffe Hill and East Stour. At this village the perimeter of the forest turned northwards to the junction of the rivers Stour and Lodden and so to Gillingham. This forest continued in existence after the passing of the Forest Charters of 1217 and 1225 and pleas of the forest were held in Shaftesbury in 1490. Disafforestation did not take place until 1628.

22   Holt Forest

This diminutive forest was situated to the south of Cranbourne Chase and west of the New Forest, the village of Holt being about three miles north-east of Wimborne Minster. Lying in the eastern half of Bradbury Hundred, the bounds of the forest ran from Mannington to Uddens Park and then turned westwards to the river Avon. After leaving the river, the perimeter continued to Horton and back to Mannington.

23   Poorstock Forest

Also known as Purstock, Porestok, Purstok and Powerstock, this small forest covered the area around the village of Powerstock which is four miles north-east of Bridport and the same distance south-east of Beaminster. The forest included Toller Porcorum, Eggardon Hill and Nettlecombe. It was originally created a forest by King John but disafforestation began in the middle of the fourteenth century. The present day Powerstock Forest is a Forestry Commission area.

24   Forest of Purbeck

The Forest of Purbeck was synonymous with the area which is known as the Isle of Purbeck and comprised the two hundreds of Hasilor or Hasler and Rowbarrow. The northern bounds of the forest followed the course of the river Frome from Poole Harbour to a point approximately midway between East Holme and East Stoke. From there the boundary turned due south passing to the west of Bovington Heath and to the east of East Lulworth until it joined the sea at Worbarrow Bay. The perimeter then continued along the coast line until it reached the mouth of the river Frome. This forest was created by King John and was divided into the East Bailiwick and the West Bailiwick which corresponded with the hundreds of Rowbarrow and Hasler respectively. Hutchins[41] makes the following observations:

> The forest extended over the whole island, and the woods were well stocked with red and fallow deer and stags, especially in the west part, but these were destroyed in the Civil Wars, and few if any have remained in the memory of man. In old evidence it is styled the Forest, Chase and Warren of Purbeck, and seems generally to have been reserved by our princes, especially in the Saxon times, for their own diversion. King James I was the last of our kings who hunted here, 1615.

DURHAM

25   Teesdale Forest

This forest lay in and around Tees Dale and included Forest and Frith, which is about seven miles north-west of Middleton in Teesdale, and Harwood a further three miles up the Dale. Some doubt exists as to the exact status of Teesdale Forest and there are virtually no references to it until the end of the fifteenth century. It is recorded that in 1538-39, there were 210 fallow and 140 red deer in the forest.[42]

26   Weardale Forest

This forest which was also known by the names of Weredale and the High Forest of Weardale, was situated beside the dale of that name. It is probable that the townships of Wolsingham and Stanhope lay within the bounds of the forest since they were each required to provide a man to act as forester during the fawning and rutting season.[43] Leland observed that 'There resorte many rede dere, strangelers to the mountains of Weredale'.[44]

ESSEX

27   Forest of Essex

Until the beginning of the fourteenth century this forest covered almost the whole of the county and Edward I claimed that it stretched from Stratford Bridge, over the river Lea (now in the east end of London) to Cattywad Bridge over the river Stour on the county boundary with Suffolk, about a mile to the north of Manningtree. In breadth it was said to extend from the Thames northwards as far as Stane Street which runs from Bishop's Stortford to Colchester (A120). Perambulations were made in 1301 and 1641 and Fisher has prepared a map showing the metes and bounds of the Forest in accordance with that of 1641.[45] By this date the Forest had been reduced to a narrow strip lying between Harlow and the Thames and the river Lea and Brentwood and a copy of this perambulation, of which the following is a summary, was included in the Fifteenth Report of the Commissioners.[46] From Stratford Bridge over the river Lea, the bounds traced the course of the river to a point about one mile east of Hoddesdon. They then turned eastwards passing to the north of Royden Hamlet and continued to Broadley Common, Little Marles and Thorrowood Common which is near to the main London — Cambridge road (A11). Here the bounds turned southwards to Rood Street which lies a little to the west of the point where the road from Epping to Ongar (A1161) now crosses the M11 motorway. At Rood Street the forest bounds followed the road to Epping and at the south end of the town they left this road and continued along the line of a minor road to Theydon Bois where they turned south-east and followed the road to Abridge on the river Roding. The bounds then turned east along the course of the Roding to a point about one mile west of Navestock where they turned due south to join the river Rom at Curtismill Green. From here they continued down the Rom almost as far as Collier Row before joining road number A1112 at Marks Gate and following it to the junction with road number A118 along which the bounds continued westwards to Stratford Bridge.

The Report of the Commissioners also records that the Forest was divided into 10 walks and although originally there were only nine, part of Loughton Walk was subsequently formed into Lambourn Walk. The 10 walks were: Chingford, Epping, West Hainault, East Hainault, Leyton and Wanstead, Lambourn, Loughton, New Lodge, Walthamstow and Woodford. The Lambourn walk was sometimes known as the Lambourn and Chigwell walk. After the beginning of the fourteenth century this area became known as Waltham Forest and included what is now Epping Forest and also Hainault Forest which was disafforested in 1851.[47]

Today the ancient Forest of Essex is mainly represented by Epping Forest belonging to the Corporation of the City of London and Hatfield Forest which is the property of the National Trust, both of which are, for the most part, woodland areas. Other remnants of the Forest are Kingswood near Colchester, Writtle near Chelmsford and Hainault near Chigwell.

GLOUCESTERSHIRE

The medieval forests of Gloucestershire can be divided into two main groups: first the Forest of Dean and second a number of small forests which lay to the north and east of Bristol. While there is a considerable amount of information available on the Forest of Dean which, over the years, has been the subject of many books and papers, exactly the opposite is the case as regards the group of forests near Bristol.

28   Alveston Forest

The Forest of Alveston was situated close to the village of that name which is on the Bristol – Gloucester road (A38) and about ten miles north-east of Bristol. It is mentioned in the Patent and Close Rolls during the early years of the reign of Henry III (1216-72) but otherwise there is little information available on this forest.

29 Forest of Corse

The Forest of Corse or Cors marched with the southern limits of Malvern Forest. Its bounds began where the Glynch Brook crosses the county boundary between Worcestershire and Gloucestershire and followed the boundary between these two counties, eastwards to Tewkesbury. It is likely that the forest bounds then followed the river Severn southwards to its junction with the river Leadon below Maisemore and then traced the course of the Leadon to the point at which it is joined by the Glynch Brook. From there it probably continued along this brook back to the county boundary where the bounds began.

Edward I gave the Forest of Corse together with Malvern Forest, to the earl of Clare, Hereford and Gloucester when he married Edward's daughter, the Princess Joan D'Acres in 1290. The forest is still commemorated in the names of Corse which lies between Staunton and Hartpury, half a mile to the west of the Gloucester – Ledbury road (A417), Corse Lawn on the secondary road from Tewkesbury to Hartpury (B4211) and also in Corse Wood Hill to the north-west of Hasfield. Reference should also be made to the notes on Malvern Forest which will be found in the section dealing with the forests of Worcestershire in Chapter 5.

30 Forest of Dean

The Forest of Dean and the New Forest are the two largest and most important ancient forests that have survived to the present day, and although their appearance has changed during the course of the centuries, there are still areas in these two forests which present a prospect which is probably somewhat similar to that in medieval times. The oak which was grown in the Dean was a valuable source of timber for the Navy and Evelyn[48] records that those in command of the Spanish Armada were ordered 'That if when they landed they should not be able to subdue our nation and make good their conquest they should yet be sure not to leave a tree standing in the Forest of Dean'.

The forest lies to the south-west of Gloucester and originally it covered a far greater area than it does today. The bounds which were recorded by a perambulation made in 1228 were approximately as follows.[49] Beginning at Leadon Bridge, about one mile to the west of Gloucester, whose modern counterpart now carries the Gloucester – Ross-on-Wye road (A40), the bounds followed the road to Newent (B4215) and from there to Gorsley ford. The bounds then continued to Burton (Burton Court), Bromsash, Bollitree Castle, Weston Penyard and so to Alton (Alton Court). From Alton the boundary turned southwards and followed, more or less, what is now the track of the old railway line to a point on the river Wye opposite Goodrich Castle. From there it followed the course of the Wye until it joined the river Severn when it turned north-eastwards besides the Severn back to Leadon Bridge where the bounds began. In the thirteenth century the forest was divided into the following ten bailiwicks: Abenhalle (Abenhall), Berse (Bearse), Bicknoure (Bicknor), Blakeney, Bleythe (Blaize) Great Dean, Little Dean, The Lea, Rywardyn (Ruardean) and Staunterne (Staunton).

Today the bounds of the forest have been greatly reduced and they now follow a circuitous course which can best be appreciated by studying the maps contained in the Forestry Commission's excellent guides to the forest.[50] The following is a very curtailed description of the present day limits of the forest. Beginning at East Dean in the extreme north, the bounds of the forest extend southwards passing to the west of Mitcheldean to Pope's Hill, then westwards to Cinderford where they turn southwards to Lower Soudley and a point about a mile to the west of Blakeney. The southern limit continues from this point to Bream where it turns to the north to Clearwell, Mile End and Berry Hill. From Berry Hill the boundary bears north-eastwards to Edge End, Lower Lydbrook and Drybrook where it turns northwards to Bailey some three miles north of Hope Mansell and then eastwards through Lane End back to East Dean where the boundary began. In 1924 the Forest of Dean was transferred from the Office of Woods and Forests to the Forestry Commission[51] and its status was further altered in 1971 by the passing of the Wild Creatures and Forest Laws Act.[52]

31 Horwood Forest

Also referred to in some instances as Horewood or Harewood, this forest was situated near the village of Pucklechurch which is two miles east of Mangotsfield (now on the outskirts of Bristol) and four miles south-west of Chipping Sodbury. The forest is referred to in the Patent and Close Rolls in the reign of Henry III while to the south and virtually adjoining it, was the Forest of Kingswood.

32 Kingswood Forest

This forest has been described as 'the mysterious Forest of Kingswood of which much is heard though little is known'.[53] At the present time, Kingswood is an urban area adjoining the Bristol–Chippenham road (A420).

Originally this forest covered an area some six miles in length and three miles in breadth and included a part or the whole of the parishes of Mangotsfield, Pucklechurch, Bitton, Bristleton (Brislington) and Hannam. Braine[54] includes a map dated 1610 showing the extent of the forest at that time and also gives details of a perambulation of 1652 which sets out the bounds. These, in relation to the present day state of the area, may be broadly summarized as follows. From the junction of Fishponds road (A432) and Stapleton road (B4058) to the junction of road B4465 with A432 and continuing along the latter road to a point east of Downend about half a mile beyond its connection with the road from Frenchay (B4427). From here, the bounds turned south and followed a line to the west of Mangotsfield and Rodway Hill along the course of the Siston Brook, to Warmley. The bounds then continued in a south-westerly direction, passing to the north of Cadbury Heath and Barrs Court to Hannam and on to Conham on the river Avon. After following the river to Crews Hole they proceeded to St George and back to the junction of Fishponds Road and Stapleton Road where the bounds began.

In early times, this forest was known as the Forest of Furches or Furcis but by the beginning of the reign of Edward I (1272) it was referred to as the Forest or Chase of Kingswood.[55] Braine states that the word 'furchis' is 'a common term applied in documents where the work of timber-cutting is going on for the purpose of commerce'.[56] About 1336 the name 'Kingswood' began to be used for that part of the forest which lay in Gloucestershire while the portion in Somerset became known as Filwood Chase, which also appears in the forms of Fillwood or Fylewood. At the same time the forest was divided into four walks or bailiwicks but much of the original forest was disafforested in 1230.[57] Reference to Keynsham Forest are sometimes found but this was generally considered to be part of Kingswood.

33   Micklewood Forest

This forest was situated about two and a half miles south-east of Berkeley and three and a half miles west of Wotton-under-Edge. Gilpin[58] refers briefly to it and the Ordnance Survey map of 1830 shows it as Michaelswood Chase. Today, the M5 motorway passes through the middle of this forest and the service area to the north of junction 14 has been built in the middle of what is now known as Michael Wood.

HAMPSHIRE

34   Alice Holt Forest

In early records the name of this forest appeared as Axisholt, Aylesholt, Alishoult or Aisholt while Gilbert White[59] referred to it simply as 'The Holt' but this should not be confused with Holt Forest in Dorset. Alice Holt Forest which is situated about three miles south-west of Farnham, Surrey, lay within an area bounded on the north by the river Wey and on the west by a series of small villages and hamlets. These include Binsted, Wyck, Binswood, West Worldham, Oakhanger and Oakwood. The southern and eastern limits of the forest passed through, or in close proximity to, Blackmore, Deadwater, Lindford and Dockenfield and then followed the county boundary as far as the river Wey. The forest was divided into three bailiwicks the North, South and West, and perambulations were made in 1300 and 1635. The forests of Alice

Holt and Woolmer were only separated by a narrow strip of land which lay outside the bounds of both forests. From 1777 onwards much of the oak from Alice Holt was used by the Navy, the timber being hauled by road to Godalming and then by boat down the river Wey to the Thames shipyards.[60] Today, Alice Holt is one of the Forestry Commission's forests and their Forest Research Station is established at Alice Holt Lodge.

35   Bere Forest

This forest was also known by the names of Beare, Bier, East Bere and the Forest of South while the southern portion was sometimes referred to as Porchester Forest. It lay to the north of the Fareham—Porchester—Havant road (A27) and extended northwards almost to Hambledon. The thirteenth Report of the Commissioners[61] contains a copy of a perambulation made in 1688 which states that the bounds were as follows. Beginning at Mislingford on the river Meon, about four miles north of Wickham, the bounds followed the northern boundary of West Walk to Huntbourn, Great Ervills, Denmead, Anmore, Wecock and Padnell. From here they turned south past Stakes and Little Park Wood to Bedhampton where they proceeded westwards to Farlington and north-westwards to Purbrookheath. They then continued to Walton Heath, Wine Cross and Wickham Common where they deviated to the south for a short distance before reaching Wickham and following the river Meon back to Mislingford where the bounds began. Bere Forest was disafforested under an Act of 1810.[62]

The forest was divided into two walks, namely the East Walk and the West Walk, and today two woods still bear these names. West Walk, immediately to the north of Wickham and close to the river Meon and East or Creech Walk about two miles north-east of the village of Southwick. Both these areas now belong to the Forestry Commission since Bere Forest was a former Crown Wood and was transferred to the Commission in 1923. The remainder of the forest was disafforested under the Act of 1810. Subsequently a Forestry Commission forest was established in this area under the name of Bere Forest, but in 1971 it became part of the Queen Elizabeth Forest.

36   Buckholt Forest

The facts relating to this forest, which was sometimes referred to as Bucholt or La Bokolt, are somewhat obscure. According to the Hundred Rolls of the thirteenth century, the parks of Buckholt, Milchet and the Forest of Panshet were parts of Clarendon Forest. Melchet and Clarendon Forests are considered separately under the county of Wiltshire and Panshet is dealt with under Clarendon. However, in 1360 Buckholt was referred to as a forest with two foresters in charge of it and was divided into the East and West Baileys.[63] It was situated to the east of, and adjoining, Clarendon Forest but lay in

Hampshire and today Buckholt Farm is still shown on modern maps being about one mile north of West Tytherley and two miles west of Broughton, close to the Romsey – Over Wallop road (B3084). John Speed shows Buckholt Forest as lying between West Tytherley and Upper Wallop.[64]

37   Chute Forest

Chute Forest covered a substantial area both in Hampshire and Wiltshire but as the larger part was in Wiltshire most of the facts concerning this forest are given under that county. However, the following information regarding the names given to the Hampshire portion are included under this section.

That part of the forest that lay in Hampshire extended from the county boundary with Wiltshire eastwards to Hurstbourne Tarrant and this included the woods of Dowles and Doiley. Dowles has now become Doles Wood which lies on either side of the road from Andover to Hurstbourne Tarrant and Newbury (A343). Doiley is now represented by Doyley Manor, about three miles north-east of Hurstbourne, and Doiley Cottages. In medieval times Doiley appeared in the form of Digerle or Derhile. Doles Wood is now part of the Forestry Commission's Andover Forest.

Four miles north-east of Andover and a mile from the southern end of Doles Wood (Ridges Copse) is Finkley House and Finkley Manor Farm and these mark the locality of what was known as Finkley Forest. In 1292, Edward I allowed the Abbess of Hurstbourne Tarrant 'to sell forty oaks in her wood of Hurstbourne within the bounds of the Forest of Finkley', while in 1302 she was permitted to sell forty acres of 'her wood of Hurstbourne in the Forest of Chute'. From this it would seem probable that what was sometimes referred to as Finkley Forest was in fact part of the Forest of Chute and that Finkley was a bailiwick of Chute. Again in 1235 mention is made of the 'royal Forest of Finkley and Derhele' (Doiley) while in 1652 reference was made to 'the wood and woody ground called the Ridges (now Ridges Copse) which was parcel of Finkley Forest' and this again would indicate that it was a part of Chute Forest.[65]

38   Harewood Forest

This forest which straddles the Andover – Basingstoke road (A303) lies about two miles south-east of Andover. In 1296 Harewood was considered to be within the metes and bounds of Chute Forest although it was held by Wherwell Abbey. In 1348 or thereabouts, the Abbess petitioned the king against his forest officers who had stated that Harewood Forest was a royal demesne and, having added it to the Forest of Chute, had appointed forest officers to control it and had subsequently prohibited the Abbess from hunting in it. At the dissolution of the monasteries it was transferred to Lord de la Warr but was sold in 1695.[66]

39   New Forest

The New Forest and the Forest of Dean are the two outstanding examples of medieval forests which still exist in England, although for the most part they now present a different scene from that of the Middle Ages. The introduction of Scots pine to the New Forest in 1776 has probably changed its appearance more than any other single factor. The forest was established by William I in about 1079 and it is interesting to note that the Verderers' Court still meets several times a year, in the Verderers' Hall which adjoins the Queen's House at Lyndhurst.

In 1682 a perambulation was made of the bounds of the forest and these do not differ to any great extent from the present day boundaries of the New Forest National Park which may be briefly summarized as follows. From North Charford in the extreme north-west approximately along the line of roads B3080 and B3078 to Bramble Hill Walk, turning north-eastwards to Plaitford and Shelley Common and then south to Cadnam. From here the boundary proceeds in a south-easterly direction to Lyndhurst Station, Applemore Hill and Buttsash to Langley and then by a devious route joins the Beaulieu river at Gilbury Hard where it turns southwards along the river and follows the coast to a point a little to the east of Pyleswell House. From there it turns northwards through Horleywood to a point near Stockley Inclosure from where it bears westward to Brockenhurst. Turning due south again to Shirley Holms, one and a half miles west of Boldre, the boundary continues in a westerly direction to a cross-road on the main Bournemouth — Southampton road (A35) about one and a half miles north of Hinton Admiral church. From this cross-road the boundary swings north to a point on the Ringwood — Romsey road (A31) about three-quarters of a mile east of the centre of Ringwood. It then continues northwards to Godshill some two miles north-west of Fordingbridge and proceeds to the west of Godshill Inclosure to reach North Charford where the boundary began. There are two main deviations from the perambulation of 1682: first, the inclusion in the new boundary of an area between Bramshaw and Plaitford and second, the exclusion from the new boundary of an area lying between Brockenhurst and Boldre.

The *Report of the Commissioners on the New Forest*[67] records that in 1789 the forest was divided into nine bailiwicks which were subdivided into 15 walks as follows.

Burley Bailiwick: Burley and Holmesley Walks
Fritham Bailiwick: Boldrewood and Eyeworth Walks
Godshill Bailiwick: Ashley Walk
Lynwood Bailiwick: Broomy Walk
Battramsley Bailiwick: Rhinefield and Wilverley Walks
South Bailiwick: Whitley Ridge and Lady Cross Walks
East Bailiwick and the Nodes: Denny Walk and the Nodes and Ashurst Walks

Inn Bailiwick: Ironshill Walk
North Bailiwick: Castle Malwood and Bramble Hill Walks

It should be noted that in medieval times there was, in addition to the New Forest in Hampshire, a New Forest which lay some six miles to the west of Richmond in Yorkshire while another New Forest was adjacent to Cannock Chase in Staffordshire.

40   Pamber Forest

This small forest was situated to the east of, and almost adjoining, the village of Tadley some three miles south of Aldermaston. It dated from the thirteenth century but ceased to be a forest at the beginning of the seventeenth century.

41   Parkhurst Forest

This former Crown Forest is located about one and a half miles north-west of Newport in the Isle of Wight and now forms a part of the Forestry Commission's Wight Forest, although the ancient forest was disafforested in 1812.[68] In 1903 the Crown Forest extended to 1,312 acres, of which 1,130 were wooded[69] but by 1969 it had increased to 1,806 acres of which 1,477 were under plantations.[70]

42   Waltham Chase

Also known in the eighteenth century by the name of Horderswood Common, this area lies about one and a half miles south-east of Bishops Waltham and adjoins the western perimeter of Bere Forest. It should not be confused with Waltham Forest which now forms part of Epping Forest in Essex. It was acquired by the Lord Treasurer in the sixteenth century and was subsequently granted to the Earl of Wiltshire but was enclosed in 1870.[71]

At the beginning of the eighteenth century this area became notorious on account of a gang of deer stealers who were known as the 'Waltham Blacks' due to their practice of blacking their faces at night, a procedure adopted by army commandos during the 1939-45 War. The violence that their actions occasioned resulted in the passing of an Act of Parliament in 1722[72] which became known as the 'Black Act' and which began with the following words:

> *Whereas several ill-designing and disorderly persons have of late associated themselves under the name of Blacks and entred into confederacies to support and assist one another in stealing and destroying deer, robbing of warrens and fish-ponds, cutting down plantations and trees and other illegal practices . . . several of them with their faces blacked . . .*

After this Act had come into force over 40 members of the gang were arrested and at a special assize held at Reading, four were executed and the remainder transported. During the same period, other gangs were engaged in poaching deer in Cranbourne Chase.

43   West Forest

Little information is available about West Forest although Spelman[73] includes it in his list of forests and Speed[74] shows it on his map of Hampshire which was published in 1610 or thereabouts. It was apparently a detached portion of Bere Forest and lay about five miles west of Winchester and within an area bounded by Houghton (two miles south of Stockbridge), Little Somborne, Sparsholt, Pitt, Farley and King's Somborne and included Parnholt Wood. The current Ordnance Survey map marks 'Forest of Bere Farm' approximately in the centre of the area described above. In close proximity to this farm lies a block of woodland, a part of which is named West Wood. It is possible that the name of the forest had its origins in this wood but it is more likely that it was so named on account of the fact that the area lay to the west of the main Forest of Bere. Bere was also known as the Forest of South and the derivation of this name may have been due to the fact that it lay to the south of the smaller portion which formed West Forest. Hursley Forest which belongs to the Forestry Commission is about two miles to the south of Forest of Bere Farm.

44   Woolmer Forest

Also known by the names of Wolvemar and Wutmer, the centre of this forest was some six miles south-east of Alton and a similar distance west of Hazlemere and was only separated from Alice Holt Forest to the north by a narrow strip of land. It was divided into two walks or bailiwicks namely Linchborough Walk and Borden Walk. Gilbert White[75] stated that Woolmer Forest was about seven miles in length and two and a half miles in breadth and was 'abutted on' by the parishes of Kingsley, Greatham and Liss on the west, Rogate and Trotton on the south and Bramshott and Headley on the east and north. He also remarked that while Woolmer only harboured red deer, Alice Holt was solely the resort of fallow. This forest was transferred to the Forestry Commission in 1923 but was sold to the War Department (now the Ministry of Defence) in 1956.

HEREFORDSHIRE

45   Acornbury Forest

The name of this forest had many forms of spelling including Aconbury, Acornburye, Acornebiri, Acorneburi and Akenbury. It was situated about four miles south of Hereford and one mile north of Much Birch and Little Birch and adjoined the road from Ross-on-Wye to Hereford (A49). In 1216, King John granted land in this forest to Margaret de Lascy in order to build a nunnery.[76] Some of the woodlands lying within the limits of the original Acornbury Forest were acquired under that name by the Forestry Commission in 1954 but in 1960 these became part of the newly designated Hereford Forest.

46   Bringewood Chase

Also known as Brindwood or Bringwood, this area lay about a mile or so to the west of Ludlow. The exact bounds are uncertain but it is likely that this chase lay within the following limits. From Bringewood Forge on the River Teme the line probably followed the river north-eastwards to the edge of Oakley Park and then turned to the south-east to join the county boundary near Ludford Park. It is probable that the line then followed the county boundary to a point about a mile north-west of Richards Castle and continued south-westwards past the Goggin and Gatley Park to Leinthall Earls. From here it followed a stream west and northwards to join the Teme near The Willows and so back to Bringewood Forge. For the length of the Teme, it adjoined Mocktree Forest which is described in section 87.

47   Deerfold Forest

The eastern limits of Deerfold Forest which was also known as Derefuld, Darvold, Darvel, Deerfield and Derwaldswood lay about seven miles south-west of Ludlow. Beginning at Adforton on the main road to Hereford (A4110), the bounds followed this road southwards through Wigmore to Aymestry. Here they turned westwards along the course of the River Lugg as far as its junction with the Lime brook which they followed through Limebrook and past Lingen until this stream reached the road from Lingen to Letton. At this point the bounds turned northwards along this road through Letton to Adforton where the bounds began. Further information about this forest can be found in an account by H. G. Bull which appeared in 1869.[77] Deerfold now forms a part of Mortimer Forest which belongs to the Forestry Commission.

48   Greytree Forest

Greytree Forest which was created by Henry II and John, covered a large part of the hundred of Greytree and lay within an area the limits of which were as follows. From Stoke Edith, some five miles to the east of Hereford, through Putley to a point where the Ross-on-Wye to Ledbury road (A449) crosses the county boundary near Preston. Then along the line of the Herefordshire— Gloucestershire boundary to Queen's Wood which adjoins the M50 motorway and lies to the north of junction 3. After crossing the motorway, the line of demarcation continued southwards to the northern perimeter of the Forest of Dean which it followed as far as Ross-on-Wye. From Ross the boundary was probably coincidental with the river Wye, continuing upstream to where it was joined by the river Lugg. From there it followed the Lugg as far as its junction with the river Frome and proceeded along the course of that river to a point close to Stoke Edith. Greytree was disafforested in 1217.

49 Haywood Forest

Haywood, Haye or Hawood Forest which was three miles south-west of Hereford and about one mile north-west of Acornbury Forest, was one of the four forests that lay to the south of the county town, namely Acornbury, Haywood, Kilpeck and Greytree.

In 1578 Haywood Forest included the manors of Allensmore, Deweswell, Grafton and Callowe[78] and the bounds probably took a line comparable to the following. From the junction of the Abergavenny—Hereford road (A465) with road B4349 near Clehonger Court, eastwards through Grafton to the Ross-on-Wye—Hereford road (A49). Then southwards along the line of this road to Callow where the bounds turned westwards to the south of Allensmore Court regaining the A465 road and so following the line of this road to its junction with the B4349 road where the bounds began.

In *The Transactions of the Woolthorpe Naturalists Field Club* for 1869 under the title of 'The Remarkable Trees of Herefordshire' is shown a photograph of 'The Haywood Forest Oak' beneath which is the following note:

> *This tree is the finest of the group of old oaks standing by the homestead of the Haywood Farm. They are the only remaining trees of the Royal Forest of Haywood of olden times. It is now about sixty feet in height and at five feet from the ground . . . measures 20 feet 7 inches in circumference.*

50 Kilpeck Forest

The village of Kilpeck which gave its name to this forest, lies some eight miles to the south-west of Hereford and a mile south-east of the village of St Devereux through which the road from Abergavenny to Hereford (A465) passes. The Forests of Acornbury, Haywood and Kilpeck were all in close proximity to each other and it is possible that at one time they formed a single forest.

HUNTINGDONSHIRE

51 Harthay Forest

This forest lay some three and a half miles due west of Huntingdon and the site is shown on modern maps as High Harthay. Records of the metes and bounds which were made in 1154 and 1299 show that this forest included Brampton and parts of Ellington.[79]

52   Forest of Huntingdon

In Norman times, the Forest of Huntingdon covered almost the whole of the county but by the middle of the twelfth century it had been greatly reduced in area. At that time it consisted of three blocks which lay in close proximity to each other and were subsequently referred to as individual forests under the names of Harthay, Sapley and Waybridge. Detailed information regarding the Forest of Huntingdon has been provided by Elizabeth C. Wright.[80]

53   Sapley Forest

Sapley, which lies on the northern outskirts of Huntingdon, is now virtually part of the town. In 1542, the perimeter of Sapley and Waybridge Forests is said to have extended for about seven miles.[81] On a map dated 1801, Cary showed Sapley Heath which was probably part of the site of this forest and also marked the Sapley Oak which was then adjacent to the heath.[82]

54   Waybridge Forest

The name Waybridge also occurs in the forms Wauberghe, Weybridge, Wabridge, Wabrig and Wanbridge. Weybridge Farm, which is shown on modern maps, is situated about four miles west of Huntingdon and one mile north-east of High Harthay (see Harthay Forest).

LANCASHIRE

In recording the forests of Lancashire, some confusion can occur on account of the fact that within a forest other smaller areas are sometimes referred to as forests, as if they were entirely separate entities. For example, the Forest of Amounderness which comprised the hundred of that name, contained the Forests of Bleasdale, Myerscough and Fulwood. It is likely that when the major portion of Amounderness was no longer subject to forest law, these smaller forests, which were possibly wards or bailiwicks of the original, continued as individual forests. There also seems to have been some interchange of the terms 'forest', 'chase' and 'park', more particularly in the hundred of West Derby which lay between the Ribble and the Mersey. The Forests of Little Bowland, Pendle, Rossendale and Trawden although invariably described as forests were more correctly chases. Volume 2 of the Victoria County History for this county also contains an excellent map showing the forests and chases of Lancashire.[83]

55   Amounderness Forest

Also known as Audernesse, this forest comprised the hundred of Amounderness which extended from Preston, along the river Ribble and the coastline through Blackpool and Fleetwood to a point near Pilling about five miles east of Fleetwood. From there the bounds followed a circuitous line to Forton, Bleasdale and southwards to Longridge and Ribchester on the river Ribble. The boundary then continued along the Ribble to Preston. Originally the Forest of Amounderness included Bleasdale, Fulwood and Myerscough Forests and these are described under their respective names.

56   Forest of Blackburnshire

This forest which took its name from the hundred of Blackburnshire, consisted of four individual forests, namely, Pendle, Rossendale, Trawden and Little Bowland, which are considered under their individual titles.

57   Bleasdale Forest

This small forest which originally lay within the bounds of Amounderness Forest, was situated about five miles north-east of Garstang on the Preston-Lancaster road (A6) and some four miles east of the M6 motorway between junctions 32 and 33. It occupied an area bounded roughly by a line running westwards from Greave Clough Head on the county boundary between Lancashire and Yorkshire, to Grizedale Fell where it turned southwards to Calder Mouth, Bleasdale and Parlick Pike. At this point the line turned north to Fair Snape Fell to join the county boundary again and so back to Greave Clough Head. Beside the county boundary, it marched with Bowland Forest.

58   Little Bowland Forest

This was another small area which was a part of the Forest of Blackburnshire and was sometimes known as Little Bowland and Leagram. On the north and west it adjoined the much larger Yorkshire Forest of Bowland, the northern bounds beginning near Fair Oak Fell and continuing along the county boundary to Hodder Bank in the east where they followed the course of the river Hodder southwards to its junction with the river Loud. Bearing south-west, the bounds followed the Loud to a point near Pale where they turned north to Chipping bearing to the west of Leagram Hall, to rejoin the county boundary at Fair Oak Fell. Chipping lies about ten miles north-east of Preston and some seven miles west of Clitheroe.

59   Burtonwood Forest

This forest, which was originally a part of West Derby Forest, lay between the present day towns of Warrington and St Helens. The village of Burtonwood still commemorates the name of this forest.

60 *Fulwood Forest*

Fulwood Forest was situated to the north of Preston and a suburb of the town now bears this name. The forest lay on either side of the Savick or Savok brook and to the north of the supposed site of the Watling Street while on the west its limit was Cowfold Bridge and on the east Grimsargh.

61 *Lonsdale Forest*

The hundred of Lonsdale, Lounsedael or Lyones Dale was divided into two distinct sections which were separated by a part of Westmoreland. The northern portion lay to the north of Morecambe Bay and included Ulverston, Cartmel and the Furness Fells. The southern portion was bounded by Morecambe Bay on the west, Westmoreland on the north, Yorkshire on the east and on the south by the hundred of Amounderness. Lonsdale Forest originally covered part of the hundred of Lonsdale and it would seem probable that this related to the southern section since within it lay the Forests of Quernmore and Wyersdale which lie east and south-east of Lancaster.

62 *Myerscough Forest*

Myerscough or Mirescowe which was originally a part of Amounderness Forest was situated about seven miles north of Preston and two miles south of Garstang. It adjoined and lay to the west of the main Preston — Lancaster road (A6) and its name is now perpetuated in Myerscough Hall, Myerscough House and Myerscough Lodge.

63 *Pendle Forest*

Pendle or Penhull Forest adjoined the county boundary between Lancashire and Yorkshire and extended southwards towards Burnley, being some four miles north of that town and in close proximity to the north-western outskirts of Nelson. In the earliest times it formed part of the Forest of Blackburnshire and although always referred to as a forest was in fact a chase.

64 *Quernmore Forest*

Known also by the names of Quarlemore and Quarmore, this small forest lay about two miles to the east of Lancaster. Its northern boundary was formed by the river Lune where it flows between Escowbeck and Brookhouse. The eastern bounds ran from Brookhouse, or thereabouts, southwards to near

Crossgill and Cragg House and on to the summit of Clougha. From there, the bounds continued to the head of Damasgill and followed the gill to approximately Hare Appletree where they bore westwards to the river Conder. The bounds then followed the course of the river to Quernmore and so on to the river Lune.

65   Rossendale Forest

The Forest of Rossendale or Rossingdale was, in the first instance, part of the Forest of Blackburnshire and was situated in an area which lies between the towns of Accrington and Bacup. In its original form, it extended westwards from Accrington to Hoddleston (about a mile to the east of Darwen) and then eastwards to Ewood Bridge to the south of Haslingden. From here the southern and eastern boundaries of the forest were provided by the river Irwell as far as its source on Thieveley Pike, the northern boundary continuing on through Hameldon Hill to Accrington.[84]

References are sometimes found to Accrington Forest but these only refer to the north-western portion of Rossendale. Rossendale was disafforested about the beginning of the sixteenth century.

66   Simonswood Forest

This forest was situated in an area lying between the modern towns of Kirkby and Skelmsdale and the site is still identified by Simonswood Hall and Simonswood Moss which lie to the north of Kirkby. It was originally part of the Forest of West Derby.

67   Trawden Forest

This forest, which was previously part of the Forest of Blackburnshire, was almost adjacent to the present day towns of Colne and Nelson and some seven miles north-east of Burnley. The bounds probably began where the river Colne meets the Yorkshire border near Monkroyd on the Colne—Keighley road (A6068) and from this point continued southwards along the county boundary to Widdop Cross to the south-west of Boulsworth Hill. From Widdop Cross, the bounds probably turned to the north-west approximately along the line of the minor road which runs past Thursdon, Float Bridge and Birchenlee to Colne. From here the river Colne is likely to have formed the northern limit until it reached the county boundary again near Monkroyd.

68   West Derby Forest

The Forest of West Derby, which took its title from the hundred of that name, was also known as the Forest of Derbyshire. It originally comprised about half of the hundred and lay to the south-west of a line running roughly from Southport to Warrington. It included the parks of Croxteth and Toxteth and the Forests of Burtonwood and Simonswood which are referred to elsewhere in this chapter.

69   Wyersdale Forest

The centre of this forest lay about eight miles to the south-east of Lancaster. It was bounded on the east by the Yorkshire Forest of Bowland and on the south by Bleasdale Forest. The western boundary ran from near Grizedale Fell to Hare Appletree while on the north it marched with Quernmore Forest from Hare Appletree to the head of Damasgill; the remainder of its northern boundary continuing eastwards to Tarnbrook Fell where it joined the county boundary and the Forest of Bowland again.

LEICESTERSHIRE

70   Charnwood Forest

Charnwood Forest occupied much of the area that lies between Leicester, Loughborough and Coalville and this district is still known as Charnwood Forest. It was sometimes known as Charley Forest or Charnwood Chase and opinions differ as to whether Charnwood was ever a royal forest. Swanimotes were apparently held regularly at Whitwick, Groby and Sheepshed until the beginning of the seventeenth century and Cox[85] holds the view that this indicates that Charnwood was a royal hunting ground in Saxon times. On the other hand McKinley[86] considers that there is no evidence that Charnwood was ever a royal forest. The forest lay within an area which included on its perimeter Swithland, Groby, Bardon, Whitwick, Grace Dieu and Garendon. Adjoining the road between Nanpantan and Woodhouse Eaves is a wood named Out Woods while beside it is Outwoods Farm and these names would suggest that they lay outside the forest. Charnwood was inclosed under an Act passed in 1808[87] and today the M1 motorway divides the forest into two parts between junctions 22 and 23.

71   Leicester Forest

In the thirteenth century this forest extended from Thurcaston in the north-east to Desford, Market Bosworth and Earl Shilton in the south-west and as far as the outskirts of Leicester. It is probable that the north-eastern portion was bounded by the Rothley Brook and the river Soar. Evidence of this forest is to be found in some of the names which occur between Leicester and Desford and these include Leicester Forest East on the south-western outskirts of the city, Leicester Forest West some two miles distant, Forest House and Forest Farm. The M1 motorway crosses the site of this forest between junctions 21 and 22.

MIDDLESEX

72   *Enfield Chase*

Enfield Chase, which in 1324 was forfeited to Edward II, lay to the north and west of the town of Enfield and extended westwards to Hadley and South Mimms and northwards to the county boundary with Essex. A survey made in 1650 records that the Chase amounted to 7,904 acres and that 2,500 oaks valued at £2,100 had been marked for the use of the Navy.[88]

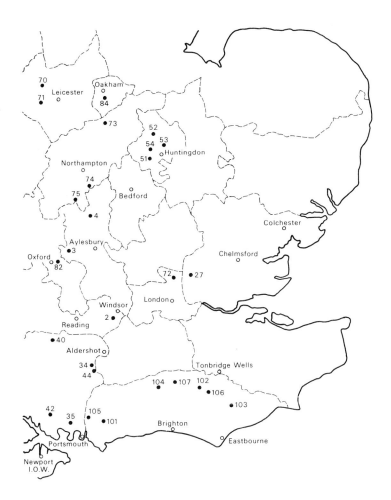

Map 1   Some medieval forests and chases in southern England

Map 2   Some medieval forests and chases in northern England

Key to Maps 1 and 2

1 Forest of Berkshire
2 Windsor Forest
3 Bernwood Forest
4 Whaddon Chase
5 Delamere Forest
6 Macclesfield Forest
7 Wirral Forest
8 Copeland Forest
9 The King's Forest of
   Geltsdale
10 Gilderdale Forest
11 Inglewood Forest
12 Nichol Forest
13 Skiddaw Forest
14 Thornthwaite Forest
15 Duffield Frith
16 Peak Forest
17 Dartmoor Forest
18 Bere Regis Forest
19 Blakemore Forest
20 Cranbourne Chase
21 Gillingham Forest
22 Holt Forest
23 Poorstock Forest
24 Forest of Purbeck
25 Teesdale Forest
26 Weardale Forest
27 Forest of Essex
   (Epping Forest)
28 Alveston Forest
29 Forest of Corse
30 Forest of Dean
31 Horwood Forest
32 Kingswood Forest
33 Micklewood Forest
34 Alice Holt Forest
35 Bere Forest
36 Buckholt Forest
37 Chute Forest
   (in Hampshire)
38 Harewood Forest
39 New Forest
   (in Hampshire)
40 Pamber Forest
41 Parkhurst Forest
42 Waltham Chase
43 West Forest
44 Woolmer Forest
45 Acornbury Forest

46 Bringewood Chase
47 Deerfold Forest
48 Greytree Forest
49 Haywood Forest
50 Kilpeck Forest
51 Harthay Forest
52 Forest of
   Huntingdon
53 Sapley Forest
54 Waybridge Forest
55 Amounderness
   Forest
56 Forest of
   Blackburnshire
57 Bleasdale Forest
58 Little Bowland
   Forest
59 Burtonwood Forest
60 Fulwood Forest
61 Lonsdale Forest
62 Myerscough Forest
63 Pendle Forest
64 Quernmore Forest
65 Rossendale Forest
66 Simonswood Forest
67 Trawden Forest
68 West Derby Forest
69 Wyersdale Forest
70 Charnwood Forest
71 Leicester Forest
72 Enfield Chase
73 Rockingham Forest
74 Salcey Forest
75 Whittlewood Forest
76 Allendale Forest
77 Hexham Forest
78 Forest of Rothbury
79 Lowes Forest
80 Forest of
   Northumberland
81 Sherwood Forest
82 Shotover Forest
83 Wychwood Forest
84 Forest of Rutland
   and Leighfield
85 Clee Forest
86 Long Forest
87 Mocktree Forest
88 Morf Forest

89 Forest of Mount
   Gilbert
90 Forest of Shirlott
91 Exmoor Forest
92 Mendip Forest
93 Forest of Neroche
94 North Petherton
   Forest
95 Selwood Forest
   (in Somerset)
96 Brewood Forest
97 Cannock Forest
98 Kinver Forest
99 Needwood Forest
100 New Forest
   (in Staffordshire)
101 Arundel Forest
102 Ashdown Forest
103 Dallington Forest
104 St Leonard's Forest
105 Stanstead Forest
106 Waterdown Forest
107 Worth Forest
108 Forest of Arden
109 Braydon Forest
110 Chippenham Forest
111 Chute Forest
   (in Wiltshire)
112 Clarendon Forest
113 Groveley Forest
114 Melchet Forest
115 Melksham Forest
116 Savernake Forest
117 Selwood Forest
   (in Wiltshire)
118 Feckenham Forest
119 Horwell Forest
120 Malvern Forest
121 Ombersley Forest
122 Wyre Forest
123 Bowland Forest
124 Galtres Forest
125 Hatfield Chase
126 Knaresborough
   Forest
127 New Forest
   (in Yorkshire)
128 Pickering Forest
129 Skipton Forest

Unlike some of the medieval forests, those of Northamptonshire included areas of woodland which contained important stocks of timber. The Reports of the Commissioners of 1787-93[1] were largely concerned with those crown forests that were able to contribute to the needs of the country, more particularly by way of oak for the Navy. These reports covered 11 forests and it is worth noting that three of them lay in Northamptonshire, namely Rockingham, Salcey and Whittlewood.

73   *Rockingham Forest*

One of the largest of the medieval forests, Rockingham or Rokingham, lay in the extreme north of the county adjoining Rutland and Huntingdon and was in close proximity to the towns of Stamford, Corby, Kettering and Oundle. The Commissioners Report[2] for Rockingham sets out at length the perambulation of 1641 which is somewhat complex and does not readily lend itself to a written description. However Pettit[3] has prepared a map of the forest showing the perambulations of 1299 and 1641 in considerable detail and reference should be made to this map in order to ascertain the exact bounds.

In 1792 Rockingham Forest was divided into three bailiwicks; Rockingham, Brigstock, the smallest of the three and Cliffe, the largest. Rockingham covered an area which is now mainly occupied by the new town of Corby, Brigstock lay around the village of that name while Cliffe stretched from Duddington in the north-west to Wansford in the east. Cliffe Bailiwick was detached from the main forest area and consequently it was sometimes, erroneously, referred to as the Forest of Cliffe. Each bailiwick was subdivided into walks, Rockingham comprising Benefield, West Walk, Gretton and Little Weldon Woods, Weedhaw and Thornhaw and Corley Woods. Brigstock comprised Coddington Woods and Farming Woods while Cliffe consisted of Westhay, Morehay, Sulehay and Shortwood.[4] Disafforestation took place over a number of years, Geddington Woods being disafforested in 1676 while statutes passed in 1795 and 1796 completed the process. Rockingham is now one of the Forestry Commission's forests and extends to over 6,000 acres.

74   Salcey Forest

Also referred to by the names of Sacy, Sawcey and Sautye, this forest lay between Northampton, Wellingborough, Newport Pagnell and Towcester and marched with Whittlewood Forest along part of its western limits. The M1 motorway cuts across the south-western portion of the forest for much of the way between junctions 14 and 16.

As in the case of Rockingham and Whittlewood, a new perambulation of the forest was prepared under the authority of Charles I in 1639 and the bounds laid down under this instrument were as follows. Beginning at the South Bridge over the river Nene in Northampton the bounds followed this river eastwards to Wellingborough Bridge where the road to Newport Pagnell (A509) crosses the river. They then turned south along the line of this road until it crossed the river Ouse at Olney and continued along the Ouse to the point where it joined the river Tove. From here the bounds followed the Tove as far as Towcester where they continued along the road to Northampton (A43) until they reached the South Bridge where the bounds began. The forest included the area known as Yardley Chase which lies to the south-west of Yardley Hastings on the Northampton—Bedford road (A428). In 1792 Salcey covered only 1,847 acres and was divided into four walks — Hanslope, Hartwell, Piddington and the Deputy Ranger's Walk; Hanslope being the largest.[5]

Salcey was enclosed under an Act[6] which was passed in 1825 and this included a provision that the allotments of land to the King and the Duke of Grafton were to be those parts best adapted to the growth of timber. After the sale of any land in order to meet the expenses incurred, the remainder of the King's allotment subsequently became a Crown Wood which was transferred to the Forestry Commission in 1923. Until 1972, Salcey Forest and Yardley Chase, which had become Commission forests, retained their old names but in that year, it is sad to note, these two historic forest areas became known as Wymersley Forest.[7] This name was presumably taken from the old hundred of Wymersley in which these two areas were situated.

75   Whittlewood Forest

The Forest of Whittlewood which was sometimes referred to as Whittlebury Forest was situated between Towcester, Stoney Stratford and Brackley and adjoined Salcey Forest which lay to the east. The Commissioner's Report[8] which is concerned with this forest contains the perambulations of 1299 together with that which was carried out at the instigation of Charles I in

1639. This Report states that the latter perambulation 'extended the bounds ... far beyond the former limits' and that in 1640 an Act[9] in effect restored the bounds of the forest to those of 1299. The perambulation of 1639 began at the bridge over the river Ouse at Thornton, three miles south-west of Stony Stratford and the bounds followed the course of the Ouse to its junction with the river Tove which they followed to Towcester. They then turned north-east along the line of the Towcester — Northampton road (A43) for about two miles before bearing due west through Tiffield and across the Watling Street (A5). Here they turned south-west between Field Burcote and Duncote to Bradden, Slapton and Wappenham and passed close to Astwell Park and Crowfield continuing along the eastern edge of Whistley Wood to reach the Brackley — Towcester road (A43) which they followed to Brackley.

At this point the perambulation ends, leaving a gap in the bounds from Brackley to Thornton Bridge where the circuit began. It would seem probable that the bounds continued along the Buckingham road (A422) as far as the county boundary and then turned north along this boundary to Biddlesden or thereabouts. From here they must have continued across country back to Thornton Bridge. Unfortunately many of the names contained in the perambulation of 1299 are now difficult to identify with any certainty and this renders any comparison between the two perambulations open to doubts and liable to inaccuracies. However among those places referred to in the first perambulation and which can be identified, are Stony Stratford, Passenham, Deanshanger, Pottersbury and Furtho in the south-east, Wappenham and Whitfield in the west and Towcester in the north. In view of this it is possible that there was not so great a discrepancy between areas covered by the perambulation of 1299 and that of 1639 as the Commissioner's Report claims.

In 1792 Whittlewood Forest extended to 5,424 acres and was divided into five walks, namely, Hanger, Hazleborough, Sholebrook, Shrob and Wakefield[10] but Pettit[11] refers to an additional walk known as Handley which was detached from the remainder and lay about a mile or so to the south-west of Towcester. However when Whittlewood was disafforested in 1853[12] there were only four walks since Hazleborough had been inclosed in 1824.[13] Hazleborough is now one of the Commission's forests.

NORTHUMBERLAND

76   Allendale Forest

Allendale or Alwendale Forest was situated to the south of Allendale Town which lies some eight miles south-west of Hexham and nine miles south-east of Haltwhistle. Hodgson[14] shows the forest extending on either side of what is now road B6295, from about two miles south of the town as far as the cross boundary with Durham. The northern part of the forest is shown as 'Low Forest' and the southern portion as 'High Forest' and this is shown on the map which is included in volume IV of Hodgson's work.

77   Hexham Forest

Although there are few, if any, references to Hexham Forest as such, this title was apparently applied to what was known as Hexhamshire. This was a district which extended southwards from Hexham for a distance of about 12 miles being five and a half miles across at its widest point. It was divided into four 'quarters' which were not in fact equal in area and known as High, Middle, Low and West Quarters. To the south lay another area which was known as Newlands and Rowley Ward and the Survey of Hexham Manor of 1547[15] refers to *fforesta infra regaliam de Hexham predictam vocata Newlands* which may be translated as 'the forest south of the aforesaid royal forest of Hexham, called Newland' but there seems to be little information regarding it.

78   Forest of Rothbury

The town of Rothbury which is situated about 10 miles south-east of Alnwick and 13 miles north-north-east of Morpeth, was originally surrounded by Rothbury Forest. Dodds[16] gives a summary of the area covered by the forest and also provides the text of a perambulation made in 1539. From these two sources the bounds of the forest were probably as follows.

Beginning at Thorney Haugh, which is likely to be Haugh which Cary[17] shows on his map of 1807 and which lay to the west of Weldon Bridge on the Morpeth — Woolmer road (A697), the bounds ran westwards to Brinkburn Priory, Hesleyhurst, Ritton Whitehouse and Fallowlees. Here they turned northwards past Simonside to Newton crossing over the river Coquet to Snitter and Debdon about two miles to the north of Rothbury. From Debdon the bounds continued in a south-easterly direction to Healey and Pauperhaugh and so back to where the bounds began.

A large part of Rothbury Forest was enclosed in 1831[18] but today a new Forest of Rothbury has been created by the Forestry Commission in this area.

79   Lowes Forest

Leland[19] observed that 'The Forest of Loughes is in Tindale on the west syde of Northern Tyne, even betwyxt the Tynnes armes'. The North Tyne and South Tyne rivers meet about a mile to the north-west of Hexham and from Leland's description it would appear that this forest covered an area lying between Wark, Haydon Bridge and Haltwhistle. In an enclosure award[20] of 1751 the name Lowes occurs as an alternative name for Ridley Moor and Hotbank and modern maps show East Hotbank to the north of Ridley Common which adjoins Greenlee and Broomlee Loughs. Immediately to the south of Greenlee Lough stands West Hotbank and half a mile or so further south are Hotbank Crags. This appears to confirm Leland's account and that the forest was situated in the area described by him.

80   Forest of Northumberland

It is probable that until the middle of the thirteenth century the individual medieval forests of the county which emerged later, were regarded as one entity under the general title of the Forest of Northumberland. The area was divided into three bailiwicks, namely, north of the river Alne, north of Rothbury and south of Rothbury[21] and subsequently different parts of the forest became known by individual names including Allendale, Hexham, Lowes and Rothbury Forests.

NOTTINGHAMSHIRE

81   Sherwood Forest

In early times this forest covered about one quarter of the county and was known as the Forest of Nottingham, variations of its later name being Schirewod, Shirewode and Shirewud. It extended from Carburton, four miles to the north-east of Warsop in the north, to Nottingham some twenty miles to the south and numerous perambulations were made during the course of time. Three of these, which were carried out in 1300, 1539 and 1674, are included in the Report of the Commissioners on Sherwood Forest[22] while Turner[23] provides a translation of that of 1300 and from this the approximate bounds of the forest may be summarized as follows.

From a ford over Rainworth Water between Edwinstowe and Wellow near Ollerton, known as the King's Ford, the bounds proceeded southwards along the road which ran from Wellow to Nottingham and after passing Rufford Abbey continued by Rainworth Water to Rainworth Ford. Here the bounds turned eastwards until they met the equivalent of what is now the Ollerton — Nottingham road (A614) which they followed to a point where the road crossed the stream known as the Dover Beck. The bounds continued along the course of the Beck until it joined the river Trent, about one and a half miles north-east of Gunthorpe Bridge. The Trent then formed the perimeter of the forest as far as Nottingham Bridge where the bounds turned northwards to follow the course of the river Leen through Radford and Basford as far as Linby Mill. Leaving the river at this point the bounds continued westwards through Linby to the Nottingham—Mansfield road (A611) or thereabouts, following this road past the site of Annesley Castle to a point near Nuncargate. They then probably followed the line of road B6021 for about two miles and passed by Kirkby Hardcastle to join the river Maun along which the bounds continued as far as the Chesterfield road (A617). After following this road to a point where it crossed the river Meden at Pleasley, the perimeter of the forest traced the course of this river as far as Budby on road A616 and so continued to Wellow where the bounds began.

The perambulation of 1674 is very similar to that of 1300 in many respects but there are two major variations. The first was a deviation of the bounds at Kirkby Hardcastle when they turned westwards to Fulwood and continued northwards along the county boundary past Huthwaite to Whiteborough. From here they passed between Treversal and Skegby along the course of the river Meden to a point between Gleadthorpe Grange and Budby where they turned north across the river to Hazel Gap. They then followed a circuitous route to Norton, along the river Poulter and across Welbeck Park to Carburton continuing through Thoresby Park and over the Ollerton — Blyth road (A614). They then bore east towards Whitewater Bridge and turned south past Ollerton to Wellow. In 1609 the forest extended to 89,406 acres[24] but by the end of the eighteenth century the area had decreased substantially on account of grants made to individuals and various Enclosure Acts[25] and in this way more than 10,000 acres were enclosed. In 1792 the forest comprised nine walks each in charge of a keeper and although, at this date, there were officially no deer in the forest except in Thorney Woods, there had been a large number in Birkland and Bilhagh until about 1770. They had then been destroyed owing to the damage they caused to farm crops and the area was enclosed by Act of Parliament in 1818.[26]

No account of Sherwood Forest would be complete without reference to the somewhat mythical figure of Robin Hood. Whether he was a real person or only one who existed in legend is a matter for conjecture and there could be some doubt as to whether Sherwood was the scene of his exploits. Leland,[27] who made a journey through England during the reign of Henry VIII, observed whilst travelling through Yorkshire:

> *Along on the lift hond a iii miles of betwixt Milburne and Feribridge*
> *I saw the woodi and famose Forest of Barnesdale wher they say that*
> *Robyn Hudde lyvid like an outlaw.*

However this does not necessarily mean that Robin Hood could not have carried out his activities in Sherwood as well since the distance from Ferrybridge to Ollerton in the northern part of the forest, was only 38 miles as the crow flies.

OXFORDSHIRE

82   Shotover Forest

The Forest of Shotover was situated on the eastern outskirts of the City of

Oxford, between Headington and Wheatley and for the most part lay between what is now the Oxford—London road (A40) and the road from Cowley to Headington (A4142). Stowood, which lies about two miles to the north, was usually regarded as being a part of Shotover, on account of its close proximity and limited extent while at various times both Shotover and Stowood were considered to be a part of Bernwood Forest. Most of Bernwood lay in the adjoining county of Buckinghamshire and it is included under that county in Chapter 4.

It is recorded that a forest eyre was held in Oxford in 1256 when pleas were heard in respect of Shotover and Wychwood Forests and those parts of Bernwood Forest which lay in Oxfordshire. On account of its nearness to Oxford, timber and underwood from Shotover was occasionally sold to some of the colleges. In 1572 the Dean of Christ Church paid five pounds for two acres of underwood although the usual price, at that time, was apparently about 33 shillings per acre. Other colleges which purchased underwood from Shotover were Queen's, New College, All Souls, Magdalen, Brasenose and Corpus.[28]

83   Wychwood Forest

Wychwood Forest lay within an area bounded on the north and north-east by the river Evenlode, on the south by the road from Witney to Burford (A40) and on the west by the Burford to Shipton-under-Wychwood road (A361). At various times it was also known by the names of Whichwude, Wichwood and Huuchwode.

The Report of the Commissioners on Wychwood[29] stated in 1792 that 'This forest is almost entirely encompassed with a stone wall, which is not however, wholly built on the boundary of the King's lands, but comprehends various coppices and open wastes, belonging to private owners and not included within the last mentioned perambulation' (1641). Cary's map of Oxfordshire shows this wall quite clearly but owing to the small scale it is difficult to identify its position accurately. Furthermore, the bounds follow such a circuitous course that it would be difficult to provide a precise written account. The approximate bounds of the forest based on the perambulation of 1641 may be summarized as follows. Beginning near Walcot, a mile to the west of Charlbury, the bounds followed the wall of Cornbury Park to Patch Hill Gate Corner and then turned south to Ramsden Heath and continued along the Hulwerk to White Oak Green. From here the bounds continued to Lowbarrow, Fordwell, Roustage Wood, Hen's Grove Wood and South Lawn. They then bore north-east to Langley, Farfield, Priest Grove and Boynal Copse and on to Ascott d'Oyley where they turned eastward to Smallstone Corner and Chilson and so back to Walcot.

In 1792, the forest covered some 3,700 acres and was divided into five walks which were known as Patch Hill, Potter's Hill, Roger's Hill, South Lawn and the Ranger's Walk. At the beginning of the nineteenth century, Wychwood Forest and its immediate surroundings were notorious for poachers, thieves and petty criminals[30] and the Forest Fair which was held in September was thought to encourage the presence of some of the less desirable members of the public. Disafforestation was brought about by two statutes which were passed in 1853[31] and 1856.[32]

RUTLAND

84   Forest of Rutland and Leighfield

Until 1235 Rutland Forest was known as the Forest of Rutland and Leicestershire but when, at that date, the area lying in Leicestershire was disafforested it became known as the Forest of Rutland or Rotelande. According to a perambulation made in 1269,[33] Rutland Forest covered the whole of the southern half of the county, its limits being approximately as follows. From the junction of the Eye Brook with the river Welland near Rockingham, the bounds followed the course of the Welland to the county boundary with Lincolnshire, near Stamford. From there the bounds turned north to Great Casterton Bridge and then followed the river Gwash to a point beyond Empingham Bridge before bearing north-westwards past Barnsdale and on through Langham to the county boundary near Cold Overton. The bounds then continued southwards along a line which is virtually the county boundary and which for the last seven miles follows the Eye Brook until it joins the Welland, thus completing the perambulation.

However, by the seventeenth century this forest had become considerably smaller in size and only covered about one-third of the original area. In 1684 Wright[34] set out a much later perambulation. This began at Fletterette Corner close to what is now Flitteris Park and the western limit followed the line given in the perambulation of 1269, southwards to Caldecote. After turning north-eastwards along the river Welland for about one and a half miles, the bounds turned north to Liddington, Uppingham, Ayston, Ridlington and Brooke. On crossing the river Gwash, the bounds continued in a north-westerly direction to join Fletterette Corner again.

Wright refers to this smaller area as 'Lifield and Beaumont Forrest' and other variations of the first name were Lyfield, Leafield, Leyfield, Leighfield and Leigh. Maps of the present day show Leighfield and Leighfield Lodge to the south and north respectively, of the river Chater and about two miles north-west of the village of Ridlington. Beaumont Chase is shown as being some two miles west of Uppingham.

SHROPSHIRE

85   Clee Forest

Clee Forest occupied an area which, until the middle of the twelfth century, included Ditton Priors, Brown Clee Hill and westwards to Culmington, some three miles east of Craven Arms. However, when Henry II granted Ditton to Wenlock Priory, and Culmington, Siefton and Corfham (or Cortham) to Walter de Clifford he also conferred Clee Forest on the same family when it became known as 'the Haye of Ernestry and Les Clives'.[35] Earnstrey Park is now situated approximately midway between Tugford and Ditton Priors. In 1199 reference was made to 'The Haye of Ernestreu and Les Clines', a further form of the name being 'Clies'.

86   Long Forest

This forest took its name from the long escarpment which is known as Wenlock Edge although the area of the forest originally stretched northwards to the outskirts of Shrewsbury. Eyton[36] provides a detailed account of the manors and townships which lay within the jurisdiction of the forest and from these it is possible to deduce its probable extent.

The limits of the forest lay within a line which may be delineated as follows. Beginning at Meole Brace on the southern fringe of Shrewsbury, the line ran eastwards to Sutton and the river Severn and then followed the direction of the river as far as Cressage where it continued along the road to Much Wenlock (A458). From there the line turned to the south-west close to the road to Craven Arms (B4378) as far as Beambridge, a mile north-east of Munslow. Here it bore south to Great and Little Sutton, Culmington and Whettleton near Craven Arms where it followed the river Onny northwards to Choulton. However before reaching this last named village, the line turned north through Myndtown, Asterton, Medlicote and Ratlinghope crossing the Wentnor – Castle Pulverbatch road which it virtually followed through Longden back to Meole Brace.

In 1300 a massive perambulation was made of the Shropshire forests and as a result almost the whole of Long Forest was disafforested except for the three areas or hayes of Lythwood, Bushmore and Haycrust which were to continue as forests. Lythwood lay about three miles to the south of Shrewsbury and stretched from Exfordsgreen north-eastwards almost to Sutton, a distance of four miles and included Lyth Hill and Pulley. The Haye of Bushmoor or Bishopmore was situated on the Craven Arms – Shrewsbury road (A49) half a mile south-west of Acton-Scott but its extent is uncertain. Haycrust, Hayhurst or Hakehurst lay to the west of Bushmore and adjoined the river Onny but its limits are also obscure. The name of Long Forest has been perpetuated by the Forestry Commission who have adopted it for one of their new forests in this area.

87   Mocktree Forest

This forest was situated between Onibury and Leintwardine, the northern half being in Shropshire and the southern portion being in Herefordshire. Beginning at Onibury, the bounds of the forest followed the course of the River Onny southwards to its junction with the River Teme at Broomfield. Here they turned westwards along the Teme and it is probable that they followed this river to the south of Tatteridge Hill, ultimately leaving the river near Trippleton. From there the bounds proceeded northwards until they reached the Watling Street which they followed to Goats Hill. At this point they deviated eastwards and continued along the contour below View Edge and Stoke Wood to rejoin the River Onny about a mile to the south of Stokesay. The bounds then followed the Onny down to Onibury where the bounds began. This forest was also known by the name of Mactry.

88   Morf Forest

Morf Forest which was sometimes referred to as the Forest of Bridgnorth lay immediately to the east of that town and adjacent to it. The perambulation of Shropshire forests of 1300 sets out the metes and bounds of Morf which may be summarized as follows.[37]

Beginning at Pendleston Mill the bounds followed the river Severn to the point where it is joined by the river Worf. They then followed the Worf to Rindleford Bridge and on to Wyken and Hilton continuing along a road (probably what is now part of A454 and B4176) to Abbots Castle Hill. From here the border of the forest marched with the county boundary with Staffordshire to a point between Claverley and Whittimere, and then passed to the north of Broughton and Beobridge where it turned south passing to the north-west of Gatacre. The bounds continued westwards through what the perambulation describes as the Cover of Morf, which was probably near Morfe valley, and so on to Mose and Quatford following the road (A442) through Bridgnorth Low Town back to Pendleston Mill.

89   Forest of Mount Gilbert

The Forest of Mount Gilbert which is more generally known as Wrekin Forest was of considerable extent and adjoined Long Forest and Shirlott Forest on the south-west and Brewood Forest on the east. Before the perambulation of 1300 which substantially reduced its size, Mount Gilbert Forest stretched from Albrighton (three miles north of Shrewsbury) on the west to beyond Sherriff Hales a distance of some 18 miles, as the crow flies. The limits of the forest prior to 1300 may be inferred from the list of villages and localities that were to be disafforested and the following is an indication of the probable extent of the forest at that time.

Beginning at Albrighton the perimeter of the forest extended eastwards to Hadnall and then south to Astley, Roden, Rodington and Wrockwardine where it turned north to Eyton upon the Weald Moors, Crudgington, Waters Upton and Great Bolas to Dodecote Grange and Howle. At this point the bounds of the forest probably followed a southerly direction approximately along the line of the Whitchurch – Wolverhampton road (A41) as far as the Watling Street (A5). Here the bounds bore to the south-west to Shifnal, Kemberton and Sutton Maddock until they reached the river Severn which they followed to a little beyond Uffington where they continued northwards to Harlescott and so back to Albrighton.[38]

The forest was divided into two bailiwicks; Haughmond, three miles north-east of Shrewsbury, which was sometimes referred to as Haumon Forest; and Wombridge, between Hadley and Oakengates, which was occasionally known as the Forest of Wombrug. The only demesne land in the forest which belonged to the King, was the Haye of Wellington.

90   Forest of Shirlott

The Forest of Shirlott which was also known as Sherlot, Schirlet and Shirlett, occupied an area between and adjacent to Long Forest and the Forests of Clee, Mount Gilbert and Morfe. On the west and north its bounds were those of the adjoining forests while to the east its limits were the Severn and, further to the south, Morfe. Its southern boundary extended approximately from Bridgnorth to Criddon and Faintree some three miles north-east of Cleobury Mortimer.[39]

The original forests of Clee, Morfe, Mount Gilbert, Shirlott and Long Forest covered a considerable area, but adjacent to the south-eastern limits of Mount Gilbert lay the Staffordshire forests of Brewood and Cannock. In close proximity to these last named were Kinver, Needwood and the Staffordshire New Forest and these ten forests formed a massive block which extended for 46 miles from Albrighton in the west to Tamworth in the east.

SOMERSET

91   Exmoor Forest

The Forest of Exmoor or Exmore lies in the extreme north-west of Somerset between the Bristol Channel and the towns of Lynton, South Moulton, Dulverton and Minehead. The area of the Norman forest was substantially increased by King John but after the Forest Charters of 1217[40] and 1225[41] steps were taken to restore it to approximately its original size.

Four perambulations of the forest have been recorded. The first was made in 1279 and the second less than a year later; the third in 1298 and the last in 1651. The bounds of the forest according to the first perambulation of 1279 were as follows. Beginning at County Gate on the Lynton—Porlock road (A39) the bounds followed the county boundary southwards along Badgworthy Water to Brendon Two Gates, Saddle Gate, Moles Chamber, Kingsford Gate and Litton Water to the junction of the Danesbrook with the river Barle. At this point the boundary line of the forest turned northwards up the Barle until it reached a point opposite Hawkridge Common where it bore due east between Ashway and Ashwayside to Mounsey Hill Gate. From there the line followed the road over Winsford Hill to Comers Cross, leaving the road at that point to continue past Room Hill to Road Castle on the Exe. After following the Exe upstream to Downscombe, the bounds continued northwards over Wellshead Allotment to Aldermans Barrow, Lucott Cross and Hawkcombe Head to join the Lynton—Porlock road. The line then turned west along this road to County Gate where the bounds began.

In the first three perambulations, the western limit of the forest was the county boundary between Devon and Somerset. However in the 1651 perambulation this limit was moved a little way into Devon although it remained roughly parallel to the county boundary for most of its length. Gresswell[42] gives a full account of each of the four perambulations.

Forest eyres for Somerset were held at Ilchester in 1257 and 1270 and the pleas heard included those relating to Exmoor Forest. The forest was the subject of several leases from the seventeenth to the nineteenth centuries but it was ultimately disafforested in 1815[43] after which the portion allotted to the Crown was sold to John Knight in 1818. The story of the remarkable efforts made by John Knight and his son Frederick to reclaim the moor is admirably recorded by C. S. Orwin.[44] The first pack of hounds recorded on Exmoor was that belonging to Hugh Pollard, the ranger of the forest, who kennelled his hounds at Simonsbath in 1598.[45]

92 *Mendip Forest*

Mendip Forest originally extended from what is now Weston-super-Mare, south-eastwards almost to Wells being in width about three to four miles. The motorway (M5) now passes through the western portion of the forest for a distance of about four miles to the south of junction 21.

In 1298 a perambulation was carried out, the details of which are given by Collinson[46] but the bounds as then described are difficult to identify today. It would appear that these did not cover an area much larger than the parishes of Cheddar and Axbridge.[47] However those who were responsible for this perambulation observed that the following townships and their woods were afforested after the coronation of Henry II in 1155 and consequently they should be disafforested in accordance with the Forest Charter.[48] Thus in the thirteenth century the forest included these townships and they provide an indication of the original extent of Mendip Forest. Beginning at St Thomas's Head on the coast four miles north of Weston-super-Mare the townships included Worle, Banwell, Churchill, Langford, Rowberrow, Shipham, Burrington Blagdon, Ubley, West Harptree, East Harptree, Chewton, Priddy, Compton, Winscombe, Christon, Loxton, Bleadon, Hutton and Uphill to which may be added Cheddar and Axbridge.

The name of Mendip Forest is still used for the Forestry Commission's new forest which has been established in this area.

93   The Forest of Neroche

This forest, which was also known by the names of Nerechirch, Nerachich, Rache, Roach or Roche, lay some six miles or so south-east of Taunton and was roughly rectangular in shape, the four corners being in close proximity to Langport, Staple Fitzpaine, Whitestaunton and South Petherton. As in the case of other forests in Somerset, Neroche was often visited by King John who was particularly fond of hunting in the county.

A perambulation of the forest was made in 1298 and as in the case of the perambulation of Mendip Forest, which was undertaken in the same year, those concerned did not record the old boundaries but instead specified the additions that had been made since 1154, chiefly by King John. Thus they claimed that the following townships ought to be disafforested in accordance with the Charter of Henry III. Beginning in the north-east of the forest these were Drayton, South Petherton, Ilton, Ilminster, Horton, Donyatt, Broadway, Sticklepath, Combe St Nicholas, Castle Neroche, Curland, Staple Fitzpaine, Bickenhall, Ashill, Stewley, Capland, Isle Abbots and Isle Brewers.[49]

When in 1830 an Act[50] was passed for the disafforestation of the Forest of Neroche it named 13 parishes in which the forest lay. In addition to the majority of those referred to in the perambulation of 1298, Barrington, White Lackington, Commett, Hatch Beauchamp and Beer Crocombe were also included. From these two sources of information, it is probable that the bounds of the forest approximated to the following. From Langport the eastern limit probably followed the line of the river Parrett to its junction with the Lopen Brook after passing under the Fosse Way (A303) at Petherton Bridge. The bounds are then likely to have followed the brook to Dinnington and on to Dowlish Wake, turning southwards along the river Isle to Wadeford, Whitestaunton and the county boundary with Devon. After bearing north along the county boundary the line probably continued past Buckland St Mary to Blackwater and Staple Hill to join the road B3170 a little to the south of Corfe. At this point the bounds are likely to have turned eastwards to Hatch Beauchamp and then joined the Taunton–Langport road (A378) which the bounds followed to Langport where the perambulation probably began.

The Forestry Commission has named one of its new forests Neroche since it lies within the bounds of the old.

94   North Petherton Forest

This forest, which was roughly triangular in outline, lay between Bridgwater, Taunton and Langport, its southern boundary being only two to three miles from the northern limit of Neroche Forest while at one point (between North Curry and Curry Mallett) little more than half a mile separated them. Perambulations were made in 1279 and 1298 of which both Collinson[51] and Greswell[52] provide details. From these perambulations it may be deduced that the bounds of the forest were approximately as follows. Beginning at Huntworth, three miles south of Bridgwater, the bounds ran eastwards to the river Parrett and continued along the river to a point about a quarter of a mile south of Stathe where the Wedgmoor Old Rhyne joins the Parrett. Here the bounds probably turned south-westwards and continued along this ryhne to the minor road from the hamlet of Newport to Greenaway and Knapp and then joined the river Tone at Ham, following the river under the M5 motorway to Bathpool. At Bathpool the bounds probably turned northwards to Gotton and Quantock Farm bearing north-east to Thurloxton and North Petherton, to continue over the motorway a little to the south of junction 24 and so back to Huntworth.

Much of the Forest of North Petherton was low-lying marshy land interlaced with streams, runnels, drains and scattered pools with their attendant sluices, hatchways and fisheries. A mile or so from Huntworth in the northern part of the forest lay Petherton Park, the site of which is now commemorated by a farm of that name. Leland[53] has recorded the following impression of this area during one of his journeys.

> From . . . Athelney I rode by a low marsch ground a 2 miles to Pedertun Park. Here at Pederton the soil westward and south west rysith agayn and ys not fenny.
>
> There ys a great numbre of dere longging to this Park, yet hath it almost no other enclosure but dikes to let the catelle of the commune to cum yn. The dere trippe over these dikes and feed al about the fennes and resort to the Park agayn.

95   Selwood Forest

The Forest of Selwood which lay partly in Somerset and partly in Wiltshire, extended from Bradford-on-Avon in the north to the county boundary between Wiltshire and Dorset in the south. However this section only refers to the smaller part of the forest that was situated in Somerset the remainder being described later in this chapter under the county of Wiltshire. The Somerset portion formed a comparatively narrow strip of land lying parallel to the forest area which lay in the adjoining county and stretched from Frome in the north to Bruton and Penselwood in the south. In 1673 this area was referred to as 'the Forest of Frome Selwood'.

A perambulation of the forest in Somerset was made in 1298 but several of the places mentioned are difficult to identify at the present day. At the same time, those who made the perambulation added a list of 19 townships or parts of them, which, they claimed, should be disafforested in accordance with the Forest Charter.[54] Collinson[55] gives the Latin text of the perambulation and its findings while Greswell[56] provides an English translation.

From this list of townships and the perambulation it is probable that the forest lay within an area bounded by the following line. From Bruton to Henley Grove and then along the course of the Bruton—Frome road (A359) to Wanstrow, Cloford and Frome where the line turned due east to Rodden to join the county boundary between Somerset and Wiltshire. The eastern limit then joined the main part of the forest which lay in Wiltshire. The dividing line between these two parts began as the county boundary east of Rodden and continued to a point on the Frome—Maiden Bradley road (B3092). The boundary line then turned south until it reached the road from Kilmington to Maiden Bradley where it followed a south-easterly direction to approximately White Sheet Hill and then westward to Kingsettle Hill. Here it turned south for about a mile before bearing east again to Stourton and then south-west to White Cross and the county boundary between Somerset and Dorset. On reaching the Mere—Wincanton road (A303) the line continued to Hunter's Lodge Inn where it followed the road to Bruton (B3081).

Until 1962, when it was decided that they should be treated as an administrative part of Mendip Forest, the Forestry Commission's woodlands in this district were known as Selwood Forest.

STAFFORDSHIRE

96   Brewood Forest

The Forest of Brewood, or Breoda as it was sometimes known, lay partly in Staffordshire and partly in Shropshire, about three-quarters of its area being in the former county. The village of Brewood is to be found six miles north-north-west of Wolverhampton and three miles to the east of Boscobel where Charles II hid among the branches of an oak in 1651.

Although no perambulations of the forest have survived, the bounds have been deduced from the record of fines in respect of forest offences which are contained in the Pipe Roll of 1166-67[57] and it would appear that they were approximately as follows. Beginning near Stretton, six miles to the east of Cannock, the bounds ran beside the river Penk as far as Bilbrook where they swung south-west through Codsall and then south to Perton. Here they turned to the north-west crossing the county boundary at its intersection with the Shifnal—Wolverhampton road (A464) and so on to Albrighton and Donnington. The bounds then ran roughly parallel to the Newport—Wolverhampton road

(A41) as far as its junction with the Watling Street (A5) at which point Brewood Forest abutted on the eastern limit of the Forest of Mount Gilbert. At this point the line of the forest bounds bore north-east passing to the north of Blymhill and Wheaton Aston where they turned south-eastwards to Stretton at which place the bounds began.

97   Cannock Forest

Although Cannock was a royal forest it appears to have acquired the title of 'chase' by virtue of the fact that in 1290 Edward I granted about one quarter of it to the Bishop of Lichfield. Despite the fact that only the area so granted became a chase, this designation was applied to the whole forest. The name Cannock has several forms including Cannok, Canoc and Cank and Leland[58] noted that 'The wodde or forest in Staffordshire communely caullid Cank Wood yn old writinges, is caullid Cannok' and he went on to say that 'Cank Foreste is a great thing, merely longging to the Bishoprick of Lichefield'. His second remark would seem to imply that the whole of the forest belonged to the Bishop but as noted above, this was not the case.

A map showing the extent of the forest including the Bishop's chase, which has been based on the forest pleas of 1286 and a perambulation of 1300, is included in the Victoria County History.[59] From this the bounds of the forest are shown to be as follows although the southern boundary is only approximate. From the junction of the rivers Penk and Sow at Stafford, the northern limit of the forest continued along the Sow to its confluence with the Trent and then followed that river until it was joined by the Thame. Holding to the course of the river Thame as far as its junction with the Bourne Brook, a mile below Tamworth, the bounds then followed the Brook past Hints, Weeford and Shenstone to its source a mile to the east of Pool Green.

From here the forest bounds continued to Aldridge Lodge where they swung north westwards to the line of road A461 which they followed as far as its junction with road A41. The bounds then turned west along road A41 to the centre of Wolverhampton where they followed road A449 northwards for about three miles before turning due west through Ford Houses to join the river Penk at Bilbrook. The river was then followed northwards through Penkridge to its junction with the Sow where the bounds started.

The bounds of the Bishop of Lichfield's chase were, broadly speaking, as follows. From the point at which the Sherbrook joined the river Sow, half a mile south of Tixhall, the bounds of the chase ran eastwards along the course of the Sow and Trent to where the river Blithe entered the Trent. Here the bounds turned due south to a point about a mile to the west of Lichfield and then bore west to approximately Burntwood Green, where they turned south to Brownhills or thereabouts. From here the bounds passed to the north of Great Wyrley and then swung northwards to the west of Cannock and so back to the Sherbrook. The forest was divided into seven hays or bailiwicks which were named Alrewas, Bentley, Cheslyn, Gailey, Hopwas, Ogley and Teddesley. Today the Forestry Commission own over 6,600 acres of Cannock Chase.

98   Kinver Forest

The bounds of Kinver Forest, based on the perambulation of 1300, were approximately as follows. From Pasford in the north, the bounds ran south-eastwards past Pattingham, across the Bridgnorth — Wolverhampton road (A454) near Trescott and on to Orton and Wombourn. They then took a south-westerly course to join the Smestow Brook which the bounds followed to Wallheath, or thereabouts, where they continued eastwards along a stream as far as the Wolverhampton — Stourbridge road (A491).

The forest limits then followed the boundary between Staffordshire and Dudley passing to the west of Stourbridge and on to a point on the Staffordshire and Worcestershire border near Lower Hagley. Here they bore due west and then to the south of Kinver and followed the county boundary to the point where Staffordshire, Shropshire and Worcestershire meet. Continuing towards the north-west along the Staffordshire-Shropshire border for about a mile, the bounds turned north-eastwards past Gilberts Cross, on the Bridgnorth — Stourbridge road (A458), and so to Hoo Farm. Here the limits of the forest took a north-westerly course to Halfpenny Green (where they marched with Morfe Forest) and on to Upper Ludstone, Shipley and Rudge and so back to Pasford. Kinver Forest was divided into three hays, namely Ashwood, Chasepool and Ilverley but by the latter part of the sixteenth century only Ilverley remained as a Crown forest, the other two hayes having been granted to the Dudleys.[60]

The name of Kinver is now applied to one of the smallest of the Forestry Commission's forests in England which extends to a little over 700 acres.

99   Needwood Forest

Needwood Forest was situated in an area which lay between Uttoxeter to the north, Lichfield to the south, Burton on Trent to the east and Abbots Bromley to the west. Its bounds, which were extremely circuitous, can be appreciated most easily by studying a plan of the forest, based on a map of 1778, which is included in the Victoria County History.[61] In shape the forest was that of a distorted cross and very briefly the bounds ran from Marchington Woodlands in the north to Wood Gate near Draycott in the Clay and on to Hanbury Woodend, Belmont Gate, Anslow Gate, Rangemore and Dunstall Gate to a point to the north-west of Barton under Needwood. Continuing in a clockwise direction, the bounds ran on to Upper Blakenhall, Woodhouses, Hadley End, Hoar Cross, Folly Hall near Newborough, Holly Bush, Tomlinson's Corner and back to Marchington. The forest was divided into five wards or bailiwicks namely Barton, Marchington, Tutbury, Yoxhall and Uttoxeter, the last named being detached from the remainder and near the town of that name.

In the sixteenth century Needwood was well stocked with deer and during his travels through Staffordshire Leland[62] observed 'The Forest of Neede Woode by Tuttebyri . . . is mervelussy plenished with dere.' Unlike many of the medieval forests, Needwood originally carried a fair stock of timber and was noted for its fine oak. However by the beginning of the fifteenth century it was apparent that it was being overcut and steps were taken to exert some control. Despite this, by 1558 the number of trees in the forest had been further reduced although a survey made in 1587 confirmed that there was still a fair quantity of oak remaining. On the return of the monarchy in 1660 all felling and sales of timber were stopped and over the next 120 years efforts were made to build up the growing stock. When the forest was transferred to the Duchy of Lancaster in 1696, further fellings took place and although some 70 years later proposals were put forward for the establishment of nurseries, in which to raise oak, nothing came of them.[63] Needwood was disafforested in 1801.[64]

100   New Forest

Although the New Forest in Hampshire is one of the best known medieval forests, there were in fact two other New Forests in England, one in Yorkshire and the other in Staffordshire which is the subject of this note. Although no perambulations of the Staffordshire New Forest are now in existence, Greenslade[65] has provided a map of the forest which is based on the record of amercements or fines which are contained in the Pipe Roll of 1166-67. The following description of the probable bounds of the forest is largely in accordance with this map.

Beginning about a mile to the north of Tunstall, the bounds proceeded in a south-easterly direction across the Stoke on Trent — Leek road (A5009) at Woodhead or thereabouts. Continuing over the Stoke — Ashbourne road (A52) near Ash Hall the bounds swung south to Weston Coyney and Stallington, about a mile south-west of Blythemarsh on the Stoke — Uttoxeter road (A50). At Stallington the boundary of the forest bore south-east almost to Bramshall on the Stone — Uttoxeter road (B5027) where it turned westwards to within a mile or so of Milwich continuing south to Weston, on the Stone — Rugeley road (A51) and so to Ingestre and Tixhall — the southern limit of the forest. Bearing north-westwards the bounds then passed about a mile to the north-east of Stafford continuing to the west of Marston and Stone to follow the line of the M6 motorway for about one and a half miles as far as junction 15. From there the bounds crossed the Newcastle under Lyme — Audlem road (A525) about a mile from the centre of Newcastle, passing to the west of Stoke on Trent and so to the north of Tunstall where the bounds began.

Reference has already been made in Chapter 4 to the fact that 'lyme' is an old English name for a large forest[66] and Newcastle under Lyme doubtless takes its name from the New Forest in which it was situated.

SUSSEX

The county of Sussex was originally divided into six districts known as rapes each of which extended across the county in roughly parallel lines from north to south. They were named, in succession from west to east: Chichester, Arundel, Bramber, Lewes, Pevensey and Hastings and each contained one, or in some cases two, forests. These were as follows: Chichester: Stanstead Forest and part of Arundel Forest; Arundel: Arundel Forest; Bramber: St. Leonard's Forest; Lewes: Worth Forest; Pevensey: Ashdown and Waterdown Forests; and Hastings: Dallington Forest.

During the Middle Ages and for some time afterwards, Sussex provided large quantities of wood for fuel which was used in the process of iron smelting. This industry thrived by virtue of the presence of easily obtainable iron ore lying below the surface and extensive supplies of fuel growing on the surface. Two important centres for this industry were Ashburnham, five miles north-west of Bexhill, and St Leonard's Forest which lies between Crawley and Horsham.

101   Arundel Forest

The Forest of Arundel lay between Chichester, Arundel and Midhurst and the course of the bounds was approximately as follows. From Fishbourne, a mile to the west of Chichester, on the Havant road (A27), the bounds proceeded eastwards on the line of this road as far as Avisford, some two and a half miles west of Arundel. Here they turned south to Cudlowe which now lies beneath the sea but was probably near Middleton which is between Bognor Regis and Littlehampton. From this point the bounds continued along the coast to the mouth of the river Arun and in all probability followed the course of this river as far as the village of Bury, which lies about a quarter of a mile to the east of the Arundel—Pulborough road (A29). While Tierney[67] suggested that the bounds of the forest crossed the high ground behind Arundel, at the same time he expressed doubts that this was correct and it would seem to be far more likely that the river formed the boundary. From Bury the bounds continued to Houghton and then bore to the west on to the top of the Downs and Up Waltham passing to the south of Cocking and on to North Marden. Here they turned south to Up Marden and Stoughton where they marched with Stanstead Forest and so back to Fishbourne at the northern end of Chichester Harbour. The name of Arundel Forest is still applied to one of the Forestry Commission forests which have been established in the area.

102   Ashdown Forest

Ashdown Forest lay between East Grinstead, Tunbridge Wells and Lewes. It is said to have covered some 18,000 acres and its bounds included the parishes of East Grinstead, Hartfield, Withyam, Buxted, Maresfield and Fletching. Part of this area is still known as Ashdown Forest, much of which is open, unenclosed land and is administered under the Commons Regulations (Ashdown Forest) Provisional Order Confirmation Act 1885. In earlier times this forest extended southwards towards Pevensey when it was sometimes known as Pevensey Forest.[68] To the east and adjoining Ashdown lay the Forest of Waterdown.

103   Dallington Forest

This forest which was sometimes known as Brightling or Burwash Forest lay about nine miles north-west of Bexhill and eight miles north-east of Hailsham. The bounds of the forest are not known in detail but they included the parishes of Dallington, Burwash, Brightling and Mountfield and may have extended as far south as Penshurst and Ashburnham.[69] The forest was situated in close proximity to one of the chief centres for iron smelting during the middle ages.

104   St Leonard's Forest

Lying between Crawley and Horsham this forest is thought to have taken its name from a small chapel which was dedicated to St Leonard and stood within the bounds of the forest. Today the hamlet known as St Leonards lies about three quarters of a mile east of the outskirts of Horsham. Although the exact metes and bounds of the forest are not recorded, it included the extensive parish of Beeding and lay within the following limits.

Beginning to the south of Ifield which is now a part of Crawley, the eastern bounds ran southwards besides the Crawley to Brighton road (A23). A little to the south of Peas Pottage the bounds probably bore to the south-west crossing the Handcross—Lower Beeding road (A279) about a mile to the east of Beeding, and then continued roughly parallel with the boundary between east and West Sussex. On reaching the road from Cuckfield to Billinghurst (A272) or thereabouts, the bounds turned westwards to West Grinstead and Knepp Castle. Here they swung to the north, approximately along the line of the road to Horsham (A24). Passing to the east of Horsham the bounds probably bore to the north-east continuing to the north of Faygate and Bewbush to where they started.

The forest was divided into ten bailiwicks or walks, six of which covered the northern part of the forest and were named Throstlehill, Thorningbroke, Beaubush (now Holmbush), Shelley, Fortesland, Whiteberewe and Hyde.[70] St Leonards is commemorated by the name of one of the Commission's forests which is situated in the area.

105   Stanstead Forest

Stanstead was the most westerly forest in Sussex and lay between the county boundary with Hampshire and the western limits of Arundel Forest. The bounds are likely to have taken the following course but this should only be regarded as an approximation.

From a point on the county boundary probably near Old Ditcham, the bounds proceeded eastwards to South Harting and then turned south to Up Marden and Stoughton. At Stoughton they took a south-westerly course and in all probability followed the course of the river Ems through Racton to its junction with the Hampshire boundary a little to the north of Westbourne. Here the bounds turned northwards and followed the county boundary back to Old Ditcham or thereabouts.

106   Waterdown Forest

Waterdown which lay to the east of Ashdown Forest, covered a large area and at one time was considered to be one of the three most important forests in Sussex. The southern portion included the whole of the parish of Rotherfield and from there it stretched northwards through what is now Eridge Park, to the county boundary with Kent.[71] To the north-east it included the district between Frant and the Kentish border and although Speed[72] delineated the forest on his map of 1610 as lying between Rotherfield, Frant and Groombridge, the area near Frant was the only part which was still shown as 'Water Down Forest' by Cary[73] in his atlas of 1809.

107   Worth Forest

Worth Forest lay between Crawley, East Grinstead and Haywards Heath and adjoined St Leonard's Forest on the west and was in close proximity to Ashdown Forest on the east. Within the limits of Worth Forest were certain areas which were referred to as forests under their individual names although they formed integral parts of Worth. These were Tilgate Forest, Balcombe Forest and Brantridge Forest and although, in 1610, Speed shows this area as Worth Forest on his map of Sussex,[74] on Cary's atlas of 1809 it is named Tilgate Forest.[75]

There are no records of the bounds of Worth Forest but it is probable that it began near the county boundary with Surrey and extended southwards as far as Cuckfield. The western boundary was coincident with that of St Leonard's Forest and the eastern limit could have been the line of the Haywards Heath — Turner's Hill — Lingfield road (B2028) with the southern boundary formed by the road which passes through Haywards Heath and Cuckfield (A272) although Legge[76] considers that Worth Forest may have extended as far as Ditchling.

WARWICKSHIRE

108   Forest of Arden

The Forest of Arden was situated in that part of Warwickshire which lay to the north of the river Avon which flows diagonally across the county from Rugby in the north-east to Salford Priors in the south-west. Leland[77] who travelled through England in the sixteenth century stated:

> Marke that the moaste part of Warwykshire that standithe on the lefte hond or banke of Avon as the ryver dessendethe, is called Arden and this countrye is not so plentifull of corne, but of grasse and woode. Such part of Warwikshire as lyethe by sowth on the left hond or banke of the Avon is baren of woode but plentifull of corne.

It should be noted that in the above passage Leland apparently made a mistake, since he first says that the part of Warwickshire which 'standithe on the left hond or banke of Avon as the river dessendethe is called Arden and this countrye is not so plentifull of corne but of grasse and woode'. He then goes on to say that 'such part of Warwikshire as lyethe by sowth on the left hond or banke of the Avon is barren of woods but plentifull of corne'. By mentioning the south (sowth) in his second sentence, he undoubtedly meant the left hand bank while in his first sentence the word 'left' should in fact be 'right'.

   Camden enlarged on Leland's remarks and said:

> The County of Warwick . . . is divided into two parts, feldon and woodland or the field and the woody country, parted from each other by the river Avon running obliquely through the middle of the county from south-east to north-west.[78]

Later he observed:

> Let us now take a view of the woodland which lies north beyond the Avon occupying a larger extent, being the most part covered with woods though not without pastures, cornfields and iron mines. As it is at present called the woodland, so it had antiently the much older name of Arden, but as I take it, to the same purport, for Arden seems to have signified a forest among the antient Britans and Gauls . . . .

There are five places in the names of which the designation 'Arden' is included and these are Arden's Grafton adjacent to Temple Grafton, Hampton in Arden three miles to the east of Solihull, Henley in Arden eight miles west of Warwick, Tanworth in Arden three miles north-west of Henley and Weston in Arden between Coventry and Nuneaton. All these places lie to the north of the Avon and so support Camden's views as to the location of the Forest of Arden.

If the river Avon formed the southern limit of the forest it is probable that the county boundary with Worcestershire and Staffordshire marked the western bounds and that with Leicestershire marked the eastern limit. How far north the forest stretched, it is difficult to say, but it is probable that it reached as far as Atherstone if not the northern boundary of the county. In 1952 the Forestry Commission created a new forest within the limits of the ancient one which they named Arden. Although part of the Forest of Feckenham lay in Warwickshire, this forest is considered under Worcestershire.

WILTSHIRE

In medieval times a larger proportion of land was afforested in Wiltshire than in almost any other county while in Dorset and Hampshire there were several forests which either adjoined those in Wiltshire or were in close proximity to them. The effect of this was to create a very large block of land which was subject to forest law. Although Braydon Forest which lay in the north of the county, was detached from the main forest complex, the distance from its southern boundary to the northern limit of Savernake was only 10 miles. From Savernake an unbroken chain of forests stretched, as the crow flies, some 47 miles to the Solent and comprised the forests of Savernake, Chute, Clarendon, Melchet and the New Forest.

Westward lay Cranbourne Chase which adjoined Clarendon Forest and extended to within two miles of the Dorset forest of Blakemore. On the north side of the Chase and adjacent to it was Groveley Forest which was only four miles to the west of Clarendon while seven miles from the western boundary of Groveley, Selwood Forest began. On the north of Selwood and marching with it, were the forests of Chippenham and Melksham. To the east of Clarendon and bounding on it was the Hampshire forest of Buckholt with West Forest beyond, while to the north and close to the Hampshire portion of Chute was Harewood Forest. An area as large as this was able to provide unlimited opportunities for hunting and other kingly recreations and this may well have influenced the choice of the site for Clarendon Palace which Henry II built as a royal residence.

Information as to the bounds and perambulations of the Wiltshire forests can be obtained from several sources including the Victoria County History. This contains a number of excellent maps and descriptions which set out the bounds of the various forests in detail and to which reference should be made for further information on their limits.

109   Braydon Forest

The Forest of Braydon, Braden or Bradene lay between the towns of Cricklade, Swindon, Wootton Bassett and Malmesbury. Beginning a mile to the east of

Cricklade, where the river Ray joins the Thames, the bounds followed the course of the Ray southwards to Lydiard Tregoze and continued as far as the motorway (M4) about a mile to the west of junction 16. The bounds then turned westwards for about a mile before bearing south past Wootton Bassett, to join the Brinkworth Brook, the course of which the bounds followed before turning north to reach the Malmesbury—Wootton Bassett road (B4042) on the outskirts of Brinkworth. After crossing this road the bounds joined the Woodbridge Brook and continued along this brook until it passed under the secondary road from Lea to Charlton. They then passed a little to the west of Charlton and Hankerton to follow the Swill Brook until it joined the Thames at Ashton Keynes and so along the course of the Thames to beyond Cricklade where the bounds began.[79]

Akerman[80] supplies copies of several perambulations including one which was made in the time of Edward III. He also provides a description of the bounds which were cited in a court order resulting from a suit brought by Charles I. In 1946 the Forestry Commission established a new forest in this area and named it Braydon Forest but in 1972 it was incorporated with Savernake Forest.

110   Chippenham Forest

During the thirteenth century, the Forests of Chippenham and Melksham were regarded as one and the bounds extended from the junction of the rivers Avon and Marden, a mile to the north of Chippenham, along the course of the Marden to Calne. Here the bounds turned south to Heddington Wick, Nether Street and Rowde where they followed the Summerham Brook to its junction with the Semington Brook. The bounds then continued along this brook until it joined the river Avon which they followed northwards through Laycock and Chippenham to its junction with the river Marden where the bounds began.

After the beginning of the fourteenth century when Chippenham had become a separate forest, the bounds still started at the junction of the Avon and the Marden. However they left the course of the Marden near Stanley and continued on a line which ran approximately through Studley, Bowood and Whetham to Sandy Lane. Here they turned westward to join the Avon about half a mile to the north of Laycock and so followed the Avon back to the starting point.[81] The Forest of Chippenham was divided into the two bailiwicks of Bowood and Bers and was ultimately disafforested in 1624. The bounds of Melksham Forest are described later in this chapter in section 115.

111   Chute Forest

The greater part of Chute Forest lay in Wiltshire with only a small section extending into the adjoining county of Hampshire and for this reason it has always been regarded as a Wiltshire forest. The Hampshire portion has already been described in section 37 of Chapter 4. The name Chute, which occurs in the forms Cheut, Chure, Char, Chutte and Cetum, is also that of a village which lies three miles east of Collingbourne Ducis, on the Marlborough — Tidworth road (A338) and five miles west of Hurstbourne Tarrant on the Newbury — Andover road (A343).

The northern boundary of the Wiltshire portion of the forest began on the river Avon about a mile to the north of Upavon, and followed the approximate line of what is now a minor road which links the Upavon — Ludgershall road (A342). From the junction with the latter road, the bounds turned north-eastwards to meet the limits of Savernake Forest near Aughton Down and continued eastwards along the southern bounds of Savernake to meet the county boundary with Hampshire about a mile to the south of Vernham's Dean. At this point the bounds turned south to follow the county boundary for more than 20 miles to a point near Middle Winterslow where the Roman road from Winchester to Old Sarum crosses the boundary. From here the bounds turned due west and followed the line of the Roman road to Old Sarum and for most of this distance they adjoined the northern limit of Clarendon Forest. At Old Sarum the bounds joined the Avon and followed this river to the point where they began, a little to the north of Upavon. Disafforestation of the Wiltshire portion of the forest took place in 1639.[82]

112   Clarendon Forest

Immediately to the south of Chute Forest and adjacent to it, lay Clarendon Forest which in turn adjoined Melchet Forest, along its southern boundary. The bounds of Clarendon Forest began at a ford through the river Bourne, a mile and a half to the south of Winterbourne Earls and continued eastwards along the Roman road through Middle Winterslow to the county boundary with Hampshire. They then followed the county boundary as far as the minor road which runs from east to west across Dean Hill and turned eastwards along this road until it joined the Salisbury — Totton road (A36) at the Pepper-box. The bounds continued beside this road for about a quarter of a mile before bearing northwards to West Grinstead where they turned due west to join the river Avon at Bodenham. After proceeding along the Avon to its junction with the river Bourne they continued along the Bourne to the ford where the bounds began.[83]

Within the bounds of Clarendon Forest and lying to the east of Clarendon Park was an area which was sometimes referred to as Panshet or Pannsett Forest. During the Commonwealth a detailed survey was made of Clarendon in 1650 and this records that the forest comprised five divisions or bailiwicks which were known by the names of Fussell's, Hunt's, Palmer's, the Ranger's and Theobald's. Forest pleas were held in Salisbury.[84]

113 Groveley Forest

Groveley Forest which was originally known as Gravelignes and later as Gravelee or Graveley, was one of the few forests that were mentioned by name in Domesday Book. Perambulations were made at various times and that of 1299, which was considered to be one of the most important, is set out by Hoare.[85] In the County History,[86] Grant provides a map of the forest which shows the bounds as they were in 1219 and also in 1300. In 1219 the forest bounds began at Wylye and followed the course of the river of that name as far as its junction with the river Nadder at Wilton. At this point the bounds turned westwards and followed the Nadder as far as the railway bridge over the river, about half a mile south of Teffont Evias. Here they left the river and continued northwards to Teffont Evias and Teffont Magna where they crossed the road from Barford St Martin to Fonthill Bishop (B3089) and followed a minor road for one and a half miles across Teffont Down. The bounds then turned due east and continued for a further mile and a half along another minor road until it joined the Dinton to Wylye road near Middle Hills, which they followed back to Wylye.

Groveley forest was originally divided into two bailiwicks, the North and the South, but by 1300 the forest had been reduced to half its size. The Lords of the Manor, the freeholders and the tenants of Great Wishford and Barford St Martin claimed various rights within the forest and in 1603 these were set out in: 'a true resitall of the old, antient and laudable customes belonging, and in right apperteyning to the Mannors of Great Wishford and Barford St. Martyn in the Countye of Wiltes'.[87] The customs included rights of pannage, grazing access and taking wood.

114 Melchet Forest

Between Clarendon Forest and the New Forest and contiguous to both, lay Melchet Forest. The bounds began at the Pepperbox on the Salisbury — Totton road (A36) and followed the line of a minor road eastwards across Dean Hill to the county boundary with Hampshire. Here they turned south and followed the boundary as far as Melchet Park where they crossed into Hampshire and continued south-eastwards along a tributary of the river Blackwater. After passing to the south of Sherfield English the bounds continued to Dandy's Ford and then turned northwards to Dunwood before bearing south-east again through Squab Wood. They then crossed the Romsey — Ringwood road (A31) and after passing through Burnt Grove and Sounding Arch continued along the western side of Embley Wood.

From here the bounds turned south-west and continued over the Salisbury — Totton road, across Forley Common to the Cadnam — Fordingbridge road (B3078) near Wittensford. After passing over this road they swung westwards and rejoined it at Brook and continued along this road to a point about a mile beyond Bramshaw Telegraph Post. The bounds then turned north to Langley Wood where they bore west along the road from Landford to Redlynch for a distance of about two and a half miles, and continued northwards past Upper Pensworth Farm and Barford Down to the Pepper Box.[88]

115 Melksham Forest

Melksham has already been referred to under Chippenham Forest since, until the beginning of the fourteenth century, these two forests were considered to be one. In the course of its history various names have been applied to Melksham Forest and in the time of Henry III it was known as the Forest of Melksham and Chippenham. After Melksham was separated from Chippenham it was sometimes referred to as the Forest of Melksham and Pewsham, variations of Pewsham being Peevisham and Pemshaur. In Tudor times the name of Blackmore Forest was not infrequently used while the area north of Spye Park was occasionally known as Bladon Forest and both these names still appear on some small-scale maps at the present time. These should not be confused with Blackmore or Blakemore Forest in Dorset or Braydon Forest which is also in Wiltshire.

When Melksham and Chippenham were divided the bounds of Melksham were established as follows. The northern boundary began at the river Avon about half a mile to the south of Laycock where the Roman road from Bath to London crossed the river. From here the bounds proceeded eastwards and shortly before reaching Spye Park they turned south and, following a devious route, crossed the Melksham—Calne road (A3012) about half a mile to the east of Sandridge Park before reaching Rowde. From Rowde the bounds continued their course along the Summerham and Semington Brooks until the latter joined the river Avon. They then turned northwards along the Avon and continued to the point where the bounds began.[89]

116   Savernake Forest

At the beginning of the thirteenth century Savernake Forest covered an area of land which, broadly speaking, lay between East Kennett, Marlborough, Hungerford, Vernham Dean, Easton Royal and Pewsey. The name Savernake also occurs as Safernoc and Savernac while in the twelfth century it was sometimes known as the Forest of Marlborough.

Beginning at East Kennett the line taken by the bounds was approximately as follows. After holding to the course of the river Kennett as far as Marlborough, the bounds followed the Hungerford road (A4) for about two miles. In 1199[90] they turned north at this point to rejoin the Kennett beside which the bounds proceeded to Hungerford. However by 1228, instead of diverging to the river Kennett they continued along the line of the road to

Hungerford (A4). From here the bounds followed the river for about two miles where they turned due south to Inkpen, Buttermere and Vernham Dean although in the perambulation of 1228, they followed the line of the county boundary from Inkpen.[91] At Vernham Dean the bounds turned westwards and ran, coincident with those of Chute Forest, to a point about a mile to the north of Aughton Down. From this point they continued to Easton Royal where they followed the Burbage road (B3087) to Pewsey and continued past Wilcot to Knap Hill where they swung north along the Ridgeway to rejoin East Kennett.

In 1200 Savernake Forest was divided into five bailiwicks, namely, Le Broyle, La Verme, Southgrove, Hippenscombe and West Bailey but by 1464 two subdivisions of West Bailey had been created, one to the south of Marlborough known as Panterwick and the other to the west of Burbage, named Iwode.[92] Forest eyres were usually held at Marlborough. Although Savernake Forest is now largely in private ownership, much of the woodland area is managed by the Forestry Commission.

117   Selwood Forest

The Forest of Selwood lay on either side of the county boundary between Somerset and Wiltshire and the smaller portion which was situated in Somerset has already been described in section 95 of this chapter. Beginning in the north-west where the river Frome flows into the Avon, the bounds ran eastwards along the course of the Avon, to its junction with the Semington Brook. From here to the point where this brook is joined by the Summerham Brook, Selwood marched with Melksham Forest. From the Summerham Brook the bounds continued across the Devizes — Trowbridge road (A361) to Bulkington, Great Cheverell and Stoke Hill and then continued across Salisbury Plain by way of the now derelict village of Imber to the junction of the Warminster — Salisbury road (A36) and the Heytesbury — Amesbury road (A344).

From this road junction, the bounds followed the course of the river Wylye for about a mile past Knook and Upton Lovell before bearing westwards to Corton and then south-west over Tytherington Hill and Pertwood, where the bounds joined the Warminster — Shaftesbury road (A350). They then followed this road through East Knoyle to the county boundary with Dorset a mile and a half south-west of Semley. Here the bounds turned north-west and proceeded along the Dorset-Wiltshire boundary to Zeals on the Mere — Wincanton road (A303). From Zeals they continued along the boundary between the Somerset and the Wiltshire portions of the forest which are described in section 95 of this chapter. The bounds ultimately rejoined the boundary line between Somerset and Wiltshire where the Frome — Maiden Bradley road (B3092) passes from one county to the other. From this point the bounds followed the division between the two counties until it joined the river Frome at Rode and the bounds then continued along the river to its junction with the Avon, where they began.[93]

The two parts of Selwood, the one in Somerset and the other in Wiltshire were administered separately for most of their history and disafforestation took place in 1627.

WORCESTERSHIRE

118 Feckenham Forest

Feckenham Forest, which in the twelfth and thirteenth centuries was sometimes known as the Forest of Worcester, lay mainly between that city and Redditch although its eastern limits extended into Warwickshire as far as the river Arrow.

To the north-west was Pepperwood also known as Pyperode or Pepperod which formed an extension of Feckenham and occupied an area which included Bromsgrove and Chaddesley Corbett and reached as far as Rushock.[94] Although it may have been regarded as a separate forest at some time in its early history, it was usually referred to as the Forest of Feckenham with Pepperwood. On the west lay the Forest of Ombersley while to the south-west stretched the Forest of Horwell and although in course of time these two forests lost their identity and became a part of Feckenham Forest they were for many years considered as individual forests and have been treated as such in this chapter.

The bounds of Feckenham Forest began at Ipsley which is now a part of Redditch and followed the course of the river Arrow southwards to its junction with the Avon,[95] and then continued along the Avon to Fladbury which marked the eastern limit of Horwell Forest. At Fladbury the bounds turned northwards and from this point their course can only be regarded as approximate. They probably ran parallel to, or coincident with, the bounds of Horwell Forest passing to the north-east of Throckmorton and White Ladies Aston and, after reaching the Worcester—Alcester road (A422) turned westwards to Worcester. From Worcester the bounds continued in a north-easterly direction probably to Salwarp and then followed the course of the river Salwarp to Stoke Prior and so to Tardebigge and Bordesley where they swung south to Ipsley where the bounds began. That portion of the forest which was in Warwickshire lay between the county boundary with Worcestershire and the river Avon.

In the Middle Ages Droitwich, which stood between the Forests of Feckenham and Ombersley, was one of the most important centres for the production of salt. In the process of manufacture it was necessary to subject the raw material to heat and to do this a large number of furnaces were needed which by the end of the fifteenth century numbered no less than 360 in the vicinity of Droitwich. These furnaces used considerable quantities of wood and it is said that during this period the surrounding countryside was denuded of trees and to satisfy the demands of the furnaces, wood was brought in from various parts of Feckenham Forest including Bromsgrove and Alcester. It was considered that the annual consumption of wood for this purpose amounted to some 6,000 loads which at 50 cubic feet to the load amounted to 300,000 cubic feet and that the most suitable material was 'young pole wood, easy to be cloven'.[96] Feckenham was disafforested in 1629.

119   Horwell Forest

This forest lay between Feckenham Forest and the river Severn and extended from Worcester in the north to within four miles of Tewkesbury in the south. Nash[97] gives an account of the bounds of the forest but some of the places mentioned by him cannot be readily identified at the present time and the following is a summary of the probable limits.

Beginning at Worcester the bounds followed the road to Spetchley (A422) crossing the motorway (M5) between junctions 6 and 7 and then proceeded to White Ladies Aston or thereabouts and after crossing the Piddle Brook they continued (probably to the north of Peopleton) to Throckmorton. From here the bounds passed by the village of Hill and after crossing the road from Worcester to Evesham (B4084), they reached the river Avon. Although Nash omits it, Fladbury which lies a mile to the east, was originally part of Horwell Forest.[98] The bounds then followed the Avon to a point probably between Upper and Lower Strensham where they turned due west crossing the motorway (M5) close to the service area immediately to the north of junction 8 and continued until they reached the river Severn. They then followed the course of the Severn back to Worcester where the bounds began. Horwell was disafforested in 1229 consequent upon the charter of 1217.

120   Malvern Forest

Writing in the middle of the sixteenth century Leland[99] observed that 'The Chase of Malverne is bigger than other Wire or Feckenham and occupiethe a greate part of Malverne Hills. Great Malverne and Litle also is set in the Chase of Malverne. Malverne Chase . . . is in lengthe in some place a xx miles, but Malverne Chase dothe not occupi all Malverne Hills.' Malvern was originally a forest but when Gilbert, earl of Clare, Hertford and Gloucester married the daughter of Edward I in 1290, he was given the Forest of Malvern together with the much smaller Forest of Corse which adjoined it.[100] This latter forest which was situated in Gloucestershire will be found under that county under section 29. As a result of this gift Malvern ceased to be a royal forest and became a chase and although some two hundred years later it returned to the possession of Henry VII, it was never formally reafforested.

The bounds of the forest began near Lulsley where the river Teme crosses the county boundary into Worcestershire and continued eastwards following the Teme until it joined the Severn. The bounds then followed the course of the Severn as far as Tewkesbury where they continued along the county boundary first with Gloucestershire and then with Herefordshire until they reached the point near Lulsley where the bounds began. To the east lay the Forest of Horwell which was separated from Malvern Forest by the Severn.

In 1664 an Act was passed which provided for the enclosing and disafforesting of the 'Forest and Chase of Malvern'.[101] Three places which lay within the bounds still carry names which are connected with the medieval forest and chase: Assarts Common, half a mile to the south-east of Little Malvern and Chase End Hall and Chase End Street which lie close to the county boundary about half a mile to the south of the Tewkesbury — Ledbury road (A438).

121   Ombersley Forest

Ombersley Forest, which was also known as Ambreslie, was situated between Stourport, Chaddesley Corbett, Droitwich and Worcester. To the north and east lay Feckenham Forest with Pepperwood while the rivers Severn and Stour formed the western boundary.

Nash[102] gives a perambulation of the forest but it is difficult to construe this in names of the present day and the probable bounds of the forest may be summarized as follows. Beginning at the North Gate of Worcester the bounds followed the river Severn northwards to its junction with the river Stour at Stourport and continued along the course of the Stour for about two miles. The bounds then turned eastwards to Torton, Bradford and Rushock and probably reached a point near Upton Warren on the Bromsgrove — Droitwich road (A38) continuing southwards, possibly along the line of this road to Worcester again. Ombersley Forest was disafforested in 1229.

122   Wyre Forest

The Forest of Wyre which was also known as Bewdley Forest was originally of considerable size and according to Eyton[103] is said to have extended from the north of Bewdley, southwards as far as Worcester. Subsequently that part of the forest that was situated in Worcestershire was substantially reduced in area so that the greater part of the forest lay in Shropshire. However, in view of the fact that Wyre gave its name to Worcester, since this was derived from Wyre-ceastre or Wyre-castra, and as its alternative name of Bewdley Forest is taken from a Worcestershire town, this forest has been included under the county of Worcester.

Leland[104] who made his itinerary in the middle of the sixteenth century recorded the following comments on this forest:

> *Wire Forest where of summe part is sett in Wicestershire but the
> moste parte in Shropshire and stretchithe up Frontholt upon Severne
> onto Bruge Northe. Bewdley is set in the Marchis of this Forest and
> stretchithe a 2 miles beyond . . . Wire is more than xx mills compas.*

Eyton[105] considers that in Saxon times, that part of Wyre that lay in Shropshire
was attached to, and probably reached, the manors of Cleobury and Kinlet. In
medieval times it is probable that Wyre Forest lay within an area, the
minimum limits of which were as follows (but it should be stressed that these
are not the bounds of the forest but simply the perimeter of the area in which
the forest probably lay). From Cleobury Mortimer, the limits followed the line
of the road to Bridgnorth (B4363) as far as the junction with the road to
Highley (B4555), a mile to the north of Kinlet. The limits then followed this
road to its crossing of the Borle Brook which it followed to the Severn. The
course of the Severn was followed as far as Bewdley where the limits probably
traced the line of the Tenbury Wells road (A450) as far as Callow Hill and then
continued past Buckridge, along the county boundary as far as the river Rea
and so back to Cleobury Mortimer.

The Forestry Commission began to acquire parts of Wyre Forest in 1925
and they now own about 2,600 acres of it.

YORKSHIRE

123   Bowland Forest

This forest which adjoined the western boundary of the county lay between
Clitheroe and Lancaster and bordered on the Lancashire forests of Wyersdale,
Bleasdale and Little Bowland. It is shown on a map prepared by Farrer[106] and
the following description of the approximate bounds are based on that map.

Beginning in the north where the river Hodder rises close to the county
boundary, the bounds followed the course of the Hodder into Stocks Reservoir
and continued along the eastern perimeter to the point at which the river flows
out again. The bounds, however, turned northwards along the water's edge for
about half a mile where they swung to the north-west to Brunton Lathe. Here
they bore to the south-west and continued for some five miles until they
reached the road from Slaidburn to Dunsop Bridge at a point about half a mile
to the east of Woodend. The bounds then swung back in a long curve through
Birkett Fell and Crimpton to the top of Marl Hill Moor where they turned south
and then west, to Hare Clough and Brownsholme Hall, where they followed a
beck to the river Hodder. At this point the bounds turned westwards and
continued along the county boundary back to the point where they began. In

1953 the Forestry Commission formed a new forest in this area which has retained the name of Bowland Forest.

124   Galtres Forest

Known also by the names of Gautries and Galteriz, this forest stretched from the city of York, northwards to a little beyond Easingwold. A perambulation of the forest which was made in 1316 is reproduced by Gill[107] and the following description of the bounds is based on this.

The bounds began 'at the foot of the wall of the city of York at the bridge of Layrthorpe, following the wall as it goes up to the Boutham gates of the same city and so following the wall to the water of Ouse'. They then continued northwards along the course of the river as far as Newton on Ouse where the river Kyle joins it. From there the bounds followed the Kyle past Tollerton and Alne to a point about one mile due north of Easingwold where they turned south-eastwards passing to the north of Crayke to join the river Foss. The bounds then followed the course of the Foss past Stillington and Strensall back to Layerthorpe Bridge where they had begun. The forest was divided into the three bailiwicks of Kyle, Easingwold and Myerscough.

Leland[108] visited 'the Forest of Galtres whereof 4 miles or more was low medowes and morisch ground full of carres, the residew by better ground but not very high . . . I saw very little wood yn this quarter of the Forest'.

During the Civil War Galtres suffered considerably and it was here that in 1644 Prince Rupert assembled his troops before the Battle of Marston Moor, the site of which is some four miles south-west of Newton on Ouse. Galtres was disafforested during the reign of Charles II but several names are still to be found within the limits of the old forest which indicate a close connection with it. These include Forest Hall near Alne, Laund House, Forest Hill and the Hunting Lodge of James I.

125   Hatfield Chase

The town of Thorne which stands almost in the centre of Hatfield Chase, lies about 10 miles north-east of Doncaster and 13 miles west of Scunthorpe. Although Hatfield came into the possession of the Crown in the fourteenth century and thus became a forest, the designation of 'chase' nevertheless continued to be used.[109]

The bounds began at God's Cross (shown by Carey[110] as Goad's Cross) which is an old stone standing on the county boundary with Lincolnshire and about one and a half miles west of the village of Wroot. From here they ran north-west almost in a straight line to the village of Kirk Bramwith on the river Don whose course the bounds followed as far as Stainforth. At this village they left the Don and after following the boundary between the Strafford and Osgodcross wapentakes which is marked by a small stream, they reached the river Went. There the bounds turned east along the Went until it joined the Don and they then continued more or less in a straight line to Holdenby Grange on the old river Don which at this point also marked the county boundary between York and Lincoln. The eastern limits of the Chase then followed the course of the old Don which for much of the way coincided with the county boundary, as far as Durkness Crooke.[111] This would appear to correspond with Dirtness Bridge which adjoins the Hatfield — Scunthorpe road (A18) a mile to the north of Sandtoft Grange. From here the forest bounds continued along the Idle river past the village of Wroot and so back to God's Cross.

Within the bounds of the Chase was an area of about 70,000 acres known as the Level of Hatfield which lay to the east of Hatfield village. This was an undrained area of marsh, bog and water and modern maps show the site in two parts, the High Levels and the Low Levels. It was estimated that there were about a thousand red deer in the Chase in 1607 but the numbers rapidly diminished when drainage of the area began in 1626. In the same year the Chase was disafforested.[112]

126   Knaresborough Forest

The Forest of Knaresborough extended from the western bank of the river Nidd at Knaresborough westwards to Bolton Abbey or thereabouts. Originally it consisted of three bailiwicks or constableries comprising Thruscross, Clint and Killinghall. The hamlet of Thruscross lies two miles north-west of Blubberhouses which is situated on the Harrogate — Bolton Bridge road (A59); Clint stands to the north of the river Nidd about a mile and a half east of Ripley on the Knaresborough — Pateley Bridge road (B6165) while Killinghall lies a mile to the south of Ripley on the Harrogate road.

Subsequently these three bailiwicks were increased to eleven, largely by subdivision, and comprised Felliscliffe, Birstwith, Hampsthwaite, Thruscross, Menwith-with-Darley, Killinghall, Bilton-with-Harrogate, Beckwith-with-Rossett, Timble, Clent and Clifton.[113] The most westerly points in the forest mentioned as being parts of these bailiwicks are Bramley, Timble and Clifton although the forest extended as far as Bolton Bridge with the river Wharf forming the western and southern boundary. This is recorded by Leland[114] who made his itinerary during the years 1534 to 1543 and observed that: 'The Forest from a mile beneth Gnarresburgh up to very Bolton yn Craven is a 20 miles yn lenght and in bredth it is in sum places an viij miles. The principal wood of the Forest is decayed.'

Consequently the forest lay within an area the limits of which are set out below but it should be emphasized that these are not the actual bounds but only define the area in which the forest was situated. From Summer Bridge, three miles to the south-east of Pateley Bridge, the line followed the road to Knaresborough (B6165) and then turned south along road B6163 to Follifoot and Spacey Houses, on the Harrogate — Yealdon road (A658). From there the line continued along this road until it reached the river Wharfe and then followed the course of this river north-westwards to Howgill about five miles to the north of Bolton Bridge. From Howgill the line turned eastwards through Simon Seat back to Summer Bridge. A new Forest of Knaresborough was created by the Forestry Commission in 1951.

127   New Forest

Between the road from Brough under Stainmore to Rokeby and Scotch Corner (A66) and the river Swale which flows through Swaledale, there are several areas which are recorded as forests. These comprise Stainmore Forest, adjoining road A66 near Bowes; Arkengarthdale Forest, five miles to the south of Barnard Castle; the New Forest, three miles north-east of Reeth and six miles north-west of Richmond and Applegarth Forest, two miles west of Richmond and adjoining the river Swale.

Spelman[115] includes the New Forest and Applegarth in his list of forests although Whitaker[116] states that Stainmore, Applegarth and Arkengarthdale belonged to the earls of Richmond to whom they were presumably granted. Subsequently the New Forest came into being and Whitaker observes that these forests 'were afterwards reduced to the New Forest, of later date (as its name imports) than the rest and lying wholly in the parish of Kirkby Ravensworth'. In 1932, the Forestry Commission established a new forest in this area which was named Arkengarthdale Forest, but in 1960 it was renamed Stang Forest.

128   Pickering Forest

Pickering Forest, which was also known as the Forest of Pickering Lythe, lay between the towns of Stokesley, Whitby, Scarborough and Malton the bounds, according to a perambulation contained in a cartulary of Whitby Abbey[117] of the early fourteenth century, being approximately as follows.

Beginning at Howe Bridge some three miles north of Malton where the Malton — Pickering road (A169) crosses the river Rye, the bounds followed the course of this river for the whole of its length and continued to Ralph Cross on Westerdale Moor in the centre of what is now the North York Moors National Park. At this point the bounds turned eastwards over Glaisdale Moor to Loose Howe and Shunner Howe where they then followed the Wheeldale Gill until it joined the Murk Esk. Continuing down this river to Grosmont, they turned south-east to Bracken Howe, Foster Howe and Lilla Howe which stands between Goatland Moor and Fylingdales Moor. From here the bounds proceeded to the source of the river Derwent and followed this river to the point where it was joined by the Tilla Beck about two miles north of East Ayton on the Scarborough — Pickering road (A170).

Here the bounds turned north-eastwards along the line of what is now known as the Sea Cut to Keld Runnels and then swung north to Prospect House Farm, a little to the east of Suffield. They then proceeded along the side of the hill to Thieves Dikes where they bore to the north-east past Silpho Brow Farm and on to Kirkless Farm. From this farm the bounds followed the course of the East Syme Beck north-westwards for about a mile before turning north again to reach the Scarborough — Whitby road (A171) at a point about three quarters of a mile south-west of the village of Staintondale. The bounds continued along this road to the Falcon Inn where they bore to the north past Pye Rigg Howe to Green Dike and so to Blea Wyke Point on the North Sea.

From here they followed the line of the coast southwards, excluding Scarborough and Falsgrove to a point to the north of Filey where they turned south-west across the marshes of Filey to join the Hertford river. The bounds continued along the Hertford river to its junction with the river Derwent and followed the course of the Derwent until it was joined by the river Rye. They then proceeded along the Rye to Howe Bridge where the bounds began. In the earliest times the eastern portion of the Forest was known as Scalby Forest but subsequently Pickering was divided into two wards or bailiwicks: the west ward which was also known as the Pickering Lythe Ward and the East or Scalby Ward.

129   Skipton Forest

The Forest of Skipton, which adjoined the western extremity of Knaresborough Forest, covered an area of land which was roughly square in outline and lay within the following limits. From Skipton in the south, the bounds probably followed the course of the river Aire to Gargrave and then turned north-eastwards through Eshton, Flasby Hetton, Cracoe and Thorpe to join the river Wharfe at Burnsall. Here they traced the course of the Wharfe past Drebly and Barden Bridge to Bolton Bridge where they swung west approximately along the line of the main road (A59) back to Skipton.[118]

PART TWO

THE DEVELOPMENT OF MODERN FORESTRY

THE OVERTURE TO FORESTRY   6

THE ECLIPSE OF THE MEDIEVAL FOREST

By the beginning of the sixteenth century, the structure of the medieval forests had begun to crumble despite the fact that the façade was to remain for another hundred years. Although there were several factors which contributed to their demise the basic reasons were financial and economic. During the latter part of the century, both the sovereign and the government were being subjected to increasing financial pressures: the war with Spain was costing nearly one third of a million pounds a year[1] and it should be remembered that such a figure would appear far greater if translated into present day values. Nor did this need for money diminish with the accession of the Stuarts, for James I, Charles I and Charles II were continually seeking ways to meet their financial obligations.

The medieval forests were created and administered with the object of providing the sovereign with preserves over which he had the right to hunt and which, as Manwood[2] observed, were 'for his princely delight and pleasure'. Although, to a limited extent, the forests provided the king with a source of income by way of amercements and grants, such revenue could never be regarded as anything more than incidental. Now, as the purse strings tightened and fresh sources of revenue were sought, the potential value of the forests began to be examined.

To the Norman and Plantagenet kings, hunting was a sport which incorporated many of the manly qualities which they admired. Gradually, however, this ardour and devotion to the chase began to fade so that by the end of the sixteenth century their successors no longer displayed the almost fanatical keenness of earlier times. This is not to say that the sovereign had lost all interest in hunting; Elizabeth I, James I, and Charles II all enjoyed it but they did not engage in it with the same vigour and determination that was displayed between the eleventh and the fifteenth centuries. At the same time, the laws of the forest tended to be applied less vigorously and to fall gradually into disuse with the result that those in authority began to lose control. This, in turn, was followed by an increase in poaching and ultimately in a decline in the value of the forests for hunting. These events may not have contributed directly to the passing of the medieval forests but they did nothing to encourage their continuation since the purpose for which the forests had been created began to be called into question.

The disintegration of the forests was hastened by the Civil War which lasted from 1642 to 1646. During this period little attention was paid to what remaining authority the officers of the forest still possessed and deer were killed and trees felled without scruple. After the war was over, this state of affairs continued while the country remained in a state of disarray and by the time the monarchy was restored in 1660, the pattern of the old forests was rapidly falling apart, expedited without doubt by the laxity and dishonesty of some forest officials.

Early in the sixteenth century there were signs that the demand for timber and firewood was beginning to outstrip the supply. The reasons for this are discussed later in this chapter but the effect of these shortages was to stress the need for action in order to improve the country's timber supplies.

THE DEMAND FOR TIMBER

When considering the position regarding timber supplies in the sixteenth and seventeenth centuries, it is as well to remember that during much of this period wood provided most of the needs of the community which were subsequently met by coal and, to a lesser extent, by iron.

From a domestic point of view, the greatest demand was for firewood which was generally known as fuel or fewelwood and serious shortages, causing great hardship, had occurred in 1436 and 1542 when there were exceptionally severe winters. It is recorded that in 1436 'The grete hard bityng frost bygan the 7 day of Decembre, and endured unto the 22 day of Feverere next, which greved the peple wonder sore; and moche pepel deyed in that tyme, for colde and skarcitie of wode and cole'.[3] An Act of 1553[4] which was concerned with the sale and measurement of firewood refers to 'the great scarcity of woods that is happened since the time of the said King Edward the Fourth' (1461-63). Although by the middle of the sixteenth century the use of coal was

becoming well established in those areas in which it was mined or in districts
to which coal could be brought by sea, it was disliked by housewives. This was
apparently on account of the smoke, soot and smell which coal produced as
compared to wood. It is recorded that Elizabeth I 'hersealfe greatly greved
and anoyed with the taste and smoke of sea cooles'.[5]

The word coal or cole was originally used with reference to charcoal, the
verb 'to charke' meaning to char or coke and was used by Fuller[6] in 1662,
while the noun 'charke' referred to charcoal or coke. In the middle of the
sixteenth century, what is now simply referred to as 'coal' was known as sea-
coal or pit-coal and was so named from the fact that it had either been

3.   *Work in the woods. A print probably of continental origin, showing felling,
cross-cutting, trimming out branch wood and the conversion of timber with a
frame saw. The produce consists of planks and bundles of rods while a stand on
which the rods are bundled and tied can be seen in the bottom left hand corner.
c. 1600.*

transported by sea or dug from a pit. This was in order to distinguish it from char-coal which was the carbon residue obtained by partially burning wood in the process known as charcoal burning. Originally the name 'colliers' was applied to those engaged in charcoal burning and not to those working in coal mines.

Next to firewood, the greatest demand was probably for timber needed in the construction of houses and other buildings. However the requirements for such purposes differed from those for fuel in two main respects. First, the material that was used in building work was of a different size and quality to that which was generally supplied for firewood. Second, the demand for building timber was substantially less and not of the same urgency as that for fuelwood, while in course of time, as stone and brick began to replace timber, this market contracted. Other domestic needs for timber included furniture, much of which was of oak since the use of foreign woods did not become general until the beginning of the eighteenth century. Household utensils, such as plates, dishes, bowls, tankards, ladles and pails were normally made of wood and were known as treen and this was not replaced until pewter, silver and tin came into common use.

In industry the consumption of timber was also considerable and this was a cause for concern over a long period. Agriculture was largely dependent on timber for carts, waggons and implements although, in the latter, the working and wearing parts were usually made of iron. Timber also provided posts and rails for fencing, hurdles, troughs, dairy utensils and the handles for practically every tool on the land. While the needs of agriculture were common to most of the country, other industries tended to be concentrated in comparatively restricted areas. By the middle of the sixteenth century the glass-making industry was rapidly expanding and considerable amounts of wood were consumed in the process of manufacture but by 1650 coal had replaced wood to a large extent.

In Kent, the clothing industry required a substantial volume of wood in order to heat the dyeing vats and in Cranbrook and the seven adjoining parishes, an average of 180 acres of woodland was felled each year, between 1553 and 1573, to supply the needs of fuel and the clothing industry. It is estimated that about two-thirds of the area felled was coppice and underwood.[7] Droitwich was the chief centre for the manufacture of salt and in the course of producing this commodity, it was necessary to heat the brine over a furnace. Early in the sixteenth century there were no less than 360 furnaces in operation and some 6,000 loads of wood were needed every year to keep them supplied. It is said that the countryside surrounding Droitwich was completely devoid of timber and consequently supplies of wood were brought in from Alcester, Alvechurch and Bromsgrove.[8]

During this period, the industry which probably caused the greatest concern and apprehension, on account of the large quantities of wood which it absorbed, was iron smelting. Although this process had been carried out from the earliest times, it had reached considerable proportions by the fifteenth century and had continued to expand during the next hundred years. The production of iron was chiefly carried out in Surrey, Kent and Sussex while at the same time these counties grew some of the finest oak in the country which was in great demand for the Navy. Gradually coal began to replace wood for smelting and as this development spread, the iron industry moved to localities where coal was readily available so that, by 1690, smelting was in decline in those areas which were dependent on wood for fuel. Another industry which had steadily grown in importance between the fifteenth and seventeenth centuries was shipbuilding and much of the concern for possible timber shortages stemmed from the fear that supplies for the Navy might be jeopardized. The whole question of the Navy's requirements as regards timber are considered in a later chapter.

Although there is little doubt that iron smelting consumed large quantities of wood, much of this, which was in the form of poles, was obtained from underwood rather than from mature timber. At the same time it should be borne in mind that in those days it was the usual practice to allow young selected poles to grow on into timber. However, the claim that future timber supplies were being seriously undermined was undoubtedly exaggerated. In some quarters there was even a movement of opinion towards the view that the iron industry encouraged the preservation and better management of woodland areas. Yarranton[9] observed that:

> *Iron-works are so far from the destroying of Woods and Timber, that they are the occasion of the increase thereof. For in all parts where Iron-works are . . . there are great quantities of Copices or Woods which supply the Iron-works: And if the Iron-works were not in being, these Copices would have been stocked up and turned into Pasture and Tillage . . . And in Glocester-shire, Worcester-shire, Warwick, Salop and Stafford Shires are vast and infinite quantities of Copices, wherein there are great store of young Timber growing; and if it were not that there would be Moneys had for these Woods by the Owners from the Iron Masters, all these Copices would be stocked up and turned into Tillage and Pasture, and so there would be neither Woods nor Timber in these places.*

Although he was no advocate of iron smelting, which he referred to as 'this wasting-oare', Evelyn[10] also had doubts as to the alleged adverse effects of the industry on the reserves of timber, as can be seen from the following remarks:

> *But yet to prove what it is to manage Woods discreetly; I read of one Mr. Christopher Darell a Surrey Gentleman of Nudigate, that had a particular Indulgence for the cutting of his Woods at pleasure, though*

a great Iron Master; because he so order'd his Works, that they were
a means of preserving even his Woods; notwithstanding those
unsatiable devourers: This may appear a Paradox, but it is to be
made out; and I have heard my own Father (whose Estate was none
of the least wooded in England) affirm, that a Forge, and some other
Mills, to which he furnish'd much fuel, were a means of maintaining
and improving his woods; I suppose, by incresing the Industry of
Planting, and care; as what he has now left standing of his own
Planting, enclosing and cherishing, in the possession of my most
honoured Brother, George Evelin of Wotton in the same County, does
sufficiently evince; a most laudable Monument of his Industry and
rare Example, for without such an Example, and such an Application,
I am no Advocate for Iron works, but a declared denouncer.

THE PROBLEMS OF SUPPLY

If the demands for timber were increasing so was the shortage and there were
two main reasons for this. The first was the fact that supplies of timber from
economically accessible sites were decreasing. Although there might be large
stocks growing in the country, if this timber could not be conveyed to the areas
of consumption, either because there was no means of transporting it or
because the cost of doing so was prohibitive, then it could make little
contribution to the nation's needs. In the sixteenth and seventeenth centuries,
the roads in rural areas consisted for the most part of unmetalled tracks which
soon broke up with the passage of heavy loads especially in wet weather. If a
laden timber wagon sank into a particularly soft section of the road, it might
remain there for several months until there was a spell of dry weather during
which it could be pulled out. The first roads constructed on modern principles
were built in 1765 by John Metcalfe who was followed, early in the nineteenth
century, by Telford and McAdam. For many years the problems of haulage
were matters of concern to those responsible for providing the naval dockyards
with supplies of timber and in 1793 the Report of the Commissioners on
Waltham Forest (otherwise the Forest of Essex) contains the following
admonishment:

> *. . . it behoves the King's Officers to be very attentive to the growth*
> *and preservation of the timber trees upon this Forest, as, in a few*
> *years, it would be the supply of Deptford and Woolwich yards; and,*
> *from its vicinity to those yards, be a saving of 50 per cent in the*
> *carriage of timber laid in from distant parts.*

The alternative to transport by road was transport by water, which in the
sixteenth and seventeenth centuries meant by sea or river, since the building of

canals did not begin until the early part of the eighteenth century and even then gained little momentum until about 1762, when the Bridgwater Canal was constructed.

On account of these transport difficulties, centres of production which needed timber tended to develop in areas where supplies were close at hand, or at least within easy haulage distance. In the case of ship building it was also necessary to have direct access either to the sea or to a navigable river flowing into it. The New Forest was especially well placed since not only were there large supplies of timber readily to hand, but these were also in close proximity to the sea and to local ship yards. The Sixth Report of the Commissioners noted that Alice Holt and Woolmer Forests were:

> . . . bounded on one side by the River Way, which becomes navigable at Godalming about ten miles from the middle of the Forest; and communicates with the River Thames, affording an easy conveyance of the forest timber to the dock yards in that river, and at moderate expence.[11]

This was an important matter since some of the largest ship-building yards were situated on the Thames at Rotherhithe, Deptford, Blackwall and Woolwich all of which lay in an area some four miles in length, the centre of which was Greenwich. The transport of timber for the Navy from forests in Northamptonshire, which lay some distance from a navigable river, provided a more difficult problem. From Whittlewood Forest timber was transported by road to the Thames at Burcot, six miles south of Oxford and from Salcey Forest to the river Lea at Hertford, to complete its journey by water.[12]

The second main reason for the shortage of timber was the lack of adequate steps in the past, to ensure a supply for the future. In medieval times trees were raised from coppice shoots or springs which grew from the stumps or stools of felled trees but these shoots were liable to be damaged by deer or domestic animals unless protected from them. Natural regeneration, that is the growth of young trees from seed which has fallen in the course of nature from larger trees and taken root, also occurred but this needed protection as well. This problem continued for many years and as late as 1792 the report on Wychwood Forest[13] stated that:

> . . . it is feared that neither the swine, nor even the deer, are kept out of the King's Coppices . . . This totally prevents the acorns from getting up, so that it is impossible for any timber ever to get up in this forest, in succession to that now growing, unless inclosures and coppices are made within the forest.

Apart from these two basic reasons for the increasing shortage of timber, other causes have been put forward but these should only be regarded as contributory and in some cases they are not altogether convincing. It has been suggested that at the time of the dissolution of the monasteries by Henry VIII, the monks set about selling many of the woodlands that formed part of their monastic estates in order to realize assets which were more conveniently removable. If there were instances of this, it is difficult to assess what effect such action had on the nation's timber supply. There was also the general exploitation of growing timber by landowners, not only in order to raise money but also to convert woodland areas into agricultural land. This had been a gradual process over a long period but how widespread it was, or what long term effect it had, is uncertain. The alienation of some of the royal forests and woodlands by Elizabeth I and the Stuarts has been said to have adversely affected the country's timber resources. However, it would have to be shown to what extent these alienated lands were used for growing timber at the time of alienation and whether, after their disposal, they were converted to uses other than timber production. During the Civil War some unauthorized and occasionally illicit, felling was carried out but this was probably more on account of political enmity than a demand for timber and it is difficult to assess what effect this felling had on existing stocks. Finally, there was the depletion of supplies brought about by the demands of certain industries which has been discussed earlier in this chapter.

THE CORRECTIVE MEASURES

Faced with the situation of expanding demands and diminishing supplies, it was necessary for action to be taken in an attempt to deal with the problem and the first steps towards safeguarding future supplies were contained in an Act[14] of 1482. This allowed an owner of woodlands which lay within the bounds of a forest, chase or purlieu, who felled any of his woods, to enclose the area immediately after felling for a period of seven years, in order to protect the young growth. Some 60 years later, in 1543, Henry VIII passed a further Act,[15] the opening sentence of which stated that:

> *The King our Sovereign Lord perceiving and right well knowing the great decay of timber and woods universally within this his realm of England to be such, that unless speedy remedy in that behalf be provided, there is great and manifest likelihood of scarcity and lack, as well of timber for building, making, repairing and maintaining of houses and ships, and also for fewel and firewood for the neceesary relief of the whole commonalty of this his said realm.*

This Statute, which contained 21 sections, was an important landmark in English forest history since it was the first attempt at establishing a system of woodland management in this country. It laid down that when coppice or underwood of 24 years growth or less was felled, 12 oaks known as standils or storers should be left per acre. If there were insufficient oak to make the count, then standils of elm, ash, aspen or beech should be left to make up the number and these standils were not to be felled until they reached a size of ten inches square within three feet of the ground. Failure to leave the requisite number resulted in a fine of three shillings and four pence for each one removed. Standils are now known as standards and coppice-with-standards is a recognized silvicultural system which is still found in the southern counties.

The Act also provided that when any coppice or underwood which was of 14 years growth or less, had been felled, the area was to be enclosed or otherwise protected from cattle and other animals for the space of four years. If this provision was disregarded, the person responsible was fined three shillings and four pence for every rood of land which, for every month after felling, remained unenclosed. Underwood of between 14 and 24 years growth was to be enclosed for six years and failure to do so resulted in a similar scale of fines. It may be noted that a rood was equal to a quarter of an acre. It was also an offence to convert to pasture or tillage any area of coppice or underwood which was two or more acres in extent and two furlongs from the owners house. Disregard of this section led to a fine of 40 shillings for every acre so converted but this did not apply where conversion had been carried out during the 20 years preceding the Act. Owners of woods that contained 'great trees' of over 24 years of age were required, when these woods were felled or thinned, to retain 12 such trees per acre and these were to be oak or, if insufficient oak were available, then elm, ash, aspen or beech. These could not be felled for a further 20 years and the land on which they stood had to be protected from cattle for seven years after the area had been thinned or the rest of the stand felled.

The actual wording in the Act refers to 'the felling and weeding' of great trees and this is one of the first occasions when thinning is mentioned. If these provisions were disregarded, the owner became liable to a fine of six shillings and eight pence for each great tree that he failed to retain, with a further fine of three shillings and four pence per rood for every month that the area remained unenclosed. However this provision did not apply to an owner who needed the timber for certain specified purposes including the building and repair of houses, fencing and ship building. Six sections of the Act were concerned with trees growing on waste or on land subject to common rights while certain exemptions were made from the provisions of the Act. These included woodlands growing in certain parts of Kent, Surrey and Sussex, trees in Cornwall growing within two miles of the sea and trees which were 'sear and dead in the tops'. Anyone who damaged the protective fences around felled areas were liable to a fine of ten shillings but after these fences had been in position for two years, the owners were allowed to turn colts or calves which were under a year old, into the woods.

The next step towards conserving supplies of timber was an Act,[16] passed in 1558, which curtailed the use of timber in the iron industry and was 'for the avoiding of destruction and wasting of timber'. It forbade the use of any timber trees of oak, beech or ash as fuel for iron making which were:

> one foot square at the stub and growing within fourteen miles of the sea or any part of the rivers of Thames, Severn, Wye, Humber, Dee, Tine, Teese, Trent or any other river, creek or stream by which carriage is commonly used by boat or other vessel to any part of the sea.

A fine of 40 shillings per tree was to be exacted from those in default but the Act did not apply to Sussex, the Weald of Kent and the parishes of Charlewood, Newdigate and Ligh in Surrey. The eight rivers that are mentioned by name are presumably those that were regarded as being the most important for transporting timber.

Further legislation[17] concerning the iron industry was enacted in 1581 on account of the erection of new iron foundries near London, the Downs and the Sussex coast since timber suitable for felling

> doth daily decay and become scant, and will in time to come become much more scarce, by reason whereof the prices are grown to be very great and unreasonable and in time to come will be much more if some remedy be not provided.

Under this Act it was an offence to use timber as fuel for making iron within 22 miles of the Thames below Dorchester (eight miles south of Oxford) or within four miles of Winchelsea, Rye or the foot of the Downs between Arundel and Pemsey (Pevensey) or three miles of Hastings. Contravention of this resulted in a fine of 40 shillings for every load of wood suppied to an iron foundry. While the Act exempted certain localities, including the Wealds of Surrey, Sussex and Kent, it also prohibited the erection of new iron works in these areas subject to a fine of £100. It also gave special exemption to Mr Christopher Darell to whom Evelyn referred in his remarks on the iron industry, as mentioned earlier in this chapter.

The last of the Statutes[18] of this period which were aimed at conserving timber, was passed in 1585 and related to the Wealds of Sussex, Surrey and Kent. It referred to 'the great plenty of timber which hath grown in those parts hath been greatly decayed and spoiled and will in short time be utterly consumed and wasted, if some convenient remedy therein be not timely provided'. Under this Act the building of any new iron mills was prohibited as was the use of 'sound timber trees or trees of oak, ash and elm which could be used for cleft wares or sawing timber'. The fine for building new mills was £300 and for the use of sound timber in smelting, 40 shillings. However, it was permissible to use the 'tops and offal' of any sound trees for fuel in iron works that were situated in certain specified districts. The second part of the Act was concerned with the damage to roads caused by the haulage of iron and 'coals', which would include wood for smelting, and the liabilities of those concerned, to repair such damage.

Although these Acts paved the way towards the conservation of the nation's timber supplies, there were three reasons why they did not, in themselves, solve the problem. First, there was the difficulty of enforcing this legislation since evasion was comparatively easy and prosecutions were few and far between. It was one thing to lay down that 12 standils were to be retained to the acre, but it was extremely difficult to check this number when the areas concerned might be scattered over several counties. The second problem which was closely connected to the first, arose from the lack of information and records relating to the country's timber resources. Without such knowledge, there was little prospect of either making an accurate appreciation of the situation or ensuring that the law was observed. Third, these Acts not infrequently contained exceptions or modifications which provided those who were so inclined, with opportunities to avoid such provisions as they found unacceptable.

THE DETERIORATION OF THE FORESTS

Although the reasons for the ultimate disintegration of the royal forests were fundamentally financial and economic, there were other more local causes which contributed to their deterioration and which were largely due to the shortcomings of the forest officers. By present-day standards many of them could only be regarded as dishonest but two aspects of this problem ought to be mentioned not in order to provide an excuse, but rather to suggest an explanation for such a state of affairs. First it should be remembered that during this period of history corruption was commonplace in many walks of life. The receiving of presents, the establishment of perquisites, the payment for positions and privileges and the manipulation of offices to the advantage of the individual concerned, were all too common and were, to a large extent, regarded as accepted practice. If those who held the higher positions in the land were guilty of such conduct, it could hardly be expected that their lesser brethren would not also become tarnished in the same way. Second, the remuneration of those who found employment within the forest hierarchy, especially in the lower grades, was often so meagre as to invite corruption and dishonesty.

Too often foresters and woodwards were inefficient and possessed little technical knowledge of their calling and this led to waste and neglect. The poorer inhabitants of the countryside, whose living standards were low, indulged in poaching and stealing wood in order to supplement their needs. The theft of young trees which would have grown into timber and the damage to protective fencing around felled areas thereby allowing animals to enter and destroy the young springs, could affect the stocking of a forest and its production of timber in the future. In some cases neighbouring villages claimed rights of grazing, pannage and gathering wood, as in the case of Grovely Forest, and this tended to aggravate the situation.

However it was the forest officers themselves who often proved to be the worst offenders. Cattle were allowed to graze in enclosed coppices while in some forests the woodwards or keepers actually mowed the young coppice areas for hay, thus effectively cutting off all the young springs and any natural regeneration that chanced to be there.[19] In order to augment their inadequate salaries, some officers claimed more than their proper entitlement of wind-blown trees and browse wood which they either used themselves or sold for firewood. This led to the removal of large limbs which, on account of their size, should not have been classified as browse and to the deliberate damaging of sound trees which were then felled on the grounds of their being defective. The cutting of excessively large limbs for browse-wood produced extensive wounds which subsequently allowed the entry of disease and the ultimate damage or loss of what otherwise might have been good timber. Other opportunities for fraud and deceit existed in the course of measuring and marketing timber, and it was not difficult knowingly to under-measure trees which were then paid for on the full measure, the difference being appropriated by the vendor. Poundage, which was in effect commission, was paid on the value of timber sold and consequently some of those concerned, indulged in over-cutting.

Behind these various opportunities for dishonesty lay a complete lack of competent management and control and it was this, as much as anything, that was the cause of the trouble and allowed such misdemeanours to continue unchecked. It would seem that little was done to improve the management of the crown forests during the next hundred years since in 1788, the Commissioners reported: '. . . so wasteful and destructive is the present system of management in those forests, that the general quantity of timber in them lessens every year.[20]

As compared to the crown forests, those woodlands that belonged to private individuals were generally managed with greater efficiency and success, largely due to the fact that they were unhampered by forest law, the rights of others or an outdated forest administration. An individual who used his initiative and business acumen was often able to make a worthwhile contribution to the nation's timber supply and, at the same time, obtain a reasonable return for his efforts. There have always been those who have regarded the cutting of timber with concern and apprehension and so it was in the sixteenth and seventeenth centuries when the felling of trees and woodlands tended to increase. Some blamed the monasteries, some the farmers and their sheep walks,[21] others the Commonwealth[22] and a few the 'Popish politicians' but, as is all too common, none blamed the hard economic facts. There could have been other reasons for the deterioration of the country's woodlands if Leland's[23] observations, which he made during his visit to Wales, were equally applicable to England, for during his itinerary he noted:

> Many hilles thereabout hath bene well woddid . . . but now in them is almost no woode. The causses be these; First the wood cut down was never copisid and this hath beene a great cause of destruction of wood through Wales. Secondly after cutting down of wooddys the gottys [goats] hath so bytten the young spring that it never grew but like shrubbes. Thirddely men . . . destroied the great woddis that thei should not harborow thieves.

During the seventeenth century a general sense of disquiet regarding the country's woodlands and timber resources began to manifest itself, as witnessed by the appearance of several publications which were concerned with these matters. The first was *The Commons Complaint*[24] by Arthur Standish which appeared in 1611 and referred to: 'The general destruction and waste of woods in this kingdom with a remedy for the same: Also how to plant wood according to the nature of every soile'. Standish also remarked that 'few or none at all doth plant or preserve by reason thereof there is not tymber left in this kingdome at this instant onely to repaire the buildings thereof . . .'

In the following year, another book appeared under the title of *An Olde Thrift newly Revived . . .*[25] the author writing under the initials of R.Ch and, although these have been attributed to R. Churton and R. Chambers, there is little doubt that the writer was Rocke Church who was the King's Surveyor in 1608. At the foot of the title page will be found, in French, the words *Tout pour l'église,* a pun on the author's name which provides his identity. In 1613 Standish published his *New Directions of Experience to the Commons Complaint*[26] which he followed two years later with *New Directions of Experience for the Increasing of Timber and Firewood*[27] in which he put forward his scheme to plant 250,000 acres in order to meet the country's timber requirements. Firewood was to be grown in hedgerows and parks but some of his proposals are not altogether easy to follow. In 1652 a small book appeared which was written by Silvanus Taylor under the title of *Common-Good or the Improvement of Commons, Forrests and Chases by Inclosure*[28] but this was mainly concerned with commons and inclosures and only indirectly with timber production.

Twelve years later the first edition of John Evelyn's *Sylva or A Discourse on Forest-Trees*[29] was printed. It ran into five editions, the last being published in 1729 while in 1776 it was republished in an annotated form by Dr A. Hunter and this included a number of illustrations chiefly depicting the foliage and fruit of different trees. The fifth and last edition of Hunter's version was placed on the market in 1825. Some have acclaimed *Sylva* as one of the great books on trees and forestry while others have spoken of it disparagingly, asserting that Hunter's edition is of far greater value, but whatever views are held it seems difficult to contest the following facts. Evelyn wrote a book that was the first to discuss and examine in detail the raising of trees and the growing of timber and much of what he said remained sound sense over the next 300 years and some of it is applicable even today. In some respects he may have paid too much attention to individual trees and too little to growing them in woodlands for the production of timber but this was a fault which was common to many writers well into the nineteenth century. Earlier writers had been more concerned with the politics of the problem; what, in the broadest terms, was wrong and what, in equally broad terms, should be done to put it right. Evelyn, on the other hand provided detailed information as to how, when and where to put the matter right. His book being the first of its kind, contained mistakes or rather statements that would not be accepted today, as indeed might well be expected, but it also contained much more that was sound and instructive and it must be regarded as a major landmark in the history of English forestry.

Twelve years after the publication of *Sylva*, Moses Cook who described himself as 'Gardiner to the Earl of Essex' brought out his book, *The Manner of Raising, Ordering and Improving Forest-Trees . . .*[30] It is possible that Cook was inspired by Evelyn's example to write this book and the second edition which is dated 1717 refers on nine occasions either to Evelyn personally or to the *Discourse of Forest-Trees*. Three of these references are distinctly complimentary: 'see Esquire Evelyn's *Discourse of Forest-Trees* who hath writ well of this and others', 'the ingenious author of the *Discourse . . .*' and 'I cannot pass by the learned Squire's good advice in his *Discourse . . .*'. As a contribution towards the planting of trees and woodlands in the seventeenth century, this book can be regarded as second only to Evelyn's *Sylva*.

THE SEARCH FOR REVENUE

In medieval times revenue from the forests was largely due to fines or amercements payable in respect of offences against forest law, to receipts from the granting of licences and privileges and to monies received from the sales of timber. As successive monarchs began to attach less importance to the forests as reserves for hunting, so the laws of the forest were enforced less strictly and gradually the whole conception of the medieval forest began to change. As forest law was relaxed so the fines decreased, and as administrative control weakened so thefts of timber increased, sales declined and revenue diminished. In any event, since the main object of the medieval forests had been to provide facilities for hunting, any income which was derived from them was regarded as being largely fortuitous.

4.   *Felling and selling timber. This print formed the frontispiece to the second edition of Moses Cook's*
The Manner of Raising . . . Forest-Trees,
dated 1717. It shows timber being felled and measured while the owner and his agent discuss the price with the timber merchant. Felling is by axe and measuring by rod and dividers while the crooks at the opposite ends of the two butts in the foreground are most probably for ship's timbers.

By the middle of the sixteenth century the general need to increase the royal revenue had become a matter of some urgency and one possible source lay in the forests. However, several major difficulties stood in the way of any action that might be taken in the matter. First, it should be borne in mind that a royal forest comprised an area of land which was subject to forest law and over which the sovereign had the right to hunt, even if it was not the property of the crown. In most cases, only a comparatively small area in a forest was royal freehold, that is to say, land which actually belonged to the king rather than land over which he exercised the right of hunting. Consequently the amount of forest land that the sovereign was free to sell or lease, was much less than would at first appear to be the case. Second, most of the royal forests were subject to rights claimed and exercised by various sections of the community of which rights of common, pannage, turbary and gathering wood are examples and such rights could cause considerable complications when disposing of the land. Third, and largely on account of the foregoing, it was difficult to assess the value of a royal forest in terms of money.

There were two general lines of approach to the problem of raising money from the old forests; the first was to try to increase their annual revenue and the second was to realize their capital value. There were several ways in which the annual income could be improved and the first of these was by expanding the sales of timber. This would appear to be a comparatively simple matter but unfortunately there were a number of difficulties. In the first place few proper records existed which provided details of the forests so that information as to their extent, age or quality was difficult to ascertain and this seriously prejudiced potential sales. Many of the medieval forests were to a large extent devoid of any trees that could be considered to be of commercial value, as for example the Peak Forest, Exmoor Forest and many of those which lay in the northern counties and consequently sales of timber were limited to those forests which carried a fair stock of individual trees or woodlands.

For various reasons any efforts to make the forests more viable and to increase their financial returns, met with opposition from several quarters. Forest officers were concerned that such action might prejudice their own interests, not only through a closer examination of their activities but also by the sale of material which might otherwise have become a part of their perquisities. Those who lived in or near a forest and claimed rights within it felt that any change would be for the worse and, on investigation, they might find it difficult to substantiate their claims. James I who had acquired a great enthusiasm for hunting, attempted, soon after his accession, to re-animate forest law and was opposed to any steps that might interfere with or impair his sport even if the purpose was to increase his income.

Another way of improving the revenue was by leasing or farming coppices and underwood which belonged to the Crown, to individuals. These were let at a fixed annual rent either for an agreed number of years or for the period which one or more named persons might live and was known as a lease for life or lives. Leasing could be beneficial and advantageous to the Crown in that it provided a certain fixed income, it also eliminated to a large extent the expenses connected with forest officials and it greatly reduced the costs of administration. Leases were not without their problems and disadvantages however, and these included difficulties created by forest rights, the fear that irresponsible and excessive felling by the lessees might prejudice future timber supplies and the possibility of damage to game, especially the deer.

A further possible source of income from the Crown forests lay in the province of the assarts. These were areas of land within a forest from which, in contravention of forest law, the trees had been removed and the roots grubbed up and which had then been converted to arable. Normally such offences were dealt with by a fine and the guilty party was then granted a licence, for which he made an annual payment, allowing him to continue in occupation of the assarted land. Such payments were known as arrentations and in *The Shorter Oxford English Dictionary*[31] the verb 'to arrent' is defined as 'to allow the enclosure of forest land "with a low hedge and small ditch" under a yearly rent'. Many of these rents had been fixed during the fourteenth century so that, by the end of the sixteenth century, their value had fallen substantially for a number of reasons. In some cases rents had not been increased for about two hundred years and consequently had failed to take into account any increase in the value of the land or any fall in the value of money; tenants had changed; areas had been disafforested; some rents had lapsed and were no longer paid while in some cases new assarts had occurred without being recorded or rented. Steps were therefore taken to improve the financial returns from these assarts and a full account of them, more particularly as regards the forests of Northamptonshire, is given by Pettit.[32]

The alternative to increasing the annual revenue from the forests, was to realize their capital value by selling them or, as it was known in the sixteenth and seventeenth centuries, by alienation, that is, by transferring their ownership to another. There were two ways in which this could be done, the first was to dispose of the land, underwood, timber and so on without disafforesting the area, so that the Crown and others beneficially interested retained their rights and the land virtually remained under forest law. The second method was by disafforestation under which all rights or privileges of the sovereign or his subjects were relinquished and forest law was brought to an end. Alienation was criticized on several counts: it resulted in the disintegration of capital reserves, it could adversely affect future supplies of timber especially for the Navy, it was opposed by those who held rights in the forest while compensation paid to forest officers who lost their employment, was an added expense. On the other hand it could be claimed that in addition to raising money, the disposal of forests which were expensive to maintain and which produced little or no revenue, could also result in a substantial reduction in costs. Alienation began to gather momentum during the latter half of the sixteenth century and continued until the accession of James I who showed considerable antipathy to the disafforestation or sale of the royal forests but after his death the process of disposal accelerated again.

A somewhat different approach to the problem of raising funds from the forests was adopted by Charles I who attempted to revive forest law and to restore the forest bounds in accordance with some of the earliest perambulations. His action had two objectives: first to exact fines from those who now found themselves not only subject to forest law but also guilty of contravening it; and second, to obtain from land owners capital sums, on payment of which their property would then be disafforested. This outrageous attempt to raise money, which savoured of blackmail, failed to a very large extent but it struck what was tantamount to the final blow which brought down the edifice of the medieval forests.

THE ELEMENTS OF EXPENDITURE

The largest item of expenditure in the Crown forests was that of the salaries and wages which were paid to forest officers of whom those in the lower grades were normally full time employees. The higher ranks tended to hold office with little or no payment but instead recouped themselves in other ways. During the middle ages the ranks of forest officers included wardens, verderers, rangers, foresters, woodwards and keepers but by the sixteenth century, some of these ranks had either lapsed or merged with others. As well as the remuneration which officers received, there were certain benefits in kind which were also recognized as being their due. However, as mentioned earlier in this chapter, the matter did not end there and in course of time, the line which divided legitimate perquisites from dishonest dealings became almost invisible. As early as 1217[33] restrictions were placed on certain activities of the king's foresters relating to these matters, while in 1350[34] it was laid down:

> *That no forester, nor keeper of forest or chase, nor any other minister,*
> *shall make or gather sustenance, nor other gathering of victuals, nor*
> *other thing by colour of their office against any man's will within*
> *their bailiwick nor without, but that which is due of old right.*

A further item of expenditure was the repair and maintenance of the lodges or houses which were provided for those who were required to work and live within the forests. These were chiefly foresters and woodwards and although timber was usually supplied from the forest for these repairs, the cost of upkeep could nevertheless be considerable in a large forest. There were also the costs of administration at the higher levels and these were chiefly attributable to salaries and emoluments. Consequently any action to diminish the expenditure had to be concerned with reducing the numbers of those employed or with their salaries or possibly with both. There were, however, inadequate records relating to those who worked in the forests and as a result, the task of reducing their numbers was prejudiced from the outset. It was also felt, and not without good reason, that any reduction in the already inadequate level of salaries would result in those concerned, recouping themselves in other ways and that this would lead to still more dishonesty. Only in the sphere of administration could a fair degree of retrenchment have been achieved satisfactorily.

THE MOVEMENT TOWARDS TIMBER PRODUCTION

As the character of the royal forests began to change, so their shortcomings as potential producers of timber became more apparent. If they were no longer to be the happy hunting grounds of kings, then at least they should become a means for raising timber and providing national wealth but how this was to be achieved was far from clear. One of the main obstacles was the lax and inefficient system of administration and this was already causing concern early in the sixteenth century. In 1541 it was laid down that the Court of the General Surveyors of the King's Lands should be a Court of Record and that its members should include the King's General Surveyors and the Master of the Woods.[35] Subsequently, two Surveyors General were nominated one of whom was concerned with crown lands in general and the other with crown woods and forests in particular. Among those who held the office of Surveyor General of Woods were Roger Taverner and his son, John, each of whom wrote a *Book of Survey,* in 1565 and 1584 respectively. In addition, local surveyors and woodwards-general (so named as to distinguish them from those woodwards who were employed in a private capacity) were appointed.

Pettit[36] has described for the first time the office of the preservators who were appointed in the latter half of the sixteenth century and whose duties were, in effect, the control and supervision of other forest officers. He has also provided an abstract of 13 articles of instruction which were drawn up for the preservators and cover such matters as the felling of trees and underwood, browsewood, sales and the protection of woodlands. These proposals aimed at improving the timber supply by controlling the felling and sale of trees which were growing naturally in the forests rather than by the organized planting of young trees. This and the fact that the preservators lacked adequate powers to deal with offenders, were two serious faults in the new plan. It was also too optimistic to think that by creating a new rank of forest officer the problems of inefficiency and dishonesty would be eliminated, and unfortunately these difficulties remained so that after the Restoration the preservators ceased to exist. Other attempts to introduce some form of management into the forests included a series of surveys which were carried out towards the end of the sixteenth and early in the seventeenth centuries and reference has already been made to those conducted by the Taverners.

Not only in the Crown woods was there a need for a new sense of purpose and the private owner and his woodlands were also the subject of criticism. In 1612 Church[37] noted '. . . how forward every man is in these days to fell down timber and grub up copies and none endeavours to plant any . . .' while later in the century Cook[38] was to observe that 'there are too many men more inclined to stock up than to plant'.

As the seventeenth century drew to a close, the curtain was finally rung down on the old forests of medieval England. Although it would still be another 200 years before modern forestry started to take shape, from now on the word 'forest' began to convey the idea of timber rather than hunting and of commerce rather than sport.

5.   *Oak for the Royal Navy. This picture is the frontispiece to*
The Modern Druid
*by James Wheeler which was published in 1747. In the centre is an oak bearing
a heavy crop of acorns; on the right Britannia sits holding an oak seedling in her
hand while in the background ships of the fleet are assembled. The Latin
inscription may be translated as 'The Glory and Protection of Britain'.*

THE WOODEN WALLS　　　　　　　　7

An island country is bound to be dependent to a large extent on shipping for its economic survival and consequently steps must be taken to safeguard its merchant ships from attack and to keep its sea lanes open. Although the need for this was very apparent during the two world wars of the present century, attention was drawn to it as early as 1635 when Lord Coventry addressed the judges of England[1] as follows.

> *The wooden walls are the best walls of this kingdom; and if the riches and wealth of the kingdom be respected, for that cause the dominion of the sea ought to be respected, for else what would become of our wool, lead and the like, the prices whereof would fall to nothing if others should be masters of the sea.*

At first, ships were small in size but by the beginning of the fifteenth century more and larger ships were being built partly on account of the activities of Henry IV and Henry V against France, during the Hundred Years War. In 1418 the *Grace Dieu* of some 1400 tons was launched and with a length of about 130 feet and a beam of 48 feet, she was the largest ship which had been built in England up to that time. By comparison the *Santa Maria* in which Columbus crossed the Atlantic in 1492, was probably not more than 75 feet in length. Larger ships also began to be built on account of the needs of commerce, since an expanding overseas trade resulted in longer voyages and required greater cargo space. For some time, when ships were needed for naval operations, it was common practice for merchant vessels to be taken over and while the master and the crew were retained in order to sail the ship, a captain and men-at-arms were put on board to provide the fighting force.

In the sixteenth century the differences in the design and construction of fighting ships and merchant ships became more evident as can be seen in the *Henry Grace à Dieu* more commonly known as the *Great Harry*, a four-masted ship of 1500 tons which was the pride of Henry VIII and was launched in

1514. The development of the galleon by the Portuguese had a marked effect on naval designs in this country and both the *Revenge* and the *Ark Royal* were based on galleons. The *Revenge* which was launched at Deptford in 1577 was rated as 500 tons and was 92 feet in length with a beam of 32 feet. As larger ships were built so the rigging became more extensive and this in turn affected the size and pattern of the masts.

So long as the nation's needs could be met by a small number of ships, whether for the Navy or the merchant fleet, the country's timber resources were able to meet the demand but as foreign trade increased and the Navy began to expand so the situation changed. The first indication of concern for future timber supplies is to be seen in the Act for the Preservation of Woods[2] of 1543 while between 1558 and 1585 other legislation was passed which restricted the felling of timber for use in iron smelting.

The exploits of the Elizabethan seafarers and adventurers, as exemplified by Drake's voyage to the Spanish West Indies in 1585, not only whetted the appetites of others for such lucrative undertakings but also goaded Spain into punitive action which resulted in the despatch of the Armada in 1588. The early years of the seventeenth century saw the development of trade with the Far East, though in keen competition with the Dutch, and the expanding of the East India Company which established a trading base or 'factory' at Surat in 1612. This was followed by others which were set up at Madras, Bombay and Calcutta during the course of the century. Apart from the expansion of foreign trade, the first and second Dutch wars of 1652 and 1665 and the war with Spain in 1656 stressed the need for a larger and more powerful navy and the creation of such a navy was to be more than justified by Nelson's triumph at Trafalgar.

During the next hundred and fifty years, Britain became involved in no less than seven wars, to say nothing of various minor engagements, in each of which the Navy was concerned to a greater or lesser extent. The wars of the English, Spanish and Austrian Successions of 1689, 1702 and 1740 were followed by the Seven Years War in 1756, the War of American Independence in 1775, the American War of 1812 and finally the Napoleonic wars which ended with Wellington's victory at Waterloo in 1815. The participation in these numerous campaigns and the development of overseas trade was only possible with a large navy and a substantial mercantile marine. The construction, repair and maintenance of the necessary ships placed increasingly heavy demands on the country's timber resources so that, by the middle of the eighteenth century, the difficulties in meeting these demands were causing the greatest concern. The availability of timber for naval construction is considered later in this chapter.

The Structure of a Wooden Ship

In order to appreciate how much timber was needed for building a large ship and also the dimensions and characteristics of the individual timbers, it is first of all necessary to consider the structure of a ship and to some extent, the method of construction. Although this section is concerned with the ships of the Royal Navy, the building of merchant vessels was also a matter of considerable importance and large quantities of timber were required for their construction. However, those who were concerned with their design were not so restricted in their choice of timber or so conservative in their methods of construction as were their naval counterparts. Even so, private shipyards were sometimes in competition with the Navy for the largest and best quality oak. Chief among these were the yards which built for the East India Company, some of whose ships were comparable in size to the smaller naval vessels. In the latter half of the eighteenth century this rivalry for the best timber reached such proportions that in 1772 an Act[3] was passed 'for the more effectually securing a quantity of oak timber of a proper growth for the use of the Royal Navy'. Under this Statute it was laid down that:

> the said United Company of Merchants trading to the East Indies . . .
> shall not build or cause any person or persons whatsoever to build
> any new ship . . . for the service of the said United Company, until the
> tonnage of ships employed . . . in the trade of the said Company . . .
> shall be reduced to forty-five thousand tons.

The ships of the Royal Navy comprised a number of types or classes and these included ships of the line, cutters, frigates, schooners and sloops. They were rated according to the number of guns they carried and the following summary is an approximate guide:

1st rate:	100 guns	4th rate:	64 guns
2nd rate:	90 guns	5th rate:	40 guns
3rd rate:	74 guns	6th rate:	26 guns

However the number of guns on a ship varied and the Eleventh Report of the Commissioners[4] gives, in an account of ships built between 25th October 1760 and 31st December 1788, the following figures:

1st rate:	100 guns	4th rate:	50 guns
2nd rate:	98 guns	5th rate:	44, 38 or 36 guns
3rd rate:	80, 74 or 64 guns	6th rate:	32, 28, 22 or 20 guns

HMS *Victory* which was a 1st rate originally carried 104 guns. Ships of the line were the largest and were so called because they formed a line of battle but the most numerous class comprised the 3rd rates which were often referred to as 'seventy-fours'. They provided the main fighting strength of the Royal Navy and made a very substantial contribution to the maritime power of this country.[5] 1st and 2nd rates were built with three gun decks and 3rd and 4th rates with two.

The largest ships were built in the Royal Dockyards the most important of which were Portsmouth, Chatham, Sheerness, Devonport, Woolwich and Deptford but some of the smaller ships were built under contract in private yards. Holland[6] has provided a detailed study of the work of privately owned yards that were established in Hampshire. Despite this it was sometimes found to be more economical to build a small ship alongside a large one so that any pieces of timber that were not big enough for the larger vessel or were left over after its construction had been completed, could be used in the smaller one.

6. *A modern timber-built trawler under construction at Messrs Dixon & Sons' yard at Exmouth in 1973.*

In building a ship of the line, oak, elm and beech were used in the construction of the hull but the masts and spars were of pine and spruce. Trees from which masts were obtained were normally imported from Europe or North America since this country did not produce material that was considered suitable. The timbers that were employed in the construction of a ship were divided into different categories according to their use and were known by specific names. 'Great timber' referred to exceptionally large pieces which were needed for such massive parts as the wing transom and stern post. 'Compass timber' comprised naturally curved pieces which were required for beam arms, breast hooks, futtocks, knees and riders. 'Plank' or 'planking' was used for covering the decks and also for the sides of the ship, both internally and externally, the thickness of the planking decreasing from the keel upwards, the bottom planks being not less than six inches thick and the uppermost about three inches. Two bands of heavier timber known as 'waling' ran along the length of the ship, on and above the waterline which were formed of the thickest planking. In giving evidence before a Select Committee in 1849, a timber inspector from Portsmouth Dockyard stated that compass timber was 'any timber that curves five inches and upwards in 12 feet', and that 'thickstuff is 4½ inches up to 10 inches thick; plank is 4 inches to 2 inches; below that is board'.[7] Although much of the timber was required to be curved or shaped, there was also a need for what was known as 'straight' while pieces which had been roughly trimmed or squared were known as 'sided' timber. Reference is made in Appendix 6 of the Eleventh Report of the Commissioners,[8] to all these categories except great timber, together with the prices which were paid for them in 1791.

The building of a wooden ship of any size was a formidable task but in the case of a ship of the line it was a tremendous undertaking and completion usually took at least five years. Very fortunately, HMS *Victory* can still be seen at Portsmouth and although a number of alterations have been carried out since she was built at Chatham in 1765, her main structure is, to all intents and purposes, the same. Many of the features which are described in this section, may be seen by visitors to the *Victory* although some are in those parts of the ship that are not normally open to the public. To appreciate fully the construction of the ship, it is well worth studying beforehand Dr Longridge's excellent book *The Anatomy of Nelson's Ships*[9] in which many constructional details are shown by admirable line drawings and photographs. In the following paragraphs some of the component parts of a 1st rate are briefly described and illustrated by drawings but for more detailed information reference should be made to Dr Longridge's book.

The basis of construction was the keel which ran the length of the ship from stem to stern. It was made of elm and was about 20 inches in depth and increased in width from 18 inches at the stem to about 20 inches amidships and then decreased to about 16 inches at the stern. In HMS *Victory* the dimensions of the keel were slightly more and its length a little over 152 feet, so that it was obviously impossible to obtain a single piece of elm of such a size. In order to overcome this, separate sections of elm, not less than 25 feet in length were joined together by scarfing them, that is to say by fastening them so that the ends overlapped each other for not less than 5 feet.

Attached to the bottom of the keel was the false keel which was 6 inches thick and the same width as the keel itself, its purpose being to protect the keel

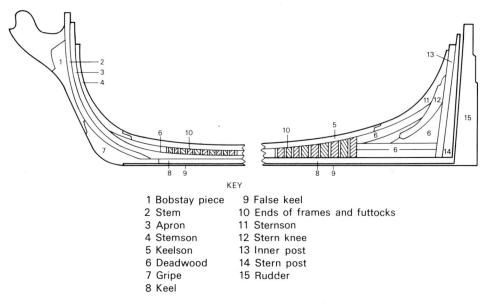

KEY

1 Bobstay piece	9 False keel
2 Stem	10 Ends of frames and futtocks
3 Apron	11 Sternson
4 Stemson	12 Stern knee
5 Keelson	13 Inner post
6 Deadwood	14 Stern post
7 Gripe	15 Rudder
8 Keel	

7.   *Longitudinal section of a timber-built ship. c.1790.*

from being damaged by underwater obstructions. On top of the keel were the floor frames and above these and fixed to them, was the keelson which ran above and in line with the keel. Square in section, the keelson was rather smaller than the keel but was made up of lengths of elm scarfed together in a similar fashion to the keel. At the forward end the keel merged into the gripe and the stem and the keelson joined the stemson while between the stem and the stemson was fixed the apron. Owing to their shape these parts were all produced from compass timber but because of their length, it was necessary to scarf two or three shorter pieces together.

The sides of the ship consisted of frames to which the planking was fixed and these formed a continuation of the floor, the ends of which were held between the keel and the keelson. The frames which extended upwards from the floor were built up of shaped sections known as futtocks or foot hooks and it was to these frames that the external and internal planking (also known as the inside and outside skin) which formed the sides of the ship, were fixed. In order to strengthen the ship still further, curved timbers known as riders which extended from the keelson to the orlop deck, were laid at intervals on top of the inner planking. The side of the ship was thus made up of the outer planking, the frames, the inner planking and the riders. Another form of strengthening were the breast hooks which were fixed internally across the bows but if they also carried the ends of the deck planking, they were termed deck hooks.

At the stern, the keel ended at the stern post and inner post, the former being about 30 feet in length and a little over 2 feet square at the top. At the base, the width was equal to that of the keel but it extended forward along the keel for about 3 feet. Not only was it a major structural member but the rudder was also attached to it and consequently it was one of the most important timbers in the ship and, since it had to be cut from one solid piece of oak, it was also one of the most difficult to obtain. On the forward face of the stern post was fixed the inner post and although not as large as the stern post, it was also a very substantial piece of timber. The keelson merged into the sternson which was fixed to the upper portion of the inner post and lay partly along the stern post knee.

Excluding the forecastle and quarter decks, there were four decks in a 1st rate. The lowest was the orlop or overlying deck, the name being derived from the Dutch *oberluppen* or overloopen, since it was the deck which overlaid or covered the hold. Above the orlop deck were the lower, middle and upper gun decks, in that order. Each of these decks was supported by oak deck pillars, those below the orlop being larger than those between the gun decks on account of their greater height and the weight which they had to bear. The deck pillars supported the deck beams which ran athwartships, that is, transversely across the ship from port to starboard. The ends of these beams were carried by hanging knees which may be compared to a present day shelf bracket, the vertical arm being fixed to the side of the ship with the horizontal arm projecting inboard to support the ends of the deck beams. The arms were usually straight but if it was necessary to avoid an opening in the side of the ship, such as a gun port, knees were used in which the vertical portion was curved to the right or the left. Other knees known as lodging knees were fixed horizontally, that is to say, parallel to the deck, so that one arm was attached to the side of the deck beam and the other to the side of the ship, thus imparting a considerable degree of rigidity.

Where the distance between the deck beams had to be increased or where extra strength was needed, as for example where the masts passed through the decks or where the capstans were located, special timbers known as 'beam arms' were used. These were in the nature of a stay or brace and extended diagonally from the side of the ship to the end of the adjacent deck beam. Set at right angles to the deck beams and running fore and aft, were the secondary deck timbers which were termed 'carlings' while at right angles to them and parallel to the deck beams were the smaller ledges.

Although this description of the timbers that were required in the construction of a wooden ship is far from complete, it may convey some idea of the very considerable quantity of timber which was used and of the specialized shapes and sizes which were needed. As will be seen, a very high proportion was compass timber and this greatly added to the difficulties of supply, the problems of which are considered in the following section.

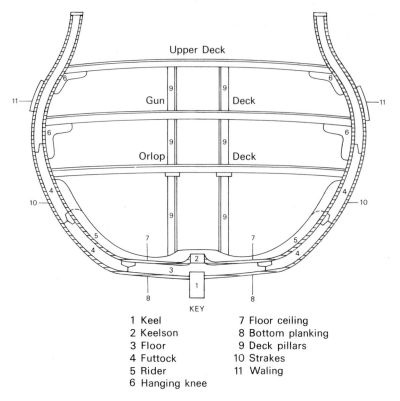

KEY

1 Keel	7 Floor ceiling
2 Keelson	8 Bottom planking
3 Floor	9 Deck pillars
4 Futtock	10 Strakes
5 Rider	11 Waling
6 Hanging knee	

8.   *Cross section of a timber-built ship. c. 1790.*

SHIPS IN TERMS OF TIMBER

The amount of timber used in the shipyards from the middle of the seventeenth century until the development of iron ships in the nineteenth century was immense, and in the last hundred years of this period, it was the cause of much concern. In 1796, Marshall[10] remarked that:

> *When we consider the prodigious quantity of timber which is consumed in the construction of a large vessel, we feel a concern for the probable situation of this country at some future period.*

He was concerned not only over the needs of the Royal Navy but also with the large quantities of timber which were being used in building ships for the merchant fleet since, between them, heavy inroads were being made into the country's timber reserves.

There is little detailed information available as to the amount of timber which was needed in building a ship and this is probably due, at least in part, to the following. Ships ranged in size from a 1st rate of 100 guns to a 6th rate of 32 guns or less and consequently the amount of timber used in their construction varied considerably. Not only did the larger ships consume more timber but in some sections they also needed more massive timbers; a substantial proportion of the trees that reached the shipyards was lost during sawing or 'conversion' into ship's timbers while there was the ever-present threat of decay. The problems of waste and decay are considered more fully in a later section.

However some information on this matter is provided by Marshall[11] who states

> A seventy-four gun ship (we speak from good authority) swallows up three thousand loads of oak timber. A load of timber is fifty cubical feet; a ton, forty feet; consequently, a seventy-four gun ship takes 2000 large well grown timber trees; namely, trees of nearly two tons each.

Three thousand loads of oak at 50 cubic feet to the load amount to 150,000 cubic feet and a tree of two tons, at 40 feet to the ton, contains 80 cubic feet and consequently 2000 such trees would contain 160,000 cubic feet so that the two figures are very comparable. A 74 gun ship was a 3rd rate which had two gun decks while the 1st and 2nd rates which were built with three gun decks would have contained a substantially larger amount of timber.

Banbury[12] records that in the *Royal George,* a first rate of 100 guns which was launched in 1756, 5,756 loads, that is 287,800 cubic feet of timber was used in the construction of the hull. This figure included 24,150 cubic feet (483 loads) in respect of the planking and 15,950 cubic feet (319 loads) for the knees. What is probably the most reliable information on this matter was provided by an inspector of naval timber at Portsmouth Dockyard when giving evidence before a Select Committee in 1849, one question which he was asked and his reply were as follows.

> How many loads (of timber) do you use in the different classes of vessels of war?
> About 6,000 loads in 120-gun ship, a three-decker; in an 84-gun ship, one of our largest class of two-deckers, we use about 4,400; then the smallest two-deckers, a 74, would have about 3,600; one of our frigates would require 2,400.[13]

At the same time, Gabriel Snodgrass who was described as 'the experienced and very intelligent Surveyor of Shipping of the East India Company' informed the Commissioners[14] in 1792 that the amount of oak timber used by the Company in the construction of their ships was in the proportion of one and a half loads (75 cubic feet) to one ton of shipping; thus a ship of 2000 tons would consume 3,000 loads.

Marshall also gives an estimate of the area of woodland which was needed in order to grow the number of trees required for the construction of a third rate of 74 guns.

> The distance recommended by authors for planting trees in a wood . . . in which underwood is also propagated, is thirty feet upwards. Supposing trees to stand at two rods (33 feet, the distance we recommend they should stand at, in such a plantation) each statute acre would contain 40 trees; consequently, the building of a seventy-four gun ship would clear, of such woodland, the timber of 50 acres. Even supposing the trees to stand at one rod apart (a short distance for trees of the magnitude above mentioned) she would clear twelve acres and a half; no inconsiderable plot of woodland. When we consider the number of King's ships that have been built during the late wars, and the East Indiamen, merchant ships, colliers and small craft that are launched daily in different ports of the kingdom, we are ready to tremble for the consequences.

However, Marshall's estimate was not entirely endorsed by the Eleventh Report of the Commissioners which had appeared some four years earlier and which stated

> The most prevailing opinion among experienced surveyors and persons conversant in the management of wood, appears to be, that on good soil, where great timber is made the principal object in management and the young trees are regularly thinned out and the finest preserved for timber, without regard to the underwood, 40 trees may be expected to grow on the acre; and that, at 100 years growth, those trees may be computed to contain, one with another, two loads of timber: but in all woodlands, of any considerable extent, there are vacant parts, where, from different causes, the trees have failed; and on referring to the surveys taken in the time of James the First, when we know there had been a very careful management, though the quantity of timber was, in general, near six times greater than is now upon the same ground, we find no example, of so many as 40 trees of two loads each per acre, through the whole of any forest. Making allowance, therefore, for such defects, we think that 34 trees of one load each, girt measure, may be expected on the acre, in a fit soil and under proper management and 34 loads of timber girt measure being equal to 50 loads square measure, the produce of one thousand acres, which would be about 50,000 loads, would be sufficient for the supply of the Navy for one year, the average yearly consumption being, as we have before stated, 50,542 loads.

If the amount of timber required for the building of a single ship was impressive, the total requirements of the Navy were even more so. Except for a period in the middle of the sixteenth century and during the reign of James II, the Royal Navy had been expanding steadily since the time of Henry VIII as can be seen from the following tonnage figures which are taken from the Eleventh Report of the Commissioners.[15] The dates are the years in which the sovereigns died unless otherwise stated.

Henry VIII	1547	12,455 tons
Edward VI	1553	11,066 tons
Mary	1558	7,110 tons
Elizabeth I	1603	17,110 tons
James I	1625	uncertain
Charles I	1649	uncertain
The Restoration	1660	57,463 tons
Charles II	1685	103,558 tons
Abdication of James II	1688	101,892 tons
William III	1702	159,017 tons
Anne	1714	167,171 tons
George I	1727	170,862 tons
George II	1760	321,104 tons

By 31st December 1778 the tonnage had risen to 413,667. The Fifth Report[16] includes as Appendix 49, 'A State of the Quantity of Oak Timber used for the support of the British Navy, from His Majesty's Accession in October 1760 to the end of the Year 1788'. This is made up of two items, first, the amount of oak timber received into HM Dockyards during this period, amounting to 768,676 loads and second, the estimated quantity of timber required for building ships that had either been purchased for the Navy or built for it in private dockyards. The total number of loads which had been used in these ways amounted to 1,285,306 and the average number of loads per annum over the period of 28 years totalled 45,904 or 2,295,200 cubic feet. The timber which was supplied to the Royal Dockyards was used either for building new ships or for repairing existing ones and Albion[17] considers that the allocation of timber for these purposes was in the proportion of two-thirds for building and one-third for repairs. In contracts for supplying timber to the Royal Dockyards, it was usual to stipulate that knees should be supplied in the ratio of four loads to every hundred loads of oak timber, and elm timber in the ratio of six or seven loads to a hundred loads of oak.

When the First Report of the Commissioners (of the second series) was published in 1812,[18] it confirmed Marshall's opinion as to the amount of timber which was required in order to build a 74-gun ship, but it varied some of the figures contained in the Eleventh Report. It was now considered that 60,000 loads of oak was

> ... *the quantity which would be sufficient annually to support, at its present unexampled magnitude, the whole British Navy, including ships of war of all sorts, but which may be taken as equivalent, together, to 20 Seventy-fours, each of which one with another, contains about 2,000 tons, or would require, at the rate of a load and a half to the ton, 3,000 loads making just 60,000 loads for twenty such ships. It is a current opinion that not more than forty oaks can be produced and grow to maturity on an acre of land, and in several of the answers to the printed queries which the Surveyor General of Woods, etc, circulated in the year 1808, and of which he transmitted a copy to the Lords of the Treasury, they had been put at a smaller number but on the other hand there is reason to believe, from the actual experience of several very intelligent owners and managers of extensive oak woods and plantations in different parts of England, that in a favourable situation and with proper management, more than eighty such trees may be produced on one acre. Adhering however, to the above average of forty to the acre and taking the average quantity of timber in each tree at a load and a half, 1,000 acres will, at the end of one hundred years, the period of time generally allowed for the full growth of an oak, produce 60,000 loads or enough to maintain the Navy on its present scale for a year.*
>
> *And according to this deduction, 100,000 acres would be requisite and adequate if so planted and managed that the timber on each 1,000 could be felled in successive years and that 1,000 immediately replanted, for maintaining a Navy like the present for ever.*

THE AVAILABILITY OF SHIPYARD TIMBER

In the two previous sections of this chapter, consideration has been given to the design of wooden ships and to the amount of timber that was used in their construction. Although ship builders were fully conversant with both these matters, there was one aspect that remained uncertain and over which they had little or no control, namely, an adequate and regular supply of suitable timber.

Broadly speaking, there were two main categories of timber which were needed in the shipyards: compass and straight. Compass timber included any pieces which were curved and which were used in such items as knees, futtocks, riders, breast hooks and in the construction of the stem. There are however some references which might suggest that knees were not always regarded as compass timber as in the following instance of 1670: 'Mr Moorcock

has tendered some knees and compass timber and asks £3 10s a load but I
expect he will take less if treated with'.[19] For the purpose of this section, the
term straight timber is used to include planking and special timbers which
were known as great timbers, such as the wing transom and stern post.
Supplies were derived from two distinct sources although in some cases a
single tree might provide timber of both categories.

As regards compass timber, oak trees growing in hedgerows and parkland,
which developed large open crowns, produced the greatest amount since, on
account of their unrestricted growth, the branches had ample room to develop
curves and bends. Sometimes the bole or trunk provided a limited amount of
straight timber but this was generally short in length, since oak grown in the
open does not actually attain any great height. Illustration 9 shows how some
compass timbers could be obtained from trees of this kind. In 1831, Matthew[20]
remarked that

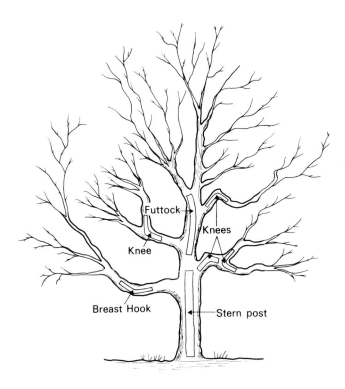

9. *The source of compass timber. This drawing shows how some of the numerous*
curved pieces, known as compass timber, which were needed in ship building,
were obtained from a tree.

In Britain crooked oak for timbers is found chiefly in hedge-rows and open forests, where the winds, casual injury, or overhanging superior branches, have thrown the tree, while young, from its natural balance; or, by the tree, from open situation or excision of lower branches, parting early into several leaders, which in receding from each other, form curves and angular bends.

At the turn of the eighteenth century the shortage of compass timber was becoming a serious matter and several suggestions were put forward for overcoming these deficiencies. One proposal was to encourage the growth of curved timber through the medium of pruning. Monteath[21] favoured the removal of the leader so as to allow a lateral branch to take over and continue growth which would become, in his words, 'a fine crook'. Illustration 10, which appeared in his book, shows his proposal.

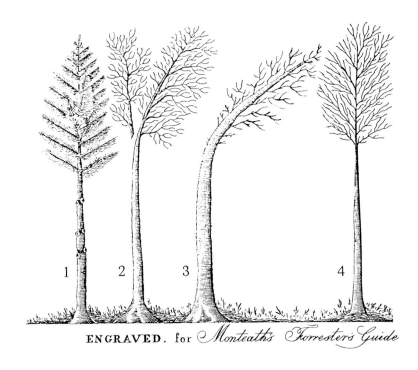

ENGRAVED. for *Monteath's Forrester's Guide*

10. *The production of compass timber. Tree no. 2, which has developed a fork, has its straight leader removed so as to encourage the growth of the limb on the right. This should subsequently develop into three no. 3. From* The Forester's Guide *by Robert Monteath, 1820.*

Marshall[22] had somewhat similar ideas except that he favoured the restriction of the growth of an unwanted branch rather than its removal. He considered that the stems of young trees should be kept free of side shoots and pruned to a single leader and when this had been done by 'throwing the main strength of the head into one principal bough (by checking, not removing the rest) a crookedness of timber is had with certainty'. In addition he claimed that 'what is equally necessary in ship timber, a cleanliness and evenness of contexture are, at the same time, produced'. Billington[23] on the other hand preferred the selective pruning of the crowns of young oaks.

Another plan for producing compass timber was based on the training of young oaks by fastening them to stakes or other trees, so that they developed curved stems as they grew.[24] A very different system was that which was based on the effect which a tree with a large spreading crown had on its less dominant neighbours which grew in close proximity to it[25] since as the less vigorous trees tended to grow away from the larger one, they produced curved stems. On the matter of obtaining knees, Matthew[26] considered that

> *The easiest way to procure good oak knees is to look out in hedge-row and open forest for plants which divide into two or four leaders, from 5 to 10 feet above ground; and should the leaders not diverge sufficiently, to train them as horizontally as possible for several feet, by rods stretching across the top or by fixing them down by stakes.*

Straight timber and plank was considerably easier to obtain than compass timber, except for those unusually large pieces known as great timber. Plank was largely used for the outer and inner skin of a ship and the trees which provided this material were 12 to 40 feet in length and at least 8 inches in diameter at the smaller end. Matthew was of the opinion that trees that were intended for plank 'ought to be reared in close forest or protected situation, drawn tall and straight or, what is preferable for a part, with a gentle regular bend, technically *sny*'.[27]

By the beginning of the nineteenth century some work had been done on what was termed the 'boiling' of timber, with a view to bending it and so obtain the gentle regular bends to which Matthew refers. Pontey[28] urged the use of 'boiling and a screw apparatus to make bends' on the grounds of economy in both labour and timber. It is probable that 'boiling' was in fact steaming and Matthew used this term when he says that 'planks bend sufficiently side-way by steaming'.

The difficulties in obtaining adequate supplies of material for the shipyards were not only confined to the matter of great and compass timber. Many of the component parts of a ship were obtained from large oaks which, owing to their slow rate of growth, needed many years to reach the required size. As a result, few land owners were prepared to postpone felling their oak until they had reached a considerable age, when they could obtain a good price for much younger trees. In addition, since farms yielded a substantially higher return than woodlands, there was an increasing tendency to convert woods into agricultural land and this further contributed to the increasing scarcity of timber.

Although by the beginning of the nineteenth century a number of canals had been built and a few of the more important roads had been improved, the transport of timber was still a major problem. By 1830, it had become the practice in some parts to convert trees for plank in the woods and Matthew noted that

> When planks are cut out where grown, they are sawn from the round log immediately after it is felled and barked, which not only prevents injury from drought-cracks, but produces also a considerable saving of timber and labour as the wood is softer when green.

He might also have added that there was a saving in transport as the volume of timber which had to be hauled to the dockyards was considerably reduced by conversion in the woods.

Another matter that affected the amount of timber which ultimately found its way into a ship, was the waste that occurred in the course of converting timber in the round into the individually prepared items needed in its construction. Abel[29] refers to the enormous wastage which occurred in conversion and considers that about one half of the wood was lost. If this was the case, a loss of 50 per cent although considerable does not appear to be excessive by present day standards when the conversion of lower grade oak in a modern sawmill can result in loss through wastage of 40 per cent and in some cases even more. Decay was another problem both before conversion and after the building of the ship and this is considered later in this chapter.

Another cause of the shortage of timber in the shipyards was the widespread abuse of the time-honoured privilege of the shipwrights to take away chips for their own use. Originally this concerned the small flakes or pieces of wood that were produced when using an adze or axe during the preparation of the timber. In course of time the so-called chips became any piece of wood that was less than three feet in length and the Eleventh Report[30] relates how men were stopping work an hour before time in order to cut up useful pieces of timber as chips. The Report observes that: 'The perquisite of chips allowed to the shipwrights in the dockyards is another source of waste of useful timber which ought certainly to be prevented.' In fact the whole system under which timber was purchased and delivered to the dockyards laid itself open to dishonesty and corruption at all levels.

As the difficulties in obtaining supplies of suitable timber increased, so consideration began to be given to the ways and means of overcoming the problem. There was, however, a large body of opinion which, influenced by the experience of the past, opposed any changes or innovations in the methods of ship construction irrespective of the need or purpose of such modifications. Despite this, two leading naval architects put forward proposals which were aimed at overcoming the increasing shortages of timber; the first was Gabriel Snodgrass who was Surveyor of Shipping for the East India Company and the second, Sir Robert Seppings who was a designer in the Royal Dockyards. The Eleventh Report (Appendix 29)[31] contains some 35 questions put to Snodgrass by the Commissioners together with his answers. His reply to the last question 'Can you suggest any means by which the consumption of oak timber may be lessened in ship-building . . .?' contained a great number of suggestions which varied from methods of storing and seasoning timber to modifications in ship design and included the following more specific points. Breast hooks and knees in general should be of iron 'as they are lighter, cheaper and stronger than wood and may be made to any size and length'. In order to strengthen the structure of a ship diagonal braces should be fixed, extending from the keelson to a point where the underside of the lower gun deck joins the side of the ship. Some 20 years later Seppings advocated among other things that the deck beams should be fastened to the ends of extended riders instead of to knees and that triangular iron braces should be bolted to the inside of the frames in order to strengthen the ship lengthways, thereby presumably reducing the size of some of the timbers.

As the supplies of homegrown oak became scarcer, the possibility of using foreign oak was investigated but it was considered that it did not attain the required standard and its use was never adopted to any extent. At the same time a search was made for a species which might provide an alternative to oak for ship construction and the Commissioners reported that: 'The larch or larix was by far the most likely to answer this purpose of any kind of tree of which we had obtained any certain information', but little seems to have been done to follow up this conclusion.

The whole question of timber supplies for the dockyards was complicated by the fact that in building a ship, it was not only the difficulty of obtaining a sufficient quantity of timber but also that of finding supplies which were of the required shapes and sizes. Ultimately the size to which ships could be built was limited by the size of the trees which provided the timber. In 1839, as the age of wooden ships was drawing to a close, Sawyer referred to the difficulty in finding an oak similar to one which had been used in the building of the *Royal Sovereign*. The tree had come from Framlingham in Suffolk and had 'squared four feet nine inches and whose length was forty-four feet' — a fine stick indeed.

THE PROBLEM OF DECAY

To the difficulties of supply were added the problems of decay which could seriously shorten the life of a ship and so add to the depletion of the already inadequate stocks of timber. In 1789 the Commissioners of the Navy expressed their views as to how long a ship could be expected to last as follows:

> *In general it is found that the ships built in the King's Yards last much longer than those built by contract or purchased; but the precise difference of their duration cannot be ascertained, as it depends on a variety of circumstances extremely contingent in their nature and not easily described. We are however of opinion that 15 years may be allowed for ships built in the King's Yards and 10 for those in Merchants yards.* [32]

McWilliam[33] writing nearly 30 years later was not quite so optimistic and put the average life of 'modern built ships of war' at 12½ years with an optimum of 14.

A ship's timbers could be subject to attack from the inside or the outside of the vessel. Internally the danger was decay and rot which could cause such extensive damage as to render a ship unseaworthy. Dry rot could be brought about by the condition of the timber or by faults in the design and construction of the ship or by both of these factors. Too often resort was had to unseasoned timber while the retention of sapwood so as to obtain a part of the required shape or size, was equally hazardous. Practically none of the timber that was imported from abroad was seasoned and if it had been rafted to the port, it would be very wet at the time of loading, so that with the humid conditions produced in the hold during a long sea voyage, ideal conditions were provided for the development of any fungi.

Constructional faults in a ship, especially those which impeded the movement of air or caused a lack of ventilation, could hasten the spread of rot. During the building of a ship the whole structure was exposed to the weather and this greatly added to the risk of decay.

The two classic examples of what could happen in extreme cases of dry rot are those of the *Royal George* and the *Queen Charlotte*. In 1782 the former, a 1st rate of 100 guns, sank in Portsmouth harbour with considerable loss of life including that of Admiral Kempenfeldt. She was at the time being 'heeled over' so that some minor repairs could be carried out a little below the water line, a procedure which was quite normal in those days. Owing to the rotten state of her timbers the strain proved to be too great and her bottom fell out so that she sank immediately. The *Queen Charlotte,* another 1st rate of 110 guns, which was built in 1810, was so rotten by the time she was completed that she had to be rebuilt before she could be commissioned. While she was being fitted out, it was found that some of the Canadian oak and pitch pine was in an advanced state of decay. This was apparently due to the fact that in an endeavour to hasten the seasoning of the ship's timbers, stoves had been placed in different parts of the hold after it had been finished. Nothing could have been calculated to encourage the growth and spread of fungi more than this and above the water line she soon became almost completely rotten. Originally she had cost £88,524 but by 1859 when no less than £287,837 had been spent in addition on repairs, it was decided to rename her *Excellent,* an appellation which could hardly have been less appropriate.[34]

As the problem of decay became more serious, so greater efforts were made to find a solution and one of the first matters which received attention was that of winter-felled timber. Since oak bark commanded a good price from the tanners and as it could only be stripped when the sap was 'running' — normally in April — it was usual for much of the oak to be felled at that time of year. However it was generally considered that the timber of trees felled during the winter months, when the tree was dormant and the sap was 'down', was more durable than that of trees felled in the spring or summer. This view is still held today although with the increasing use of kiln drying, whereby timber can be artificially seasoned, winter felling is now of less importance than it was. In order to encourage the felling of oak in winter the Navy were prepared to pay an increased price for it to which the Eleventh Report refers as follows.

> *The bark of winter-felled timber being lost, the Commissioners of the Navy allow for such timber an advanced price of 7¼% to compensate that disadvantage; but bark having risen very much in value, no great quantity of winter-felled timber is obtained.*[35]

Closely connected with the subject of winter and spring felling was the theory that when the bark was removed, a change took place in the sapwood or outer annual rings of a tree. This matter was raised by Dr Robert Plott in 'A Discourse concerning the most seasonable time of Felling Timber' which he submitted to James II, through Samuel Pepys, in 1687. In this paper[36] he observed that

> *. . . if it be bark't in the spring, and left standing naked all summer, exposed to the sun and wind, as is usual in Staffordshire and the adjacent counties, whereby they find by long experience, the trunks of their trees so dried and hardened, that the sappy part in a manner becomes as firm and durable as the heart itself.*

In 1739 De Buffon[37] expressed similar views when he remarked that 'there is no more to be done but to bark the trees . . . The white wood by this operation becomes as hard as the heart of an oak.' It was later suggested that trees that had been stripped should remain standing for three years after the bark had been removed.

The Commissioners were, however, somewhat sceptical and observed that it may 'be thought extraordinary, that if it was found to have such beneficial effects, the practice should not have become more general'. At the same time they questioned that this may have been accounted for by the damage which might be caused to the young coppice or underwood by delaying the felling of trees for three years after they had been barked or by the increased cost of stripping a standing tree as compared to one that had been felled. Whatever the true facts of the case, it seems that this procedure was never adopted to any great extent.

One of the undoubted causes of decay was the use of unseasoned timber and this was a matter which was stressed by Snodgrass in his reply to the Commissioners, when he referred to the imprudence

> of building ships . . . with green materials, which certainly is the principal cause of the rapid decay of ships that are built in this manner and of the bad state of many of the ships of the present Navy and also of the extraordinary expence and consumption of timber in building and repairing them.[38]

In anticipation of a national emergency, the Commissioners of the Navy considered it necessary to have three years supply of timber in their dockyard. Although this action may have created a feeling of security, such confidence was largely misplaced owing to the excessive waste which occurred in these stocks, through decay. Most of the timber was delivered to the dockyards in what was termed 'its rough state' which presumably means in the condition in which it was after it had been felled and trimmed out or, as it is termed today, 'in the round'. On arrival at the yard, it was sorted according to the year in which it had been felled and that which was brought in first, was the first to be used. On the subject of storing and stacking the Commissioners passed the following comments.

> The part called the sap, being full of juices, soon begins to corrupt: and that corruption spreads, not only to the rest of the same tree, but to those lying next to it. To prevent this waste, very proper orders have been given by the Navy Board, 'that if there be otherwise room, there shall not be more than three heights, or ranges of great timber,' but from want of room those regulations, necessary for the free admission of air, cannot always be followed; and so much is the timber injured from this cause, that a very considerable part of it is rendered unfit for ship-building.[39]

Other steps that were taken to try and combat decay included the charring of timber which was placed over a fire for a short time in order to produce a protective layer of partially burnt wood. This method, which had been in use for a very long time, was still employed in some parts of the country during the present century for protecting fencing posts, until preservatives such as creosote were introduced. Although charring provided a safeguard against the entry of fungi, its use in shipbuilding was very limited since it had a number of disadvantages: a piece of timber could be unwittingly reduced in size by excessive burning; the charred surface could be broken or removed before the timber was fixed in position and charred timber could not be used for mortices, tenons or other joints or for any accurate work.

In order to assist in the movement of air through the less accessible parts of the ship and so reduce the conditions favourable for the spread of decay, holes were bored with an auger through some of the timbers and this process was termed 'snail creeping'. The Eleventh Report to the Commissioners contains the following extract from a letter from the Officers of Portsmouth Yard dated 23rd June 1791, regarding the condition of the timbers of the *Royal William* when she was broken up in 1757:

> . . . *the ends of the beams, the faying parts of the breast hooks, crotches, riders, knees, etc. etc. were gouged in a manner then practised, and which was called snail creeping by which means the air was conveyed to the several parts of the ship, which otherwise could not have received that advantage and which we apprehend was very useful to her preservation.* [40]

Other action which it was suggested should be taken to reduce the risk of decay in timber, was the provision of a roof or cover over a ship during its construction, in order to protect it from the weather. The procedure which was followed in Venetian dockyards was described in detail by John Strange who had been British Minister in Venice, but little if any action appears to have been taken as a result of his report. [41]

A ship's timber could be subject to attack from the outside of the hull as well as from the inside and the cause of the trouble was the shipworm or marine borer, *Teredo navalis.* By boring into the side of the ship this mollusc could cause extensive damage and at first all attempts to deal with it proved quite ineffective. However the problem was ultimately solved in the latter half of the eighteenth century, by covering the underwater portion of the hull with small copper sheets or plates, the procedure being known as 'sheathing'.

THE ADVENT OF THE IRON SHIP

When the first iron ships were built at the beginning of the nineteenth century, they were small and largely of an experimental nature and it was not until 1837 that one of them, the *Sirius,* proved to be commercially successful. A few years later when Brunel's *Great Britain* was launched at Bristol in 1843, she was not only the first major iron ship to be built but, at that time, was the biggest ship in the world.

Although HMS *Warrior,* which was the first iron ship in the Royal Navy, was built in 1860, the use of iron appears to have made comparatively little impact on naval construction despite the fact that with the increasing scarcity of suitable timber, iron provided a valuable alternative. As it was, nearly three quarters of a million pounds were spent in buying timber for the Navy in 1860 while the proposed expenditure for the following year amounted to almost one million. In the highest quarters, opinions were voiced to the effect that iron would never entirely supersede timber in ship construction but early in 1862 an event occurred which changed the whole situation, virtually overnight.

The year 1861 marked the outbreak of the American Civil War and early in 1862 a naval encounter occurred in Hampton Roads which lie between Newport News and Norfolk, Virginia near the mouth of the James River. It was a minor engagement in that only three ships were involved, the ironclad *Merrimac* and the wooden ships *Congress* and *Cumberland,* but it was a major event since it signalled the end of the long era of wooden ships in the Royal Navy. During this action the *Merrimac* sank both the *Congress* and the *Cumberland,* one blowing up and the other being rammed and sunk, the guns of the two wooden ships being quite ineffective against the armour of the *Merrimac.*

When the news reached England in March 1862 it was immediately realized that, unless the Navy was provided with ironclads, the Country's role as a great sea power was at an end. It is difficult to appreciate the widespread effect that this turn of events had on the machinery for providing the Royal Navy with timber. The future of those woodlands that had been planted with oak, specifically for the Navy, was called into question; the channels through which timber had been purchased were drastically curtailed; those who were concerned with the transport of timber to the dockyards soon realized that their services were no longer required, while many of the smaller shipbuilding yards found themselves in jeopardy.

The replacement of timber by iron, and subsequently steel, for the ships of the Royal Navy had a profound effect on forestry in this country during the latter half of the nineteenth century, and this is considered in Chapter 9.

THE OLD FORESTRY 8

Although the object of the medieval forests was to provide sport and not to produce timber, other than the occasional tree, the first milestone on the long road that was to lead to the forests of the twentieth century, was a statute of 1482.[1] This Act laid down that if a man owned a wood within the bounds of a forest, chase or purlieu he could, after felling it, enclose the area with 'sufficient hedges' to keep out cattle and other animals and maintain these hedges for seven years after felling. The purpose of this was to protect the young shoots which grew from the cut stumps until they had reached a size when they were no longer attractive to grazing animals. While the Act was doubtless intended to ensure that such woods provided cover and, later, browse for deer, it was nevertheless the first step which was taken to promote the growth of trees and underwood.

In 1543 the Act for the Preservation of Woods[2] was passed but, unlike the preceding one, its purpose was to safeguard future timber supplies. This was to be achieved by providing that, when an area was felled, 12 trees were to be left to the acre to grow on until they reached a specific size. Further information regarding the provisions of this Act is set out at some length in Chapter 6 in the section entitled 'The Corrective Measures'. This Statute, as amended by sections 18 and 19 of a later Act of 1570,[3] is of particular interest since it is not only concerned with timber production but also sets out the first system of woodland management recorded in this country. Enclosures which were made under this Act were known as 'encoppicements' but subsequently this term was often applied to any area of woodland which was enclosed after felling so as to protect the young growth or 'springs'.

In the sixteenth century there were two principal methods by which a crop of trees could be raised other than by natural regeneration: coppice and coppice-with-standards. The word 'coppice' is derived from the French *couper* meaning to cut and in the sixteenth and seventeenth centuries there were many variations of this term in use such as coppse, copys or coppis while other forms will be found in the Vocabulary of Old Forestry Terms in Appendix I. Coppice had developed over a great many years by the simple process of felling an area of woodland. If this was done in the winter, the 'stools' or stumps which had been cut produced young shoots during the following summer which, if protected from animals, would in the course of the next 12, 16 or 20 years or so, provide the succeeding crop. The length of time for which the coppice was grown before being cut depended mainly on the size of the produce that was required, since, other things being equal, the longer it was grown the larger it would be. Coppice growth was known as 'springs' and areas of coppice were often referred to as 'spring woods'. Evelyn recommended that the cutting of coppice areas should follow a definite plan so as to obtain a regular return and this is known in modern forestry as sustained yield.

> If copses were so divided as that every year there might be some fell'd, it were a continual and a present profit: seventeen years growth affords a tolerable fall, supposing the copse of seventeen acres, one acre might be yearly fell'd for ever; and so more according to proportion, but the seldom fall yields the more timber.[4]

Thus, more than 300 years ago, Evelyn established one of the basic principles of forest management.

Originally coppice was formed from whatever species had established themselves on a particular area and this depended largely on the soil and other site conditions. It is possible, at the present time, to form some idea of the variety of species of which the coppice of the middle ages was probably composed, by examining any woodland which has been cleared and then left to its own resources. Among the species growing on such an area may be found ash, birch, blackthorn, hawthorn, hazel, holly, field maple and oak and on more restricted sites alder, buckthorn, hornbeam and spindle. In some cases the oak was subjected to a form of pollarding which was carried out only two or three feet above ground level and this practice was still being carried out in areas of hornbeam coppice in Hertfordshire until about 1920.

Later the system of growing coppice was expanded so as to obtain two crops at the same time from one area. The first was gathered from the coppice itself while the second was obtained by allowing a limited number of trees to grow up among the coppice until they had reached timber size. Although the Act of 1543[5] laid down that 12 trees should be retained to the acre, Evelyn considered this number was the absolute minimum and he advised that 37 or 38 trees should be left which he subdivided as follows.

> As to what numbers you are to leave on every acre, the Statutes are our general guides, at least the legal. It is very ordinary copse which will not afford three or four Firsts, that is Bests; fourteen Seconds, twelve Thirds, eight Wavers according to which proportion the sizes of young trees in copsing are to succeed one another.[6]

In the Act, those trees that were to be retained were referred to as standils or storers but in course of time they became known, more generally, as standards although they enjoyed many local names of which some 20 will be found in Appendix I. Standards were normally restricted to oak but under the Act ash, aspen, beech and elm were acceptable if there were insufficient oak to make up the required number of 12 per acre.

The fact that it was felt necessary to pass this Act shows that there was a growing concern for the country's timber supplies and this anxiety was shared by private individuals as well as by the officers of the Crown. Standish writing in 1611 addressed himself to the King in the following terms:

> *We doe in all humblenesse complaine unto your Majesty of the general destruction and waste of wood, made within this your Kingdom more within twenty or thirty last yeares than in any hundred yeares before.*[7]

During the next year, Rocke Church who was the King's Surveyor expressed equal concern.

> *Then must there needs be some speedy means used for prevention of felling whole woods of timber, and grubbing up of copies at pleasure to convert them into pasture, arrable or meadow ground, else in short time, this waste and scarcitie will grow to a consummation of the whole.*[8]

New Thoughts on Raising Timber

As the supply of timber began to diminish and the demand to increase, so the need for more productive woodlands became apparent and consideration was given to ways of growing timber, other than that of coppice-with-standards. The first development in this direction was the sowing of acorns and mast in woods which was known as 'setting' or 'planting'. This method probably began in the latter part of the fifteenth century and Roger Taverner, in his survey of 1565, refers to the sowing or setting of acorns and beech mast in this way.

The old terms used in connection with the establishment of young trees can be somewhat confusing for while the verb 'to sett' acorns or young trees was to plant them, the noun 'setts' or 'sets' referred to cuttings and sometimes to seedling trees. Discussing hornbeam, Evelyn[9] remarked that it 'is planted of setts, though it may be raised from the seeds . . . but the more expeditious way is by setts'. However he later observed 'I do by no means approve of the vulgar praemature planting of sets as is us'd throughout England'. He also used the term 'setling' in connection with willows but this was presumably to describe a small set while the word 'pilcher' was occasionally used.[10]

Although it was claimed by some that the sowing of acorns in the woods was the most satisfactory way of raising a new crop, there were several practical difficulties, largely due to damage by birds and mice and the competition of excessive weed growth. In order to overcome these problems, the practice was evolved at the beginning of the seventeenth century whereby seeds were, instead, sown in a small piece of ground which could be kept weeded and in which damage by mice or birds could be eliminated or greatly reduced. The land that was used for this purpose was often part of a garden but it soon became known as a 'nursery' or 'seminary'. One of the earliest references to a nursery was made by Church in 1612 when he was describing the raising of young oak: 'And in this garden or nurserie thus made, you may, when they are grown to three foot high, remove of them how many you please.'[11] Nurseries continued to increase in importance during the seventeenth century and Evelyn devoted a complete chapter to 'The Seminary' in the second edition of *Sylva* in 1670.

Although mice were recognized as a serious obstacle when growing oak by direct sowing, there is little mention of the rabbit which in later years was to cause such extensive damage in English woodlands. Rabbits, which were then known as conies, were introduced into this country by the Normans[12] and during the Middle Ages they were present in sufficient numbers to justify them being recognized as one of the beasts of the warren. In the virtual absence of tree planting in the forests, any damage which they might cause was doubtless of little consequence. Even so it is recorded that in 1374 the parker of Earnwood near Kinlet, on the northern limits of Wyre Forest, paid six pence for a pottle of tar for painting trees so as to prevent, or at least discourage, rabbits from eating them. Almost 200 years later, Thomas Tusser[13] advised:

> *Sow acornes, ye owners that timber do love*
> *Sow hay and rie with them, the better to prove*
> *If cattle or coney may enter the crop*
> *Young oak is in danger of losing his top.*

It was not long before it was realized that nursery work needed special knowledge and skills, some of which are still practised today. Cook[14] describes in detail how to store ash keys in layers of sand, a process which is now known as 'stratification', while Evelyn advises on 'barrelling' acorns, mast, keys, nuts, haws and holly berries by placing them between layers of sand or earth in a barrel or tub. He also gives the following advice on the treatment of young seedlings after frost-lift: 'Your plants beginning now to peep should be earthed up and comforted a little; especially after breaking of the greater frosts and when the swelling mould is apt to spue them forth.'[15] Views were now being expressed on such matters as the preparation of the ground, the depth at which seeds should be sown and when young seedlings should be lifted.

Nurseries had originated through the need to protect the larger hardwood seeds such as acorns and beech mast but these enclosed plots were to prove equally valuable for raising the far smaller conifer seeds. However, conifers did not come into general use until new species had been introduced from abroad since the only native conifer of timber value was the Scots pine. At first such introductions were few and far between and they gained little momentum until the nineteenth century. The first conifers which were introduced into this country and which were subsequently recognized for the value of their timber, were Norway Spruce which is usually considered to have been brought into England in about 1548, the common silver fir *Abies alba* in 1603, the European larch in 1620 or thereabouts and the Corsican pine in 1759. However, towards the end of the seventeenth century conifers were already being recognized as having a commercial value and Evelyn discusses them at some length in a chapter entitled 'Of the Fir, Pine, Pinaster, Pitch-tree, etc'. In this he observes

> Abies, Pinus, Pinaster, Picea *etc are all of them easily rais'd of the Kernels and Nuts which may be gotten out of their cones and clogs, by exposing them a little before the fire or in warm water, till they begin to gape and are ready to deliver themselves of their numerous burthen.*[16]

This is probably the earliest instance of specific information on conifer seed extraction.

After raising young trees in nurseries, the next logical step was to plant them out in the woods or on the site of new woodlands. What is considered to be the first area in England to be planted with young trees, as opposed to being sown or dibbled with acorns, is Cranbourne Grove, in Windsor Forest. This was carried out between 1550 and 1560[17] but planting did not become common practice until the middle of the eighteenth century. Evelyn[18] refers to 'plantations' in 1670 but there is nothing to suggest that this was in respect of planted areas rather than those that had been sown, but in 1745, Ellis,[19] when discussing beech, explains how to 'obtain a wood by transplantation'. At the same time there was still a body of opinion which favoured the establishment of woodlands by means of direct sowing. Bradley,[20] in 1718, urged 'I would advise that every plantation of oaks be set from acorns on the very spot where they are to remain' and this view was shared by Langley[21] who, in 1740, stated 'I advise that you plant acorns etc in the places where they are designed to remain; for they not only produce the straightest timber, but much sooner than those that are checked by often transplanting.'

The removal of certain trees in a stand or plantation in order to improve the growth and vigour of the remainder, which is now termed 'thinning', was originally known as 'weeding' and this word is used, in that sense, in the Act of 1543.[22] Rather more than a hundred years later, Silvanus Taylor[23] employed the word 'garble' to describe thinning and this is defined in *The Shorter Oxford English Dictionary*[24] as 'to select out the best' or 'to make selections from with a purpose' both of which definitions very aptly describe the operation of thinning.

Reference has already been made to those rudiments of forest management that were contained in the Act for the Preservation of Woods[25] and to those suggestions that were put forward by Evelyn on the subject of sustained yields for coppice.[26] There is, however, little evidence that any practical steps were taken in the management of woodland areas and, in retrospect, one can appreciate the reason for this. In the first place there was little knowledge of the subject, largely due to the fact that there had never been any need for it. Second, that as far as the royal forests were concerned, there were so many rights, restrictions and privileges in or over them which had become established over a long period of time, that any attempt at effective management was seriously prejudiced. Third that since private woodlands were so fragmented, any overall plan of management was faced with major difficulties and last, it is doubtful if those concerned had any clear idea as to what the objects of management should be.

However in 1607 James I, who took a great interest in the country's woodlands, set up a Commission with the following terms of reference.[27]

> *These things are to be considered in the execution of the Commission by the Commissioners and the Jury that is to say — A Survey of the number of coppice woods; how many acres each coppice containeth; of how many years' growth the same is; what every coppice is worth by the acre; in whose possession the same is; if granted to any person, then for what term and upon what consideration; whether the trees and the standels be preserved in every coppice according to the Statute; and what waste and spoil hath been made in the same coppices or any of them and by whom . . . To consider how many acres of coppice woods will be necessarily reserved for the fencing and enclosing of new woods to be raised that the number of the trees sold may be trebled by that planting and whether the aldermores, lops of thorns, and such like underwoods will be sufficient for continuing the enclosure.*

A year later, in 1608, the King initiated a survey of the timber that was growing in the royal forests and at the same time gave orders for the preparation and sowing of land for new woodland areas. Proposals were also drawn up for establishing an additional 51,000 acres of coppice over a period of 15 years or 3,400 acres a year.[28] Further evidence of the King's interest in the country's timber resources may be found in a small book by Arthur Standish which appeared in 1615, entitled *New Directions of Experience for the Increasing of Timber and Firewood,*[29] the title page of which describes it as: 'authorised by the King's most excellent Majesty, as may appeare for the increasing of timber and firewood with the least waste and losse of ground'.

Charles I did not display the same interest in the royal forests as his predecessor had shown except to regard them as a means of raising revenue. His attempts to reimpose the bounds and limits of the medieval forests and to restore the system of fines, amercements and impositions led to the passing, in 1640, of what is sometimes referred to as the Act of Limitations of Forests.[30]

As the country began to settle down again after the Restoration, steps were taken to deal with the problem of damage to trees and woodlands which had seriously increased during the period of the Commonwealth. Consequently, in 1663, legislation was passed for dealing with 'unlawful cutting or stealing or spoiling of wood' and with 'destroyers of young timber-trees'.[31]

In 1666 the gradual movement towards some form of elementary forest management was given an added impetus by a survey which was carried out in the Forest of Dean. A year later this was followed by an Act which was largely concerned with inclosures, rights of common and the felling of timber within the forest.[32] Some 30 years on similar action was taken in respect of the New Forest[33] while, in 1705, a further survey was made of that forest and, in due course, a rudimentary plan of management was drawn up. During the first year of the reign of George I, legislation was passed with a view to encouraging the planting of trees for timber, shelter, ornament or fruit and also to deal with the problem of woods which might be set on fire maliciously.[34] Other statutes relating to the cultivation and protection of trees were enacted in 1763, 1766, 1769 and 1773, the titles of which will be found in Appendix II.

THE ENTHUSIASM FOR PLANTING

The second half of the eighteenth century was marked by a new interest in planting and by the emergence of new thoughts and ideas on growing timber. This was due to three main factors, the first of which was the enclosure of large areas of land under the numerous Enclosure Acts, and some idea of the extent of this can be gathered from the following figures.[35]

1700-1760	237,845 acres
1761-1801	2,428,721 acres
1802-1844	1,610,302 acres
1845 and after	187,321 acres
	4,464,189 acres

While these enclosures incorporated the existing woodlands there were other areas which, on account of their shape, size, soil or site conditions, were clearly more suitable for planting as woods or spinneys, than for agriculture. Common land was also included by the passing of an Act[36] in 1756 which provided for the enclosure of commons in order to plant trees on them, subject to the mutual consent of the parties concerned. In some cases provision was made for breaks, belts or shaws so as to protect exposed buildings or fields or to mark the boundary of a farm or estate and it was largely through these enclosures that the English woodland became such an integral part of the English countryside.

Although, in the initial stages, enclosures were often the cause of felling large numbers of trees to provide material for new fences or to straighten boundaries, in course of time the resulting hedges or banks were instrumental in supplying timber. Acorns dropped by birds or animals, ash keys carried by the wind and elm suckers spreading along the length of the hedge, supplemented by planting by far-sighted owners, in course of time provided vast numbers of hedgerow trees which subsequently provided a valuable source of timber.

The second factor which acted as an incentive to planting was the undiminishing demand for timber by the Royal Navy, the Merchant Navy and the country as a whole, the population of which was growing steadily larger. The third factor was the increase in wealth especially among landowners who were prepared to spend considerable sums of money on their estates. Evelyn's influence was still very apparent and it received a fresh impetus with the publication of Dr Hunter's annotated edition in 1776. The fact that of those books that were solely concerned with woodlands and timber-growing, seven were published between 1700 and 1750, and no less than twenty between 1751 and 1799, is some indication of the increasing attention that was being paid to these matters.

This new interest in planting was greatly encouraged by The Society of Arts (now The Royal Society of Arts) which was founded in 1754. In 1758, in order to encourage landowners, the Society offered medals and other awards for the successful establishment of young plantations of exceptional merit. Fortunately, details of the plantations for which awards were made have been recorded and these provide a great deal of information as to the acreages planted, the spacing of the plants, the species used and the location of the planting site.

One of the first silver medals was awarded to Mr M. Lee of Ebford, near Exeter, who, in 1761, had planted an area of Weymouth pine (*Pinus strobus*), a species which had first been grown in this country at Badminton in 1705. In 1764 Mr R. Fenwick of Edlingham in Northumberland planted 102,000 Scots pine and when, two years later, he put in a further 100,000 two-year-old trees at a planting distance of 'two to five feet', he was awarded a gold medal by the Society. In addition to oak, the hardwood species that were also being planted included alder, plane, elm and Lombardy poplar but the largest areas were devoted to conifers.

In 1808 Dr Bain planted 5,146 Maritime pine (*Pinus pinaster*) in Dorset while Mr Congreve of Aldermaston planted 684,560 larch from 1808 to 1811 in addition to 73 acres which he planted with acorns during the same period.

At first he used one-year seedlings which had been raised in Scotland and had cost five shillings per thousand but he found that during the long journey from the North many had become heated. Subsequently he lined out the seedlings in his nursery for a year before planting them out and observed that this 'is the plan I always mean to adopt in future'. He was awarded two gold medals, one for his larch and the other for his oak. In 1810, Mr Cowlishaw received a silver medal for planting 75,000 larch on 14¾ acres in Nottinghamshire. Assuming that they were evenly distributed over the area, this represents 5,153 trees to the acre and if 'planted on the square', they would have been spaced at about 3 feet apart.

In Durham, the three Mr Backhouses — William, Jonathan and Edward — each achieved remarkable results on their respective estates. During 1809-10, William planted 300,000 larch and 50,000 other species on 131 acres which, if regularly distributed and square planted, would have been spaced at about 4 feet apart. In 1812, Jonathan planted 271,000 larch mixed with oak, spruce and Scots pine at a spacing of 5 feet by 3 feet with 2,500 larch and 400 oak, spruce and pine per acre. He was an advocate of ploughing 'peat earth' before planting on it as this broke up the ground and helped to drain it. In the following year, Edward reached the peak by planting 363,000 larch on 197 acres which with even distribution and square planting, would have been spaced at about 5 feet by 5 feet. For these outstanding achievements, William and Edward were awarded gold medals and Jonathan a silver one.

On the Duke of Devonshire's estate in Inglewood Forest, Cumberland, no less than 1,981,065 trees were planted on 550 acres of waste land in 1820. The species comprised one million larch, half a million Scots pine with the remainder being made up of some 13 different species. Not surprisingly, His Grace was duly awarded a gold medal. As regards hardwoods, Sir William Templar Pole of Axminster, Devon, planted 98 bushels of acorns in his nursery in 1821 while in Shropshire, Mr Wilkinson dibbled 240 bushels of acorn on 260 acres with the acorns 2½ to 3 feet apart; both received gold medals.[37]

Other evidence of the considerable interest that some landowners took in their woodlands during the second half of the eighteenth century may be found in the records which were kept by some estates. Two examples of these are the books that were in use on the Duke of Bedford's Estate near Tavistock, Devon, and on the Gunby Hall Estate near Spilsby in Lincolnshire.

The Tavistock book which was compiled in 1758 contains a coloured plan of each wood on the estate drawn to a scale of 2½ chains to an inch followed by details of sales which took place over the succeeding years. A schedule of all the estate woodlands is provided and this gives the following particulars for each wood: the name; the acreage 'according to ye old survey'; the acreage by a new survey stated in both 'customary' and 'statute' measure; the difference between these measures and the number of years growth in 1753. The

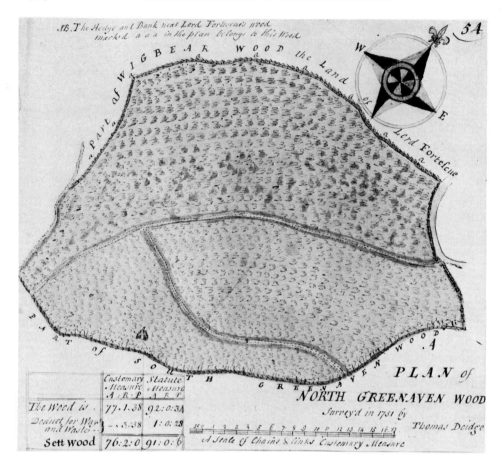

	Customary Statute Measure Measure A . R . P . A . B . P .		
The Wood is .	77.1.38	92:0:34	
Deduct for War and Waste . .	— .3.38	1:0:28	
Sett wood	76.2.0	91:0:6	

PLAN of
NORTH GREENAVEN WOOD
Survey'd in 1751 by
Thomas Deidge
A Scale of Chains & links Customary Measure

11. *This map of North Greenaven Wood is reproduced from the Bedford Estates Woods Book containing plans and descriptions of the woods which belonged to the Duke of Bedford in Devon. Although the book is dated 1758, the maps which it contains were drawn at various times prior to that date. North Greenaven Wood lay four miles west of Tavistock.*

following summary of information relating to Maddacleave Wood is an example of a typical entry in the book. After stating that the wood lies about 4 miles west of Tavistock it is recorded that it was sold on 10th October 1695 by Martyn Ryder to Henry Williams and Henry Ham of Beer Ferris for £10 per acre. It was calculated that the wood extended to 58 acres but one acre was reserved for timber and 3 acres had been burnt so that the total amount received was £540: two years were allowed for felling. Other entries providing comparable information are given for the years 1713, 1741, 1758, 1782, 1799 and 1803. References to leaving 'the old standills and fifteen new ones for every acre' show that Maddacleave Wood was composed of coppice-with-standards. The fact that the underwood was sold by someone who was not apparently connected with the estate suggests that the individual woods were let on lease by the estate to lessees who then sold the underwood as and when it was fit to cut. The variations in dates is due in some cases to different sections of the wood being sold at varying times.

Another example of recording the history of planting on an estate is provided by the *Gunby Hall Tree Book* which contains details of the trees and plantations on the Gunby Estate which is situated some 4 miles from Spilsby in east Lincolnshire. This property belonged to the Massingberd family for several hundred years until it passed to the National Trust in 1944. Although the book dates from about 1765, it contains information relating to trees and woodlands which had been planted as early as 1661. The particulars include the species, the numbers planted, the date of planting and other relevant facts which were judged worthy of inclusion. One member of the family, Peregrine Massingberd, who was an artist of some merit, took a special interest in the estate and its trees and in the early years of the nineteenth century included a number of delightful studies of trees in the book. Some idea of the extent of the work which was undertaken can be gained from the fact that 26,000 trees were planted in 1808; 83,416 in 1809 and 45,375 in 1810 while the total number of trees planted between 1804 and 1824 amounted to 402,323. The species grown were ash, oak, sweet chestnut, walnut, spruce, larch and Scots pine although the conifers were used mainly as nurses for the ash. In addition to planting and replanting woodland areas, large numbers of oak, sweet chestnut and Scots pine were established in the hedgerows.[38]

THE UNFOLDING PATTERN

It could be said that neither these records nor the awards by the Society of Arts, reflect the position on the ordinary estate and that these results were only achieved by exceptionally keen and dedicated landowners and this may well be true. Fortunately, however, other information exists which provides a general picture of the various activities relating to woodlands throughout the country at the turn of the eighteenth century. Shortly after the Board of Agriculture had been set up in 1793, it was decided to carry out surveys of the agriculture and farming operations that were practised in each country throughout the Kingdom. Most of the reports which arose out of these surveys were published before 1796 but these were in the nature of an introduction and were later considerably enlarged in the second edition by accounts contributed by local observers and landowners. The title of each report began with the words *General View of the Agriculture of the County of . . .* and every volume contained a chapter on woodlands which was generally headed 'Woods and Plantations'. The amount of space that was devoted to such matters varied considerably and presumably depended on the writer's interest in the subject. Vancouver's report on Devon[39] includes a chapter which extends to 26 pages and is divided into four sections, entitled respectively, 'Copse Woods', 'Beech and Other Woods', 'Plantations' and 'Timber'. In some reports the subject receives considerably less space and attention.

In 1808 the first of five reviews or summaries of the county reports written by William Marshall was published and covered the 'Northern Department of England'[40] and this was followed during the next 10 years by similar summaries for the Western,[41] Eastern,[42] Midland[43] and Southern and Peninsular[44] Departments. These summaries provide a valuable insight into the management of the woodlands on English estates at the beginning of the nineteenth century.

During this period, coppice, whether grown by itself or under oak, ash or other standards, formed the commonest woodland crop although an increasing number of young plantations were being established. Numerous species were accepted as coppice and in addition to ash, oak, birch, hazel and alder, mention is made of willow (often referred to as sally), mountain ash, wild cherry, beech, hornbeam, maple, whitethorn and blackthorn. The most frequently grown were ash, hazel, oak, birch, alder and willow, in that order, while the length of the rotations were usually from 10 to 15 years. However, in some counties, rotations of less than 10 years were adopted but these were practised in order to supply material for special markets such as 3-4 years for corfe rods in Northumberland, 6 years for crate rods in Staffordshire and 6-9 years for hurdles in Hampshire and Dorset. At the same time, when bigger produce was required, the rotation was lengthened and in Shropshire where 'large quantities of oak poles are used for different purposes in the coal-pits; as they are required to have some strength, they are seldom fallen before 24 years growth', while 'near Bewdley, in Worcestershire, is a large tract of underwood fallen at 18 to 21 years growth, for converting into charcoal for making bar-iron'.[45]

As regards hedgerow timber, this was described in Herefordshire as 'most plentifully dispersed over most of the district. The elm is the most general'. In Worcestershire 'the hedgerows are everywhere crowded with elm and . . . they often produce timber of considerable dimensions' but there were also 'as fine oak and ash as the kingdom produces'. Of Cheshire, it was said that 'the number of trees in the hedgerows and coppices is so considerable that, from some points of view, the whole county has the appearance of an extensive forest'.[46] It is clear that in some parts of England the enclosures were now making a substantial contribution to the supply of timber but this was not the case everywhere. In Nottinghamshire the neglect of landowners in failing to raise timber trees in hedgerows is severely criticized.

It is to be lamented, that in the new inclosures very little attention should have been paid to raising hedge-row timber, which is done at

first with no more expence of fencing than the raising of the quick.
Whole tracts of country may be seen without a single tree growing up
for farming use.[47]

Of Dorset it was remarked that 'this county is extremely barren, both in timber and wood'[48] while Warwickshire was described as 'the county that should be a pattern to others'. Of the Cotswolds it was said that 'the country is almost naked (of trees) and straw an article of fuel'.

Although at the beginning of the nineteenth century English woodlands consisted largely of coppice, the practice of planting instead of coppicing was gaining ground in many districts. Apart from the awards that had been made by the Society of Arts, evidence of this can be found in the reports for two widely separated counties. In Northumberland it was said that 'plantations on an extensive scale are rising in every part of the county' while in Shropshire it was remarked that 'there are many modern plantations of various sorts of firs and pines'. However there was still a considerable difference of opinion as to whether seeds, more particularly acorns, should be sown direct on the planting area or whether they should be sown in nurseries and the young trees subsequently planted out. There were two basic methods of sowing acorns; the first which was applicable to unplanted land consisted of sowing them with, or shortly after, a cereal crop which was usually wheat and the second was by dibbling and was normally used when replanting old woodland. On Lord Bagot's estate in Staffordshire both direct sowing and the planting out of young trees were practised as the reporter describes.

> *The young plantations are made sometimes by sowing acorns with*
> *wheat, after summer-fallow, and sometimes by planting out young*
> *plants of oak and other wood; in which case, at the end of one or two*
> *years, when such plants have taken well to the ground, they are cut*
> *off at the surface and the second shoot trusted for the tree; this*
> *second shoot thriving with much more luxuriance and vigour than*
> *the first, checked by transplanting. Also after cutting down a wood,*
> *the replanting is sometimes effected by striking in with the pick-axe a*
> *sufficient number of acorns and other seeds of forest trees or*
> *underwood; and all the methods have been attended with success.*[49]

In Surrey a somewhat different procedure was followed by 'some of the most experienced and successful woodmen of the weald'.

> *The field in which it is intended to sow the acorns, is completely*
> *summer-fallowed and during this operation it is thoroughly cleaned*
> *of all root-weeds, and has a good dressing of manure and sometimes*
> *of lime given it. At the last ploughing it is ridged up so as to keep it as*
> *dry as possible during the winter. Wheat is then sown in it at the*
> *usual season and after the wheat is well harrowed in, acorns are put*

in with a dibble, at about one foot distant from each other. When the
wheat is reaped the ensuing autumn, the seedling oaks are not
sufficiently high to be cut or injured by the sickle; the stubble serves
as a kind of protection to them during the winter. Sowing the acorns
at the same time the wheat is sown and harrowing them in together,
is much preferable to dibbling them in; especially on a tough retentive
soil such as the oak delights in. The holes formed by the dibbles are
liable to hold water and thereby to rot the acorns which can scarcely
be deposited too loosely and shallow in the ground.[50]

The procedure for dibbling acorns and the subsequent treatment of the crop, as practised in the Forest of Dean at the end of the eighteenth century, was as follows.

The usual time of planting acorns in the Forest is as soon after
Christmas as the weather will permit. This practice is founded on the
idea that they are likely to be eaten by mice and other vermin, if
planted before; but an intelligent planter belonging to the Forest is of
the opinion that autumn planting is best, because at that time there is
sufficient food for these animals and more easily obtained; and that
in spring, after the acorns have lain in the ground for the winter, they
become sour and unpalatable.

The method of planting is, first, to mark out the ground; then
taking off about a foot square of turf, to set two or three acorns with a
setting-pin; afterwards to invert the turf upon them and, by way of
raising a fence against hares and rabbits, to plant two or three strong
whitethorn sets round. They are seldom thinned till they have attained
the size of hop-poles and then are left at twelve feet distance from
each other, with the view of again thinning them by taking out every
other one, when they are thirty years old, and have attained the size
of five or six inches diameter. By growing thick, no side-shoots are
thrown out, which supersedes the necessity of pruning.

The young trees which are drawn at the first thinning are
transplanted and, as it is thought, grow equally well with those that
have not been removed and produce timber as full at the heart,
compact, strong and durable as that which is raised immediately
from the acorn.[51]

Despite the continuing demand for oak in the shipyards, other species were now being grown in the new 'plantations' that were being established, but lack of experience rendered the choice of species somewhat haphazard. In Westmoreland the Bishop of Llandaff, Dr Richard Watson, planted more than 100 acres of 'high ground' near Ambleside with oak, ash, elm, beech, sycamore, Scots pine and larch but after 7 years, although the hardwoods were 'alive but stunted' they 'did not promise well'. On the other hand, the two conifers, especially the larch, were thriving as well as the Bishop could wish. On the Howardian Hills in the North Riding it was reported that 'the plantations . . .

have a pretty large mixture of firs and other trees' but that 'the larch grew particularly well'. In Northumberland, larch was described as being 'pre-eminent', far outstripping 'many species of firs and pines'.[52] Its rate of growth and its ability to succeed where other species failed, soon made larch a popular choice and it was planted in many parts of the country; its prestige continued for the next hundred years.

As the new plantations grew in number, so the demand for young trees increased and this in turn encouraged the formation of nurseries: 'There are two or three considerable nursery-gardens in this Riding that raise large quantities of forest-trees and shrubs for the supply of the public, the proprietors of which contract to plant on an extensive scale and at reasonable prices.'[53] This is probably one of the first references to contract planting. On a Yorkshire estate the following method of raising larch transplants was practised.

> *The beds on which the seeds are to be sown are dug in the spring and the larch cones laid upon their surface; these the sun and wind drying, cause them to open and shed a considerable part of their seed and the cones are afterwards beaten to get out the remainder; they are then covered very slightly with earth and kept weeded. At first, great care is necessary to keep the birds from them, otherwise they will pick off the seed from the head of the plants just peeping above ground.*
>
> *The plants are pricked out at one year old and . . . it (is) best to transplant them a second time and finally plant them out at four years old though those which have been only once removed, answer to be planted out at three or four years old, but the roots are not so good as those which have been twice transplanted.*[54]

The Report of 1811 contains extracts from correspondence between Sir Cecil Wray of Summer Castle, Lincolnshire, and the reporter. He was undoubtedly a very shrewd and observant landowner and some of the opinions on woodland management which he expressed almost 170 years ago are still sound today.

> *As regards general observations, gentlemen differ so much respecting their modes of planting and management of trees, that I can only give you my opinion. First, that I would always plant each species of trees by itself — at least I would never plant Scotch firs intermixed with others on the idea that they are good nurses: . . . the Scotch fir soon becomes from its spreading branches, a bad neighbour. Gentlemen say they would weed them out but they never do it in time to prevent the mischief. Second, that I would never plant a tree older than two year seedlings. Third, that I would never put so many on an acre as the nurserymen persuade us to do: 2,000 the very utmost; 1,200 full sufficient. Fourth, that I would always trim off the side branches, . . . I know this article is much controverted.*

His views on the advantages of Scots pine are also of interest.

> *Having rather spoken against Scotch fir, give me leave to say a word*
> *in their favour. First, they grow fast and the wood is of sufficient use*
> *for farm houses, etc. Second, the poor people supply themselves with*
> *very good fuel by gathering the fir-apples and rotten wood; you will*
> *sometimes see twenty children in my plantations appleing as they*
> *call it. Third, the green boughs keep deer completely well in winter*
> *and save much hay if given to sheep, particularly in snows: I have*
> *sometimes 3 or 400 sheep grazing on them at once. Fourth, the*
> *boughs are of great use in ovens, firewood, fencings, etc.*[55]

In addition to this enthusiasm for planting, a new interest in silviculture and woodland management was beginning to emerge. Coppice was now being grown on fixed rotations instead of being cut at random, with the area divided into falls of equal size. Since the number of falls corresponded to the number of years in the rotation, the same acreage was cut each year and this was the principle of sustained yield. The need to maintain a good growing stock of stools or springs was now being recognized and this was carried out by layering or planting. In Berkshire, woodmen were allowed to grub out old unproductive stools for firewood, provided that they planted a new set and replaced it with another, if it failed. The importance of providing drains in woodlands was now being realized and it was noted that 'much benefit would arise by making open grips to carry off the water which should be opened every third year at furthest'.

The economic value of natural regeneration in beech stands was not overlooked and in Buckinghamshire it was noted that 'these woods require but little attention as the old trees shed a sufficient quantity of seed to keep the wood constantly full of young plants'. The beechwoods on the Cotswold escarpment 'reproduce themselves from seeds self-sown' and 'they generally come up so thick as to require to be constantly drawn [i.e. thinned] for the first twenty or thirty years'. In Berkshire it was recorded that 'the beech woods in this county are exceedingly well managed'.

Further thought was also given to the economic aspects of timber production and especially to the question as to whether it was more profitable to fell oak at 50 to 60 years or to retain it until it was 80 or 100 years old, when it would be fit for the Navy. Dr Watson, who was both a woodland owner and Bishop of Llandaff, made the following observation:

> *If profit is considered, every tree of every kind ought to be cut down*
> *and sold when the annual increase in value of the tree, by its growth,*
> *is less than the annual interest of the money it would sell for.*

To which, Marshall added 'together with the annual value of the land it grows upon'. The Bishop went on to say:

> . . . particular soils or the greater or less thriving condition of the wood, may render it useful to cut down trees before they are worth 30s. or to let them stand a while longer. It ought to be remarked also that large trees sell for more per foot than small ones do, yet the usual increase of price is not a compensation to the proprietor for letting his timber stand to a great age.[56]

The reluctance of woodland owners to sell their oak to the Navy was attributed to the low prices which the shipyards offered for naval timber, after taking into account the length of time that an owner had to wait until his trees reached the required size. Although the naval dockyards had increased their price for oak by 7¼ per cent in order to compensate owners for the loss of bark on winter-felled oak (which would have commanded a good return from the tanneries in the spring), this increase was soon overtaken by a rise in the price of bark.[57] One proposal for overcoming the shortage of timber for the Navy was to grant tax exemption to owners who planted oak, although there was no provision that the oak should ultimately be sold to the Navy.

> If for one or more acres covered with a given number of thriving oak plants, the owner was to be exempted from the operation of certain taxes; if, for instance his house was to be exempted from window tax or he was to be allowed . . . some gratification and exemption equal to the good he did his country, new forests would soon spread themselves over the Kingdom and become a security for its future safety and prosperity.[58]

THE PLIGHT OF THE ROYAL FORESTS

While many woodlands in private ownership were now showing signs of improvement and prosperity, unfortunately the same could not be said of the woods and forests belonging to the Crown. It was remarked, that as regards

> the state of these forests and chaces compared with those woods which are private property . . . the difference is obvious to the most cursory observer. In the one, a young thriving oak-tree is scarcely to be seen, whereas in the other, a regular succession appears in every quarter. The miserable state of the Royal Forests does not originate from any want of public spirit in those who have at present the charge of them, but necessarily arises from the errors of an ancient system which had in view more the preservation of deer than timber; and consequently sacrificed the preservation of the latter for the purpose of securing food for the former.[59]

12. *An epitome of the New Forest. This illustration which appeared in 1811 in a book on the Forest by Percival Lewis, shows four of its facets. The shield and arms indicate that it is a Royal Forest; timber production is shown by the timber feller with his axe and the felled trees; hunting is implied by the deer and two hounds while ship building is represented by the ship under construction.*

There were several reasons for this state of affairs. These included a lack of ability among those responsible for the management of the forests; the unsatisfactory system of remuneration of those employed in them which encouraged dishonesty; the damage caused by deer and the effect of commoners exercising their rights in respect of underwood, timber, grazing and so on. Some idea of the damage which could be caused by deer and cattle can be gained from the following account of the position in Northamptonshire.

> *The depredations and ravages committed by the deer and cattle upon the young sprigs and coppices at so early an age, not only prevent even the smallest possibility of obtaining a regular succession of oak timber but cause a daily diminuation in the growth of the underwood. The injury sustained by the deer being admitted into the young spring wood in the first instance is very considerable, but that injury is small indeed when compared to the destructive havock made by the devouring jaws of a herd of hungry cattle, admitted into the young coppice just as the leaves have begun to appear . . . All the townships using a commonage in these woods . . . are in an open field state and . . . in consequence of the inability of the occupier of an open field farm to procure a sufficiency of food for their support in the winter season [the cattle] are reduced to an extreme state of leaness and poverty at the time they are turned into the woods, when whole herds of them rush forward like a torrent and everything that is vegetable and within their reach, inevitably falls a sacrifice to their voracious and devouring appetite.[60]*

Although these critical observations were made in 1815, the state of the Crown forests had been a matter for concern for over 200 years. Eventually, in 1786, legislation[61] was passed under which Commissioners were appointed to enquire into the state and condition of the Crown woods and forests. Their First Report dated 25th January 1787, consisted of schedules of the properties that were held on lease from the Crown and this was followed in June of the same year by a Report dealing with the rents payable to the Crown. The Third Report which appeared in 1788, was concerned with the Forest of Dean while the Fourth Report, which extended to only three pages, contained further observations on rents. The Fifth Report together with the succeeding five, dealt respectively with the New Forest, Alice Holt and Woolmer Forests and the Forests of Salcey, Whittlewood, Rockingham and Whichwood. The Eleventh Report was confined to the subject of timber for the Navy and the Twelfth, with the Crown Estates in general and includes comparatively few references to the woods and forests. The Thirteenth, Fourteenth and Fifteenth Reports which were issued between 1792 and 1793 cover the Forests of Bere, Sherwood and Waltham respectively. The Sixteenth Report contains further information on rents while the Seventeenth Report describes the management and administration of the forests.

At this time the Crown Forests were under the supervision of the Surveyor-General of Woods who was assisted by two deputy-surveyors in London and one itinerant deputy. In addition there were six other surveyors who were

HERTFORDSHIRE.

Capital Oak Timber.

A

CATALOGUE

OF

1,538

OAK, ASH, AND ABELE OR POPLAR TREES,

MANY OF

LARGE DIMENSIONS, AND OF THE BEST QUALITY,

WITH THE

LOP, TOP, AND BARK,

WELL ADAPTED FOR THE

NAVY, MILLS, AND OTHER LARGE WORKS,

NOW GROWING

ON SEVERAL WOODS AND A FARM,

AT,

HARMER GREEN,

IN THE

PARISHES OF WELWYN AND DIGSWELL,

IN THE

COUNTY OF HERTFORD,

WHICH WILL BE

Sold by Auction,

On THURSDAY the 17th Day of APRIL, 1817, at TWELVE O'CLOCK,

AT THE WHITE HART INN AT WELWYN,

IN LOTS..

The Tenant of the Farm, and Wm. GIDDONS the Woodman, will shew the
Timber

13.   *The cover of a catalogue for a timber sale held in 1817.*

responsible respectively for six forests or groups of forests, namely: the Dean Forest, the New Forest, Alice Holt with Woolmer and Bere, Whittlewood with Salcey, Sherwood Forest and Waltham Forest. The management of Whichwood Forest was entrusted to assistants since there was no resident deputy for the Forest. The Surveyor-General received a net salary of £66.18s per year together with allowances of £638.15s which included 'riding charges' of £313. This figure was supplemented by fees and perquisites which included 5 per cent charges on all Navy timber, woodsales and expenditure on works and salaries, 'chip money' of two shillings per tree for all Navy timber felled in the New Forest and three pence per cord for all cord wood in the Forest of Dean. The itinerant deputy received a salary of £300 per annum, the two deputies in London £100 each and the remainder, amounts varying from £50 to £20 a year except in the case of Waltham Forest where the deputy was unpaid. These salaries were supplemented by various allowances and perequisites such as firewood and payment for marking trees to be felled at the rate of 4d to 6d per tree.[62] It is obvious that such a system would inevitably lead to dishonesty and encourage exploitation of the forests. However, this was not all, since fraudulence was accompanied by an absence of both professional knowledge and competent management.

> *But it is not by profusion in felling the timber or in the execution of works done in the forests, that the property of the Crown has alone been injured: the total want of any uniform plan of management and care of trees, while growing has perhaps been still more destructive in its effects. In our Report on New Forest, we observed that the extensive inclosures planted there in the beginning of this century, were, from the neglect of thinning them while young, become filled with trees which though of a great height contain very little timber; and it is to be feared will never be of much use to the Navy. And in the same manner . . . in the Forest of Whittlewood . . . the trees are left to grow as accident directs, no care having been taken to plant in vacant places or to thin out the trees where they stand too near each other.[63]*

Subsequently, in 1810,[64] the management of the Forests and Land Revenues of the Crown was transferred to the Commissioners of Woods and Forests and this arrangement continued until 1923 when the Forestry Commission accepted responsibility.

In their Eleventh Report, the Commissioners calculated that it would require 100,000 acres of productive woodland in order to provide the Royal Navy with a regular supply of timber every year. This was based on the assumption that 1,000 acres of oak, 100 years old, would constitute one year's supply. The total area of land on which the timber belonged to the Crown amounted to approximately 115,000 acres and was situated in the New Forest, the Dean, Alice Holt, Woolmer, Salcey, Whittlewood, Whichwood, Waltham, Sherwood, Bere and Sulehay Walk in Rockingham Forest. The

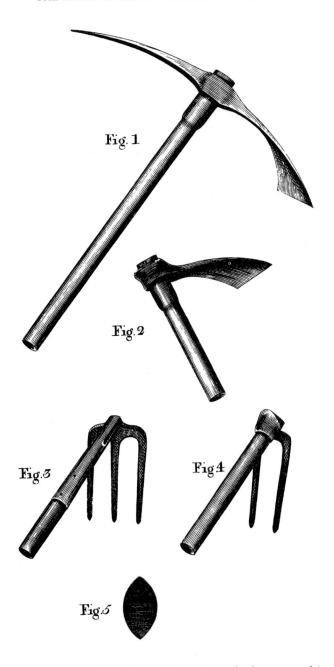

14.   *Tree planting tools in 1809. This illustration which appeared in*
The Profitable Planter
*by W. Pontey shows the following tools. Fig. 1, a planting mattock; fig. 2, a
planting hoe; figs. 3 and 4, hoes with tines or prongs for use on stony ground or
on heavy soils while fig. 5 shows a section through one of the tines of the hoe in
fig. 3.*

Commissioners considered that of this area, 60-70,000 acres would be suitable for growing oak and action to make better use of this land was accordingly recommended.[65]

Consequently a policy of disafforestation, followed by inclosure and planting was adopted from 1809 onwards. In this context disafforestation referred to the release of areas from forest law and the termination of the rights claimed under such law. On disafforestation, allotments of land within the forest were made to the Sovereign and to others who could substantiate their claims. This process enabled the Crown to carry out the inclosure and planting of the land which had been allotted to it. However, there was still a difference of some 30-40,000 acres between the 100,000 that were needed and the 60-70,000 acres which would be available after disafforestation. It was accordingly proposed to make up this deficiency by planting forest land in the Duchy of Lancaster, by utilizing wastes on Crown lands and in the Duchies of Cornwall and Lancaster, by acquiring land and by resuming possession of Crown lands which were let on lease.[66]

By 1823 this policy had begun to achieve some results and the Commissioners reported that the area of young plantations in the Royal Forests now extended to some 51,627 acres. It was also estimated that an additional 11,000 acres could be made available in the New Forest and the Forest of Dean by throwing open existing inclosures, in which the trees were no longer liable to damage by animals, and then enclosing unplanted areas of equal size. Despite this the extent of the land which became available for planting, failed to reach the figure of 100,000 acres. This was partly due to the fact that the funds allocated for the purchase of additional land had been exhausted and consequently little was acquired after 1823 although planting continued unabated on land that was available.[67]

In 1819 or thereabouts the practice of planting Scots pine as a nurse for oak was adopted and in some cases the pine was planted one or two years before the oak. This method of raising oak proved to be very satisfactory but it was essential to remove the Scots pine before it began to suppress the oak.

THE CURTAIN FALLS

As the nineteenth century gained momentum so the old forestry imperceptibly moved to its close, though few of those who were concerned appeared to be aware of it. The fact that the Commissioners had just put forward proposals to ensure supplies of oak for the Navy for the next hundred years, did not suggest that they entertained any doubts as to the future demands for oak by the shipyards. On the other hand, woodland owners were showing an increasing interest in growing conifers for timber and in the raising, planting and tending of forest trees, and this interest was reflected in the publication, between 1800 and 1850, of some 26 books that dealt with such matters. Unfortunately, the value of some of these was diminished by the fact that the authors tended to regard their books mainly as a vehicle for putting forward their own views and theories which, not infrequently, other authors vehemently denounced. Of these books, *The Forester* written by James Brown in 1847, was one of the best and those by William Withers, published between 1826 and 1829, the most cantankerous.

The year 1827 marked the first of a series of events which, collectively, were to have a major effect on forestry in Britain during the twentieth century. This was the introduction of conifers from Western North America which began with the Douglas fir and was followed in 1831 by the Sitka spruce and the Giant silver fir. These three species were introduced by David Douglas, and have since proved to be of very great importance in British forestry. Other conifers which were introduced from North America during this period and which have been planted extensively in English woodlands are the Western hemlock introduced in 1851, the Western red cedar in 1853, the Lodgepole pine in 1853-54 and the Lawson cypress in 1854.

When in 1810, the management of the Royal Woods and Forests was vested in the Commissioners of Woods, the Commissioners were at the same time made responsible for the management of the Crown estates which included manors, lands and houses in various parts of the country. In 1827 the Land Revenues of Ireland were placed under the management of the Commissioners and in 1832 they were entrusted with the Land Revenues of Scotland while in the meantime they had been made responsible for the Crown Revenues in Alderney and the Isle of Man. Furthermore, in 1832, the office of the Surveyor-General of Works and Public Buildings was added to the Department of Woods and Land Revenues. In 1813 the Commissioners were given the task of the formation of Regent's Park and Regent's Street and subsequently, Victoria Park Spitalfields and other improvements in London.[68] It is therefore very evident from this catalogue of responsibilities, that the Commissioners were deeply involved in many matters other than the woods and forests and when, in 1833, a Select Committee was appointed to examine the Land Revenues of the Crown, they directed their attention mainly to matters concerned with the land revenues rather than the forests.

However in 1848 the House of Commons appointed a Select Committee on the Woods, Forests and Land Revenues of the Crown and their findings were published later in the same year. In their report the Committee stated that: 'The management of the Forests and Woodlands of the Crown have never been investigated since the period (1787) when Commissioners were specially appointed by Parliament for that purpose.'[69] Although the First and Second Reports, of 1812 and 1816 respectively, had been published after 1787, these were apparently regarded simply as reports and not as investigations.

In addition to examining various matters which affected the Crown forests as a whole, such as their administration, organization, revenue and expenditure, the Committee considered four individual forests. Approximately 50 per cent of the Report dealt with the New Forest, about 20 per cent with Epping (also referred to as Hainault or Waltham Forests) and about 10 per cent with Whittlewood and Wychwood Forests together. Their investigations cover many points including forest courts; the officers of the forests and their remunerations; enclosures and planting; deer and cattle in the forests; sales of timber and bark and methods employed in measuring timber.

With the exception of any inclosures which could be made in the New Forest and the Dean after throwing open equivalent areas, almost all the land in the Crown forests which was suitable for growing oak had been planted by about 1850. Since the object was to raise a final crop of some 40 to 60 trees per acre, with large crowns in order to obtain a high proportion of compass timber, heavy thinnings were necessary at frequent intervals. These usually took place every five years but in some cases the interval between thinnings was even less. Heavy thinnings were also influenced by the high prices which could be obtained for oak bark and small timber and in some cases the wish to obtain an improved income clashed with the best interests of the stand.[70]

In 1849 another Select Committee was appointed which issued two reports in July of that year. Of the evidence contained in the First Report[71] about 33 per cent was concerned with the Forest of Dean, 30 per cent with the New Forest, 15 per cent with Salcey and Whittlewood Forests while some 10 per cent covered the Forests of Bere, Delamere, Holt, Parkhurst and Woolmer, with general matters affecting these forests making up the balance. The Second Report was largely concerned with urban properties belonging to the Crown.

By this time almost all the land which was capable of being used and which was suitable for growing timber had been planted, with the exception of sites in the New Forest and the Forest of Dean which might be made available by inclosures.[72] It was probably for this reason that during 1849 an Act[73] was passed authorizing the appointment of a Commission to examine the rights and claims in and over the New Forest and Waltham Forest. In the following year, the Commission issued its report and this resulted in the passing of what is generally referred to as the Deer Removal Act.[74] Under this statute the Crown gave up its right to deer in the New Forest which were to be removed within two years of the passing of the Act. In place of this right, the Crown was empowered to inclose and plant with trees an area not exceeding 10,000 acres, in addition to the 6,000 acres that were already enclosed. When the trees that had been planted in these inclosures were no longer in danger from cattle and deer, the area could be thrown open and other land, equal in extent, inclosed instead. This Act caused such a public outcry that 16 years later, after a Committee of the House of Commons had considered the whole question of

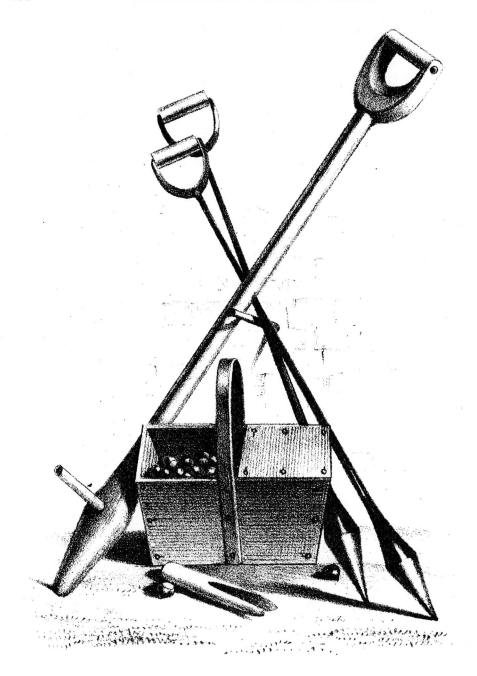

15.   *This illustration is taken from*
            A Treatise on . . . Timber Trees
*by G. W. Newton which was published in 1859. It was entitled 'Implements to
be used in dibbling acorns, nuts and keys'.*

the New Forest, an amending Act[75] was passed in 1877.

In 1854 a Select Committee[76] was appointed:

> . . . to inquire into the present management and condition of the Crown Forests in England, with a view of ascertaining the responsibility of the present Commissioners and whether it would be in the public interest that some of the smaller forests should be sold, as being unfit for the growth of timber for Her Majesty's Navy.

The Committee's Report which was issued in July 1854 contains a number of observations and among these are the following (some of which probably applied equally to woodlands, which were in private ownership.)

Since the life of a mature tree was longer than that of a man, there was a special need for continuity of management in the case of woodlands. The shortage of timber for the Navy had now become extremely serious as can be appreciated from the undermentioned extract.

> Except in the Forest of Dean and the New Forest, there is scarcely any timber at present of sufficient age for Navy purposes; nor is there likely to be for many years to come. The Forest of Dean, which lately contained 22,000 loads, now contains only 4,000. The Forests of Alice Holt, Woolmer and Delamere contain none. The Forests of Hainault and Epping have long since ceased to bear timber, and are now devoted to agriculture. In the New Forest, out of 2,635 loads felled, consisting of 3,115 trees, only 936 loads were accepted by the Surveyor of the Navy, so large is the proportion of faulty to sound trees.[77]

Delamere Forest and those who were concerned with its management, received severe criticism in contrast to Bere and Alice Holt.

> With regard to Delamere Forest, . . . its condition is most unsatisfactory; the soil is very variable and is, in a large portion of this forest, poor and unproductive. Nor has the management . . . been judicious, and it appears to have been in the hands of persons incompetent for the duty. With reference to the smaller forests of Alice Holt and Bere . . . the management by the present surveyors, has been satisfactory and judicious.[78]

The conditions in Woolmer Forest were considered to be so unsuitable for growing timber that the Committee felt that consideration should be given to its sale. In fact, no action was taken for over a hundred years until, in 1956, the forest was sold to the War Department (now the Ministry of Defence). The policy which had been adopted for thinning and felling was also subject to criticism since oak was not felled or thinned when it was necessary for silvicultural reasons but rather when the needs of the Navy dictated it. There was also a considerable variation in the intensity of thinning which was adopted while the policy of only planting oak in the Crown Forest was called into question.

> *Your Committee think it well worthy of the most serious consideration whether legislation has not made it too generally and strictly an obligation to produce oak timber, qualities of soil, local markets and other circumstances pointing, in certain situations, to a different description of tree as a far more profitable source of revenue and more worthy of adoption.*[79]

The Report also records that a sawmill had recently been erected in the Forest of Dean and that the possibility of building other mills elsewhere, was under consideration. It was not intended that these mills would convert any 'crooked or knee timber' for the Navy since 'ship and boat builders are alone competent judges of what is best adapted for their own purposes'.

By the middle of the nineteenth century a wider interest had begun to develop throughout the general public as well as among landowners, in what was later referred to as 'forestry', although that term was not, as yet, generally used. In 1855 *The Quarterly Review*[80] contained an article which extended to nearly 30 pages and was based for the most part on the second edition of *The Forester*[81] which had appeared in 1851. This described the planting and tending of a wood of 50 acres and covered in some detail the site conditions, drainage, fencing, choice of species, planting, weeding, thinning and pruning. Although this article expresses some views that would not be accepted today, such as a mixture consisting of oak, ash, sycamore, elm, larch and Scots pine or the advice never to prune conifers, it contains enough to show that present day forestry methods were not far distant.

The latter part of the article is a criticism of the Crown Forests and includes the copy of a document setting out the shortcomings of the Forest of Dean which, it was alleged, was written by Nelson in 1803. Whoever the writer was, his account provides a record of ignorance, incompetency and dishonesty which it would be difficult to outmatch. Perhaps it was as well that the old forestry, based on the concept of growing oak for the Royal Navy, was now in its last throes. It was, however, the naval action of Hampton Roads in 1861 which finally administered the *coup de grâce*.

THE NEW FORESTRY   9

Although the engagement of Hampton Roads in 1862 had been a short-lived affair, its effect on the woods and forests of this country was to be felt for another 50 years, though today it is difficult to appreciate the full implications. From the earliest times ships had been built of timber and since the beginning of the sixteenth century, oak had provided the key to British sea power and had consequently dominated both the shipyards and the woodlands of this country. The need for it had been emphasized by the Act of 1543[1] and since that date increasing quantities of oak had been sought for both the Navy and the mercantile fleets.

For 300 years contemporary writers such as Evelyn (1664), Wade (1755), Nichols (1793) and Matthew (1831) had appealed to the patriotism of landowners and had urged them to plant oak, in the hope that it would grow to the size which the dockyards needed. Some had responded like Admiral Collingwood who, whenever he walked or rode around his estate, took a pocketful of acorns which he scattered wherever there was a chance for them to germinate and grow. Since the end of the sixteenth century the main purpose of the Royal Forests had been to provide oak for the Navy, although their success in doing so had fallen far short of their real potential.

All this had come to an end with incredible abruptness and in the hiatus which followed, the country's woodlands faced a period of unprecedented uncertainty. Since there was no longer any need to grow oak for the Navy, any sense of urgency to raise timber, especially in the Crown Forests, soon evaporated. Nisbet[2] remarked that:

> *All the former concern as to the national importance of British woodlands appears to have become completely forgotten; it seems to have passed absolutely and entirely from the recollection of the public, and of their representatives in Parliament.*

It is difficult to assess the extent to which this sense of anti-climax affected those woodlands that were in private ownership. As some estates had planted large areas of conifers and were no longer substantial producers of oak, it is unlikely that they were involved to the same degree as the Royal Forests. Eventually, these changes came to be accepted and the fact that in 1877 the Deer Removal Act[3] was amended,[4] so that the area to be inclosed for planting oak in the New Forest was substantially reduced, is some indication of this. By 1880 there were already signs of a new approach to forestry.

The Influence of Covert Shooting

Since the beginning of the nineteenth century game shooting in England had been increasing in popularity while at the same time new developments had been taking place in the design of sporting guns. Although flint locks had been introduced into this country at the end of the seventeenth century, it was not until 1815 that J. Manton, the London gunmaker, is said to have perfected this mechanism for sporting guns. Until about 1800, practically all sporting guns were single-barrelled and it was not until after that date that double-barrelled guns came into general use.

The next development was the introduction of the copper percussion cap in about 1820 which in turn affected the design of the firing mechanism, although guns were still muzzle-loaded. In 1857, the Lefauchieux gun was imported into England from France and this incorporated two important new features. In the first place it was breech-loading and secondly, it was a pin-fire gun, that is to say, a cartridge was used (instead of loose powder) which was fired by means of a projecting pin. However, this method was short-lived since in 1867 it was superseded by the central-fire system which is basically that which is in use today. The year 1871 saw the manufacture of the first hammerless guns while three years later, W. Greener, a Birmingham gunsmith, introduced choked barrels with which the effective range of a gun could be noticeably increased.

As a result of these improvements in guns and ammunition, it was possible to achieve more accurate shooting at a faster rate and at a longer range. Prior to this, game shooting consisted of walking up birds in order to flush them and this method allowed the line of guns to halt after a shot had been fired, without more birds being flushed, until the line was ready to move on. This gave a gun time to reload which, when using a muzzle-loader, might take two or three minutes and could only be done when standing still. When breech-loading central-fire guns came into general use, the situation changed completely. Reloading could now be done in a matter of seconds, especially when a gun was fitted with cartridge ejectors, while birds could be killed at a longer range.

All that was now needed were more birds to shoot and in many parts of the country these could readily be provided by pheasants. They were easy to rear and were completely at home on many country estates where the woodlands afforded cover and protection and at the same time enabled them to be driven over the guns, often providing high fast-flying birds. Pheasants did best in woodlands which consisted of mixed broadleaved species such as oak, sweet chestnut and beech with a scattering of conifers in which they could roost. Acorns, chestnuts and beech mast also provided a supply of attractive food early in the shooting season which discouraged the birds from straying. The type of woodland which fulfilled these requirements most readily were those managed as coppice-with-standards or those which had been heavily thinned and now tended to be understocked. These included stands of oak which had been planted to provide timber for the Navy and had since degenerated.

As the new methods of shooting were widely adopted so the woodlands came to be regarded simply as pheasant coverts in the management of which the keeper took precedence over the forester. It was now the head keeper who decided which areas should be felled and which should be retained and the quality of the crop or the replacement of deteriorating stands by young plantations which could provide timber for the future, was not considered. On some estates this unsatisfactory state of affairs continued until the outbreak of war in 1939, and it was not until after the Forestry Commission's Dedication Scheme[5] for private woodlands had been announced in 1947, that on some estates, forestry began to receive the attention which it deserved.

THE REKINDLING OF INTEREST

It was not until 1880, almost 20 years after Hampton Roads, that a new interest in forestry began to emerge and one of the first indications of this was the founding of the English Arboricultural Society (now the Royal Forestry Society of England, Wales and Northern Ireland) in 1882. The formation of the Society was largely due to the initiative of Henry Clark who was forester on the Blenkinsopp Hall Estate near Haltwhistle and J. W. Robson, a nurseryman at Hexham in Northumberland.[6] The fact that the Scottish Arboricultural Society (now the Royal Scottish Forestry Society) had been established 28 years previously, in 1854, and that the English Society was formed by those who lived only 25 miles or so south of the Border, suggests that the greatest interest in forestry existed in the North.

In 1884 an International Forestry Exhibition was held in Edinburgh which was the first of its kind to be concerned solely with forestry. The exhibits were arranged in 10 classes and these comprised practical forestry, forest products, scientific forestry, ornamental forestry, illustrations of forestry, forest literature and history, essays and reports, collections on loan, economic forestry and miscellaneous exhibits. A competition was held for essays on matters relating to forestry and trees and a very comprehensive report on the exhibition which contains 21 prize-winning essays (of which 14 are concerned with British forestry) was published in 1885.[7]

One result of this exhibition was to focus attention on forestry education and training and a Select Committee was appointed in 1885 'to consider whether, by the establishment of a forest school or otherwise, our woodlands could be rendered more remunerative'. However, Parliament was dissolved before the Committee had time to complete its investigations and it was accordingly reappointed in 1886 and although interim reports were published in 1885 and 1886, the final report did not appear until 1887.[8] In this, the Committee made a number of observations and recommendations which may be summarized as follows.

> Although the woodlands which belonged to the State were comparatively small in extent, the total acreage of private woodlands in England amounted to 1,466,000 acres while those in Wales and Scotland covered 163,000 acres and 829,000 acres respectively.
>
> Apart from the actual profit derived from the timber, the value to agriculture by planting trees for shelter should not be overlooked.
>
> Landowners might also make their woods more profitable if additional attention was paid to the choice of species planted and subsequently to their management.
>
> A board to be known as the Board of Forestry should be set up which would include delegates from the English Arboricultural Society, the Royal Agricultural Society of England, the Office of Woods and Forests, the Surveyors Institution, the Linnean Society, the Scottish Arboricultural Society, the Highland and Agricultural Society of Scotland and the Royal Dublin Society. The functions of this Board should be the organisation of forest schools or courses of instruction, the institution of examinations and the preparation of a syllabus and official text-book. The subjects for such examinations to include practical forestry, botany, geology, entymology, surveying, drainage and timber measuring.
>
> Serious consideration should be given to the unsatisfactory situation which had arisen in the New Forest as a result of the Act of 1877.[9]

Two years after the publication of the Select Committee's final report, an Act[10] was passed establishing a Board of Agriculture but this legislation did little to meet the recommendations of the Committee. As regards forestry, the functions of the Board were limited to the collection and preparation of forest statistics, the inspection of schools in which instruction was given in matters relating to forestry, the qualified assistance of such schools and the collection of information for the promotion of forestry. One of the more satisfactory results of the Act was the grant of £250 towards the salary of a Professor of

Agriculture and Forestry at Durham College of Science in 1891.

The observations on the unsatisfactory position which existed in the New Forest resulted in another Select Committee being appointed in 1889 'to enquire into the administration of the Department of Woods and Forests and Land Revenues of the Crown'. The Committee's report was published in 1890[11] and while the administration of the Crown Woods and Forests was considered to be satisfactory, action was suggested as regards certain individual forests. On the grounds that timber was no longer required for the Royal Navy, it was recommended that the New Forest and the Forests of Alice Holt, Bere, Dean and Parkhurst should no longer be devoted to timber production. Very fortunately, the Committee's recommendations were not accepted.

Although it was only to have an indirect influence on forestry in this country it may be noted that in 1885 courses in forestry were introduced at the Royal Indian Engineering College at Coopers Hill near Egham in Surrey. These were for those who wished to enter the Indian Forest Service and were only available to students who intended to take up forestry in India.

16. *Charcoal burning in the seventeenth century. This drawing which appeared in*
John Evelyn's
Sylva
in 1670 shows three stages in the construction of a charcoal kiln. In the centre, the initial preparations are carried out; on the left is the completed kiln before covering it with earth and on the right is the kiln after firing.

Towards the end of the century, forestry began to be recognized more widely and in 1893 an Exhibition of Horticulture and Forestry was held at Earls Court in London. Developments were also taking place in the fields of education and forest management and in 1897 the English Arboricultural Society held its first examinations in forestry and these were to continue for the next 80 years. In the Crown Forests attention was now being paid to woodland management and in 1897 a working plan was prepared by H. C. Hill who had been a Conservator of Forests in India, for the Forest of Dean[12] and for the adjoining Highmeadow Woods.[13] The purpose of the plans was

> to introduce . . . a more scientific and systematic system of forest cultivation than has hitherto been adopted . . . It is desired not only to improve the prospective yield of the Forest, but also to establish such a system of management as may serve those who desire to study forestry in this country with a good practical object-lesson, such as at the present time they have to go to France or Germany to find.[14]

Two years after the publication of these reports, E. P. Popert who, like Hill, had been a Conservator of Forests in India, was appointed Superintendent Forester in the Dean and in 1907 was made Consulting Forest Officer. In taking up these duties he became the first technically-trained forest officer to be employed by the Crown.[15] It is interesting to note that his son, A. H. Popert, who entered the Forestry Commission in 1920, became Acting Deputy Surveyor for the Forest of Dean in 1936 and subsequently Conservator for the South West England Conservancy.

THE SIGNIFICANCE OF CONTINENTAL PRACTICE

With the approach of the twentieth century, continental forestry practice, more particularly that which was expounded in Germany, began to exert an increasing influence in this country and this may be attributed, at least in part, to the following circumstances.

Up to this time, English forestry had chiefly consisted of allowing trees to grow and then felling them, and forest management, as it is known today, was non-existent. As a new interest in forestry began to develop, so a demand arose for more information, improved techniques and a new approach to growing timber. The obvious source of help lay in the Continent where the French and the Germans had applied themselves to the management of their forests over a long period. However in India, the Government of that country had already been actively concerned with the creation of a forest service and in 1855, a permanent policy for forest administration had been laid down. From the following year until the end of the century, the success of the Indian Forest Service was largely due to three outstanding German foresters.

In 1856 Dietrich Brandis (later Sir Dietrich Brandis) joined the Service and 'with this appointment the dawn of scientific forestry in India began'.[16] He was appointed the first Inspector General of Forests in 1864 and after being placed on special duties in 1881, retired in 1883. He was followed by Dr William Schlich (later Sir William Schlich) who held the position of Inspector General until 1885 when he left India in order to establish the new forestry department of the Royal Indian Engineering College at Coopers Hill. He, in turn, was succeeded as Inspector General by Berthold Ribbentrop who subsequently retired in 1900, having served in India for 33 years.

It is probable that many of the principles and practices which were followed in German forestry were introduced into the Indian Forest Service and when members of the Service returned to England it is very likely that they were instrumental in dispersing these ideas. Reference has already been made to H. C. Hill and E. P. Popert who, after leaving India, took an active part in forestry in this country but it was Sir William Schlich who made the greatest impact on British forestry in the early years of the present century. When Coopers Hill closed in 1906, the forestry section was transferred to Oxford where Schlich continued to lecture, while from time to time he advised landowners on forestry matters and prepared working plans for several large estates. In this way he was able to pass on much that was based on German forestry practice.

Books provided another channel through which German forestry practice was disseminated in this country and in 1889 the first volume of *Schlich's Manual of Forestry* appeared. This classic work on forestry was published in five volumes between 1889 and 1896, the first three being written by Schlich himself. The fourth which dealt with forest protection, was a translation by W. R. Fisher of *Der Forstschutz* written by Dr Richard Hess, Professor of Forestry at the University of Giessen, while the fifth, on forest utilization was a translation, also by Fisher, of *Die Forstbenutzung* by Dr Karl Gayer, Professor of Forestry at Munich University. Fisher who had been a Conservator in the Indian Forest Service was Assistant Professor of Forestry at Coopers Hill when he undertook these translations.

In 1893 John Nisbet completed the translation of *The Protection of Woodlands* written by Dr Hermann Furst who was the Director of the Bavarian Forest Institute at Aschaffenburg in the Spessart. Nisbet, who was himself the author of several books on forestry, had served in the Forest Service in India under Ribbentrop and later became Professor of Forestry at the West of Scotland Agricultural College. In his book *Studies in Forestry* which was published in 1894 Nisbet gives a list of 11 German publications on forestry which he remarks in the preface 'have been frequently quoted throughout the various chapters of this book'. In the same year a *Text-book of the Diseases of Trees* by Professor R. Hartig of the University of Munich which had been translated by William Somerville (later Sir William Somerville) and H. Marshall Ward was published, while in 1904 the translation of Dr Adam Schwappach's *Forstwissenschaft* by Fraser Storey and E. A. Nobbs appeared under the title of *Forestry*. During this period only one book on French forestry was translated into English, namely *Elements of Sylviculture* by G. Bagneris who had been a Professor at the Forest School at Nancy. The translation which was made by E. E. Fernandez and A. Smythies, both of the Indian Forest Service, appeared in 1882.

It is difficult to assess what impact these continental ideas and opinions made on English forestry at the time. The effect was probably limited in extent since few estates were either sufficiently interested in forestry or prepared to put these new ideas into practice. When Schlich visited private estates in England in order to prepare working plans for them, he tried to encourage the idea of systematic forest management which he had been taught in Germany. In his later years when he looked back on this work, he regarded it as some of the least successful of his career and he attributed this to the frequent changes in the ownership of private estates and to the absence of any tradition of forestry in this country.[17]

In the meantime steps were being taken to deal with the Crown Woods and Forests which were now feeling the full effect of the use of iron and steel in place of timber for naval construction. After the appointment of Mr E. S. Howard (afterwards Sir Stafford Howard) as commissioner of Woods in 1893, considerably more attention was devoted to the technical management of the Crown Forests than had previously been the case. During this period there were large areas of oak, much of which had been planted at approximately the same time and which subsequently had been so heavily thinned that the density of the remaining stock had been reduced to a minimum. The system of thinning that had been followed in the past was designed to produce timber that was suitable for shipbuilding but the demand for oak for the Navy no longer existed and this open-grown timber was of restricted value for other purposes. At the same time the price of bark had fallen to such a level that stripping was no longer an economical proposition.

Under such circumstances the following steps were proposed in an attempt to overcome these problems. No further thinning was to be undertaken and the poorer stands of oak were to be clear felled and replanted with conifers. When this had been done, the middle quality oak was to be replaced by other more suitable species but the best oak was to be allowed to grow on for a considerable time, on a regular rotation.[18]

THE THRESHOLD OF THE TWENTIETH CENTURY

The early years of the new century were marked by a series of events which provided ample evidence that forestry was now rapidly gaining momentum.

Unfortunately, it was not until a war of unprecedented magnitude had occurred, that the value of the nation's forests were to be fully appreciated. One of the first events of the century was the acquisition by the Crown, in 1901 and 1902, of the Tintern Woods which lay on the Monmouthshire side of the Wye Valley. This area extended to some 3,000 acres and since it was situated close to the Forest of Dean, it formed an important addition to the Crown Estates.

17. Hauling charcoal in the Forest of Dean. c.1911.

Although the Select Committee which had been set up in 1885 had made its final report in 1887, little had resulted from it and in 1902 a Departmental Committee was appointed by the Board of Agriculture to enquire into and report on British forestry. The Committee's terms of reference were

> . . . *to enquire and report as to the present position and future prospects of forestry, and the planting and management of woodlands in Great Britain, and to consider whether any measures might with advantage be taken, either by the provision of further education facilities, or otherwise, for their promotion and encouragement.*

The Committee's Report was published in November 1902[19] and the Minutes of Evidence taken by the Committee, in 1903.[20] The general opinion of the members which is contained in paragraph 5 of the Report was as follows: 'We endorse the conclusions of the Select Committee of 1885-87 as regards the neglected condition of forestry in Great Britain, the possibility of improvement, and the necessity for the provision of better means of education.'

Below is given a summary of the conclusions and the nine recommendations that are set out in paragraph 36 of the Report.

> *That forest areas should be provided for practical demonstrations in England and Scotland and that Alice Holt Woods should be used for this purpose in England.*
>
> *That lecturers in forestry should be appointed at Oxford and Cambridge Universities and that small demonstration areas should be provided in this connection.*
>
> *That agricultural colleges should include forestry in their courses of study and should provide short courses for young foresters. Instructors should also be available to advise owners on the management of their woods.*
>
> *That provision should be made for the education of foresters and woodmen by employing them as student-foresters in demonstration forests.*
>
> *That in districts which contain large areas of woodland County Councils should arrange lectures in forestry and provide financial assistance for foresters who wished to attend.*
>
> *That action should be taken as regards estate duty on timber.*
>
> *That legislation should be introduced to protect woodland owners against loss from fires caused by railway engines.*
>
> *That an inquiry should be undertaken to ascertain the area of the country's woodlands and their composition.*
>
> *That the attention of local authorities should be drawn to the importance of planting trees in water catchment areas.*

Some indication of the interest that was being taken in continental forestry may be gathered from the fact that in 1902, the English Arboricultural Society held its first overseas tour in order to visit forests in France. In the field of education, lectureships in forestry were established during the following year at the University College of North Wales at Bangor and at the Armstrong College at Newcastle-on-Tyne. Two years later, at the Royal Show which was held at Park Royal in Willesden, London, the Royal Agricultural Society of England staged the first forestry exhibition to be held at one of its shows. Since 1904 forestry exhibits have been included in every Royal Show up to the present time (1980) with the exception of 1915 and 1916 and during those years when, on account of the two world wars, the Royal Show was not held, namely in 1917 and 1918 and from 1940 to 1946.

18. *Bark stripping. A team of eight stand beside an oak from the lower six feet of which the bark has already been removed; the remainder will be stripped after the tree has been felled. The date is probably about 1905.*

January 1904 marked the opening of the School of Forestry for Woodmen at Parkend in the Forest of Dean. C. O. Hanson who had been a Deputy Conservator of Forests in India and whose excellent book *Forestry for Woodmen* was subsequently published in 1911, was placed in charge of the School which continued to train woodmen until July 1971 when it was closed. During 1905 further evidence of the increase in the status of forestry in this country was apparent when H M King Edward VII graciously conferred the prefix of 'Royal' to the title of the English Arboricultural Society.

Following the example of the Royal Agricultural Society, the Bath and West and Southern Counties Society staged a forestry exhibition at its show at Newport, Monmouthshire in 1907. This was the first time that a forestry exhibit had been arranged by the Society and since then there has been a forestry section at every show except in 1914 and 1915 and in those years when, owing to the wars, it was not possible to hold a show, namely from 1916 to 1919 and from 1940 to 1946. In the province of education, the year 1907 also saw the establishment of a readership in forestry at Cambridge University.

The increasing number of those who were out of work was now causing concern throughout the country, and in June 1907 an Afforestation Conference was held in London in order to consider what steps could be taken to plant new woodland areas and so provide work for the unemployed. The matter had been raised initially by the Association of Municipal Councils which had been approached by several corporations with regard to the planting of land in the vicinity of waterworks and sewage disposal plants. Subsequently the Association had written to the Secretary of the Local Government Board and had conveyed to him the following resolution which the Association had passed:

> That this Council expresses its opinion that the time has now arrived when the question of afforestation should be seriously considered by the Government, and that it be referred to the Law Committee to take steps for urging upon the Government the necessity for initiating afforestation schemes.
>
> And I am directed by the Law Committee to invite your Honourable Board to consider, in the interests of the unemployed and also in the interests of municipalities, whether a National Scheme could be put forward.

That considerable importance was attached to this Conference may be inferred from the fact that the President of the Board of Agriculture (Lord Carrington) presided over it and that he was accompanied by the President of the Local Government Board, the Commissioner of Woods and Forests and several Members of Parliament. Among others who attended were representatives of a number of municipalities, Professor Schlich, W. R. Fisher, H. J. Elwes (President of the Royal English Arboricultural Society), Fraser Storey and A. C. Forbes. Although this matter was discussed at great length little seems to have been achieved and Lord Carrington is reported to have said 'that the Conference had knocked on the head the delusion that afforestation was a great cure for want of employment'.[21] It is difficult to say whether this was only a personal view or whether it was the opinion of the whole Conference but two years later a very different sentiment was expressed in the Royal Commission's Report of 1909.

This Commission had been appointed in 1906 and its original terms of reference were concerned with coastal erosion and the reclamation of tidal lands. Subsequently, in March 1908, the following additional reference was added.

> Whether in connection with reclaimed lands or otherwise, it is desirable to make an experiment in afforestation as a means of increasing employment during periods of depression in the labour

market, and if so by what authority and under what conditions such experiment should be conducted.

The findings of the Commission on this reference were published as Volume II, entitled *Second Report (on Afforestation)* and was divided into two parts; Part I comprising the actual Report[22] and Part II the Minutes of Evidence.[23]

The Report was divided into six parts which dealt with British forestry in general, unemployment and afforestation, the nature and extent of suitable land, administration, finance and a summary of conclusions and recommendations. These last named covered a number of points among which were the following.

> *It was agreed that a policy of afforestation was desirable and that there were approximately 9,000,000 acres in the United Kingdom which could be planted without substantially encroaching on agricultural land. In order to obtain a sustained yield, the best rotation would be 60 years and the area to be felled and planted each year would consequently amount to 150,000 acres.*
>
> *Permanent employment would be provided on the basis of one man per 100 acres planted.*
>
> *After 80 years the net revenue should show a return of 3¾% on the net cost.*
>
> *A special Board of Commissioners, having powers of compulsory purchase, should be set up to deal with the work of afforestation.*

In contradiction of Lord Carrington's view which, as President of the Board of Agriculture, he had expressed at the Afforestation Conference in 1907, the Commissioners recorded the following opinion on the subject of unemployed labour in relation to afforestation: '. . . your Commissioners are of opinion that a national scheme of afforestation would contribute to the solution of the unemployed problem . . .'

The question of afforestation and unemployment had now aroused considerable public interest and in the *Quarterly Journal of Forestry* for January 1909[24] it was noted that 'The question of afforestation in the British Isles is rapidly gaining ground' and then adds that 'An excellent article on that subject . . . appeared in the *Daily Mail* of 27th November'. Nor did the matter escape the attention of the Editor of *Punch*[25] who, on 27th January 1909, published the cartoon which appears in illustration 19.

Probably in view of the success of the forestry exhibitions which the Royal Agricultural Society had been holding on the showground since 1904, the Society decided to give practical encouragement to private estates by holding competitions for growing woodlands. The first of these, known as a 'Plantation Competition', was held in 1909 but as in the case of the showground

PUNCH, OR THE LONDON CHARIVARI.—JANUARY 27, 1909.

AFFORESTATION'S ARTFUL AID.

WOOD NYMPHS. "THANK YOU SO MUCH. THIS'LL MAKE A BEAUTIFUL HOME FOR US IN YEARS TO COME."

EX-UNEMPLOYED. "THAT MAY BE, MISS. BUT WHAT I LIKE ABOUT IT IS, IT'S MAKING A JOB FOR ME TO-DAY."

19. *Two different views on afforestation. A cartoon which appeared in* Punch *on 27th January 1909.*

exhibitions, they did not take place in the war years. Although the competition was not held in 1947, 1957 or 1975, it has otherwise been a regular feature of the Royal Show in the remaining years. Among the recommendations of the Departmental Committee of 1902 was one relating to damage caused by railway fires and, as a result, the Railway Fires Act 1905[26] was passed. This came into force on 1st January 1908 and provided limited compensation for fires due to railway locomotives but it was subsequently amended in 1923.[27]

During the course of his Budget speech in 1909, Lloyd George announced that the Government intended to introduce development grants with a view to making better use of the country's natural resources. In the case of forestry, grants were to be available for such undertakings as 'schools of forestry', the acquisition of land for planting and the creation of 'experimental forests'.[28] With these and other objects in view, the Development and Road Improvement Fund Act[29] was passed in 1909 and in 1911 the newly appointed Development Commissioners issued their First Report. In order to deal more specifically with forestry, a Forestry Committee was formed consisting of four of the Commissioners who drew up the policy that was to be adopted when considering applications for grants. Briefly, this was based on the following principles: first, any expansion in forestry must be founded on effective education and research; second, no scheme for large scale afforestation by the State should be considered until it had first been established where, from an economic and financial aspect, the most suitable areas for any new forests were situated; and third, no action should be taken until a sufficient number of trained foresters were available.[30]

THE NEW APPROACH TO FOREST MANAGEMENT

As the first decade of the century came to an end there were signs that a new appreciation of the technical aspects of forestry was beginning to emerge and this was especially so in the case of forest management and silviculture. Until now most of the available information on these matters was of German origin but this new interest was now focused on forestry practice which was applicable to this country. The third volume of *Schlich's Manual of Forestry*, which covered forest management, had been published in 1895 and was based entirely on German methods. As the author remarked in his preface to the third edition of 1905, his object was 'to give a clear picture of economic forestry' and therefore

> *I took my illustrations from the country where economic forestry had been most highly developed and not from Britain, . . . even if they are stamped with the well-known mark 'Made in Germany'.*[31]

Although this volume contained yield tables for eight different species, these had been compiled in Germany from growth statistics recorded in that country. When Nisbet's *The Forester*[32] appeared in 1905, it was clear that the author had also been influenced to a large extent by German practice although those sections in the second volume which cover forest management are neither as detailed nor as extensive as in the *Manual of Forestry.* Nevertheless the yield tables which Nisbet included were all of German origin.

Although in 1809, Charles Waistell had drawn up what are thought to be the first yield tables for species growing in this country,[33] it was not until the publication of *The Practice of Forestry* by P. T. Maw[34] in 1909, that detailed information relating to the management of English woodlands became available. While the author did not mention working plans, he included a chapter on 'Measurements for purposes of forest management' followed by another on 'Estimation of increment on crops of timber' which covered such matters as basal areas, form factors, increment and the measurement of sample plots. This book also included tables giving the expected yield from seven species as well as thinning tables and tables for calculating volumes, basal areas and heights.

For the first 25 years or so, of this century, the only periodical devoted to English forestry was the *Quarterly Journal of Forestry,* published by the Royal English Arboricultural Society, and it was in this publication that many of the current views and interests of the day were reflected. For this reason it is interesting to note that in 1911 a paper by C. O. Hanson appeared in the *Quarterly Journal*[35] comparing the form factors which the writer had prepared for larch growing in England with those calculated for Scots pine in Germany. Arising out of this article, the next number of the *Journal*[36] contained a further contribution on the subject of form factors which was considerably more technical than those which usually appeared in this periodical. The author was R. L. Robinson who in later life was appointed Chairman of the Forestry Commission and subsequently became Lord Robinson.

In 1912, Maw followed up his book with the publication of yield tables for use in British woodlands.[37] These were based on 'the adaptability of any particular area for the successful growth of timber' and sites were divided into four classes, Quality I being the best and Quality IV the worst. A somewhat similar system was adopted by the Forestry Commission in the preparation of the Commission's yield tables which were first published in 1920. Maw produced tables for ash, beech, birch, oak, poplar, sweet chestnut, Douglas fir, larch, Norway spruce, Scots pine, silver fir and Sitka spruce and soon after they were published they were reviewed in the *Quarterly Journal of Forestry*[38] by R. L. Robinson.

Although in the course of the next few years the war was to interrupt these investigations, enough had already been done to ensure that further action would be taken when peace returned.

The Vanishing Scene

There can be little doubt that the inadequacy of the country's woodlands were an increasing cause of concern to the Government and in 1912 only a year after the Development Commissioners had issued their first report, the President of the Board of Agriculture appointed an Advisory Committee on Forestry.[39] The membership of this Committee which was under the chairmanship of Sir Stafford Howard included Sir William Schlich, E. R. Pratt, President of the Royal English Arboricultural Society, Professor William Somerville, a past President of the Society with R. L. Robinson as Secretary.

It was intended that the Committee should consider any appropriate matters which might arise but in the minute of appointment it was asked, initially, to deal with the three following matters.

> *To consider and advise upon proposals for a forestry survey.*
> *To draw up plans for experiments in sylviculture and to report upon questions relating to the selection and laying out of forestal demonstration areas.*
> *To advise as to the provision required for the instruction of woodmen.*

In July 1912 the Committee completed its report on the first of these three references and recommended that a forestry survey should be carried out in two stages. The first, which was to take the form of a 'preliminary enquiry or flying survey', would be concerned with the general location of land suitable for afforestation; while the second, termed a 'minute enquiry or detailed survey' would examine more specifically any suitable land which was disclosed by the initial investigation. It was also recommended that, for the purpose of the preliminary survey, England should be divided into seven districts and Wales into two. If the preliminary reconnaissance disclosed any land suitable for afforestation, a detailed examination should follow with a view to the State acquiring an area of not less than 5,000 acres as an 'experimental forest'.

In the case of the second reference, the Committee divided their report into two parts, the first dealing with demonstration areas and the second with forestry experiments. After setting out the requisites of a demonstration area, the Committee expressed the view that the Forest of Dean would best meet these needs. As regards forestry experiments it was recommended that an approach should be made to landowners in order that the Board of Agriculture might obtain permission to set out experimental plots in private woodlands. As to the third reference which related to the instruction of woodmen, the Committee considered that the courses provided by the School for Woodmen at Parkend and at Chopwell Woods, the management of which had been entrusted to Armstrong College in Newcastle on Tyne in 1906, should be extended. It was also recommended that two scholarships of £50 should be offered to the best students who had passed through a woodman's school so as to help them to proceed to higher training.

At the same time a movement was taking place in private forestry which showed that some owners were turning their thoughts to the financial aspects of woodland management. Due to the efforts of M. C. Duchesne, who was Ranger of Burnham Beeches and agent for the Corporation of the City of London, the English Forestry Association was formed in 1912 with the following objects.

> To encourage the demand for English timber (and coppice), to advertise its superior qualities, to encourage its use by consumers, to organise the markets and to assist the consumer to secure sufficient and regular supplies with the least possible trouble.
>
> To supply all information relating to English timber (and coppice), especially its marketing and to assist members in every way possible.

When reading a paper on the new association to the Surveyor's Institution in 1912 Duchesne made it clear that it was not intended to encroach on the activities of other forestry bodies: 'We limit our ground to the marketing and the commercial utilisation of timber, so that we do not interfere with the Royal English Arboricultural or any other existing society'.[40] Until the Home-Grown Timber Committee was formed in November 1915, the Association was active in organizing supplies of timber and pitwood and in so doing, it was probably unique by reason of the fact that, since it was not a trading association in the accepted sense, it charged neither fees nor commission on sales. In 1921 the Association went into voluntary liquidation and a trading company was formed under the name of The English Forestry Association Ltd which, in addition to carrying on the activities of the original Association, also sold forest trees and undertook a certain amount of contract planting. This company went into liquidation in 1926 and a new public company was floated which continued until 1970 when it merged with another forestry concern. The English Forestry Association can well be regarded as the forerunner of the Home-Grown Timber Marketing Association which was formed in 1934.

During 1913, in a further attempt to bring about an improvement in forestry, the Board of Agriculture introduced an Advisory Scheme to assist and advise owners on matters connected with their woodlands. So as to facilitate the operation of the scheme, England and Wales were divided into five regions which were designated Northern, Welsh, Central and Southern, Eastern and South Western Districts and an advisory officer was appointed in each of these.[41]

By this time the clouds had begun to gather over Europe and before the end of the following summer, war had been declared. Although many thought that it would only be a matter of months before it was all over, few realized that after 4th August 1914 life in this country would never be the same again. Few things were to survive unchanged and least of all the woodlands of England.

THE FIRST WORLD WAR
AND ITS AFTERMATH

10

When war broke out in August 1914 the position regarding supplies of home-grown timber was anything but satisfactory. Between 1850 and 1913 six Royal Commissions, Select Committees or Departmental Committees had been appointed to consider various aspects of forestry but they had achieved very little and Sir William Schlich must have voiced the feelings of many people when he made the following comments.

> *. . . very little has as yet been done to increase the area under forest. Too much talking and too little action — that is the long and the short of it . . . Demonstration areas and Schools of Forestry are all very well, but they will not materially increase the timber supply of the country; nor will the attempts at producing fresh species or new varieties of trees, which some people think will be the salvation of the forestry question. . . . Action, and again action, is what we need rather than these ever recurring Commissions and Committees.*[1]

Instead of taking steps to ensure that there were adequate supplies of home-grown timber, successive governments had relied on imports from abroad to meet most of the country's requirements and by 1914, the United Kingdom was importing approximately 10 million loads (400 million cubic feet) of unmanufactured timber per annum. When war was declared the season for importing timber from Northern Europe was at its height and reasonably good stocks were held in this country, while at the same time it was not considered that the war would create any great demand for timber. Even so, some anxiety was felt as regards the supply of pitprops for the collieries since coal provided the Royal Navy and much of industry with the main source of power and, in view of this, a survey of the country's timber resources was made, as a matter of urgency. It was subsequently estimated that the supplies of pitwood were sufficient for a period of about eighteen months to two years and as a measure of control a Pitwood Department was set up by the Board of Trade. The situation was helped to some extent by the fact that in 1915, the volume of imported timber was maintained at almost 75 per cent of the pre-war average although it fell to about 65 per cent in 1916. In order to conserve supplies of timber in this country the French Government agreed to supply the British Expeditionary Force with timber from the French forests. This operation was organized through a Directorate of Forestry under Major-General the Lord Lovat who later became the first chairman of the Forestry Commission.[2]

During 1915 an event occurred which, in effect, marked the beginning of a new form of hostilities which was to have a very considerable influence on the prosecution of the war during the next two years. This was the sinking of the Cunard liner *Lusitania* by a German submarine off the Old Head of Kinsale on 7th May 1915 with a loss of 1,198 lives. From this date until the end of the war the British Empire suffered tremendous casualties among its merchant ships as the following figures show. During 1915 approximately 885,000 gross tons of shipping were sunk and this rose to some 1,231,800 tons in 1916, the losses in the last three months of that year totalling some 524,500 tons. In 1917 the figure reached 3,660,000 tons while that for April 1917, 526,400 tons, was the highest total for any single month. By November 1918 the losses for that year had fallen to 1,632,200 tons.[3]

As an increasing number of ships were sunk, so more vigorous action was taken to ensure that the maximum use was made of the natural resources that were available in this country. With this in mind the President of the Board of Agriculture (the Earl of Selborne) appointed the Home-Grown Timber Committee in November 1915 under the chairmanship of the Rt Hon. F. D. Acland M.P. This Committee had three main objectives: first, to save shipping by organizing supplies of home-grown timber and thereby reducing imports; second, to obtain adequate quantities of timber for use on the Western Front, and third, to meet the general needs of the Services. The country was accordingly divided into Districts each of which was placed under the control of an Advisory Officer.

Initially the Committee had assumed that the existing sawmills throughout the country would be able to deal with the increased volume of timber that was to be felled, but this did not prove to be the case. Consequently it became necessary not only for the Committee to establish its own mills, but also to provide the staff to operate them. Such was their success that by the end of 1916, in spite of poor equipment and unskilled labour, the Committee had despatched 4½ million cubic feet of converted timber, 13,000 cubic feet of round timber and 1½ million cubic feet of pitwood and similar produce.[4]

On 31st March 1917, the Home-Grown Timber Committee came to an end and its duties and responsibilities were transferred to the Directorate of Timber Supplies which had been set up by the War Office in February of that year. Under this Directorate, the country was again formed into Divisions each of which was provided with a Forestry Staff for dealing with the acquisition of timber and a Works Staff for carrying out felling, transport and conversion.

Among the first steps taken by the Directorate were the fixing of maximum prices for timber and the prohibition of felling except by licence. After a few weeks of activity the Directorate was transferred to the Board of Trade in May where it became the Timber Supply Department under the Controller of Timber Supplies (Sir James Ball). Although the Department possessed compulsory powers for the acquisition of timber, they were rarely used and by the end of the war it was buying timber in England and Wales at the rate of 7 million cubic feet per month.[5] It is estimated that during and immediately after the Great War no fewer than 450,000 acres of woodlands in Britain were felled.[6]

At the time of the Armistice, the Timber Supply Department was responsible for the employment of a considerable labour force which included about 2,000 women.[7] In the early days of the war women were employed in forestry on an individual basis without receiving any properly organized training and consequently it was found, very understandably, that they needed a considerable amount of supervision and direction. Later in the war after the Women's Forestry Corps had been formed, the situation changed fundamentally. Many tasks which previously had been carried out by men, were undertaken by members of the Corps and their contribution to the nation's war effort was considerable.

During the last two years of the war, steps were taken to control the prices and supplies of timber by means of Orders issued by the Army Council or the Board of Trade. These included the *Standing Timber (United Kingdom) Order* which was made in 1917 with the object of preventing the purchase of timber by those who did not intend to fell and convert it but simply to hold it until the price rose. Under this Order, sales of standing timber in excess of a value of £300 were prohibited except by licence. The *Home Grown Timber Prices Order* 1917 which fixed the maximum prices for timber 'of the ordinary qualities' was followed by the *Home-Grown Timber Prices Order* 1918. This laid down the maximum prices that could be charged or paid for standing or felled timber, timber in the log delivered by rail or barge and for converted hardwood or softwoods delivered in the same way. In the following July, the *Timber Control Order* 1918 was made which imposed further restrictions on the purchase and sale of home grown timber. The same month saw the publication of the *Pitwood Order* 1918 which not only prohibited the movement of pitwood from one area of supply to another except under permit, but also controlled prices. Later in 1918 the *Fuel Wood Order* was issued which set out in considerable detail the regulations affecting firewood. However, by March 1919, all restrictions regarding the sale and prices of home-grown timber had been removed except those relating to pitwood.

As the war continued, it soon became apparent that timber, like coal and iron, was essential for the economic survival of the country and in July 1916 a Forestry Sub-Committee of the Reconstruction Committee was appointed. Its terms of reference were: 'To consider and report upon the best means of conserving and developing the woodland and forestry resources of the United Kingdom having regard to the experience gained during the war.' The Rt Hon. F. D. Acland, M.P., was appointed chairman and the other 13 members included Sir William Schlich, A. C. Forbes and Major General the Lord Lovat with R. L. Robinson as secretary. This committee became known as the Acland Committee and its findings as the Acland Report and these designations have been frequently used in after years.

The Sub-Committee's Final Report,[8] which was published in May 1917, was of the greatest importance since it laid the foundations of British forest policy for the future. The Report contained a summary of the findings and some idea of the significance that was attached to these may be gathered from the fact that in 1943, some 26 years later, they were again included in the Forestry Commissioners report entitled *Post-War Forest Policy.*[9] The following is a precis of the summary.

(1) The total area of woodland in the United Kingdom before the war was estimated at 3 million acres. The annual yield from this area was believed to be 45 million cubic feet and this was considered to be only one-third of what it should have been under efficient silvicultural management.

(2) From 1909 to 1913 the average annual imports of timber, similar to that produced in this country, were equivalent to 550 million cubic feet of standing timber while the costs of imports in 1915 and 1916 was £74 million or £37 million in excess of their pre-war value.

(3) The area of land used for rough grazing but capable of growing first class conifer timber was not less than 3 and probably more than 5 million acres of which 2 million acres could be used for growing timber without reducing the home production of meat by more than 0.7 per cent. If this land was so used it would give employment to at least ten times the number of men who were previously working on this area.

(4) The conduct of the war had been prejudiced by the country's dependence on imported timber and in future the United Kingdom must safeguard its supplies of timber.

(5) In order to ensure that, in the case of an emergency, the United Kingdom would be independent of imported timber for at least three years, it would be necessary to afforest 1,770,000 acres. If an average rotation of 80 years was adopted, two-thirds of this area should be planted in the

first 40 years. However, in view of the difficulties that might arise in the early stages, only 200,000 acres should be planted in the first 10 years. Of this area, 150,000 acres should be planted by the State and 50,000 acres by public bodies and private individuals, assisted by grants or by cooperation with the State.

(6) It was not proposed to plant any arable land although a certain amount of such land should be acquired in order to provide smallholdings for forest workers.

(7) From the 15th year onwards, the proposals for afforestation would provide supplies of pitwood from the quicker-growing species on the better mountain sites. By the 40th year the areas planted during the first 10 years should contain enough timber to keep the pits supplied, during an emergency, for two years at the existing rate of consumption.

(8) The first essential was the establishment of a Forest Authority which had the necessary funds and powers to acquire and plant land.

(9) The Authority should be enabled to make grants to public bodies and private individuals for afforestation or replanting during the first 10 years after the war.

(10) The estimated cost for the first 10 years was £3,425,000 and it might be necessary to invest £15 million in the undertaking during the first 40 years, after which time it should be self-supporting. The financial return was difficult to forecast since it depended on wages, prices, rates of interest and so on. Even if forests yield less than the current rate of interest on the capital invested, they are nevertheless, a national necessity. The whole amount involved would be less than half the loss that occurred in 1915 and 1916 due to the country's dependence on imported timber.

(11) The Committee's proposals were made in the interests of national safety and this meant that more timber should be grown in the British Isles. The only large reserves of timber in the British Empire were in Canada and unless agreement could be reached with the Canadian Government for the conservation of these reserves, provision must be made in this country on a far larger scale than the above proposals which are for the purpose of defence.

The Report of the Forestry Sub-Committee was generally accepted, the only major difference of opinion arising over to whom the Forest Authority should be responsible. In due course this matter was resolved and the proposals accepted by the War Cabinet. Subsequently, in November 1918 an Interim Forest Authority was set up, preparatory to the appointment of a permanent body after the necessary legislation had been prepared.[10] The Interim Authority was composed of the following members: The Rt. Hon. F. D. Acland, M.P. (chairman), Lord Clinton, Major David Davies, M.P., Colonel Walter Steuart-Fothringham, Lord Lovat, T. B. Ponsonby, R. L. Robinson and A. MacCullum Scott, M.P.

In the meantime the Authority began to make arrangements as to the future administration and to select personnel to fill the various appointments that would have to be made. Steps were also taken to encourage landowners and their agents to take a greater interest in forestry and with this in mind, a conference was held at the headquarters of the Surveyors Institution (now the Royal Institution of Chartered Surveyors) in January 1919. On this occasion various matters were discussed and these included supplies of seedlings, the taxation of woodlands, wire netting and the training of land agents in forestry.[11]

Eventually, on 19th August the Forestry Act received Royal Assent and shortly afterwards came into effect on 1st September 1919.

A NEW SENSE OF DIRECTION

The passing of the Forestry Act marked the beginning of a new era in English forestry and in order to appreciate the full implications of this, it is necessary to bear in mind the condition of forestry before and after the outbreak of war.

Until the wartime fellings had begun to take their toll, English woodlands were largely composed of broadleaved trees, more particularly oak, and this was especially so in the Crown forests. On some private estates in the midlands and the south of England, the woodlands consisted almost entirely of coppice or coppice-with-standards and where this was the case, little or no planting was carried out. Both these systems were well suited to shooting and game preservation and in many cases the woods were managed with pheasants in mind rather than timber production. The fact that rabbits and hares, when allowed to range unchecked, could quickly ruin an area of young trees, did nothing to improve matters.

As the full impact of submarine warfare began to be felt, so the demands on the country's woodlands increased and by the middle of 1916 considerable areas were being felled. Private woodlands bore the heaviest burden of these fellings simply because there were few other sources of supply. As an example of the spirit of the times, Lloyd George quoted in his war memoirs, a letter which he had received from Alfred de Rothschild in February 1917. In it he offered the beechwoods on his estate at Halton, between Tring and Wendover, as a gift to the nation and 'before long the splendid slopes of beech forest on the Chilterns were laid low by Canadian lumberjacks'.[12] However it was not only the better stands of timber that were felled since as the demand became more pressing so the prices rose and the less accessible woodlands of second and third quality were acquired. There can be little doubt that owners of these low grade woodlands benefited to a considerable extent since in peace time such areas would not have realized sufficient money to meet the cost of clearing and replanting.

By 1900 many of the conifers which had been introduced into Britain during the nineteenth century had reached an age and size that clearly demonstrated their value as timber trees and, in some cases, their adaptability to grow on the poorer quality sites. Sitka spruce, Douglas fir, the giant silver fir, *Abies grandis*, the western red cedar, *Thuya plicata*, and Japanese larch are examples of some of these introductions. Although by the beginning of the present century the species had not been used to any great extent, they later proved to be of the greatest value for replanting the areas felled during the war and in the creation of the new postwar forests.

Not only were changes taking place in the woods but also among those who worked in them. On many private estates were to be found woodmen who might well have traced their descent from the woodwards of the middle ages and A. C. Forbes gives the following description.

> *This type of man was chiefly found on the estates in coppice with standards districts, and was of purely local extraction. To regard him as little more than an ignorant woodman or labourer would be a great mistake. He may not have been a great reader, and probably had never heard of many species of trees now familiar to every forest labourer, nor was he acquainted with modern forest terminology. But in all matters relating to the growing of coppice and its conversion, the measurement of timber by the tree, the barking of oak, and the ancient lore associated with this class of woodland, he was entirely at home ... Many of these men could tell at a glance the number of cubic feet in a rough-headed oak, ash or elm, not perhaps with mathematical accuracy but as near as was necessary to estimate its value ... Many of them knew what an acre of underwood could turn out to within a dozen hurdles or bundles of peasticks. They recognised trees which were going back from those which were putting on a good increment, although growth borers and increment tables were outside their world of knowledge, and in the barking season their recognition of those trees which would 'run' and those which would not, saved their employers a good many pounds in the value of bark. Even in planting matters, they were not entirely ignorant, although their methods may not have produced good showing in costing returns.[13]*

With the passing of the years this patriarchal figure has been gradually replaced by the forestry worker of today who, unlike his predecessor, is now concerned with a wide range of mechanical equipment from chainsaws to tractors, with the increasing use of fertilizers and herbicides and who works for most of his time among conifers rather than hardwoods.

On many private estates before the First World War, woodland management was virtually non-existent and this state of affairs was due to several factors. In most cases the agent had very little knowledge of forestry although there were some notable exceptions such as P. T. Maw, and consequently the

20.   *The old tradition. Felling a Scots pine at Puslinch
near Yealmpton, South Devon in 1890 or thereabouts.*

management of the woods was left to the head forester who, like the agent, had seldom received any technical training in forestry. In addition to this there existed a general antipathy to forestry among many owners and their agents, based on the views that 'trees took a long time to grow' and unlike farm crops gave no quick return and consequently that 'forestry does not pay'. There was also the influence exerted by the sporting interests on an estate which frequently interfered with the management of the woods. The Report of the Royal Commission on Coast Erosion and Afforestation contains the following observation with reference to the evidence given by the head forester on a well known estate:

> *So intimate is the association in the United Kingdom between sport and forestry that even on an estate that is considered to possess some of the best managed woods in England, the sylvicultural details have to be accommodated to the hunting and shooting and trees must be taken down 'in different places to make cover for foxes, and so on'.*[14]

By the end of the war, forestry in this country was ready for a change and it only needed a key to unlock the door which could lead 'to-morrow to fresh woods and pastures new'. That key was provided by the Forestry Act of 1919.

THE ESTABLISHMENT OF THE FORESTRY COMMISSION

The purpose of the Forestry Act 1919[15] was to establish a Forestry Commission for the United Kingdom and to promote afforestation and timber production and the following is a summary of its main provisions. The Act which contained 11 sections, provided for the appointment of eight Commissioners, one of whom was to be chairman, and not less than two of whom were to have special knowledge and experience of forestry in Scotland; at least one was to have scientific attainments and a technical knowledge of forestry and one was to be a member of the House of Commons. Commissioners would serve for a period of five years and not more than three of them would receive salaries, the total sum of which would not exceed £4,500 but the Parliamentary Commissioner would be unpaid.

The Act laid down that it was the duty of the Commissioners to further the interests of forestry and to develop afforestation and timber production. It additionally provided that the powers and duties of the Board of Agriculture and Fisheries, the Board of Agriculture for Scotland and the Department of Agriculture and Technical Instruction for Ireland should, in so far as they applied to forestry, be transferred to the Commissioners. Powers were also given to the Commissioners to buy or lease land required for afforestation or in connection with it; to sell, let or exchange land which proved unsuitable for planting; to acquire standing timber and to dispose of such timber as belonged to them.

They were further empowered to make grants or loans in respect of afforestation or replanting and to undertake the management of, or give advice on the planting or management of, any woods belonging to individuals or local authorities or under the control of the Commissioners of Woods or any Government Department. The Commissioners could also establish and operate woodland industries or assist others to do so; undertake training and instruction in forestry; carry out research and experiments and publish the results of such work. If an occupier of land failed to deal with rabbits, hares and vermin (which was specifically stated to include grey squirrels) and consequently trees were damaged or likely to be damaged, the Commissioners could take action to control them.

Also authorized by the Act were the appointments of Assistant Commissioners for England and Wales, for Scotland and for Ireland and the establishment of four consultative committees for England, Wales, Scotland and Ireland respectively. Provision was also made for the Commissioners to acquire land compulsorily where such action was considered to be necessary. The financial arrangements for the Commission were provided by a fund known as the Forestry Fund and during the first ten years the sum of £3,500,000 was to be paid into it by annual instalments of such amounts as Parliament might think fit.

The Act came into force on 1st September 1919 and the Commissioners were appointed on 29th November: Lord Lovat (Chairman), The Rt Hon. F. D. Acland, M.P., Lord Clinton, L. Forestier-Walker, M.P., Sir John Stirling-Maxwell, Bt, T. B. Ponsonby, R. L. Robinson and Colonel W. T. Steuart-Fothringham. A. G. Herbert was appointed secretary to the Commissioners.

On 8th December 1919 the first trees were planted by the Forestry Commission and the following is an account of the events that are said to have preceded this historic occasion. At a meeting held in London on 7th December the Commissioners decided that the time had come for their programme of afforestation to begin and later that evening when Lord Lovat boarded the night train for Scotland, he intended to plant the first trees at Monaughty on the following day. However, Lord Clinton, who lived in Devon, evidently felt that, for tree planting, England was just as good a place as Scotland and before leaving London he got in touch with C. O. Hanson who was Divisional Officer at Exeter and Tom Brown, one of the Commission's foresters. Arrangements were made for them to meet Lord Clinton at Eggesford station early the next morning equipped with planting spades and trees to plant.

It would appear that Lord Clinton was accompanied by H. Murray (afterwards Sir Hugh Murray) who was Assistant Commissioner for England and Wales. On arrival at Eggesford, which lies approximately midway between Crediton and Barnstaple, the party proceeded to a site in what is now known as Eggesford Forest, where they planted a number of beech and larch. Having done so, Lord Clinton sent a telegram to Lord Lovat which was handed to him as he got off the train at Elgin. This informed him that the Commission's first tree had already been planted. Later a plaque was erected on the site bearing the following inscription.

THESE TREES WERE PLANTED
8TH DECEMBER 1919
BY

LORD CLINTON	COMMISSIONER
H. MURRAY	ASST. COMMISSIONER
C. O. HANSON	DIVISIONIAL OFFICER
T. BROWN	FORESTER

AND WERE THE FIRST PLANTED BY THE
FORESTRY COMMISSION IN THE
UNITED KINGDOM

The spelling is that which appears on the actual plaque.

During the initial period the organization of the Commission was briefly as follows. The main headquarters were located in London as also were the headquarters for England and Wales, these two countries being divided into five Divisions numbered one to five with their own headquarters at York, Shrewsbury, Cardiff, Exeter and London respectively. The headquarters for Scotland was situated in Edinburgh while that country was divided into four Divisions named the South Eastern, Western, North Eastern and Northern with individual headquarters at Edinburgh, Glasgow, Aberdeen and Inverness respectively. Ireland was formed into two Divisions, the Northern and Southern with the national and divisional headquarters all in Dublin.

The final stage in the establishment of the Commission was marked by the passing of the Forestry (Transfer of Woods) Act 1923[16] when the Crown Forests, which had previously been administered by the Office of Woods, were formally transferred to the Commission.

BETWEEN THE WARS

After the end of the war, conditions in this country gradually returned to normal and the first major event which took place in connection with forestry was the British Empire Forestry Conference. The United Kingdom delegates to the Conference, which was held in London in July 1920, were led by Lord Lovat and included the Rt Hon. F. D. Acland, Sir William Schlich and R. L. Robinson. Among the various matters that were considered by the Conference were forest policy, forest resources, research and education but two of the main points that emerged were first, the need to establish a centre for the training of forest officers and, second, the demand for a bureau for the collection and distribution of information on forestry.[17] One result of the Conference was the appointment by the Forestry Commissioners in November of that year, of an Inter-Departmental Committee under the chairmanship of Lord Clinton, to prepare a scheme for setting up a central institution for the training of forest officers.[18]

Concurrently with the Conference, an Empire Timber Exhibition was staged in London and this included an extensive display of timber grown in this country and its utilization. 'The object aimed at was to combine the efforts of the sylviculturalist, the timber merchant and the manufacturer into one educational exhibit'.[19] The success of this exhibition may be gathered from the fact that the interest shown by members of the public was so great that its duration was extended from two to three weeks.

The year also saw the issue of the first three bulletins prepared by the Forestry Commission, two of which were concerned with the rate growth of timber trees and one with forest insects.[20] The fact that the Commission had only been formed on 1st September 1919 and that these bulletins appeared early in 1920, suggests that much of the preliminary work had been carried out by the Interim Forest Authority. In 1921 the *First Annual Report of the Forestry Commissioners* which contained an account of the work of the Commission during its first year, was published.[21]

The *Forestry Act* 1919 provided for the establishment of Consultative Committees for England, Wales and Scotland and directed that each of these Committees should include among its members representatives of certain bodies and also persons who had appropriate interests and knowledge. These were the Board of Agriculture and Fisheries (in the case of England); county councils or other local bodies interested in forestry; societies concerned with afforestation; woodland owners; representatives of labour and persons who had practical experience of matters relating to forestry, woodcraft and woodland industries. It was not until the passing of the Forestry Act 1945 that these Consultative Committees were replaced by National Committees.

The Act of 1919 also enabled the Commissioners to carry out experiments and research and shortly after the Act had come into force two Research Officers were appointed, one for England and Wales and the other for Scotland. In December 1929 the Commissioners set up an Advisory Committee on Forest Research under the chairmanship of Mr R. L. Robinson but it was not until 1946 that Alice Holt Lodge was selected as the Commission's Research Station.[22]

Early in 1921 the country began to feel the effect of the economic and financial pressures of the post-war period, so that by March steps were being taken by the Government to reduce public expenditure and in this, forestry proved to be no exception. By the end of the year however, unemployment had increased to such an extent that the Forestry Commissioners were instructed to acquire additional land for planting, in order to provide employment in those areas that were most seriously affected.[23] At the same time an Unemployment Fund was set up of which £250,000 was allocated to forestry. From this sum, woodland owners and local authorities who provided work for the unemployed, were eligible to be paid grants in respect of planting and scrub clearance.[24]

The Committee on National Expenditure which the Government had appointed in 1921 under the chairmanship of Sir Eric Geddes and which was frequently referred to as the 'Geddes Committee', published its Second Interim Report in 1922.[25] This contained recommendations that the State Scheme for afforestation should be discontinued and that the Forestry Commission should be merged with the Ministry of Agriculture, but this catastrophe was averted largely as a result of Lord Lovat's ability and diplomacy.

After the passing of the Government of Ireland Act[26] in 1920 and the subsequent creation of the Irish Free State, all matters concerning forestry in Ireland were handed over either to the Free State Government or to the Government of Northern Ireland on the 1st April 1922. In the following year the Forestry (Transfer of Woods) Act became law and under it the Crown Forests were formally transferred to the Forestry Commissioners so that the Commission became the sole forest authority in this country. Shortly afterwards, the Railway Fires Act (1905) Amendment Act 1923[27] was passed and this increased the limit of a claim which could be made by a woodland owner from £100 to £200.

On 13th October 1924, the recommendations of the British Empire Forestry Conference of 1920 and those of the ensuing Inter Departmental Committee finally bore fruit. On that day, the Imperial Forestry Institute started work in temporary accommodation at the School of Forestry in Oxford, Professor R. S. Troup having been appointed Director of the Institute and Lord Clinton, Chairman of the Board of Governors.[28]

For some years the adverse effect of the atmospheric conditions upon many of the conifers at the Royal Botanic Gardens at Kew had been causing concern. Eventually at the suggestion of Sir John Stirling-Maxwell who was then a Forestry Commissioner, it was agreed that a new national pinetum should be established at Bedgebury near Goudhurst in Kent, under the joint control of the Royal Botanic Gardens and the Forestry Commission. The new pinetum, which was formed out of a part of Bedgbury Forest, came into being on 1st April 1924, the first trees being planted in the following year. Originally 50 acres were allocated for the pinetum but by 1972 it had been increased to 80 acres. In addition to the pinetum, an adjoining area was laid out in 1929 in a series of forest plots in which different species were planted. In 1972 this area extended to approximately 45 acres on which 151 plots had been laid out and in which 97 species were represented.[29]

In 1925 forestry lost one of its outstanding figures with the death of Sir William Schlich. He had been a member of the Indian Forestry Service from 1867 to 1885, had then become Professor of Forestry at the Royal Indian Engineering College at Cooper's Hill for 25 years and had subsequently moved to Oxford University for a further 15 years, where he became Professor of Forestry. He had been a member of several important committees including the Acland Committee and had given evidence before a number of others. He was the author of the first three volumes of the *Manual of Forestry* and, over a long period, had written many papers on silviculture and forest management. In an appreciation of his work, the following tribute was paid to him by the Forestry Commissioners: 'To him, rather than to any other one man belongs the credit of the spread throughout the Empire of modern ideas on forest policy and silviculture.'[30]

The same year saw the formation of a new forestry society entitled The Society of Foresters of Great Britain (now The Institute of Foresters) and its constitution was formally adopted at a meeting held in Oxford on 5th August 1926. The object of the Society was 'to advance and spread in Great Britain the knowledge of technical forestry in all its aspects' and subsequently R. L. Robinson was elected as the first President. Its members were for the most part professional foresters who were drawn from the Forestry Commission and from the teaching and research departments of those universities that were concerned with forestry. The first copy of the Society's journal appeared in 1927 under the title of *Forestry.*

Although the Department of Scientific and Industrial Research had appointed the Forest Products Research Board in 1921, it was not until 1925 that the Forest Products Research Laboratory was established. Accommodated at first at the Royal Aircraft Establishment at Farnborough, it moved, two years later, to a permanent site at Princes Risborough, near Aylesbury. When, in 1965, the Department of Scientific and Industrial Research was dispersed, the Laboratory became a part of the Ministry of Technology but in 1970, it was transferred to the Department of Trade and Industry and a year later to the Department of the Environment.[31]

In March 1927 Lord Lovat resigned from the Forestry Commission to take up his appointment as Parliamentary Under-Secretary for Dominion Affairs. As the first chairman of the Commission he had guided its development, influenced its policy and saved it from early extinction and his services to the Commission cannot be over-estimated. He was succeeded by Lord Clinton who, like Lord Lovat, was an owner of extensive woodlands in which he took great interest and who had also been a Commissioner from the start. During April another Forestry Act[32] became law which increased the number of Commissioners from eight to ten and enabled them to make bye-laws in respect of any land under their control. In an attempt to encourage private owners and local authorities to undertake more planting, the Commission drew attention to the grants that were available. These were up to £2 an acre for conifers and up to £4 for approved hardwoods and a notice issued by the Commissioners in August 1927 contained the following somewhat optimistic paragraph: 'These grants will no doubt induce greater activity in systematic planting by municipalities and others, and also provide increased employment, especially during the winter months.'[33] When, three years later, the Tenth Annual Report was published, it was, however, remarked that the provision of grants and technical advice 'have not been successful in arresting the deterioration of the home woodlands in private ownership much less in restoring the pre-war position.'[34]

By 1930 the country was facing further economic problems so that it again became necessary to examine the country's finances and in 1931 another Committee on National Expenditure was appointed.[35] This Committee recommended that the Commissioners should not undertake any new acquisitions of land 'for the present', that no new forest workers holdings should be formed and that planting should be curtailed to 20,000 acres for the ensuing five years and should only be on land that had already been acquired. However, after the Commission's case had been put to the Chancellor of the Exchequer, it was agreed that the allocation to the Commission should be reduced to £450,000 per annum for the next five years. After taking into account the Commission's income from its own resources this figure would be increased to about £600,000 and this was to be spent as the Commissioners saw fit. In this way an overall limit was placed on the Commissioners expenditure without specifying how the necessary saving should be achieved.[36]

A census of woodlands and home-grown timber production had been put in hand in 1924 under the direction of the Forestry Commission but it was not until 1928 that the report, in which the results appeared, was published.[37] This gave the total woodland area in Great Britain as 2,958,672 acres and it is interesting to note that 50 years later, the area of productive woodlands in Great Britain amounted to approximately 4,218,000 acres. In addition, there were in 1978 some 716,500 acres of scrub and felled woodland giving an overall total of about 4,934,500 acres.[38] The report also contained the following observation in respect of privately owned woodlands: 'It is unlikely that the area of effectively productive woodland in private ownership will in the future exceed 1½ million acres, if indeed it reaches that figure.' In point of fact, in March 1978, the area of privately owned productive woodland in Great Britain extended to well over 2 million acres.

Since the end of the war the status of forestry in this country had undergone a dramatic change, largely due to the work of the Forestry Commission. At the same time a new approach to forestry was beginning to develop on many private estates and as evidence of this, the Royal English Arboricultural Society changed its name in 1931 to the Royal English Forestry Society.

During 1932 Sir Roy Robinson, who had been knighted in the previous year, succeeded Sir John Stirling-Maxwell as Chairman of the Forestry Commission and so attained the position which he was to hold until his death in 1952.

If the last ten years before the First World War were concerned with forestry and the establishment of a forest authority, then the last ten years before the Second World War were correspondingly concerned with the disposal of the timber that the country was now producing. Although the rate of planting was not as fast as had been anticipated in the Acland Report, by 30th September 1929 the Forestry Commission had, nevertheless, planted 138,279 acres while private owners and local authorities had achieved 76,736 acres.[39] It was consequently very evident that as afforestation and replanting continued, more attention would have to be paid to the utilization and marketing of home-grown timber. With this in mind the Commissioners appointed an Inter-Departmental Home-grown Timber Committee in December 1931[40] with Sir John Stirling-Maxwell as chairman, and in September 1933 the Committee issued its interim report.[41] The matters which it considered included the transport of timber, its disposal in small lots and in fluctuating quantities and the lack of seasoning and grading. In its Report the Committee recommended that more attention should be paid to the requirements of those industries that consumed large quantities of timber and as a result the Commission issued four booklets which set out in detail the demands for timber in coalmining, shipbuilding and in the box, packing-case and wood-turning industries.[42]

In the meantime and before the publication of the Inter-Departmental Committee's Report, the Central Landowners' Association (now the Country Landowners' Association) had called a conference on the marketing of home-grown timber at the end of 1932. Representatives of eight bodies which were concerned with forestry were invited to attend and these comprised the Royal English Forestry Society, the English Forestry Association Ltd, the Chartered Surveyors Institution and the Land Agents Society together with four Scottish societies having similar interests. There was little doubt that there were many matters on which action was needed and the editorial of the *Quarterly Journal of Forestry* for January 1933 contained the observation that 'present conditions in the marketing of home-grown timber are nothing short of chaotic', and concluded with the comment that 'The fact that these societies are getting together for the purpose of constructing a scheme (for marketing) is one of the most hopeful auguries for English estate forestry.'[43]

In November 1933 a second conference, sometimes referred to as the Home-Grown Timber Conference, was held under the chairmanship of Lord Clinton and those attending included representatives of woodland owners, timber merchants and the several societies and institutions that were interested in the matter. On this occasion reports from 27 counties on the original proposals which had been put forward at the previous conference were considered. It was subsequently agreed that the Chairman should draw up a detailed scheme for the formation of a marketing association and this was prepared by Lord Clinton in December 1933.[44]

In spite of these efforts to improve the marketing of timber and woodland products there was a general feeling of uncertainty about the future and in February 1934 a national deputation from those concerned with forestry, visited the House of Commons. The object was to impress upon the Government that unless some assistance was forthcoming, the forestry industry would decline to such an extent that not only would there be a massive increase in unemployment, but also a dangerous situation would be created from a national point of view. The deputation which included representatives of the forestry societies, land owners, professional institutions connected with the land and timber merchants in both England and Scotland, was received by the Financial Secretary to the Treasury, L. Hore Belisha.[45]

The Home-Grown Timber Marketing Association was formed in January 1934 and in November it issued the first bulletin of timber prices and marketing information. At the first General Meeting, held on 30th January 1935, Lord Clinton was elected President of the Association and by the middle of 1935 five branches had been formed.

In May 1934 the Forestry Commissioners appointed a subcommittee to examine and report on the various matters relating to the marketing of timber. In the following February the subcommittee put forward its proposals and acting on these, Sir Roy Robinson announced the setting up of the National Home-Grown Timber Council in March 1935. This body would be concerned with economics and statistics, trade information and propaganda and a limited amount of research which would not normally be carried out at the Forest Products Research Laboratory. The Council would not become involved in any commercial transactions and would have an independent chairman. Its composition, excluding the chairman, would be as follows.

Four timber growers — two English and two Scottish.
Four timber merchants — two English and two Scottish.
Four users of English or Scottish timber.
One representative of the Forestry Commission.
One representative of the Forest Products Research Laboratory.

The Commission undertook to make a grant towards the expenses of the Council of £7,500 over a period of five years on condition that the other bodies on the Council contributed not less than £500 between them.[46] The Editor of the *Quarterly Journal of Forestry* in commenting on this new development said: 'We welcome the formation of the Council as being the most important step in the advancement of British forestry since the establishment of the Forestry Commission.'[47] The National Home-Grown Timber Council was constituted as a limited company in February 1936 with Sir Edward Grigg as chairman while Lord Clinton and W. E. Hiley as members of the Home-Grown

Timber Marketing Association represented the English timber growers and
H. E. Newsum and J. W. C. Agate of the Federated Home-Grown Timber
Merchants' Association represented the English timber merchants.[48]

At the same time two matters were giving rise to increasing concern: the
first, which was obvious to all, was the problem of unemployment while the
second, which was only apparent to those who were conversant with such
matters, was the condition of those woodlands that were in private ownership.
Early in 1936 the Government increased the Forestry Fund from £450,000 a
year to £500,000 and it was intended that this sum together with the
Commissioners own income, would allow the planting programme to be
increased by 50 per cent and so provide work for the unemployed. In this way,
it was possible to take some positive steps to deal with the problem of
unemployment; but to provide a remedy for the debility of private forestry was
a very different matter.

In December 1936 the Royal English Forestry Society appointed a committee
'to prepare a report on the methods which should be adopted to encourage
better forest management on private estates' and in March 1937 a meeting
was held to consider the problem when the discussion was opened by Sir Roy
Robinson, Chairman of the Forestry Commission. It was not difficult to
diagnose the reasons for this unsatisfactory state of affairs and although
various suggestions were made as to how these might be overcome, the fact
remained that it was on the individual woodland owner that the success or
failure of private forestry ultimately rested. 'A real comprehensive improvement
depends in the first instance on the arousing of forest consciousness among
owners, and in providing them with the means to acquire knowledge. That is
the first step, the most important step and the most difficult step.'[49]

In its efforts to encourage private owners to take more interest in their
woodlands the Royal English Forestry Society published a booklet in 1937
entitled *Estate Woodlands* which provided concise information for woodland
owners. For their part, the Forestry Commissioners held two conferences in
February 1938 and in May 1939 respectively which were attended by
representatives of the various bodies concerned with forestry. One of the
results of the first conference was the appointment of an Experimental
Advisory Committee in 1939 to ascertain the demand for advice on woodland
management in Kent, Surrey and Sussex but its work was brought to a halt by
the outbreak of war.[50]

THE GATHERING CLOUDS

Although the situation in Europe had been deteriorating for some time, it was
not until the Munich Agreement in September 1938 that the dangers began to
be fully appreciated by the public as a whole. However, the possibility of
another war had already been anticipated in some Government departments
and preliminary steps taken to meet this contingency. Discussions had been

held in 1936 regarding the control of timber supplies and a scheme was drawn up in 1938 for the subsequent formation of the Timber Control.[51] In 1937 representations were made to the Forestry Commissioners by the National Home-Grown Timber Council, supported by the two Royal Forestry Societies, that a new census of woodlands should be carried out and this was commenced in January 1938.[52] Unfortunately the progress of the work was overtaken by events and when, by the middle of 1939, only 18 per cent of the country had been covered, less accurate methods had to be adopted for the remainder.[53] At the beginning of 1939 the Home-Grown Timber Advisory Committee was appointed. This was composed of representatives of the timber trade, woodland owners, the Board of Trade and the Forestry Commission and was at first concerned with drawing up the maximum prices for timber which were to come into operation in the event of war being declared.[54]

As the clouds began to gather, the difficulties which lay ahead began to appear with increasing clarity. Had the country possessed extensive reserves of good quality timber there would still have been problems but, with the plantations which had been established by the Forestry Commission still under 20 years of age and with many acres of private woodlands largely unproductive, the prospect was far from encouraging.

> The international crisis has left us with a sense of insecurity such as we have not felt since the Great War. We are conscious of this insecurity not only in the political field in that we might at any time find ourselves at war, but also in the field of economics and commerce. . . . Estates are being broken up and the woodlands are being devastated with little prospect of replanting; in other words the best timber is being skimmed with little regard for the growth of what remains . . .[55]

In this atmosphere of uncertainty and impending danger, a dynamic figure passed from the forestry scene when on 9th June 1939 Sir Francis Dyke Acland died. Although he owned large estates his chief interest in forestry lay in its social aspect since he regarded it as a means of improving the conditions of rural life and of contributing to the well being of the countryside. In July 1916 he was appointed chairman of the Forestry Sub-Committee of the Reconstruction Committee and its report which became known as the 'Acland Report' laid the foundations of the Forestry Commission. He was one of the original Commissioners who were appointed in 1919 and he remained one until his death, 20 years later. While he was more interested in forest policy than silviculture, he took great interest in his woods and was responsible for the first edition of *Forestry Practice* which was published in 1933 as Forestry Commission Bulletin No. 14.

As the summer of 1939 drew to a close the nation once again stood on the threshold of a major war in which, as in 1914, the country's woodlands were to play a vital part.

THE SECOND WORLD WAR 11

THE CALM BEFORE THE STORM

Although war was declared on 3rd September 1939, seven months elapsed before the British Army became involved in any major action and in this respect the situation was very different to that which had existed in the First World War. Whereas by the end of November 1914 the battles of Mons, Le Cateau, the Marne and the first battle of Ypres had been fought, it was not until April 1940, when the operations in Norway began, that the Army was involved in its first action of any importance. The country was thus accorded a period of comparative calm before the storm broke and this provided further time for making the nation's resources more readily available.

At the outbreak of war immediate action was taken to put into operation two prearranged plans, in order to safeguard the country's timber supplies. The first of these placed the Forestry Commission on a wartime footing while the second brought about the control of the felling, use and prices of timber.

On 3rd September the Forestry Commission was divided into two parts: the Timber Production Department which was to be responsible for the supply of home-grown timber and the Forest Management Department which was to manage the Commission's forests. On the same day the Timber Control Department of the Ministry of Supply, generally referred to as 'the Timber Control' came into being under Major A. I. Harris (afterwards Sir Archibald Harris) who was President of the Timber Trade Federation and who had been appointed Controller. With its headquarters at Bristol, it was divided into four Departments: I, Imported Timber Supplies; II, Home-Grown Timber Supplies; III, Requirements, Distribution, etc., and IV, Finance.

The main task of the Timber Control was to regulate the supply of timber and, if this fell short of requirements, to decide how the timber available could be used to the best advantage. Department II, which was also known as Forestry Commission Timber Supply, was administered by the Commission with Sir Roy Robinson as Deputy Controller and three Forestry Commissioners, W. L. Taylor (afterwards Sir William Ling Taylor), Sir Samuel Strang Steel and L. Ropner (afterwards Sir Leonard Ropner) as Assistant Controllers for England and Wales, Scotland and Headquarters, respectively. Among other senior members of the staff were two Acquisition Officers, the Hon. Nigel Orde-Powlett (afterwards Lord Bolton) who was President of the Royal English Forestry Society and who was responsible for England and Wales, and Lord Kinnaird who was responsible for Scotland.[1] Early in September the Timber Control issued three Orders which fixed the prices for standing timber and set out the regulations regarding the sale of trees and the issue of felling licences.[2]

It had been agreed that the Timber Control should deal only in sawn timber and, if necessary, in pitprops from the Forestry Commission and that it would not purchase standing timber. Consequently there was a tendency for Department II which was concerned with Home-Grown Timber Supplies and which was administered by the Forestry Commission, to be regarded as a separate entity. It was subsequently decided in December 1939 that, as from 1st January 1940, the Commission should operate independently of the Timber Control but at the same time would continue to work in close contact with it. Further difficulties arose however, when these new arrangements were put into operation and in May 1940 a Timber Control Board was appointed for the purpose of co-ordinating the outturn and utilization of home-grown timber.

The Board was composed of three members under an independent chairman and consisted of Major A. I. Harris, the Timber Controller; Sir Roy Robinson, Chairman of the Forestry Commission and a representative of the Mines Department with G. Dallas as chairman. However, the Ministry of Supply announced in January 1941 that the work of home timber production would be transferred from the Forestry Commission to a new Home Timber Production Department in the Ministry of Supply with Sir James Calder as Director.[3] This change came into effect on 1st February 1941 and although from that date the Forestry Commission reverted to its normal role, those of its members who had been working in the Timber Production Department, were seconded to the Ministry of Supply for the remainder of the war.

THE STORM BREAKS

On 9th April 1940 German forces invaded Norway and Denmark and any hope of further supplies of timber from Scandinavia ended abruptly. Even before these events had taken place the President of the Royal English Forestry Society had sent the following message to woodland owners through the medium of the Society's journal.

> *In normal times amongst the most important of our endeavours are the conservation of woodlands and the prevention of excessive fellings. Our function, in fact, is to promote good forestry and to*

increase woodlands — not to destroy them. But war alters all things
. . . and is essentially destructive and, now that our country is at war,
every resource, every posession, every means, must be devoted in
their entirety, and without any hesitation whatsoever, to its successful
prosecution and the maintenance of our essential industries.[4]

In view of this, it is interesting to note that Sir Roy Robinson, when speaking after the Society's Annual General Meeting on 19th April, announced that up to the end of March 1940, that is, since September 1939, licences had been issued for felling 58 million cubic feet in England and Wales and 35 million feet in Scotland which were substantial amounts by any standard.[5]

On 10th May Germany attacked Holland, Belgium and Luxemburg and when, on 14th, the French frontier towns of Sedan and Longwy fell, the German army advanced across France. On 17th May Holland capitulated, the Germans entered Brussels and the eastern sector of the Maginot Line collapsed while ten days later Belgium surrendered. By 4th June the evacuation of the British Army from Dunkirk had been completed and on 22nd June France negotiated an armistice with Germany.

Between 3rd September 1939 and 9th April 1940 the losses of British merchant shipping amounted to approximately 339,000 gross tons and those of allies and neutrals to 349,000 making a total of 688,000 tons. From 10th April 1940 to 17th March 1941, however, British losses increased to 1,677,000 gross tons and allied and neutral losses to some 637,000 tons which together amounted to 2,314,000 gross tons.[6] At the same time the intensity of enemy air attacks greatly increased and in 1941, during March, April and May, heavy raids were carried out on a number of cities and ports including London, Coventry, Manchester, Merseyside, Bristol, Hull, Portsmouth and Plymouth. In addition to causing heavy casualties and extensive damage to buildings and port installations, some of these raids destroyed stocks of timber and pitwood. Somewhat incongruously, the recovery of timber from bombed buildings provided a considerable volume of useful material which was later supplemented by the utilization of timber from packing cases which contained goods imported from abroad.[7] The effect of these calamitous events was to place even greater pressures on the country's woodlands, since timber supplies from Europe no longer existed while those from across the Atlantic had become increasingly hazardous both at sea and on their arrival in British ports.

By June 1942 imported timber had been replaced by home-grown produce for a large number of purposes some of which were of the greatest importance and included the construction of small naval craft. 'Many hundreds of vessels were built such as drifters, minesweepers, Motor Torpedo Boats and speedboats almost entirely of home-grown wood.'[8] Home-grown timber was also used in aeroplane construction and the de Haviland 'Mosquito', one of the most versatile of aircraft, was built of plywood formed from English beech.

As the summer of 1942 passed the pattern of events became painfully clear, for as shipping losses increased, so more ways were sought for replacing imported timber with timber grown in this country and this in turn, resulted in still greater demands being made on Britain's woodlands. In a letter addressed to the Deputy President of the Royal English Forestry Society on 7th August 1942, the Director of the Home Timber Production Department, G. Lenanton (afterwards Sir Gerald Lenanton), stressed the urgent need for more timber and pitwood.

> The shipping situation makes it absolutely essential that our home production of timber should be speeded up still further. During the last six months British woodlands have been felled at the rate of approximately 1,800 acres a week, in itself a startling figure, but in future some 2,200 acres a week must be felled if we are to produce that volume of timber which is required for the effective prosecution of the war.
>
> While all kinds of utilizable timber are in demand, the most urgent need is for pitwood, of which supplies are limited. I know that pitwood production entails the sacrifice of young plantations which have not yet attained financial maturity, but the maintenance of supplies for the pits is of vital importance, and I must appeal to owners to part readily with their pitwood stands when asked to do so.[9]

On 1st January 1943 the Ministry of Supply announced that as from that date the organization of trade production in England and Wales would be based on the nine divisions of the Home Timber Production Department instead of the areas of the Timber Control. It was also announced that as from the same date the Timber Control Board had been disbanded since the purposes for which it had been set up had now, for the most part, been achieved.

ARMY FORESTRY UNITS

During the war, forestry units of the British, Australian, New Zealand and Canadian Armies played an important part in the felling and conversion of timber both in this country and overseas and a full description of their activities and movements has been provided by Meiggs.[10]

In the British Army the first forestry unit, the 129th Forestry Company, Royal Engineers, was formed shortly after the outbreak of war, largely due, it is said, to the efforts of Colonel A. H. Lloyd who was lecturer in Forestry Engineering at Oxford and who had previously served in the Royal Engineers. After proceeding to France in January 1940, the Company worked in the

Forest of Crécy producing timber for the British Expeditionary Force but after the fall of France it was evacuated from St Malo on 23rd June.[11] When it returned to England the unit was, at first, employed on coast defence in the south of England but was later transferred to the Forest of Dean where it remained until the autumn of 1943 when it moved to Cirencester.

During the summer of 1940, two more Forestry Companies were raised, the 130th and 131st, the former being stationed in Sherwood Forest while the latter joined the 129th Company in the Forest of Dean. During the summer of 1942, the 130th Company was posted to Sierre Leone in West Africa while the 129th and 131st Companies remained in this country until the end of June 1944 when they proceeded to Normandy.[12] As the front advanced so the Companies moved forward and their various tasks included the provision of piles for bridges over the Rhine and material for log roads in Holland. During these operations both Companies carried out other tasks which were allocated to the Royal Engineers as the occasion demanded, and the Officer Commanding the 131st Forestry Company was killed in the Ardennes when the unit was engaged in lifting mines.[13]

The 11th New Zealand Forestry Company, Royal New Zealand Engineers, arrived in this country on 20th June 1940 and in view of the threat of an invasion was at first employed in connection with coast defence works in Kent and Sussex, but in August the Company moved to Cirencester. Early in November, the 14th and 15th Forestry Companies landed in England and subsequently worked in Berkshire, Hampshire and Wiltshire with head-quarters in Chippenham. In August 1943 the 14th Company proceeded overseas to Algeria and later operated in Italy while the other two companies returned to New Zealand in September of that year.[14]

Although it was originally intended that the 1st and 2nd Australian Forestry Companies, Royal Australian Engineers, were to proceed to the Forests of the Landes which lie between Bordeaux and Biarritz, the collapse of France necessitated a change in plan and in July 1940 they disembarked in this country. Shortly after their arrival they moved to Northumberland where they were in operation near Hexham and at Chathill, some eight miles north of Alnwick. A year later, in August 1941, the 3rd Australian Forestry Company reached England and took over from the 1st Company at Chathill which, with the 2nd Company, moved to Dumfriesshire. They were joined by the 3rd Company in February 1942. During May 1943 the 2nd and 3rd Companies moved to Sussex but within a short time they received orders to return to Australia and left this country in September, the 1st Company following them in November 1943.[15]

The Canadian Forestry Corps was the largest of all the army forestry units that operated in the United Kingdom during the war and, in the first half of 1941, no less than 20 companies landed in this country to be followed by an additional 10 companies in 1942. On arrival they moved to Scotland where they operated in the area between Perth and Inverness. In 1943, 10 companies returned to Canada but after the allied landing in France in June 1944, five companies joined the 129th and 131st Forestry Companies RE in Normandy. A further five companies proceeded to France and Belgium at the end of 1944 while the remaining companies returned to Canada in 1945.[16]

CIVILIAN FORESTRY UNITS

In addition to the Army units which have been described in the previous section, two civilian formations from overseas, the Newfoundland Forestry Unit and the British Honduras Unit, operated in this country during the war.

It had been evident from the beginning of the emergency that if the war continued for any appreciable length of time, considerable demands would be made on labour resources. It was feared that as more men joined the forces, the ensuing shortage of labour might well be a limiting factor in obtaining supplies of timber and pitprops from the country's woodlands. With this in mind the Newfoundland Government was asked, in November 1939, if it could recruit 2,000 timber fallers for work in the United Kingdom and on 18th December the first 350 men landed at Liverpool. In the middle of February the last draft arrived, bringing the strength of the unit up to 2,150. At first the men worked in Scotland and on the Border but later detachments were moved to Yorkshire and the New Forest. At the end of six months service about one-third of the original contingent either joined the armed forces or returned to Newfoundland, and these were replaced by another draft of 1,000, the first of whom arrived at the end of June 1940. The Unit continued to work in this country for the remainder of the war and it was not until the spring of 1946 that the last 600 men returned to Newfoundland.[17]

In spite of the great assistance which had been provided by the formations already referred to in this chapter, by the spring of 1941 still more men were needed to help in the extensive fellings which had to be undertaken. Consequently, in May of that year, the Governor of British Honduras was asked if the colony could provide 500 skilled woodmen and in August the first contingent arrived, which in due course commenced operations in Scotland. In November 1943 a second contingent of 341 men landed at Glasgow and subsequently moved to the north of Scotland. However, as the shipping situation improved so that more timber could be imported, it was no longer necessary to retain the unit in this country and the main body sailed for home shortly before Christmas. Except for 200 men who decided to remain in this country on other war work, the remainder returned to British Honduras at the end of April 1944.[18]

THE WOMEN'S TIMBER CORPS

During the First World War members of the Women's Forestry Corps had shown themselves to be remarkably competent in various fields of timber production and it is not surprising that their successors achieved equally good results 25 years later. After the outbreak of war, members of the Women's Land Army, which had been formed in the summer of 1939, were given the opportunity of working in forestry and subsequently about 1,000 chose to do so. In due course the suggestion was put forward that an independent forestry unit for women should be established but this did not meet with official approval. Eventually in March 1942, consent was given for the formation of a special section, within the Women's Land Army, to be known as the Women's Timber Corps. Under this new arrangement the responsibility for the welfare of members of the Corps became that of the Home Timber Production Department in place of the Women's Land Army.

The establishment of the Timber Corps had a marked effect on the number of women who chose forestry work and recruitment increased from 80 per month in April 1942 to 180 in February 1943. Before the Corps came into being, women who wished to become timber measurers were given a short period of training at Park End in the Forest of Dean but the remainder had to acquire what knowledge they could after they arrived on the working site. While this arrangement may have been acceptable when the intake was small, with the large increase in numbers which occurred after April 1942 an improved system was needed. From that time all recruits were sent to a training centre for a month's course before starting work and these centres included Park End, Culford near Bury St Edmunds and Wetherby. Members of the Corps were now employed on many forestry operations, one example of which is shown in illustration 21.

In July 1943 the strength of the Women's Timber Corps reached a total of 4,700 in England and Wales and 1,500 in Scotland and at the same time recruiting for the Corps was brought to an end. Meiggs summarized their successes and achievements in the following words.

> During this period women replaced men in every branch of production. They drove tractors and lorries, they worked on saw benches, they felled, they measured, they even sharpened saws. They became forewomen and acquisition officers. They became in fact an integral part of the great production machine. Without them the targets could not have been achieved.[19]

In August 1946, the Women's Timber Corps was disbanded.

21. *The Women's Timber Corps, 1943. Cutting pitprops to length on a portable push bench.*

Planning for the Years Ahead

In July 1916 a Forestry Sub-Committee of the Reconstruction Committee had been appointed in order to consider the future of forestry after the First World War and by 1941 a similar problem had begun to receive attention. In 1940 the Royal Scottish Forestry Society prepared a report on the future of estate forestry and this was followed, during the next year, by a memorandum drawn up by the Royal English Forestry Society. This was submitted, in November 1941, to the Greenwood Committee on Post-War Reconstruction, the Forestry Commission and Lord Justice Scott's Committee[20] while the Central Landowner's Association (now the Country Landowner's Association), the Royal Agricultural Society of England and other bodies which were interested in forestry, also put forward their views.

Eventually, in June 1943, the report[21] which had been prepared by the

Forestry Commissioners on post-war forest policy was published and the following is a summary of some of the main points that it contained.

It was proposed that the future forest area in this country should be 5 million acres which would not only be planted but also be systematically managed and developed. The area of 5 million acres should comprise: 3 million acres of bare land which would be afforested; and 2 million acres of existing woodlands which would be selected from those which were better suited for forestry than for any other national purpose. In order to ensure that private woodlands were properly managed, it was proposed that any which were included in the 2 million acres should either be dedicated to forestry by their owners or acquired by the state.

The objective of 5 million acres should be achieved over a period of 50 years and to accomplish this, two alternative programmes were submitted. The first, referred to as the 'Desirable Programme', envisaged the planting of 1,100,000 acres in the first decade and 1,500,000 acres in the second, that is, a total of 2,600,000 acres in the first 20 years. The second, described as the 'Intermediate Programme' entailed the planting of 875,000 acres in the first decade — 225,000 less than in the Desirable Programme.

As to finance, it was estimated that the 'net outlay' for the Desirable Programme would be £41.2 million and for the Intermediate Programme, £32 million. Due attention would be paid to amenity, recreational facilities and the creation of new National Forest Parks.

The Report also laid down the following 'five essentials for successful British forestry':

> Firstly, the recognition by the Government of the importance of growing timber in this country.
> Secondly, the need for continuity in the national forestry policy including the financial aspect.
> Thirdly, the existence of a Forest Authority for formulating and implementing Government policy.
> Fourthly, the maintenance of a unified Forest Service of highly qualified personnel.
> Fifthly, the provision of adequate services for research, education and information.

The third chapter of the Report considered the future of private woodlands under four main headings: basic considerations, dedication of woodlands, taxation and marketing. Under the first, the Commissioners enunciated what they considered to be the seven fundamental principles on which the future of private forestry depended. These were as follows.

> That rehabilitation of the woodlands must proceed with certainty and rapidity.
> That all planting and natural regeneration acceptable instead of

replanting, must be properly looked after up to the stage of satisfactory 'establishment'.

In every case the owner must reach an early decision as to whether he is prepared to proceed with the work of rehabilitation.

If an owner is so prepared and can give satisfactory assurances he is deserving of financial assistance from the State.

Where no satisfactory assurances are forthcoming within a stated period the State should acquire the land.

That the wartime system of felling licences must continue until the reserve of standing timber can be adjudged satisfactory.

That some degree of control of the silviculture of private woodlands is necessary.

The second section, which was concerned with the Commissioner's proposals for dedication, contained the following undertakings which an owner would be required to give if he wished to dedicate his woods.

To use the land in such a way that timber production is the main object.

To work to a plan, to be approved by the Forest Authority, which would lay down the main operations to be undertaken.

To employ skilled supervision.

To keep adequate accounts.

In return an owner would receive financial assistance which, it was proposed, would be an amount equal to 25 per cent of the approved net annual expenditure together with loans in respect of the remaining 75 per cent. Other arrangements were proposed in the case of 'small woods'. As regards the marketing of forest produce, the Commissioners put forward two principles. First, that a reserve of standing timber should be created as quickly as possible and second that an efficient home-grown timber trade should be maintained which could be expanded in a time of emergency.

In January 1944 a supplementary report[22] on private woodlands was published. This was the result of discussions on the proposals contained in Chapter III of the first Report which had taken place between the Commissioners and representatives of the forestry societies and landowning bodies in England and Scotland. The Report was chiefly concerned with the financial assistance which should be given to woodland owners and contained the following agreed proposals.

A planting grant of £7.10s [£7.50p] for every acre planted or replanted, whether hardwoods or softwoods.

Loans (in addition to planting grants) up to an amount to be fixed with reference to individual circumstances, the rate of interest to be that at which the Forest Authority is financed plus a small operating charge.

> *A maintenance grant for 15 years of 2s 6d [12½p] per acre per annum on every acre planted and properly maintained.*
>
> *A maintenance grant for 15 years of 2s 6d per acre per annum from the date of dedication on all productive woodlands other than new plantations (which are covered by the previous paragraph).*
>
> *Grants to be revised after 5 years on the basis of ascertained costs.*

When the scheme for the dedication of woodlands was subsequently adopted by the Government these proposals became known as Basis 2.[23]

As an alternative to the foregoing proposals, a grant of 25 per cent of the approved net annual expenditure (as proposed in the first Report) together with the loans referred to above, were to be available to owners. This arrangement was later referred to as Basis 1. In the case of small woods that is to say, those that were not suitable for dedication, the planting grant of £7.10s would be available on the understanding that they could be felled in an emergency. The Dedication Scheme was eventually confirmed by the passing of the Forestry Act 1947.[24]

The Acland Report of 1916 and the Report on Post-War Forest Policy of 1943 bear a direct relationship to each other since they both had the same common purpose — the well-being and advancement of British forestry. The Acland Report however, must be regarded as being of the greater consequence since it was instrumental in creating the Forestry Commission which, in itself, was one of the most important events in the history of forestry in this country. At the same time the Post-War Report not only brought about a reinvigoration of British forestry but it also provided a firm foundation for private forestry through the medium of the Dedication Scheme. This gave owners a new incentive to replant their woods and to manage them in accordance with the rules of good forestry.

THE TASK ACCOMPLISHED

By the end of 1943 the country's woodlands had suffered extensively from the heavy wartime fellings which had become necessary, and in order that 'the damage to woodlands should be as small as possible consistent with the maximum war effort' a Consultative Commitee was set up by the Home Timber Production Department in January 1944. In addition to the Director, the Chief Acquisition Officer and other senior members of the Department, the Committee included representatives of the Forestry Commission, the Forest Products Research Laboratory, the Royal English Forestry Society, landowners and land agents.[25]

In March 1944 a new timber Order[26] came into force which consolidated the previous regulations regarding the acquisition and disposal of growing trees and home-grown timber in the round, and extended the maximum prices payable in respect of them. Later in the year the Ministry of Supply announced that, with the exception of the above Order and one relating to kiln drying, all orders that were still in operation were to be revoked and replaced by five new orders, three of which were concerned with home-grown timber.[27]

On 6th June 1944 the Allied Forces landed in Normandy and no further proof was needed to show that the tide was now flowing strongly in their favour. Despite heavy resistance and the reverses suffered at Arnhem in September and in the Ardennes in December, the Allies pressed on to victory in Europe which they achieved on 9th May 1945.

Within six weeks the Forestry Act 1945[28] became law and as a result a number of changes were made in the constitution of the Forestry Commission. The Act laid down that the Commission should consist of a chairman and not more than nine Commissioners; that at least three of them should have experience in forestry and a special knowledge of it; that one Commissioner should possess scientific attainments and a technical knowledge of forestry and that members of the House of Commons were no longer eligible for appointment as Commissioners. The Act also placed the Commissioners under the direction of the Ministry of Agriculture and Fisheries or the Secretary of State for Scotland and transferred to the appropriate Minister, the Commissioner's powers regarding the acquisition of land. In addition the Commissioners were required to appoint three National Committees for England, Wales and Scotland respectively.[29] Consequent upon the passing of this Act several changes occurred in the membership of the Commission, Sir Roy Robinson being appointed Director-General while at the same time continuing as Chairman.

On 15th August, three months after the successful termination of the war in Europe, Japan was defeated and so, after nearly six years the task was accomplished and victory finally achieved. Some idea of the contribution which was made by the country's woodlands during this period can be gathered from the following figures. During the course of the seven years from 1940 some 29,500 acres of Forestry Commission forests were felled. As regards private woodlands, the census which had been carried out between 1947 and 1949 showed some 484,000 acres either as 'Felled since September 1939' or as 'Devastated', that is to say 'that all the worthwhile timber had been cut'.[30] Of this total, English woodlands provided 254,000 acres.[31]

THE POST-WAR ERA 12

REORGANIZATION AND READJUSTMENT

After the passing of the Forestry Act in June 1945 steps were taken to implement its provisions and at the same time to carry out a major reorganization of the Forestry Commission. Previously England had been divided into seven Divisions: namely, the North West, the North East, the East, the South East, the South West, the New Forest and the Dean Forest; Wales comprised two Divisions: the North and South; and Scotland four: the North, South, East and West. These 13 Divisions were now re-formed into 11 Conservancies, the New and Dean Forests becoming parts of the South East and South West Conservancies respectively with their own Deputy Surveyors. Except in the case of the North East Conservancy and the South Conservancy of Wales, the boundaries of those Divisions which lay south of the Border were altered very considerably, the South East Division being reduced to about half its size.[1]

At the Commission's Headquarters the posts of Director-General and Deputy Director-General were established while Directors of Forestry were appointed for England, Wales and Scotland.[2] In addition to the three National Committees which had been set up under the Act, Regional Advisory Committees were formed in 1946 for each Conservancy so as to provide a ready channel for communication between the Conservator and those in the Conservancy who were interested in forestry.

In putting forward their proposed scheme for the Dedication of Woodlands, the Commissioners had expressed the view that it 'should consult freely with the Central Landowners' Association, the Scottish Land and Property Federation and the Royal Scottish and Royal English Forestry Societies'.[3] Arising out of this suggestion two committees representing private forestry interests in England and Wales and in Scotland respectively were formed in 1946 and were known as Private Forestry Committees. During the summer of 1948 it was agreed to set up one committee for the whole of the country and this became known as the United Kingdom Forestry Committee.[4]

For some time after the end of the war many of the country's problems remained and not the least of these was the continuing demand for timber. After making a preliminary survey it was resolved, at the end of 1945, that steps should be taken by the Home Timber Production Department to obtain supplies of timber from the German forests. Consequently it was decided that a new organization should be set up to be known as the North German Timber Control and at the end of February 1946 a party of volunteers from the Department left for Germany. By the end of 1947 the Control had completed its task and its members returned to this country.

In April 1946 a Committee was appointed to examine the state of the New Forest and to recommend any action that was thought necessary in the light of modern conditions. The Committee's Report[5] which was published in 1947 contained much information about the Forest and numerous recommendations regarding its administration and other matters affecting it. During 1946 Northerwood House at Lyndhurst in the New Forest was given to the Forestry Commission by Major Herbert Aris for the purpose of promoting forestry. For a number of years courses were held there but in 1974 it was sold and the proceeds used to provide an Aris Travelling Scholarship each year for two forest officers.[6]

As the country returned to peace-time conditions so more attention began to be paid to education and research. During April 1946 the Royal English Forestry Society recommenced its annual forestry refresher courses for landowners and land agents, the first course having been held in 1938 and, except for the war years from 1940 to 1945, these continued until 1956. In May the Forestry Commission's Forester Training School at Parkend in the Forest of Dean re-opened and at the same time a Forest Workers Training Scheme was organized for ex-Service men. In the field of scientific investigation, the Commission decided to establish a research station at Alice Holt Lodge near Farnham, Surrey and this came into operation during the ensuing 12 months. Finally, as 1946 was drawing to a close the prices of growing and felled timber were raised by 25 per cent with effect from 2nd January 1947.[7]

One of the earlier tasks which the Forestry Commission undertook, after its formation in 1919, was to carry out a census of woodlands. This was begun in 1924 and the Report[8] setting out the results was published in 1928 but in some respects these were considered to be somewhat incomplete. Early in 1938 work began on another census but owing to the outbreak of war in 1939, this was never completed. Consequently, it was felt that one of the more urgent post-war tasks was to make an up-to-date census and work on this was started in January 1947 and completed in June 1949, the results being published in two reports which appeared in 1952[9] and 1953.[10]

The Forestry Act 1947[11] which received the Royal Assent in March of that year dealt with various matters arising out of the dedication scheme for private woodlands. Another statute which, to a limited extent, was concerned with private forestry was the Town and Country Planning Act 1947[12] under section

28 of which local authorities were given powers to make Tree Preservation Orders. At the same time, the Act provided that no Order could be made in those cases where a dedication covenant was in operation under the Forestry Act 1947 or where advances had been made under the Forestry Acts of 1919 to 1947.

In June 1947 the Fifth British Empire Conference was held in London when representatives from 33 countries attended and during which visits were paid to several of the Commission's forests and also to woodlands on private estates. In the same month a barony was conferred on Sir Roy Robinson in recognition of his outstanding work for British forestry. A month later the Royal English Forestry Society announced that it had changed its name and that in future its title would be that of the Royal Forestry Society of England and Wales.

Although in 1943 the Report on Post-War Forest Policy had announced the Dedication Scheme and had given a general description of it, several years elapsed before the scheme was finally accepted by woodland owners. In July 1948 the *Quarterly Journal of Forestry* contained a note by the President of the Royal Forestry Society of England and Wales, Lord Merthyr, regarding the uncertainty which existed among members as to whether they should dedicate their woods or not. He concluded that '. . . at the meeting of the Council on July 21 . . . it was agreed that for the moment, and until certain points are clarified, members should take no decision.'[13] Eighteen months later progress had been made in resolving many of the outstanding points and by January 1950 it was largely on matters of prices and marketing that there were differences of opinion. However in February of that year, after further assurances had been given by the Forestry Commission, Lord Merthyr made an announcement which included the statement: '. . . the Council now advises all members of the Society who own land which is suitable for dedication, to proceed with dedication'.[14] And so, nearly seven years after it had first been proposed, the Dedication Scheme for private woodlands was finally accepted.

THE FIRST STEPS FORWARD

By September 1949 the Forestry Commission had been established for 30 years and many of the more important events which took place during this period have already been mentioned. It may be added however, that in spite of financial restrictions and the Second World War, the Commissioners had acquired an estate of some 1,560,000 acres and had planted 557,000 acres while, with the help of grants, private owners had planted 182,000 acres. Of the original Commissioners who had been appointed in 1919, only Lord Robinson was still serving.[15]

Although four years had passed since the end of the war, extensive fellings of timber continued throughout the country due largely to the restrictions that had been imposed on the importation of timber from abroad. Felling licences were still in operation and although these acted as a form of control, the volume licensed to be felled during the year ending 30th September 1948 amounted to 67 million cubic feet which was an increase of 12 million feet over the previous year.[16] Subsequently the Board of Trade announced that a considerable reduction would be made in the quantity of timber for which licences would be granted and that an overall limit of 38,136,000 cubic feet would be fixed for the whole of Great Britain for 1949.[17]

In November 1948 a Select Committee of the House of Commons was appointed to examine the estimates of the Forestry Commission and its Report was published in December 1949.[18] By this time the Commissioners had become the largest landowners in the country since they owned some 1½ million acres. Although the Committee was primarily concerned with the Commission, evidence was also heard from representatives of both The United Kingdom Forestry Committee and The Federated Home Timber Association.

During the course of 1949, two matters arose which concerned the financial aspect of private forestry. The first was the introduction, in April, of a thinning grant which was to be paid to private woodland owners in order to encourage them to thin their plantations. The grant was payable either at the rate of 3d (1¼p) per cubic foot standing or at £3.15s (£3.75) per acre, subject to a minimum out-turn and area and was only applicable to conifer stands. These grants were generally considered to be inadequate and were the subject of adverse criticism by the United Kingdom Forestry Committee.[19] No alterations were made in licensing arrangements and felling licences were still required. The second matter which was of the greatest importance to both woodland owners and the timber trade was the decontrol of the prices of home-grown timber. As from 1st December 1949 the prices of all home-grown timber whether standing, in the round, converted or mining timber were freed from price control and so, after 10 years of restriction, prices were once again allowed to find their own level in the open market.

In the same month the Commissioners set up a new committee on the use and marketing of timber under the title of the Advisory Committee on Utilisation of Home-Grown Timber, with the following terms of reference: 'To advise the Commissioners on measures designed to promote the utilisation and sale of produce from British woodlands.' The Committee included representatives of the Commission, the Board of Trade, the Forest Products Research Laboratory, the Rural Industries Bureau, the United Kingdom Forestry Committee, the Timber Development Association, the Home Timber Merchants Association of England and Wales and the Home Timber Merchants Association of Scotland.[20]

On 1st January 1950 control over the felling and sale of growing trees in

England and Wales was transferred from the Board of Trade to the Minister of Agriculture and Fisheries, and the responsibility for felling licences passed to the Forestry Commissioners. At the same time the task of regulating the felling proposals during 1950, in accordance with the quota that the Board of Trade and the Home-Grown Timber Advisory Committee had agreed, was taken over by the Commission. The Advisory Committee which consisted of representatives of the Board of Trade, the Forestry Commission, the National Coal Board, the United Kingdom Forestry Committee and the Timber Traders Associations was accordingly assigned to the Forestry Commission and a Commissioner, Lord Radnor, replaced the Timber Controller as Chairman.[21] The system which was followed for fixing felling quotas has been described in detail by the Commission.[22]

Although an Advisory Committee on Forest Research had been constituted by the Commissioners in December 1929[23] it was not until 1950 that the first annual report on research was published.[24] This was produced under the supervision of James Macdonald who had been appointed Director of Research and Education in 1948 and since 1950 annual reports on the subject have appeared each year. Another significant event which took place in 1950 was the opening of the new Imperial Forestry Building in Oxford by HRH Princess

22. *A horse drawn timber carriage: the traditional method of transporting timber.*

Margaret. Although it had been decided to establish the Institute shortly after the First World War, progress had been delayed by a shortage of funds and the outbreak of war in 1939.

The main purpose of the Forestry Act, 1951,[25] which came into operation on 1st October of that year, was to ensure that sufficient stocks of standing timber were accumulated in this country. The first section of the Act stated very clearly that the duties of the Commissioners, as laid down in section 3 of the Forestry Act 1919 now included that of 'promoting the establishment and maintenance in Great Britain of adequate reserves of growing trees'. With a view to achieving this object, the Act contained provisions regarding felling restrictions, felling licences, the procedures to be followed when licences were refused, felling directions and the position in relation to Tree Preservation Orders. It also introduced the principle of requiring an area to be replanted as a condition of granting a felling licence but this did not apply to fellings which were carried out in accordance with working plans approved by the Commissioners. Under the Act the Home-Grown Timber Advisory Committee which had been appointed early in 1939 and the Regional Advisory Committees which had been set up in 1946, were reconstituted as statutory committees. The Act further provided that at least one Commissioner should have 'special knowledge and experience of the timber trade'.

In the province of forestry education an important development took place when, after a joint meeting of representatives of the Royal Scottish Forestry Society and the Royal Forestry Society of England and Wales in September 1951, a new examining body was set up. This became the Central Forestry Examination Board of the United Kingdom which subsequently established, and now conducts, advanced examinations in forestry and awards the National Diploma of Forestry to successful candidates.

The thinning grant which had been introduced in April 1949 did not produce the results which were anticipated and in October 1951 it was replaced by an amended scheme. The new grant covered both conifers and broadleaved species and was limited to stands of a specified average top height or, alternatively, a stated quarter girth, although it remained at £3.15s (£3.75) per acre. During the same month the Commissioners made two sets of regulations relating to the felling of trees, by virtue of the powers which had been granted to them under the Forestry Act 1951.[26]

Forestry in this country suffered a great loss when, on 5th September 1952, Lord Robinson died while he was leading the British Delegation at the Sixth Commonwealth Forestry Conference in Ottawa. After studying at Oxford under Sir William Schlich, he began his forestry career in 1909 when he was made Assistant Inspector for Forestry in the Board of Agriculture and Fisheries. In 1916 he was appointed Secretary to the Forestry Sub-Committee under the chairmanship of the Rt Hon. F. D. Acland and when the Forestry Commission was established in 1919, he was included in the list of

Commissioners. On the resignation of Sir John Stirling-Maxwell in 1932 he became Chairman of the Commissioners, a position which he held until his death 20 years later. The Annual Report for 1952 contained a tribute to him which concluded with the following words: 'He more than anyone, has advanced the cause of forestry in this country . . .'[27]

Although a number of estates had accepted the Dedication Scheme there were some woodland owners who, while they were prepared to manage their woodlands in accordance with a plan approved by the Commission, did not wish to be tied by dedication. These estates which were termed 'Approved Estates' were officially recognized by the Commissioners in 1952 and were defined as 'estates whose owners have decided not to dedicate but to manage their woodlands in accordance with a working plan approved by the Commissioners'.[28] However it was not until 1953 that owners of approved estates received any financial assistance and even then they were only paid a planting grant equal to half the amount of that paid in respect of dedicated estates while they were entirely excluded from receiving maintenance grants.[29]

For some time concern had been felt regarding the depletion of hedgerow trees since they had been subject to extensive fellings with apparently little effort being made to replace them. Consequently when the Minister of Agriculture and Fisheries and the Secretary of State for Scotland appointed a committee in January 1953 to examine the whole matter, their action received general approval. The Committee which was known as the Committee on Hedgerow and Farm Timber subsequently published its report in 1955.[30]

COOPERATION IN PRIVATE FORESTRY

The marketing and disposal of timber, thinnings and other produce has always been a difficult problem in the management of the smaller woodland estates, and it was in an attempt to overcome this that the Home-Grown Timber Marketing Association was established in January 1934. The events leading up to the formation of the Association have already been described in Chapter 11 and by the beginning of 1938, seven branches had come into operation. Two of the most active were the South Devon Woodland Owners Association and Northern Forestry Products Ltd but with the outbreak of war in 1939 the Home-Grown Timber Marketing Association fell into abeyance. With peace the problems of marketing returned but at that time the attention of woodland owners was mainly focused on the Dedication Scheme so the matter did not receive the consideration which otherwise it might have done.

One of the first indications of a new interest in cooperative marketing was the formation of the Dorset Woodlands Association in August 1946 and this was followed by two articles on forestry cooperation by Sir William Lewthwaite in the *Quarterly Journal of Forestry* in 1948[31] and 1949.[32] The Forestry

Commissioners in their Report for 1948 gave further support to this movement when they remarked that 'there was great scope for the development of co-operative schemes in private forestry' and 'expressed their willingness to assist any scheme which appeared worthy of encouragement'.33 However, progress was slower than was expected and five years later the Commissioners had come to the conclusion that forestry cooperation was not expanding as quickly as the situation warranted. In 1953 they expressed the view that 'It is regrettable that there are still large areas, particularly in England, where no co-operative organisation exists to help the private woodland owner.'34 By the middle of 1953 private woodland owners were facing an increasingly difficult situation with rising costs and falling timber prices. Eventually, in November of that year, the United Kingdom Forestry Committee approached the Minister of State for Scotland, the Minister of Agriculture and Fisheries being unavoidably absent, and placed the facts before him. As a result the Committee on Marketing of Woodland Produce was set up in May 1954 under the chairmanship of H. Watson with the following terms of reference.

> *With the object of promoting confidence and stability, and bearing in mind both the output from the Forestry Commission woodlands and the need to develop markets, to consider what measures might be taken within the home timber industry to improve the arrangements for marketing produce from privately owned woodlands; and to report.*35

The work of the Committee was completed in May 1956 and its Report which was published at the end of that year, contained two major recommendations. The first was that 'a strong and effective association of woodland owners' should be formed and the Committee visualized a Woodland Owners Association for the whole of the United Kingdom divided into three sections for England, Wales and Scotland respectively. The Committee considered that the proposed Association had three 'essential functions': first, to represent the interests of private woodland owners, second, to ensure that owners were aware of current financial assistance and the facilities offered by cooperative societies, consultants and contractors as regards silviculture and marketing, and third, to collect information as to costs, prices, markets and available supplies of timber.

The Committee's second major recommendation was that a central consultative body should be set up to represent all the principal interests concerned with the marketing of home-grown timber. It was intended that this body would ensure that the country's timber resources were utilized to the fullest extent and that adequate security was provided for the home timber industry. In order to achieve these objectives, it was proposed that the existing Home Grown Timber Advisory Committee should be reconstituted under an independent chairman in place of one who was a member of the Forestry Commission. In addition, the membership of the Committee should be strengthened by the inclusion of representatives of the Department of Scientific and Industrial Research and the Timber Development Association together with three independent members who would represent the general public's interest in home-grown timber.

The steps which were subsequently taken as a result of the Watson Committee's recommendations are considered later in this chapter but in 1957, the year following the publication of the Committee's Report, the Commission's Annual Report contained the following observation on the matter of cooperative forestry societies: 'The Commissioners believe that the advantages of such societies are now being realised to a greater extent than before by woodland owners in general.'[36] Perhaps this greater realization was, to some extent, due to the proposals contained in the Report of the Committee on Marketing of Woodland Produce. Whether or not this was so, 1957 was the last occasion when reference was made to forestry cooperation in any of the Commission's Annual Reports, at least until the 58th Report of 1977-78.

THE SURVIVAL OF THE RABBIT

The rabbit was introduced into this country by the Normans[37] and during the succeeding 900 years or so, they have become one of the most serious pests in forestry and agriculture. Known in medieval times as conies, rabbits appear to have multiplied greatly during the nineteenth century and this may not have been unconnected with the increasing interest in covert shooting to which reference has been made in Chapter 9. By 1939 the rabbit population in this country had reached a prodigious size and in some parts of the United Kingdom, notably the Breckland of Norfolk and Pembrokeshire, the trapping of rabbits for food had become an important feature in the rural economy.

It was therefore a matter of considerable importance to those who regarded rabbits as a part of their livelihood, as well as those who considered them as a major pest when, during the summer of 1953, an epidemic among rabbits was reported from Kent. This was subsequently diagnosed as a virus disease known as *Myxomatosis cuniculi* which caused a high mortality rate and spread with great rapidity. By 1955 it had reached every county in England and Wales and was to be found in many parts of Scotland, so that a unique opportunity was provided for exterminating rabbits in this country. With this in mind, rabbit clearance areas were formed in 1955 under the auspices of the Ministry of Agriculture in an attempt to deal with those rabbits that had escaped infection.

However, despite the devastating effect of the disease on rabbit communities, it failed to reach some of the more remote areas which in due course provided centres for repopulation. Consequently in February 1957, the Rabbit Clearance Committee which had been set up by the Ministry of Agriculture, reported that there had been an increase in the rabbit population in no fewer than 20 counties in England and Wales, although at the same time a decrease had been recorded in 12 others.[38] By the end of the year it was clear that in spite of *myxomatosis* and the further efforts which had been made to eradicate them, rabbits were beginning to re-establish themselves. This was frequently occurring in areas from which they had previously been eliminated and the matter was viewed with considerable apprehension by the Forestry Commission. 'It is feared that the advantage given by *myxomatosis* may be fast slipping away and that unless a practical, co-ordinated and sustained campaign is pursued against rabbits, they will again become an unmitigated and expensive pest to both agriculture and forestry.'[39] The next year the Commissioners noted that in spite of the prevalence of *myxomatosis* rabbits were still increasing although at a rather slower rate. In 1960, in a final attempt to save the situation Rabbit Clearance Societies were formed with the help of County Agricultural Executive Committees and grants from the Ministry of Agriculture[40] but it was clear that the battle had been lost and that the future of the rabbit was once again secure.

GRANTS FOR PRIVATE WOODLANDS

The principle that the Forestry Commission should provide grants in order to encourage planting on private estates has its origin in the Report of the Acland Committee which was published in 1918 when, after considering the matter the Committee reached the following conclusion: 'We recommend that the basis upon which the assistance should be reckoned should be a grant of up to £2 an acre towards the cost of planting conifers, and up to £4 an acre towards the cost of planting approved hardwoods.'[41] When in due course the Forestry Act 1919 became law the Commissioners were given powers to make advances either by means of grants or loans on such terms and conditions as they thought fit. It would appear that at first grants were made on an *ad hoc* basis but in the Commissioners Report for 1922, it was stated that the sum of £50,558 had been expended in assisting corporate bodies and private individuals. This assistance had taken the form of:

> grants for planting (£4.10s per acre to corporate bodies and £3 per acre to private individuals), preparation of ground to be planted subsequently (not exceeding £3 per acre in each case), and scrub clearing in preparation for planting (£2 per acre, or one-third the net cost with a limit of £4 per acre to corporate bodies, and not exceeding £2 per acre to individuals).[42]

Appendix I of the Report contained a form of application for what was termed 'Unemployment Grant' which set out the details of the grants, the regulations affecting them and a section entitled 'Estimate of Expenditure' which was subdivided into labour and materials.

In 1927 several changes were made in the conditions applying to these grants, the most important being that those in respect of planting were based on the species adopted and not on the type of ownership. Planting grants were now fixed at up to £2 per acre for conifers and up to £4 per acre for hardwoods, irrespective of the legal status of the owner. At the same time the scrub clearing grant was reduced from £2 per acre to £1 with a proviso of 'exceptionally up to £2 per acre', and was limited to selected schemes involving not less than 50 acres. These rules remained in operation until 1933 when two alterations took place, the first of which related to the planting grant which was payable in respect of hardwoods. This was now divided into three categories according to species, in each of which the grants varied. Thus for oak and ash the grant was fixed at £4 per acre; for beech, sycamore and chestnut at £3 and for 'other approved species' at £2 while the rate for conifers remained at £2 per acre. The second change was the discontinuation of the scrub clearing grant and these arrangements remained in operation until 1946 when, in anticipation of the Dedication Scheme an 'interim planting grant' of £7.10s (£7.50) was introduced.

During 1947 this was increased to £10 per acre while, in the following year, a maintenance grant was introduced which was payable first, on every acre that was dedicated and subsequently planted and properly maintained and second, on all productive woodlands in addition to the foregoing, at the rate of 3s 4d (17p) per acre for a period of 15 years.[43] The original terms of the Dedication Scheme also provided that grants should 'be reviewed, and revised as may be necessary, after 5 years from 1946-47, on the basis of the ascertained cost'.[44] In 1949 a thinning grant was introduced the details of which have already been given earlier in this chapter and this was followed during 1950 by the introduction of grants for planting poplars. These were payable either at the rate of £8 per acre or at 2s (10p) per tree if planted in lines or rows and in this way it was hoped to encourage planting by farmers as well as by woodland owners. In the same year planting grants, at the current rate, were made available for small woods that were not considered suitable for dedication. Briefly, these were defined as detached woodlands which were less than 5 acres in extent or those with a bad access which were not more than 15 acres if of 'a good shape', or those with a bad access and up to 30 acres, if of 'a bad shape'. They also included belts of woodland subject to certain qualifications.[45]

Eventually, in 1953, planting grants were authorized for approved woodlands although they were fixed at a rate which was only equal to half the amount which was paid in the case of dedicated woodlands. This reduced rate was not increased to the full amount until July 1959 and from that date dedicated and approved woodlands received the same planting grant. In order to assist in clearing unproductive growth, much of which was the result of war time fellings, a scrub clearance grant was introduced in October 1953 for areas that were eligible for grants under the Dedication, Approved Woods and Small Woods Schemes.[46] This was fixed at £7.10s (£7.50) per acre where the cost of clearing was estimated to be from £15 to £25 per acre and £12.10s (£12.50) where the cost was estimated to be over £25.

The next major change took place in 1959 when the maintenance grant which was then 5s 6d (27½p) per acre was replaced by a management grant. This was payable at the rate of 18s (90p) per acre for the first 100 acres, 12s (60p) for the next 100 acres and 7s (35p) for the remainder. At the same time the planting grant was raised from £17 to £20 per acre while the thinning and poplar grants were discontinued as was the scrub clearance grant in 1963. Except for changes in the rates of payment, no further alterations were made until October 1974 when a new Dedication Scheme was introduced which entailed a different system of grants and is referred to in the next chapter. A summary of the changes in Forestry Commission grants to private estates which occurred between 1946 and 1974 is given in table 3.

Planting grants for small woods were introduced in 1950 and these were fixed at the same rate as for dedicated woodlands. Approved woodlands were officially recognized in 1952 and were eligible for planting grants at half the rate paid to dedicated woodlands, until 1959 when they were raised to the full amount.

THE EXPANDING PROSPECT

With the passing of the post-war years conditions began to stabilize and the prospect for forestry gradually improved. The forest year which ended on 30th September 1953 was notable for the fact that during the course of it, the Forestry Commission had planted 67,610 acres which was the largest area completed by the Commission in any one year up to that time. Of this total 21,508 acres were planted in England, 11,765 acres in Wales and 34,337 acres in Scotland while the number of young trees used in planting these acreages amounted to no less than 104,400,000.[47] North of the Border, an event of considerable interest took place when, in 1954, the Royal Scottish Forestry Society celebrated its centenary. Originally known as the Scottish Arboricultural Society, it was the first forestry society to be formed in Great Britain and James Brown whose book *The Forester* was published in 1847 and subsequently ran into six editions, was elected as the Society's first President.

Although a committee had been appointed in 1946 to consider various

Table 3

Forestry Commission grants operative from 1945 to 1973

Year	Planting grant	Maintenance grant	Management grant	Thinning grant	Scrub clearance grant	Poplar planting grant
1945	£2 to £4	—	—	—	—	—
1946	£7.10s	—	—	—	—	—
1947	£10	—	—	—	—	—
1948	£10	3s 4d	—	—	—	—
1949	£12	4s	—	£3.15s	—	—
1950	£12	4s	—	£3.15s	—	£8 or 2s
1951	£14	4s 6d	—	£3.15s	—	£8 or 2s
1953	£15	5s	—	£3.15s	£7.10s or £12.10s	£8 or 2s
1955	£17	5s 6d	—	£3.15s	£8.10s or £13.10s	£8.10s or 2s
1959	£20	—	18s, 12s & 7s	—	£8.10s or £13.10s	—
1960	£21	—	19s, 13s & 8s	—	£8.10s or £13.10s	—
1962	£22.4s	—	20s, 13s 6d & 8s 6d	—	£8.10s or £13.10s	—
1963	£22.4s	—	20s, 13s 6d & 8s 6d	—	—	—
1964	£22.12s	—	20s 3d, 13s 9d & 8s 9d	—	—	—
1967	£23.3s 6d	—	21s 3d, 14s 3d & 8s 9d	—	—	—

aspects of the New Forest, it was not until 1955 that similar steps were taken in respect of the Forest of Dean. Under its terms of reference the Committee was required to review the situation in the Forest and to recommend such action as might be necessary to ensure that its administration took into account the demands of the present day. Its report, which was published in 1958, provided much valuable information relating to the Forest and contained

39 recommendations.[48] The year 1955 also marked the occasion of the Jubilee of the School of Forestry at Oxford which had been founded in 1905 by Dr W. Schlich (later Sir William Schlich) following the decision to close the Royal Indian Engineering College at Coopers Hill. After a modest beginning the School increased in both size and influence and was instrumental in training a large number of forest officers, many of whom subsequently served throughout the world.

The end of the first decade of post-war forestry in 1956 provided a suitable opportunity to review the progress which had been made in planting and acquiring land. During these 10 years it had been the intention of the Forestry Commission to afforest or replant 900,000 acres but in fact only 548,000 acres or 61 per cent of the proposed total was achieved. As regards the acquisition of land for planting the situation was rather worse since only 493,000 acres had been acquired as against an intended 1,850,000 or only 27 per cent of the total. Although difficulties had been experienced both as regards shortages of labour and the purchase of suitable land, the Commissioners were of the opinion that it was not the total size of the programme that was at fault but that the rate of achieving this was originally set too high.[49] On private estates the results were more encouraging since out of an anticipated total of 200,000 acres some 165,000, that is 82 per cent, had been planted. If these facts struck a somewhat discouraging note, the Forestry Commissioners nevertheless had much about which they could be both satisfied and proud. On 8th May 1956 Her Majesty the Queen accompanied by His Royal Highness the Duke of Edinburgh, unveiled a commemorative stone in Eggesford Forest which recorded the planting of the millionth acre by the Commission. The plaque which is fixed to the stone bears the following inscription.

> *This stone, unveiled by*
> *Her Majesty Queen Elizabeth II*
> *on 8th May, 1956, commemorates*
> *the planting by the Forestry Commission*
> *of one million acres in Great Britain.*
> *The Commission's first trees were*
> *planted on 8th December 1919,*
> *in Eggesford Forest.*

Another event which took place a few days later and which created a precedent in such matters, was a demonstration of forestry machinery which had been initiated by the Chartered Land Agents Society and the Royal English Forestry Society of England and Wales. This was held at Hatfield Park by permission of the Marquis of Salisbury and the Gascoyne Cecil Estates Company, and was organized by Colonel D. A. Campbell who was at that time agent for the Hatfield Estate. Many items of forestry equipment and machinery including scrub cutters, cultivators, planting machines, graders and items used in timber extraction were shown at work on typical woodland sites.[50] Finally, to complete a year of considerable interest, it was announced that Westonbirt Arboretum near Tetbury in Gloucestershire had been acquired by the Commission and in due couse this magnificent collection of trees was opened to the public.

During the summer of 1957 a report which had been produced by the National Resources (Technical) Committee under the chairmanship of Sir Solly Zuckerman (later Lord Zuckerman) was published under the title of *Forestry, Agriculture and Marginal Land*. Frequently referred to as the 'Zuckerman Report', it was concerned with the proper use of marginal land which may be said to comprise the rough grazings which exist in the moorland, upland and hill districts of the United Kingdom. Among the points which were stressed by the Committee were first, the need to plan the development of forestry and agriculture as a whole and second, the importance of finding new outlets for forest produce as markets changed and demands altered. Third, it was emphasized that although there were not the same strategic conditions as in 1945, there were greater economic reasons for investing in the planting of trees than had previously been the case.

In May 1958 the Forestry Commission organized an exhibition of forest machinery at Bramshill in Hampshire which, as the Commissioners generously acknowledged, was 'inspired by the success of an exhibition of forest machinery ... at Hatfield in 1956'. The display continued for two days and was attended by over 4,000 visitors which was an indication of the increasing interest which was now being shown in mechanization.[51] The exhibition at Bramshill was the first of four displays of forestry equipment and machinery which were arranged by the Commission, the others being held at Harrogate in 1960, Bush near Edinburgh in 1962 and Blackbushe near Camberley in 1964. A forestry exhibition was also held at Bush in 1969 in connection with the Jubilee of the Forestry Commission but this covered the whole range of forestry and was not only concerned with machinery. On 24th July the Minister of Agriculture speaking in the House of Commons, made a statement on the Government's forest policy of which the following is a brief summary. In future the Forestry Commission's planting programmes were to be fixed for periods of ten years at a time and these were calculated to be about 300,000 acres for 1959 to 1963 and 235,000 acres for 1964 to 1968. As regards private woodlands, the maintenance grant was to be replaced by a more beneficial management grant, approved woodlands were to receive the full planting grant but thinning grants and grants for planting poplars were to be terminated. These increased grants which have been referred to earlier in this chapter were conditional upon 'the formation of an effective woodland owners association' in accordance with the recommendations of the Watson Committee. The Minister also announced that in future when reviewing grants, the income received from private woodlands would be taken into account as well as the expenditure on them. Felling licences were to continue in operation but the system of fixing a quota in respect of the total amount of timber that could be felled each year was to be discontinued.[52]

As 1958 moved to a close, two events occurred which were of considerable importance to woodland owners, the first being the opening, in October, of a hardwood pulpmill at Sudbrook in Monmouthshire. This was of particular interest not only because it provided another outlet for woodland produce but also because it demonstrated that coppice and small hardwood thinnings could be successfully used in the manufacture of wood pulp. The second event was the formation, in December, of The Timber Growers Organisation Ltd to represent woodland owners in England and Wales as envisaged by the Watson Committee. Although this new organization was established under the auspices of the Country Landowners Association, its membership was open to all woodland owners but in May 1960 it became an entirely independent body with its own constitution.

Another year of interest and activity followed in 1959 which also marked the 40th anniversary of the establishment of the Forestry Commission and the Commissioner's report for the year contained the following paragraph.

> *British forestry has reached the point at which substantial progress has been made in repairing the damage caused by 19th century neglect and the excessive fellings of two wars. The problems of creating and establishing the country's forest estate have largely been solved; the problems of how to manage it so as to reap a return on the investment, while at the same time preserving the asset so laboriously built up, are now to be faced.[53]*

During the course of the year an Advisory Committee on Machinery Research which included in its membership representatives of landowners, timber merchants and engineering institutions was appointed by the Commissioners.[54] In May the Home-Grown Timber Marketing Corporation was established by the home timber trade with the object of promoting the use of home-grown timber, finding new markets and generally assisting both the consumers and the suppliers of timber grown in this country. Earlier new regulations had been made by the Commissioners under section 2 of the Forestry Act 1951 which excepted certain dedicated land from felling restrictions, other exceptions having been made previously under the regulations of 1951.[55] A further advance in the field of marketing and utilization took place during the year when, following the opening of the pulpmill at Sudbrook, another mill came into operation at Ellesmere in Cheshire.

As more land was planted and an increasing number of young trees were raised in nurseries throughout the country, more attention began to be paid to the quality and source of the seed which was being sown. Although the Scottish Forest Tree Seed Association had been formed in 1956, it was not until 1959 that the Forest Tree Seed Association of England and Wales was established, the object of the Association being 'to improve the quality of all species of forest trees grown in England and Wales by encouraging in all possible ways the use of seed and plants of the best known origins'.[56] On 1st April 1966 the two Associations united to form the Forest Seed Association but when it became apparent that the functions of the Association would be absorbed by the European Economic Community, the Association was wound up in 1973.

After the formation of the Timber Growers Organisation in 1958 and the Scottish Woodland Owners Association in the following year, coordination between these two bodies was effected through the Forestry Committee of Great Britain. Composed of woodland owners this committee replaced the United Kingdom Forestry Committee which was consequently terminated in 1959. A new forestry organization known as the Association of Professional Foresters was formed in 1960 with the object of providing a society for those whose occupations lay in private commercial forestry including managers, consultants, foresters, nurserymen and contractors as well as corporate bodies and forestry companies.

British forestry suffered a great loss when, in September 1961, W. E. Hiley died. He had spent the early part of his career as a mycologist at the School of Forestry in Oxford, but later he transferred his interests to forest management and economics and on leaving Oxford in 1930, he moved to Devon where he was in charge of the woodlands at Dartington Hall. From then until his death he played a leading part in forestry in which he was recognized as an authority whose reputation was world wide.

On 24th July 1963 a Ministerial statement on forestry was made in both Houses of Parliament which was concerned with the following matters. For the decade from 1964 to 1973 the Forestry Commission intended to plant 450,000 acres and much of this would lie in the upland areas of Wales and Scotland. However, other land could be acquired if it was economically sound to do so or if, by so doing, it would benefit the landscape. In future the Commission was to pay more attention to the need for public access and recreation as well as to landscape considerations. Grants to private owners were to continue unchanged, but the rates of such grants would be examined every three years in order to take into consideration any changes which occurred in either costs or receipts. As the out-turn of the country's forests and woodlands increased, so greater attention would be paid to the marketing and utilization of home-grown timber although some action had already been taken on this point. This included the reconstitution of the Advisory Committee on the Utilisation of Home Grown Timber in October 1960 and of the Home Grown Timber Advisory Committee in 1963 as recommended in the Watson Report. In the same year Marketing Liaison Committees were set up for each region in England and Wales, the membership of which comprised representatives of the Timber Growers Organisation, the Federated Home Grown Timber Association and the Commission.[57]

In forestry education another milestone was reached in January 1963 when the first formal forestry course was held at the Cumberland and Westmorland Farm School (now Cumbria College of Agriculture and Forestry) at Newton Rigg near Penrith. Some indication of the success of this venture can be gathered from the fact that by January 1978 no less than 2,824 students had attended forestry courses at the College. After an interval of 15 years the affairs of the Forestry Commission were again examined by the Estimates Committee which completed its task in July 1964.[58] Among those who gave evidence were representatives of the Forestry Committee of Great Britain and the Federated Home Timber Associations. During the summer of that year another Act relating to the New Forest received the Royal Assent.[59] This was chiefly concerned with alterations to the perambulation of the Forest, the completion of the perimeter fence, the erection of fencing beside the Southampton to Christchurch road (A35) and the formation of ornamental woods. In October it was announced that Ministerial responsibility for forestry was to be transferred from the Minister of Agriculture to the Minister of Land and Natural Resources. However, this arrangement did not continue for very long and in February 1967 the situation was reversed and once again the Minister of Agriculture became accountable for forestry.[60]

23. *Timber haulage by means of a steam traction engine. Until the introduction of the tractor, traction engines were frequently used for this work.*

During 1965 several important changes were made in the organization of the Forestry Commission as a result of the recommendations which had been put forward by the Estimates Committee in the previous year. These were made on the grounds that as the Commission's forests became more productive their management should be brought into line with other comparable commercial undertakings. Accordingly the Director General was appointed a Commissioner together with three new full time Commissioners who were to be responsible respectively for Administration and Finance, Forest and Estate Management and Harvesting and Marketing. At the same time the three Directorates for England, Wales and Scotland were to be terminated and consequently the Conservancies were brought directly under the control of the Commission's headquarters. However, in order to maintain a direct link between the Commissioners and the forestry and other associated interests in Wales and Scotland, two new posts were established known as the Senior Officer for Wales and the Senior Officer for Scotland. With the end of the national Directorates, the role of the National Committees changed from that of an executive authority to one of a purely advisory nature and new terms of reference were therefore drawn up.[61]

During the course of 1967 four Acts of Parliament were passed which, to a greater or lesser extent, were concerned with forestry. The most important of these was the Forestry Act 1967 which, with the exception of one subsection in the Forestry Act 1919, repealed the whole of the Forestry Acts of 1919, 1927, 1945, 1947 and 1951 together with the Forestry (Transfer of Woods) Act 1923.[62] Its provisions also covered felling licences, the felling of trees subject to a preservation order, felling directions and appeals as well as dealing with matters relating to the administration and finances of the Commission. The Plant Health Act was concerned with the control of pests and diseases that were injurious to trees and bushes as well as those affecting agricultural and horticultural crops.[63] The Agriculture Act contained a number of provisions relating to forestry on hill land and more particularly the control of afforestation in a Rural Development Board area.[64] The remaining statute, the Civil Amenities Act, included provisions regarding the planting of trees in development areas and increased the penalties for felling trees illegally.[65] In 1968 the Countryside Act gave the Commission powers to plant and manage trees for amenity purposes and provided for compensation to be paid where the making of a Tree Preservation Order prevented a woodland area from being managed commercially.[66]

Although the Jubilee of the Forestry Commission was celebrated at various centres throughout the country, the main event was a Forestry Exhibition held on the Bush Estate near Edinburgh in June 1969. This included every aspect of forestry and exhibits were not only staged by the Commission but also by private estates, the home timber trade and many firms concerned with forestry. The final ceremony in the Jubilee Year was held in Eggesford Forest on 8th

December 1969 when commemorative trees were planted next to those which had been set on the 8th December 1919. Among those who took part in the ceremony was Lord Clinton, the grandson of the Commission's second chairman who had personally planted some of the original trees in 1919.

The year 1970 represented an important landmark for private forestry by virtue of the fact that the area of woodlands which had been accepted under the Dedication Scheme passed the total of one million acres, the exact figure being 1,047,300 acres. At the same time the area under the Approved Woodland Scheme reached a total of 171,950 acres.[67]

Although a census of woodlands had been carried out between 1947 and 1949, it was not until 1970 that the results of the next census, which covered the years 1965 to 1967, were published. These showed that the total woodland area of Great Britain amounted to some 4,305,100 acres of which 2,189,400 acres were in England, 495,700 in Wales and 1,620,000 in Scotland. Of the total of 4,305,100 acres, 2,686,700 acres were privately owned and 1,618,400 acres were Forestry Commission forests, while in England private woodlands accounted for 1,611,900 acres and those of the Commission for 577,500 acres. However, the total area of private woodlands in England included 407,300 acres of what was termed 'unutilisable scrub' and if this figure was deducted the acreage of private woodlands was reduced to 1,204,600 acres.[68]

In their 51st Annual Report the Commissioners provided some limited information regarding the species which comprised the 77 million trees that had been planted during the year. Of this total, 44 million were Sitka spruce, 15 million pines, 'especially lodgepole pine', 3.5 million larch and 4.5 million silver fir, western hemlock and red cedar, no additional specific descriptions being provided other than those stated above. No information was given regarding the remaining 10 million trees except that, in the case of the broadleaved species which had been planted, beech was 'the most commonly used' and amounted to 0.28 million. During 1970 further legislation dealing with forestry was added to the statute book when the Trees Act became law. This provided that Tree Preservation Orders would apply to dedicated woodlands and to those in respect of which grants had been paid, if they were no longer managed under a plan of operations approved by the Commission. The consent of the Commission was however always necessary prior to the making of an Order. The Act also provided for replanting conditions to be attached to any felling licences that were issued for dedicated woodlands if such woodlands were not being managed under an approved plan.[69]

When the Agricultural, Horticultural and Forestry Industry Training Board was set up in 1967 it was intended that it should cover those industries that dealt with 'produce from the land' and forestry was accordingly included. However, when as a result of opposition by the agricultural and horticultural sectors, the individual levy on employers in these two fields was replaced by a central levy, it was necessary in 1969 to meet the cost of forestry training by continuing the individual levy on employers in forestry.[70] Unfortunately as a result of this and for other reasons, the cost to the employer rose considerably and in 1971 it was announced that the Board would no longer be responsible for forestry training. In its place the Forestry Training Council was formed and its first meeting was held in November of that year. The membership of the Council is made up of representatives of the owners associations, the forestry societies, educational interests, trades unions and the Forestry Commission and its function is similar to that which had previously been undertaken by the Training Board.[71]

In 1963 a Ministerial statement had referred to the need for public access and recreation and by 1970 it was evident that the general public was becoming increasingly interested in relaxation in the countryside and that the Commission was in a unique position to meet the demand for recreational areas. Arising out of this, two events took place in 1971 which had an important bearing on the matter. The first was the formation of an advisory body for the New Forest, known as the New Forest Consultative Panel, in order to provide a means by which local public opinion could be ascertained on matters relating to the management of the Forest. After visiting the area in May, the Minister of Agriculture announced a new directive for the management of the Forest and this was primarily concerned with the conservation of the ancient and ornamental woodlands without regard to timber production, and with the retention of hardwoods in the timber inclosures. Later in the year the Chairman of the Forestry Commissioners, Lord Taylor of Gryffe, held a press conference at which he explained the Commission's policy on the matter of recreation and the text of the statement which was issued on that occasion was included in the Annual Report for that year.[72]

As if to mark the changing approach to forestry an Act was passed in July 1971 the contents of which were more concerned with the middle ages than the middle of the twentieth century. This was the Wild Creatures and Forest Laws Act which, with a very few exceptions, removed the last vestiges of the ancient forest rights and franchises, many of which had their origins in the Norman forests. Although this Act brought the old forest laws to an official end, it laid down that the appointment of verderers should continue and that any existing right of common or pannage should remain in operation but without the seasonal restrictions of the fence month or the winter heyning.[73]

THE CHANGING SCENE   13

By the time that the twentieth century had reached its seventieth year, changes had already begun to take place in the accepted pattern of forestry which had developed since 1919. At first these were not very apparent but by 1970 they were gaining momentum and it soon became clear that significant changes were taking place in both forest policy and forest practice.

In 1972 a consultative document which contained a review of forest policy was published jointly by the Minister of Agriculture and the Secretaries of State for Wales and Scotland.[1] This was based, to a large extent, on an investigation undertaken by economists employed in Government departments who had carried out what the report described as 'a detailed cost benefit analysis' and their findings were considered in relation to both the Forestry Commission and private woodland owners.[2] In the case of the Commission, the review dealt with three points affecting future policy, the first of which was concerned with limiting the area to be planted to a maximum of 55,000 acres per annum and this was to include both afforestation and re-afforestation. The second point emphasized the need to pay greater attention to the effect of woodlands in the landscape while the third dealt with recreation and amenity. The fact that reference to the second and third points had already been included in the Ministerial statement of 24th July 1963 and that the subject of recreation had received considerable publicity at a press conference held by the Chairman of the Commissioners in 1971, indicates the importance that was attached to these matters.

As regards the future policy for private woodlands, the Government considered that the Dedication Scheme had 'clearly outlived its main original purpose'. This view was based on the assumption that the scheme had been introduced in order to assist private owners to replant woodlands which had been felled during the war, but that now some 80 per cent of the planting on private estates was being carried out on bare land. It was also felt that changes were needed in respect of the existing grants and that in order to qualify for financial assistance any proposed work should either provide employment or produce 'an environmental gain such as creating or preserving amenity'. In addition, with a view to reducing administrative costs, grants should be made on a 'once and for all basis' the rates of payment being reviewed at intervals of three years. It was further considered that the responsibilities and functions of the Commission and planning authorities with regard to the 'environmental aspects of private forestry' should be examined. The Forestry Commission had accordingly been instructed to consult with the various interests which were concerned with private forestry and no new applications for dedication or other existing schemes would be considered while these consultations were in progress. Subsequently, on 28th June 1972 the Minister of Agriculture made a statement on the matter in the House of Commons.

The contents of the consultative document met with considerable criticism from both the Royal Forestry Society of England, Wales and Northern Ireland and the Timber Growers' Organisation and steps were taken to convey the views of these two bodies to the Minister. The *Quarterly Journal of Forestry* described the Report dealing with cost benefit analysis as 'The joint work of a team of Government economists which does forestry a considerable disservice; indeed, the dubious assumptions, the curious conjectures and the questionable arithmetic suggest that this was the intention'.[3] After submitting a written statement to the Minister in July, representatives of the Society met him in September to present their case. In this statement the Society contested some of the observations contained in the consultative paper, including the following.

> *The Society seriously questions the wisdom of applying a 10% discount rate to forestry. This rate is historically high, and has only reached 10% because the Treasury has been so unsuccessful in controlling the value of money in recent years, and is, therefore, rightly having to pay dearly for its money ... The Society regrets that the document is factually wrong in its history of the Dedication Scheme. Dedication was not invented to make good the damage done to private woodlands by the war. Its origins go back much earlier than that, to the early 1930s.[4]*

The Timber Growers' Organisation considered that by the publication of the consultative paper and cost benefit study: 'the Government plunged British forestry — and particularly private forestry — into the greatest crisis for a generation'. It further accused the Government of having 'allowed its fashionable preoccupation with the environment to blind it to the great potential which exists in Britain for the development of a viable forestry industry'.[5] Within a few weeks the Timber Growers' Organisation and the Scottish Woodland Owners' Association commissioned Professor J. N. Wolfe, Professor of Economics at Edinburgh University, to carry out a critical appraisal of the cost benefit study. The results of Professor Wolfe's investigations were published in May 1973 and the following paragraph contained in the recommendations of the Report provides a guide to its findings.

It does appear that, while no gross theoretical error is to be found in the Cost/Benefit Study, the accumulation of points of doubt seem to indicate the need for a much more substantial Study . . . considerations include uncertainty about future Government or private policy towards road location and factory location, uncertainty about the planting intentions of other landowners, the imperfect character of the market for timber and wood, and the difficulty of giving proper weight to market conditions 40 or 50 years in the future . . . we have no hesitation in urging a much more complete and deeper study of this industry and its problems than has hitherto been undertaken . . . it would be wise to avoid taking any action which would commit Government to large and long-lasting changes, while bearing in mind the difficulties which may arise from protracted indecision.[6]

Sixteen months after the publication of the consultative paper, a statement was made by the Minister of State, Ministry of Agriculture, in the House of Commons on 24th October 1973. Many of the points which had been contained in the original document were dealt with in this statement and these included the following.

Grants would be made on an acreage basis by a single payment when planting or replanting was carried out.

To qualify for grants, owners would be required not only to manage their woodlands in accordance with the principles of good forestry but there would also have to be 'effective integration with agriculture and environmental safeguards together with such opportunities for recreation as may be appropriate'.

Where a 'significant proportion of hardwoods were planted a higher grant would be paid'.

Owners whose woods were already covered by one of the previous schemes could either continue under those schemes or could transfer to the new one.

In future when dealing with grants to private estates, the Commission would consult with the agricultural departments and the planning authorities, regarding the amenity and land use aspects of the proposals as submitted by the woodland owner.

Regional Advisory Committees would be reconstituted so that their membership included representatives of agricultural, planning and amenity interests as well as those of the forestry industry.

A new Dedication Scheme which would replace the previous schemes for dedicated, approved and small woodlands, would be introduced with revised terms.

Dedication covenants would normally end when felling took place
but provision would be made for these to be renewed.[7]

The statement also endorsed the figure of 55,000 acres as the area that was to be planted each year by the Commission.

After 24th October 1973 further consultations took place between the Forestry Commission, the Government departments which were concerned with the proposals, the Forestry Committee of Great Britain and other interested organizations. The matter was subsequently brought to a conclusion with a third Ministerial statement which was made in the House of Commons on 5th July 1974 by the Minister of Agriculture, the contents being similar to the statement of the previous October although rather more detailed. The new Dedication Scheme which was known as Basis III, subsequently came into operation on 1st October 1974 and under its provisions an owner was required to discuss arrangements for public access with the local planning authority if the matter arose. For drawing up the Plan of Operations, simpler forms were introduced while it was possible for the Dedication Scheme to be terminated either by the owner or the Commission when felling took place, although an area could remain in the Scheme if it was restocked. The basic grant for planting 'an approved crop' was fixed at £18.21 per acre (£45 per hectare) while the planting of a species in order to establish a hardwood crop which would provide 'a predominantly hardwood appearance in the landscape' would receive an additional grant of £50.59 per acre (£125 per hectare). Since the new scheme for dedication was introduced various amendments have been made and details have been published of the grants and conditions which were in force on 1st August 1977 together with those which came into effect on 1st October of that year.[8] The latter included the introduction of a Management Grant and a Small Woods Scheme both of which had been discontinued when the previous Dedication Scheme had come to an end.

In 1972 a new periodical appeared under the title of *Forestry and Home Grown Timber* which, unlike other contemporary publications concerned with forestry, was written for the general public and not for the members of a society or association. Later, in 1976, the name was changed to *Forestry and British Timber*. In March 1973, the Society of Foresters of Great Britain adopted a new constitution in order to become a professional body while at the same time maintaining its character as a learned society. The opportunity was also taken to change the name of the Society to that of the Institute of Foresters of Great Britain.

Although the occasion was not directly concerned with forestry, 1973 was designated 'The Year of the Tree' otherwise 'Tree Planting Year' which had as its objects, the planting of trees as a contribution to the beauty of the countryside and the improvement of urban localities. Emanating from the Department of the Environment the scheme was supported by the Forestry Commission and the forestry societies. Largely as a result of this project, the

Tree Council was set up in March 1974 for the purpose of promoting the planting and care of trees in urban and rural surroundings, for dispensing information on trees and for providing a discussion centre for bodies concerned with such matters. The inauguration of the Council gave rise to the following editorial comment in the *Quarterly Journal of Forestry:*

> *It is perhaps paradoxical that the increasing interest in trees amongst amenity societies, and the proliferation, in the last decade or so, of societies directly connected with trees should necessitate the formation of yet another body to co-ordinate their activities.*[9]

Such proliferation did not end with the formation of the Tree Council for in June 1978, the Tree Foundation was established in order to provide financial support for the Tree Council.

During the spring of 1974, the Committee which had been appointed to examine the policies adopted in the National Parks, published its Report.[10] Frequently referred to as the 'Sandford Committee' it was mainly concerned, as regards forestry, with the question of afforestation in National Parks, not only from the point of view of land utilization but also with the planting of broadleaved species. The Committee recommended that the planting of 'bare land' should be subject to planning control and that consideration should be given to implementing in the National Parks, the decision which the Government had taken in 1971, as regards the conservation of broadleaved species in the New Forest.

Taxation and Private Forestry

In August 1974, the Government published a White Paper on Capital Transfer Tax and a Green Paper on a proposed Wealth Tax, both of which caused the gravest concern among private woodland owners. Action was immediately taken by the Forestry Committee of Great Britain to bring to the notice of the Government the effect that these forms of taxation would have on private forestry. Representations were also made to many Members of Parliament, irrespective of party, and the matter culminated in a debate in the House of Commons in January 1975. However with the passing of the Finance Act in March, most of the provisions relating to forestry which were previously covered by Estate Duty, were repealed and Capital Transfer Tax came into operation. It was not long before the inevitable reaction of woodland owners became apparent, as the Forestry Commission noted.

> *1975-76 was notable for the continued decline in planting, particularly in the afforestation of bare land. Results of sample surveys carried out by the woodland owners' organisations for the*

1974-75 planting season had indicated a fall of up to a half in some
parts of the country compared with the 1973-74 season.
    A number of reasons have been suggested for this lower level of
activity. These include . . . a reluctance to enter the long-term
commitments implicit in forestry, . . . the incidence of capital transfer
tax, the possibility of the introduction of a wealth tax and the fact that
grants under Basis II Dedication Scheme have not increased since
1967.[11]

Some idea of the extent to which planting on private estates declined between 1971 and 1977 can be gained from the figures in table 4 in respect of England and Great Britain as a whole, which have been taken from the 52nd to 58th Annual Reports of the Forestry Commission. In publishing these figures the Commission has drawn attention to the fact that they 'are compiled on the basis of financial years rather than planting seasons and relate to grants paid for planting done up to a year earlier'.[12] Even so they provide a clear indication of the general trend during this period.

Table 4

Record of planting: 1971-77

| | England | | Great Britain | |
	acres	hectares	acres	hectares
1971	16,007	6,478	60,500	24,496
1972	15,325	6,202	60,705	24,545
1973	12,474	5,048	58,445	23,658
1974	9,800	3,966	51,266	21,747
1975	6,738	2,727	31,251	12,647
1976	5,500	2,226	23,207	9,548
1977	5,221	2,113	21,475	8,681

On the initiative of the Royal Forestry Society of England, Wales and Northern Ireland, a Liaison Committee was set up in 1975 for the purpose of coordinating representations on behalf of private forestry. This Committee comprised the heads and chief officers of all those organizations that were concerned with the future of private woodlands and forestry, and subsequently the Committee issued a memorandum entitled *Forest Policy for Great Britain.* This was sent to all Members of Parliament and was considered in detail at a conference held at Oxford in April 1976.

Such was the weight of opinion against the operation of the new taxes that during a debate on the Finance Bill in July 1976, the Minister of State,

Treasury, announced that an Interdepartmental Review of Forestry Taxation and Grants was to be carried out with the following terms of reference.

> To review, in the light of changes since 1972 in capital taxation and in grant arrangements through the dedication scheme, the taxation and grant arrangements for private forestry taking account of economic, fiscal and environmental considerations: and to report by 31st December 1976.

At the same time the Minister stated that the Government wished to find out how forestry was affected by various policies and not only by taxation and he added that the Government was committed to forestry which it considered to be 'extremely important'.[13]

THE FORESTRY COMMISSION

Evidence of the changes which were now taking place in forestry soon became apparent within the Commission itself and one of the first of these was the adoption of metric measurement as from 15th February 1971 thus coinciding with the decimalization of the country's coinage.

After the Minister of Agriculture's statement on 5th July 1974, to which reference has already been made in this chapter, the Commission redefined its objectives in the following terms:

> To advance knowledge and understanding of forestry and trees in the countryside.
>
> To develop and ensure the best use of the country's timber resources and promote efficiency and development in the home timber industry.
>
> To undertake research relevant to the needs of forestry.
>
> To combat forest and tree pests and diseases and to initiate Plant Health Orders when appropriate.
>
> To advise and to assist with safety and training in forestry.
>
> To administer controls and schemes for assisting private woodland owners and by so doing, encourage the practice of sound forestry, secure good land use and — where relevant — effective integration with agriculture and ensure the use of forest management systems and practices which safeguard the environment.
>
> To develop forestry and increase the production of wood for existing industries or industries yet to be established, by extension and improvement of the forest estate.
>
> To protect and enhance the environment.
>
> To provide recreational facilities.
>
> To stimulate and support the local economy in areas of

*depopulation by the development of forests, including new
plantations, and of wood-using industry; and in pursuit of these
objectives and in the extension of the forest estate, to further the
integration of forestry and agriculture and to manage the estate as
profitably as possible.*[14]

After 1970 the Commission began to experience difficulties in obtaining
sufficient land for planting and although substantial areas continued to be
acquired in Scotland, the acreage purchased south of the Border was greatly
reduced. During the 10 years from 1961 to 1970 an average of 4,740 acres
(1918 hectares) per year were acquired in England but in the seven-year
period from 1971 to 1977 the area purchased fell to an average of only 570
acres (230 hectares) per annum. This situation was due to a number of factors
which included the reluctance of owners of hill farms to sell, owing to a general
improvement in sheep farming; a hesitation to part with land until the
implications of the Common Market were known; an increased demand for
agricultural land of all types and a consequent rise in land prices.

The decision to move the headquarters of the Forestry Commission to
Edinburgh came to fruition when in December 1974 occupation of the new
building in Corstorphine Road began. By the end of March the transfer was
complete and the new building was officially opened by the Secretary of State
for Scotland on 16th May 1975. A year later Lord Taylor of Gryfe, the retiring
Chairman of the Commission, unveiled a commemorative stone at New Fancy
View, in the Forest of Dean, to mark the planting of two million acres in Great
Britain by the Forestry Commission.

In 1973 new terms of reference were drawn up for the Home-Grown Timber
Advisory Committee, in view of the changes which were taking place in
utilization and marketing, while in 1974 the Regional Advisory Committee
were reconstituted so as to include representatives of farming, planning and
amenity interests. During the same year the Forestry Safety Council was set
up for the purpose of promoting safety in forestry in its widest context.

EDUCATION AND TRAINING

Between 1970 and 1976 a number of major changes took place in forestry
education of which the following is a brief account. In 1970 the responsibility
for training foresters was transferred from the Forestry Commission to the
Education Departments and consequently by the end of July 1971 the
Commission's training Schools at Gwydyr, Faskally and Park End had closed,
training at Benmore having been brought to an end in 1965. In 1973, a further
change took place when the Forester's Certificate, as issued by the
Commission, was replaced by the Ordinary National Diploma in Forestry.

This could be obtained after a three-year sandwich course at the Cumberland and Westmorland College of Agriculture and Forestry (now the Cumbria College of Agriculture and Forestry) at Newton Rigg. The Forester's Certificate of the Royal Forestry Society of England, Wales and Northern Ireland continued to be awarded until 1976 but the Society's Woodman's Certificate was terminated in the previous year.

Changes also occurred in the general administration of forestry training when, in 1971, the Agricultural, Horticultural and Forestry Industry Training Board relinquished its responsibilities for forestry. These were taken over by the Forestry Training Council which was set up later in the same year, under the auspicies of the Forestry Commission.

As regards the training of forest officers, it had been possible for a number of years, to read forestry at the Universities of Aberdeen, Bangor, Edinburgh and Oxford but as the numbers of those who wished to study forestry declined, changes inevitably took place. At Oxford the Schools of Forestry and Agricultural Science were combined in 1970, to form the School of Agricultural and Forest Sciences while at Edinburgh forestry became a part of Ecological Science.

FOREST RESEARCH

The history of forestry research from 1920 to 1970 has been fully covered by R. F. Wood[15] and this section is only concerned with the more important events which took place between 1970 and 1976. In the case of research organizations three major developments took place during this period the first being the establishment of the Forestry Commission's Northern Research Station on the Bush Estate near Edinburgh which was opened in May 1970. From then on the new Station became responsible for all research on silviculture, soils, forest tree physiology and genetics throughout Great Britain.[16] During the same year, the Natural Environment Research Council created a new body for the research of fundamental problems in forestry, under the title of the Institute of Forestry Research. Subsequently this became known as the Institute of Tree Biology and later the Unit of Tree Biology which is now part of the Council's Institute of Terrestrial Ecology. In January 1971, the Forest Products Research Laboratory was transferred from the Department of Trade and Industry to the Department of the Environment and this was followed by an extensive reorganization. As a result, the Laboratory was amalgamated with the Building Research Station and the Fire Research Station and, with effect from January 1972, became known as the Princes Risborough Laboratory of the Building Research Establishment.[17]

Of the various matters which were the subject of research at this time, one of the most important was elm disease, *Ceratocystis ulmi,* a particularly virulent outbreak of which occurred in 1970. Efforts to contain this disease failed completely and it is estimated that by 1978, 11 million elms had been killed by it.[18] Research was also carried out in connection with the damage caused to beech by the fungus *Nectria coccinea,* the presence of which became more apparent after the long drought of 1976. The effects of the Spruce Sawfly, *Gilpinia hercynia,* and the Pine Beauty Moth, *Panolis flammea,* on conifer woodlands were also the subject of investigation.

By 1971 research into the raising of tree seedlings in plastic tubes had made considerable progress and although only suitable for planting on peatland, the survival rate on such sites amounted to 90 per cent. In addition the rate of planting was such, that in the course of six hours it was possible to plant from 3,500 to 5,000 seedlings.[19] Investigations into the fertiliser requirements of conifers by analysing their foliage, also provided valuable information.

FORESTRY COMPANIES AND COOPERATIVES

Towards the end of the 1950s a new conception of woodland ownership began to emerge, as city investors became attracted to forestry in their search for alternatives to stocks and shares. The rules under which woodlands were treated for tax purposes gave further encouragement to prospective owners who were faced with high taxation and, as a result, a considerable amount of fresh capital was invested in the afforestation of marginal and hill land. It was largely this injection of new funds which caused the area that was planted by private resources, to rise so dramatically between 1970 and 1973. Some idea of this increase can be gained from the fact that while grants were paid on 32,046 acres in Great Britain in 1966, this figure had risen to 60,705 acres by 1972 and had thus almost doubled. Linked to this new development were the forestry companies which acted as agents and undertook the acquisition, preparation and planting of suitable land, and subsequently carried out the management of the resulting plantations.

Established for a very different purpose were the forestry cooperatives to which reference has been made in the previous chapter. These had their origins in the Home-Grown Timber Marketing Association which was formed in January 1934 and which laid the first foundations of cooperation in private forestry. In due course, local branches, each with its own individual title, were established within the Association and initially these were concerned with the provision of marketing facilities for woodland owners. However, after the second war, the services of those cooperatives that were still in existence, were extended in most cases to include woodland management, planting and contract work. In 1970, the Association of Forestry Co-operatives of Great Britain was formed by five cooperatives with the objects of strengthening and encouraging cooperation in forestry and of improving the marketing of home-grown timber.

TECHNICAL DEVELOPMENTS

Since 1946 many technical changes have taken place in forestry and these have enabled operations to be carried out which previously would not have been regarded as feasible. For the most part, these changes and developments have taken place within three operational provinces; first, the increased use of aircraft, second, the wider application of fertilizers, herbicides and pesticides and third, the employment of machinery on a greatly increased scale.

During recent years the utilization of light aircraft and helicopters for forestry purposes has been greatly extended, especially in connection with aerial surveys and inspections, fire spotting, applying fertilizers, transporting materials and extracting thinnings. Of these various operations, the distribution of fertilizers from the air has probably achieved the greatest results in terms of ultimate value. Although in the past, when young plantations had been established on the poorer upland sites, they had received an application of fertilizers at the time of planting, the use of aircraft has enabled top dressings to be distributed over sites where application by hand or tractor would be too difficult, too costly or virtually impossible. Some indication of the extent to which this technique has been adopted by the Forestry Commission, is reflected in the fact that during 1971-72 aerial applications of fertilizers covered some 69,200 acres (28,000 hectares) in Scotland and the Border.[20] Herbicides have also been applied to coppice and perennial weed growth from the air but the treatment of coppice in this way has not always proved to be completely successful. Aerial applications of insecticide have also been carried out in the case of the Pine Looper Moth, *Bupalus piniarius.*[21]

Such operations would not have been possible without the increased availability of the appropriate chemicals in their various suitable forms. In contrast to the occasional treatment of scrub and coppice from the air, widespread use has been made of chemicals in both liquid and granulated forms, for controlling weed growth in young plantations by surface application while infection by conifer heart rot, *Fomes annosus,* has been controlled, to a large extent, by the treatment of stumps with sodium nitrite and subsequently with urea.

After the end of the Second World War, greater interest began to be shown in forestry machinery and equipment and the notable success of the demonstration which was held at Hatfield Park in 1956 was a clear indication of this. Forestry machinery can be divided broadly into two main categories; that which is employed in the establishment of young plantations and that which is available for harvesting thinnings and timber. The first category comprises equipment used in preparing land for planting and this includes bulldozers for forming rides or, when fitted with open tines for ground clearance, ditching machines and rotary flail cutters. In addition, the Forestry

Commission had been developing ploughs for use in planting moorland sites since the 1920s and by 1970 these had achieved a high degree of efficiency.

Of the machines which are included in the second category, possibly the most successful and certainly the smallest is the chainsaw which was first produced by Andreas Stihl in Germany in 1927.[22] Although these saws did not come into general use in this country until the end of the 1950s, they have, since then, completely revolutionized the felling of timber while in the conversion of thinnings, the introduction of de-barking machines have reduced production costs by a substantial amount. However, the most impressive results have been achieved in the design and construction of harvesting equipment which have produced such machines as tree harvesters and processors, forwarders, skidders, loaders and timber cranes.

24. *Extracting thinning by helicopter. The ultimate development
in transporting forest produce.*

In Conclusion

On 1st January 1973, Great Britain joined the European Economic Community but it is not yet clear to what extent this will affect the future of British forestry. In view of continuing forecasts that a world timber shortage would occur within the foreseeable future, increasing concern was expressed regarding the production of timber in this country, especially as the import bill for timber and timber products had amounted to £2,154,000,000 in 1977.[23] In the light of these events, the Forestry Commission undertook a review of the country's timber resources and their report was published later in 1977.[24] In this it was suggested that it might be wise to increase the forest area in Great Britain by 1,800,000 hectares (4,417,900 acres) by the year 2025.

By 1977 it was also clear that supplies of oil and natural gas could not be expected to continue for many more years, although coal would remain available for a rather longer period. Of all the four sources of energy — wood, coal, oil and natural gas — wood alone can be renewed by man, but if future needs are to be met, it will be necessary not only to replace the timber that has been consumed, but also to increase the area of the existing forests. It is with this task that the foresters of the future should be chiefly concerned.

REFERENCES

CHAPTER 1   EARLY DEVELOPMENT AND LAWS

1   Ernle, Lord *English Farming Past and Present,* 4th edn, 1927.
2   Cox, J.C. *The Royal Forests of England,* 1905.
3   Darby, H.C. 'Domesday Woodland', *Economic History Review,* 2nd series, vol. III, 1950-51.
4   Wright, Elizabeth C. 'Common Law in the Thirteenth Century English Royal Forests', *Speculum,* vol. III, 1928.
5   Gilpin, W. *Remarks on Forest Scenery and other Woodland Views,* edited by Sir Thomas Dick Lauder, vol. II, 1834.
6   fitz Nigel, Richard 'Dialogus de Scaccario, 1179', in *English Historical Documents,* vol. II, edited by David C. Douglas and George W. Greenway, 1953.
7   Manwood, J. *A Treatise of the Laws of the Forest,* 3rd edn, 1665.
8   Turner, J.G. *Select Pleas of the Forest,* 1901.
9   Ibid.
10 Cox *Royal Forests.*
11 Gresswell, W.H.P. *The Forests and Deer Parks of Somerset,* 1905.
12 Smith, Elsie *The Sarum Magna Carta.* n.d.
13 Manwood *Laws of the Forest.*
14 Cox *Royal Forests.*
15 Fisher, W.R. *The Forest of Essex, its History, Laws, Administration and Ancient Customs and the Wild Deer which lived in it,* 1887.
16 Nisbet, J. *The Forester,* vol. I, 2nd impression, 1925.
17 Finn, R. Weldon *Domesday Book,* 1973.
18 *The Assize of the Forest* or *The Assize of Woodstock,* 1184, 30 Hen. 2.
19 Wright 'Law in Thirteenth Century'.
20 Smith *Sarum Magna Carta.*
21 *The Charter of the Forest,* 1217, 1 Hen. 3.
22 *The Charter of the Forest,* 1225, 9 Hen. 3.
23 Turner *Select Pleas.*
24 *The Custom and Assize of the Forest,* 1277, 6 Edw. 1.
25 *A Confirmation of the Great Charter and the Charter of the Forest,* 1297, 25 Edw. 1.

26 *Ordinatio Forestae,* 1306, 34 Edw. 1.

27 *A Confirmation of the Great Charter and the Charter of the Forest. Perambulations of the Forest,* 1327, 1 Edw. 3.

28 *How he shall be used that is taken for any Offence in the Forest. Bailment of him,* 1327, 1 Edw. 3.

29 *How every Person may use his Woods within the Forest,* 1327, 1 Edw. 3.

30 Manwood *Laws of the Forest.*

31 Ibid.

32 fitz Nigel 'Scaccario'.

33 *How every Person may use his Woods within the Forest,* 1327, 1 Edw. 3.

34 *An Act for inclosing of Woods in Forests, Chases and Purlieus,* 1482, 22 Edw. 4.

35 Turner *Select Pleas.*

36 *How he shall be used that is taken for any Offence in the Forest. Bailment of him,* 1327, 1 Edw. 3.

37 *An Act for the Increase and Preservation of Timber within the Forest of Dean,* 1668, 20 Cha. 2, c.3.

38 Turner *Select Pleas.*

39 Cox *Royal Forests.*

40 Turner *Select Pleas.*

41 *The Assize of the Forest,* 1184, 30 Hen. 2.

42 *The Charter of the Forest,* 1225, 9 Hen. 3.

43 Manwood *Laws of the Forest.*

44 Cox *Royal Forests.*

45 Turner *Select Pleas.*

CHAPTER 2   ADMINISTRATION OF THE LAWS

1 Cox, J.C. *Victoria County History — Derbyshire,* vol. I, 1905.

2 Turner, J.G. *Select Pleas of the Forest,* 1901.

3 *The Charter of the Forest,* 1225, 9 Hen. 3.

4 Turner *Select Pleas.*

5 *The Charter of the Forest,* 1225, 9 Hen. 3.

6 *The Custom and Assise of the Forest,* 1277, 6 Edw. 1.

7 Manwood, J. *A Treatise of the Laws of the Forest,* 3rd edn, 1665.

8 Turner *Select Pleas.*

9 *The Custom and Assise of the Forest,* 1277, 6 Edw. 1.

10 *Ordinatio Forestae,* 1306, 34 Edw. 1.

11 Manwood *Laws of the Forest.*

12 Turner *Select Pleas.*

13 Manwood *Laws of the Forest.*

14 Ibid.

15 Coke, Edward *Fourth Part of the Institutes of the Laws of England,* 1644.

16 Turner *Select Pleas.*

17 Manwood *Laws of the Forest.*

18 *The Assize of the Forest,* 1184, 30 Hen. 2.

19 *The Custom and Assise of the Forest,* 1277, 6 Edw. 1.

20 *How he shall be used that is taken for any Offence in the Forest. Bailment of him,* 1327, 1 Edw. 1.
21 Manwood *Laws of the Forest.*
22 *The Charter of the Forest,* 1225, 9 Hen. 3.
23 Turner *Select Pleas.*
24 Manwood *Laws of the Forest.*
25 *The Assize of the Forest,* 1184, 30 Hen. 2.
26 *The Custom and Assise of the Forest,* 1277, 6 Edw. 1.
27 *In what cases the killing of offenders in forests, chases and warrens is punishable and when not,* 1293, 21 Edw. 1.
28 Cox, J.C. *The Royal Forests of England,* 1905.
29 *The Charter of the Forest,* 1225, 9 Hen. 3.
30 *Keepers of a Forest or Chase shall gather nothing without the Owners Goodwill,* 1350, 25 Edw. 3.
31 *The Charter of the Forest,* 1225, 9 Hen. 3.
32 *They whose woods are disafforested shall not have Common or other Easement in the Forest,* 1305, 33 Edw. 1.
33 *An Act concerning the Breed of Horses of Higher Stature,* 1540, 32 Hen. 8.
34 Turner *Select Pleas.*
35 Ibid.
36 Ibid.
37 Ibid.
38 *The Charter of the Forest,* 1225, 9 Hen. 3.
39 Ibid.
40 Manwood *Laws of the Forest.*
41 Lewis, Percival *Historical Inquiries concerning Forests and Forest Laws with Topographical Remarks upon the Ancient and Modern State of the New Forest in the County of Southampton,* 1811.
42 *The Charter of the Forest,* 1225, 9 Hen. 3.
43 Manwood *Laws of the Forest.*
44 *The Charter of the Forest,* 1225, 9 Hen. 3.

CHAPTER 3   VERT AND VENISON

1 Manwood, J. *A Treatise of the Laws of the Forest,* 3rd edn, 1665.
2 Turner, J.G. *Select Pleas of the Forest,* 1901.
3 Southern, H.N. (ed.). *The Handbook of British Mammals,* 1964.
4 Barnes, Dame Juliana *The Book of St Albans,* 1486.
5 Collyns, C.P. *Notes on the Chase of the Wild Red Deer in the Counties of Devon and Somerset,* 2nd edn, 1902.
6 Southern *British Mammals.*
7 Barnes *Book of St Albans.*
8 Thursby, Sir George 'Deer Hunting in the New Forest', in *Deer, Hare and Otter Hunting,* Lonsdale Library, vol. XXII, 1936.
9 Ibid.
10 Cox, J.C. *The Royal Forests of England,* 1905.
11 Ibid.

12   York, Edward, Duke of *The Master of Game,* c.1410.
13   Manwood *Laws of the Forest.*
14   Ibid.
15   Holinshed, R. *Chronicles of England, Scotland and Ireland,* edited by H. Ellis, 1807 (1st edn, 1577).
16   Barnes *Book of St Albans.*
17   Turner *Select Pleas.*
18   Twici, W. *Le Art de Venerie,* c.1325.
19   Turner *Select Pleas.*
20   Turberville, G. *The Book of Hunting,* 1575.
21   Cox *Royal Forests.*
22   Ibid.
23   Hare, C.E. *The Language of Sport,* 1939.
24   Ibid.
25   *The Assize of the Forest,* 1184, 30 Hen. 2.
26   Hare *Language of Sport.*
27   Barnes *Book of St Albans.*
28   Manwood *Laws of the Forest.*
29   Cox *Royal Forests.*
30   Ibid.
31   Turner *Select Pleas.*
32   *The Charter of the Forest,* 1225, 9 Hen. 3.
33   Turner *Select Pleas.*
34   Manwood *Laws of the Forest.*
35   Fisher, W.R. *The Forest of Essex, its History, Laws, Administration and Ancient Customs and the Wild Deer which lived in it,* 1887.
36   *The Charter of the Forest,* 1225, 9 Hen. 3.
37   Ibid.
38   Cox *Royal Forests.*
39   York, Edward, Duke of *Master of Game.*
40   Cox *Royal Forests.*

CHAPTER 4   SOME ENGLISH FORESTS OF THE MIDDLE AGES I

1   Cox, J.C. *The Royal Forests of England,* 1905.
2   Spelman, Sir Henry *Glossarium Archiaologicum,* 3rd edn, 1687.
3   Cowel, J. *A Law Dictionary or the Interpreter of Words and Terms used either in the Common or Statute Laws of Great Britain,* 1727.
4   St John, Henry, Viscount Bolingbroke *Observations on the Land Revenue of the Crown,* 1787.
5   Norden, J. *Map of Windsor Forest,* 1607, Harleian MSS No 3749.
6   Ibid.
7   Cox, J.C. *Victoria County History — Berkshire,* vol. II, 1907.
8   *An Act for vesting in His Majesty certain parts of Windsor Forest in the County of Berks and for inclosing the Open Commonable Lands within the said Forest,* 1813, 53 Geo. 3, c.158.

9   Gilpin, W. *Remarks on Forest Scenery and other Woodland Views,* edited by
     Sir T. Dick Lauder, vol. II, 1834.

10   Cox, J.C. *Victoria County History — Buckinghamshire,* vol. III, 1914.

11   Ibid.

12   Cox *Royal Forests.*

13   Cowel *Law Dictionary.*

14   Leland, J. *The Itinerary of John Leland the Antiquary,* 3rd edn, 1769. (The
     itinerary was made between 1534 and 1543.)

15   Cary, J. *New English Atlas,* 1809.

16   Ekwall, E. *The Concise Oxford Dictionary of English Place-Names,* 4th edn,
     (reprinted), 1964.

17   Cox, J.C. *Royal Forests.*

18   Ormerod, G. *The History of the County Palatine and City of Chester,* 2nd edn,
     revised by T. Helsby, 1882.

19   Ibid.

20   Nisbet, J. *Victoria County History — Cumberland,* vol. II, 1905.

21   Leland *Itinerary.*

22   Nicolson, J. and Burn, R. *The History and Antiquities of the Counties of
     Westmorland and Cumberland,* vol. 2, 1777.

23   Cary *Atlas.*

24   Cox, J.C. *Victoria County History — Derbyshire,* vol. I, 1905.

25   *Journal of the Derbyshire Archaeological Society,* 1903.

26   Cox, J.C. *Royal Forests.*

27   Carrington, N.T. *Dartmoor,* 1826, preface by W. Burt.

28   Prowse, A.B. 'The Bounds of the Forest of Dartmoor,' *Transactions of the
     Devonshire Association,* vol. 24, 1892.

29   Rowe, S. *A Perambulation of the Ancient and Royal Forest of Dartmoor,* 3rd
     edn, revised by J. Brooking Rowe, 1896.

30   Leland *Itinerary.*

31   Hutchins, J. *The History and Antiquities of the County of Dorset,* 3rd edn, by
     W. Shipp and J.W. Hodson, vol. 4, 1870.

32   Bath, M. 'King's Stag and Caesar's Deer,' *Dorset Natural History &
     Archaeological Society Proceedings for 1973,* vol. 95, 1974.

33   Camden, W. *Britain or a chronographical description of the most flourishing
     Kingdomes, England, Scotland and Ireland,* translated from the 1607 edn by
     R. Gough, 1806.

34   Coker, J. *A Survey of Dorsetshire containing the Antiquities and Natural
     History of that County,* 1732.

35   Hutchins *History and Antiquities of Dorset,* vol. 4.

36   Ibid., vol. 3.

37   Ibid.

38   Cox *Royal Forests*

39   Coker *Survey of Dorsetshire.*

40   Leland *Itinerary.*

41   Hutchins *History and Antiquities of Dorset,* vol. 1.

42   Cox *Royal Forests.*

43   Cox, J.C. and Forbes, A.C. *Victoria County History — Durham,* vol. II, 1907.

44 Leland *Itinerary.*

45 Fisher, W.R. *The Forest of Essex, its History, Laws, Administration and Ancient Customs and the Wild Deer which lived in it,* 1887.

46 *The Fifteenth Report of the Commissioners appointed to enquire into the State and Condition of the Woods, Forests and Land Revenues of the Crown,* 1793.

47 *An Act for disafforesting the Forest of Hainault in the County of Essex,* 1851, 14 & 15 Vict., c.43.

48 Evelyn, J. *Sylva or a Discourse of Forest Trees,* 2nd edn, 1670.

49 Grundy, G.B. 'The Ancient Woodland of Gloucestershire', *Transactions of the Bristol and Gloucestershire Archaeological Society,* vol. 58, 1936.

50 Forestry Commission, The *Dean Forest and Wye Valley,* 3rd edn, 1964, and *Short Guide to the Dean and Wye Valley Forest Park,* 1963.

51 *The Forestry (Transfer of Woods) Act,* 1923, 13 & 14 Geo. 5, c.21.

52 *The Wild Creatures and Forest Laws Act,* 1971, 19 Eliz. 2, c.47.

53 Grundy 'Ancient Woodland' vol. 58.

54 Braine, A. *The History of Kingswood Forest,* 1891.

55 Nisbet, J. and Vellacott, C.H. *Victoria County History — Gloucestershire,* vol. II, 1907.

56 Braine *Kingswood Forest.*

57 Grundy 'Ancient Woodland' vol. 59.

58 Gilpin *Forest Scenery.*

59 White, G. *The Natural History of Selborne,* 1st edn, 1789.

60 *The Sixth Report of the Commissioners,* 1790.

61 *The Thirteenth Report of the Commissioners,* 1792.

62 *An Act for disafforesting the Forest of South, otherwise East Bere otherwise Bier, in the County of Southampton and for inclosing the open commonable lands within the said Forest,* 1810, 50 Geo. 3, c.218.

63 Cox *Royal Forests.*

64 Speed, J. *Map of Wiltshire,* 1610.

65 Brough, F. *Victoria County History — Hampshire,* vol. IV, 1911.

66 Bickley, F.L. *Victoria County History — Hampshire,* vol. IV, 1911.

67 *The Fifth Report of the Commissioners,* 1789.

68 *An Act for disafforesting the Forest of Parkhurst in the County of Southampton and for inclosing the open commonable lands within the said Forest,* 1812, 52 Geo. 3, c.171.

69 Nisbet, J. and Lascelles, G.W. *Victoria County History — Hampshire,* vol. II, 1907.

70 Forestry Commission *Forty-ninth Annual Report and Accounts of the Forestry Commission for the period ended 31st March 1969.*

71 Wilmot, C. *Victoria County History — Hampshire,* vol. III, 1908.

72 *An Act for the more effectual punishing wicked and evil-disposed persons going armed in disguise and doing injuries and violences to the persons and properties of His Majesty's subjects, and for the more speedy bringing the offenders to justice,* 1722, 9 Geo. 2, c.22.

73 Spelman *Glossarium.*

74 Speed, J. *Map of Hampshire,* 1610.

75 White *Selborne.*

76   Matthews, J.H. *Collections towards the History and Antiquities of the County of Hereford*, 1912.

77   Bull, H.G. 'The Ancient Forest of Deerfold', *Transactions of the Woolhope Naturalists Field Club*, 1869.

78   Phillips, T. 'The Royal Forest of Haywood', *Transactions of the Woolhope Naturalists Field Club*, 1870.

79   Russell, A. *Victoria County History — Huntingdonshire*, vol. III, 1936.

80   Wright, E.C. 'Common Law in the Thirteenth Century English Royal Forests', *Speculum*, vol. III, 1928.

81   Simkins, M.E. *Victoria County History — Huntingdonshire*, vol. II, 1932.

82   Cary *Atlas*.

83   Farrer, W. *Victoria County History — Lancashire*, vol. II, 1908.

84   Ibid.

85   Cox, J.C. *Royal Forests*.

86   McKinley, R.A. *Victoria County History — Leicestershire*, vol. II, 1954.

87   *An Act for allotting and inclosing the Forest or Chase of Charnwood otherwise Charley Forest or Chase and Rothley Plain in the County of Leicester*, 1808, 48 Geo. 3, c.133.

88   Cox, J.C. *Victoria County History — Middlesex*, vol. II, 1911.

CHAPTER 5   SOME ENGLISH FORESTS OF THE MIDDLE AGES II

1   *The Reports of the Commissioners appointed to enquire into the State and Condition of the Woods, Forests and Land Revenues of the Crown*, First Series, 1787-93.

2   *The Ninth Report of the Commissioners*, 1792.

3   Pettit, P.A.J. *The Royal Forests of Northamptonshire*, 1968.

4   *The Ninth Report of the Commissioners*, 1792.

5   *The Seventh Report of the Commissioners*, 1790.

6   *An Act for dividing, allotting and inclosing the Forest of Salcey in the Counties of Northampton and Buckingham and of certain lands in the Parish of Hartwell in the said County of Northampton*, 1825, 6 Geo. 4, c.132.

7   Forestry Commission *Fifty-Second Annual Report and Accounts of the Forestry Commission for the year ended 31st March 1972.*

8   *The Eighth Report of the Commissioners*, 1792.

9   *An Act for the Certainty of Forests and of the Meets, Meers, Limits and Bounds of the Forests*, 1640, 16 Cha. 1, c.16.

10   *The Eighth Report of the Commissioners*, 1792.

11   Pettit *Royal Forests of Northamptonshire*.

12   *An Act for disafforesting the Forest of Whittlewood otherwise Whittlebury*, 1853, 16 & 17 Vict., c.42.

13   *An Act for dividing, allotting and inclosing that Portion of the Forest of Whittlewood called Hasleborough Walk in the Parish of Whitfield and Liberties or Precincts of Silston otherwise Silverstone otherwise Silveston Burnham in the County of Northampton and of the Open Fields of Silston otherwise Silverston otherwise Silveston Burnham aforesaid*, 1824, 5 Geo. 4, c.99.

14   Hodgson, J.C. *A History of Northumberland*, vol. IV, 1897.

15 Hinds, A.B. *A History of Northumberland*, vol. III, 1896.

16 Dodds, M.H. *A History of Northumberland*, vol. XV, 1940.

17 Cary, J. *New English Atlas*, 1809.

18 *An Act for inclosing lands in the Parish of Rothbury in the County of Northumberland*, 1831, 1 & 2 Wm. 4, c.12.

19 Leland, J. *The Itinerary of John Leland the Antiquary*, 3rd edn, 1769. (The itinerary was made between 1534 and 1543.)

20 Gard, R.M. in correspondence, 1977.

21 Cox, J.C. *The Royal Forests of England*, 1905.

22 *The Fourteenth Report of the Commissioners*, 1793.

23 Turner, J.G. *Select Pleas of the Forest*, 1901.

24 *The Fourteenth Report of the Commissioners*, 1793.

25 *An Act for dividing and inclosing the Open Fields, Meadows, Forest, Commons and Waste Lands within the Parish of Arnold in the County of Nottingham*, 1789, 29 Geo. 3. There are also other such Acts.

26 *An Act for vesting in His Majesty certain Parts of the Hayes of Birkland and Bilhagh and of certain Commonable Lands and Open Uninclosed Grounds in the Township of Edwinstowe within the Forest of Sherwood in the County of Nottingham*, 1818, 58 Geo. 3, c.100.

27 Leland *Itinerary*.

28 Cox, J.C. *Victoria County History — Oxfordshire*, vol. II, 1907.

29 *The Tenth Report of the Commissioners*, 1792.

30 Young, A. *General View of the Agriculture in the County of Oxfordshire*, 1809.

31 *An Act for disafforesting the Forest of Whichwood*, 1853, 16 & 17 Vict., c.42.

32 *An Act to amend the Whichwood Disafforesting Act 1853*, 1856, 19 & 20 Vict., c.32.

33 Turner *Select Pleas*.

34 Wright, J. *The History and Antiquities of the County of Rutland*, 1684-87.

35 Eyton, R.W. *The Antiquities of Shropshire*, vol. V, 1853-60.

36 Ibid., vol. VI.

37 Ibid., vol. III.

38 Ibid., vol. IX.

39 Cox, J.C. *Victoria County History — Shropshire*, vol. I, 1908.

40 *The Charter of the Forest*, 1217, 1 Hen. 3.

41 *The Charter of the Forest*, 1225, 9 Hen. 3.

42 Greswell, W.H.P. *The Forests and Deer Parks of Somerset*, 1905.

43 *An Act for vesting in His Majesty certain parts of the Forest of Exmoor otherwise Exmore in the Counties of Somerset and Devon; and for inclosing the said Forest*, 1815, 55 Geo. 3, c.138.

44 Orwin, C.S. and Sellick, R.J. *The Reclamation of Exmoor Forest*, new edn, 1971.

45 Collyns, C.P. *Notes on the Chase of the Wild Red Deer in the Counties of Devon and Somerset*, 2nd edn, 1902.

46 Collinson, J. *The History of Somersetshire*, vol. III, 1791.

47 Greswell *Forests of Somerset*.

48 *The Charter of the Forest*, 1217, 1 Hen. 3.

49 Collinson *History of Somersetshire*, vol. I.

50   *An Act for Inclosing the Forest of Roach, otherwise Neroach, otherwise Neroche in the Parishes of Broadway, Bickenhall, Beercrocombe, Ilton, Barrington, Ashill, Ilminster, Whitelackington, Curland, Donyatt, Isle-Abbots, Hatch-Beauchamp and the Tithing of Domett in the Parish of Buckland St Mary, or some or one of them in the County of Somerset,* 1830, 11 Geo. 4, c.2.

51   Collinson *History of Somersetshire,* vol. I.

52   Greswell *Forests of Somerset.*

53   Leland *Itinerary.*

54   *The Charter of the Forest,* 1217, 1 Hen. 3.

55   Collinson *History of Somersetshire,* vol. III.

56   Greswell *Forests of Somerset.*

57   Greenslade, M.W. *Victoria County History — Staffordshire,* vol. II, 1967.

58   Leland *Itinerary.*

59   Greenslade *VCH — Staffordshire.*

60   Ibid.

61   Kettle, A.J. *Victoria County History — Staffordshire,* vol. II, 1967.

62   Leland *Itinerary.*

63   Kettle *VCH — Staffordshire.*

64   *An Act for dividing, allotting and inclosing the Forest or Chase of Needwood in the County of Stafford,* 1801, 41 Geo. 3, c.56.

65   Greenslade, M.W. *VCH — Staffordshire.*

66   Ekwall, E. *The Concise Oxford Dictionary of English Place-Names,* 4th edn, (reprinted), 1964.

67   Tierney, M.A. *The History and Antiquities of the Castle and Town of Arundell,* 1834.

68   Legge, W. Heneage *Victoria County History — Sussex,* vol. II, 1907.

69   Ibid.

70   Ibid.

71   Ibid.

72   Speed, John *Map of Sussex,* 1610.

73   Cary, J. *Atlas.*

74   Speed *Map of Sussex.*

75   Cary *Atlas.*

76   Legge *VCH — Sussex.*

77   Leland *Itinerary.*

78   Camden, W. *Britannia or a Chorographical Description of the Flourishing Kingdomes of England, Scotland and Ireland,* translated from the edition of 1607 by R. Gough, 1806.

79   Grant, R. *Victoria County History — Wiltshire,* vol. IV, 1959.

80   Akerman, J.Y. 'The Ancient Limits of the Forest of Braden', *Archaeologia,* vol. 37, 1857.

81   Grant *VCH — Wiltshire.*

82   Ibid.

83   Ibid.

84   Cox *Royal Forests.*

85   Hoare, Sir Richard C. *The Modern History of South Wiltshire,* vol. 4, 1822-52.

86   Grant *VCH — Wiltshire.*

87   Hoare *History of South Wiltshire.*
88   Grant *VCH — Wiltshire.*
89   Ibid.
90   Ailesbury, the Marquess of, *A History of Savernake Forest,* 1962.
91   Grant *VCH — Wiltshire.*
92   Ailesbury *History of Savernake Forest.*
93   Grant *VCH — Wiltshire.*
94   Nash, T. *Collections for the History of Worcestershire,* vol. I, 1781.
95   Turner *Select Pleas.*
96   Pillans, E.B. *Victoria County History — Worcestershire,* vol. II, 1906.
97   Nash *Worcestershire.*
98   Moger, O.M. *Victoria County History — Worcestershire,* vol. III, 1913.
99   Leland *Itinerary.*
100   Nash *Worcestershire.*
101   *An Act for Confirmation of the Enclosure and Improvement of Malverne Chase,* 1664, 16 Cha. 2, c.5.
102   Nash *Worcestershire.*
103   Eyton *Antiquities of Shropshire,* vol. IV.
104   Leland *Itinerary.*
105   Eyton *Antiquities of Shropshire,* vol. IV.
106   Farrer, W. *Victoria County History — Lancashire,* vol. II, 1908.
107   Gill, Thomas *Vallis Eboracensis,* 1852.
108   Leland *Itinerary.*
109   Cox, J.C. *Victoria County History — County of York,* vol. I, 1907.
110   Cary *Atlas.*
111   Hunter, J. *South Yorkshire,* 1828.
112   Cox *Royal Forests.*
113   Calvert, M. *The History of Knaresborough,* 1844.
114   Leland *Itinerary.*
115   Spelman, Sir Henry *Glossarium Archaeologicum,* 3rd edn, 1687.
116   Whitaker, T.D. *A History of Richmondshire in the North Riding of the County of York,* vol. I, 1823.
117   'Cartularium Abbathiae de Whiteby', *North Riding Record Society Journal,* vol. I, New Series, 1894.
118   Whitaker, T.D. *The History and Antiquities of the Deanery of Craven in the County of York,* 3rd edn, 1878.

CHAPTER 6   THE OVERTURE TO FORESTRY

1   Bindoff, S.T. *Tudor England,* 1950.
2   Manwood, J. *A Treatise of the Laws of the Forest,* 3rd edn, 1665.
3   'The Brut or The Chronicle of England', *The Early English Text Society,* original series, vol. 136, 1908.
4   *An Act for the Assize of Fuel,* 1553, 7 Edw. 6, c.8.
5   *Calendar of State Papers (Domestic),* 1547-80.
6   Fuller, Thomas *History of the Worthies of England,* vol. II, 1662.
7   Straker, Ernest *Wealden Iron,* 1931.

8   Pillans, E.B. *Victoria County History — Worcestershire*, vol. II, 1906.
9   Yarranton, Andrew *England's Improvement by Sea and Land . . .*, 1677-81.
10 Evelyn, John *Sylva or a Discourse of Forest-Trees*, 2nd edn, 1670.
11 *The Sixth Report of the Commissioners*, 1790.
12 Pettit, P.A.J. *The Royal Forests of Northamptonshire*, 1968.
13 *The Tenth Report of the Commissioners*, 1792.
14 *An Act for inclosing of Woods in Forests, Chases and Purlieus*, 1482, 22 Edw. 4, c.7.
15 *An Act for the Preservation of Woods*, 1543, 35 Hen. 8, c.17.
16 *An Act that Timber shall not be felled to make Coals for Burning of Iron*, 1558, 1 Eliz. 1, c.15.
17 *An Act touching Iron-Mills near unto the City of London and the River of Thames*, 1581, 23 Eliz. 1, c.5.
18 *An Act for the Preservation of Timber in the Weilds of the Counties of Sussex, Surrey and Kent and for the Amendment of Highways decayed by Carriages to and from Iron-Mills there*, 1585, 27 Eliz. 1, c.19.
19 Pettit *Royal Forests of Northamptonshire*.
20 *The Third Report of the Commissioners*, 1788.
21 Harrison, William *An Historical Description of the Islande of Britayne*, 1577.
22 Evelyn *Sylva*.
23 Leland, J. *The Itinerary of John Leland the Antiquary*, 3rd edn, 1769. (The itinerary was made between 1534 and 1543.)
24 Standish, Arthur *The Commons Complaint*, 1611.
25 Church, Rocke *An Olde Thrift newly Revived Wherein is Declared the Manner of Planting, Preserving and Husbanding yong Trees of Divers Kindes for Timber and Fuell . . .*, 1612.
26 Standish, Arthur *New Directions of Experience to the Commons Complaint, for the planting of Timber and Firewood*, 1613.
27 Standish, Arthur *New Directions of Experience for the Increasing of Timber and Firewood*, 1615.
28 Taylor, Silvanus *Common-Good or the Improvements of Commons, Forrests and Chases by Inclosure*, 1652.
29 Evelyn *Sylva*.
30 Cook, Moses *The Manner of Raising, Ordering and Improving Forest-Trees*, 1676.
31 Onions, C.T. (editor) *The Shorter Oxford English Dictionary*, 1975.
32 Pettit *Royal Forests of Northamptonshire*.
33 *The Charter of the Forest*, 1217, 1 Hen. 3.
34 *A Statute of Purveyors*, 1350, 25 Edw. 3.
35 *An Act concerning the Erection of the Court of Surveyors of the King's Lands and Names of the Officers there and their Authority*, 1541, 33 Hen. 8, c.39.
36 Pettit *Royal Forests of Northamptonshire*.
37 Church, Rocke *Olde Thrift*.
38 Cook, Moses *Forest-Trees*.

CHAPTER 7   THE WOODEN WALLS

1   Rushworth, John *Historical Collections,* vol. II, 1721. (Thomas, Lord Coventry's speech to the Judges of England on 17th June 1635.)
2   *An Act for the Preservation of Woods,* 1543, 35 Hen. 8, c.17.
3   *An Act for the more effectually securing a Quantity of Oak Timber for the use of the Royal Navy,* 1772, 12 Geo. 3, c.54.
4   *The Eleventh Report of the Commissioners appointed to enquire into the State and Condition of the Woods, Forests and Land Revenues of the Crown,* 1792.
5   Albion, R.G. *Forests and Sea Power,* 1926.
6   Holland, A.J. *Ships of British Oak,* 1971.
7   *First Report from the Select Committee on the Woods, Forests and Land Revenues of the Crown,* 1849.
8   *The Eleventh Report of the Commissioners,* 1792.
9   Longridge, C. Nepean *The Anatomy of Nelson's Ships,* 6th impression, 1974.
10   Marshall, William *Planting and Rural Ornament,* vol. I, 2nd edn, 1796.
11   Ibid.
12   Banbury, P. *Ship Builders of the Thames and Medway,* 1971.
13   *First Report from the Select Committee on the Woods, Forests and Land Revenues of the Crown,* 1849.
14   *The Eleventh Report of the Commissioners,* 1792.
15   Ibid.
16   *The Fifth Report of the Commissioners,* 1789.
17   Albion *Forests and Sea Power.*
18   *The First Report of the Commissioners of His Majesty's Woods, Forests and Land Revenues,* 1812.
19   *Calendar of State Papers, Domestic Series,* 3rd January 1670.
20   Matthew, Patrick *On Naval Timber and Arboriculture,* 1831.
21   Monteath, Robert *The Forester's Guide,* 1820.
22   Marshall *Planting and Rural Ornament.*
23   Billington, William *A Series of Facts, Hints, Observations and Experiments on the Different Modes of Raising Young Plantations of Oaks . . .,* 1825.
24   Matthew *On Naval Timber.*
25   Pontey, William *The Forest Pruner,* 3rd edn, 1810.
26   Matthew *On Naval Timber.*
27   Ibid.
28   Pontey *Forest Pruner.*
29   Abell, Sir Westcott *The Shipwright's Trade,* 1948.
30   *The Eleventh Report of the Commissioners,* 1792.
31   Ibid.
32   Ibid., Appendix 31.
33   McWilliam, Robert *An Essay on the Origin and Operation of the Dry Rot,* 1818.
34   Albion *Forests and Sea Power.*
35   *The Eleventh Report of the Commissioners,* 1792.
36   Ibid.
37   De Buffon, M. *A Memorial on Preserving and Repairing Forests,* 1739.
38   *The Eleventh Report of the Commissioners,* 1792.

39 Ibid.

40 Ibid., Appendix 34.

41 Ibid., Appendix 38.

CHAPTER 8 THE OLD FORESTRY

1 *An Act for inclosing of Woods in Forests, Chases and Purlieus*, 1482, 22 Edw. 4, c.7.

2 *An Act for the Preservation of Woods*, 1543, 35 Hen. 8, c.17.

3 *An Act for reviving and continuance of certain Statutes*, 1570, 13 Eliz. 1, c.25.

4 Evelyn, J. *Sylva or a Discourse of Forest-Trees*, 2nd edn, 1670.

5 *An Act for the Preservation of Woods*, 1543, 35 Hen. 8, c.17.

6 Evelyn *Sylva.*

7 Standish, Arthur *The Commons Complaint*, 1611.

8 Church, Rocke *An Olde Thrift newly Revived Wherein is Declared the Manner of Planting, Preserving and Husbanding yong Trees of Divers Kindes for Timber and Fuell . . .*, 1612.

9 Evelyn *Sylva.*

10 Worlidge, I. *Systema Agriculturae: The Mystery of Husbandry Discovered*, 1681.

11 Church *Olde Thrift.*

12 Southern, H.N. (editor) *The Handbook of British Mammals*, 1964.

13 Tusser, Thomas *Five Hundred Pointes of Good Husbandry*, 1577.

14 Cook, Moses *The Manner of Raising, Ordering and Improving Forest-Trees*, 2nd edn, 1717.

15 Evelyn *Sylva.*

16 Ibid.

17 Nisbet, J. *The Standard Cyclopedia of Modern Agriculture and Rural Economy*, vol. I, 1909.

18 Evelyn *Sylva.*

19 Ellis, William *The Timber-Tree Improved*, 4th edn, 1745.

20 Bradley, Richard *New Improvements of Planting and Gardening*, 2nd edn, 1718.

21 Langley, Batty *A Sure and Easy Method of Improving Estates*, 2nd edn, 1740.

22 *An Act for the Preservation of Woods*, 1543, 35 Hen. 8, c.17.

23 Taylor, Silvanus *Common Good or The Improvement of Commons, Forrests and Chases by Inclosure*, 1652.

24 Onions, C.T. (editor) *The Shorter Oxford English Dictionary*, vol. I, 1975.

25 *An Act for the Preservation of Woods*, 1543, 35 Hen. 8, c.17.

26 Evelyn *Sylva.*

27 *Calendar of State Papers (Domestic)*, 1607.

28 'Cottonian Mss Titus BIV', *Treasury Office: Increase of Revenue*, temp. James I (1603-1625).

29 Standish, Arthur *New Directions of Experience for the Increasing of Timber and Firewood*, 1615.

30 *An Act for the Certainty of Forests and of the Meets, Meers, Limits and Bounds of the Forests*, 1640, 16 Cha. 1, c.16.

31 *An Act for the Punishment of unlawful cutting or stealing or spoiling of Wood and Underwood, and Destroyers of young Timber-Trees,* 1663, 15 Cha. 2, c.2.

32 *An Act for the Increase and Preservation of Timber within the Forest of Dean,* 1667, 20 Cha. 2, c.3.

33 *An Act for the Increase and Preservation of Timber in the New Forest in the County of Southampton,* 1698, 10 Will. 3, c.36.

34 *An Act to encourage the Planting of Timber-Trees, Fruit-Trees and other Trees for Ornament, Shelter or Profit; and for the better Preservation of the same; and for the preventing the Burning of Woods,* 1715, 1 Geo. 1, c.48.

35 Johnson, A.H. *The Disappearance of the Small Landowner,* Ford Lectures, 1909.

36 *An Act for inclosing by the mutual Consent of the Lords and Tenants, Part of any Common, for the Purpose of planting and preserving Trees fit for Timber or Underwood; and for more effectually preventing the unlawful Destruction of Trees,* 1756, 29 Geo. 2, c.36.

37 Somerville, W. 'Old Records of Planting', *Quarterly Journal of Forestry,* vol. XII, 1918.

38 Hussey, Christopher 'An Estate Forestry Record', *Country Life,* 26th May 1944.

39 Vancouver, Charles *General View of the Agriculture of the County of Devon,* 1808.

40 Marshall, W. *A Review of the Reports to the Board of Agriculture from the Northern Department of England: comprizing Northumberland, Durham, Cumberland, Westmoreland, Lancashire, Yorkshire and the Mountainous Parts of Derbyshire etc,* 1808.

41 Marshall, W. *A Review of the Reports to the Board of Agriculture from the Western Department of England: comprizing Cheshire, Flintshire, Shropshire, Herefordshire, Worcestershire, Glocestershire, North Wiltshire, North Somersetshire,* 1810.

42 Marshall, W. *A Review of the Reports to the Board of Agriculture from the Eastern Department of England: comprizing Lincolnshire, Norfolk, Suffolk and Northeast Essex with The Marshes and Fens of Yorkshire, North Lincolnshire, South Lincolnshire, Northamptonshire, Huntingdonshire, Cambridgeshire, Norfolk and Suffolk,* 1811.

43 Marshall, W. *A Review (and complete abstract) of The Reports to the Board of Agriculture from the Midland Department of England: comprizing Staffordshire, Derbyshire, Nottinghamshire, Leicestershire, Rutlandshire, Warwickshire, Huntingdonshire, Northamptonshire, Oxfordshire, Buckinghamshire, Bedfordshire and a principal part of Cambridgeshire,* 1815.

44 Marshall, W. *A Review (and complete abstract) of The Reports to the Board of Agriculture from the Southern and Peninsular Departments of England: comprizing Hertfordshire, Berkshire, Middlesex, South Essex, South Wiltshire, Southeast Somerset, Dorsetshire, Hampshire, Surrey, Kent, Sussex, Cornwall, Devonshire, West Somersetshire,* 1817.

45 Marshall *Review from the Western Department.*

46 Marshall *Review from the Western Department.*

47 Marshall *Review from the Midland Department.*

48 Claridge, J. *General View of the Agriculture of the County of Dorset*, 1793.

49 Marshall *Review from the Midland Department*.

50 Marshall *Review from the Southern and Peninsular Departments*.

51 Marshall *Review from the Western Department*.

52 Marshall *Review from the Northern Department*.

53 Marshall *Review from the Northern Department*.

54 Marshall *Review from the Northern Department*.

55 Marshall *Review from the Eastern Department*.

56 Marshall *Review from the Northern Department*.

57 *The Eleventh Report of the Commissioners appointed to enquire into the State and Condition of the Woods, Forests and Land Revenues of the Crown*, 1792.

58 Marshall *Review from the Western Department*.

59 Marshall *Review from the Midland Department*.

60 Marshall *Review from the Midland Department*.

61 *An Act for appointing Commissioners to enquire into the State and Condition of the Woods, Forests and Land Revenues belonging to the Crown and to sell or alienate fee farm and other unimprovable rents*, 1786, 26 Geo. 3, c.87.

62 *The Seventeenth Report of the Commissioners*, 1793.

63 *The Eighth Report of the Commissioners*, 1792.

64 *An Act for uniting the offices of Surveyor General of the Land Revenues of the Crown and Surveyor General of His Majesty's Woods, Forests, Parks and Chases*, 1810, 50 Geo. 3, c.65.

65 *The Eleventh Report of the Commissioners*, 1792.

66 *The First Report of the Commissioners of His Majesty's Woods, Forests and Land Revenues*, 1812.

67 Board of Agriculture and Fisheries, Office of Woods, Forests and Land Revenues *Joint Annual Report of the Forestry Branches for the Year 1912-1913*.

68 *Report from the Select Committee on the Woods, Forests and Land Revenues of the Crown*, 1848.

69 Ibid.

70 Board of Agriculture *Joint Annual Report of the Forestry Branches*, 1912-1913.

71 *First Report from the Select Committee on the Woods, Forests and Land Revenues of the Crown*, 1849.

72 Board of Agriculture *Joint Annual Report of the Forestry Branches*, 1912-1913.

73 *An Act to authorise Her Majesty to issue a Commission to inquire into and report upon rights or claims over the New Forest in the County of Southampton and Waltham Forest in the County of Essex*, 1849, 12 & 13 Vict., c.81.

74 *An Act to extinguish the right of the Crown to deer in the New Forest, and to give compensation in lieu thereof; and for other purposes relating to the said Forest*, 1851, 14 & 15 Vict., c.76.

75 *An Act to amend the administration of the law relating to the New Forest in the County of Southampton; and for other purposes*, 1877, 40 & 41 Vict., c.121.

76 *Report from the Select Committee on Crown Forests*, 1854.

77 Ibid.

78 Ibid.

79 Ibid.

80 Anonymous 'The Forester', *The Quarterly Review*, vol. XCVI, 1855.

81 Brown, James *The Forester*, 2nd edn, 1851.

CHAPTER 9   THE NEW FORESTRY

1 *An Act for the Preservation of Woods*, 1543, 35 Hen. 8, c.17.
2 Nisbet, J. *The Forester*, vol. I, 1905.
3 *An Act to extinguish the right of the Crown to deer in the New Forest and to give compensation in lieu thereof, and for other purposes relating to the said Forest*, 1851, 14 & 15 Vict., c.74.
4 *An Act to amend the administration of the law relating to the New Forest in the County of Southampton; and for other purposes*, 1877, 40 & 41 Vict., c.121.
5 Anonymous *The Dedication of Woodlands*, Forestry Commission Booklet no. 2, 1948.
6 Davidson, J.E. 'The History of the Royal English Forestry Society', *Quarterly Journal of Forestry*, vol. XXVI, 1932.
7 Rattray, J. and Mill, R.M. *Forestry and Forest Products*, Prize Essays of the Edinburgh International Forestry Exhibition, 1885.
8 *Report from the Select Committee on Forestry*, 1887.
9 *An Act to amend the administration of the law relating to the New Forest in the County of Southampton; and for other purposes*, 1877, 40 & 41 Vict., c.121.
10 *An Act for establishing a Board of Agriculture for Great Britain*, 1889, 52 & 53 Vict., c.30.
11 *Report from the Select Committee on the Woods, Forests and Land Revenues of the Crown*, 1890.
12 Hill, H.C. *Report on the Forest of Dean, with Suggestions for its Management*, 1897.
13 Hill, H.C. *Working Plan Report for the Highmeadow Woods*, 1897.
14 *Annual Report of Commissioner of Woods and Forests*, 1897.
15 Board of Agriculture and Fisheries, Office of Woods, Forests and Land Revenues *Joint Annual Report of the Forestry Branches for the Year 1912-1913*.
16 Ribbentrop, B. *Forestry in British India*, 1900.
17 Anonymous 'Sir William Schlich's Work in Britain', *Quarterly Journal of Forestry*, vol. XX, 1926.
18 Board of Agriculture *Joint Annual Report, 1912-13*.
19 *Report of the Departmental Committee appointed by the Board of Agriculture to enquire into and report upon British Forestry*, Cd 1319, 1902.
20 *Minutes of Evidence taken before the Departmental Committee appointed by the Board of Agriculture to enquire into and report upon British Forestry*, Cd 1565, 1903.
21 Anonymous 'Afforestation Conference in London', *Quarterly Journal of Forestry*, vol. I, 1907.
22 *Royal Commission on Coast Erosion and Afforestation. Volume II (Part I). Second Report (on Afforestation) of the Royal Commission Appointed to inquire into and to report on certain questions affecting Coast Erosion, the Reclamation of Tidal Lands and Afforestation in the United Kingdom*, Cd 4460, 1909.
23 *Royal Commission on Coast Erosion and Afforestation. Volume II (Part II).*

Minutes of Evidence and Appendices thereto accompanying the Second Report (on Afforestation) (Volume II — Part I), Cd 4461, 1909.

24   Anonymous 'Afforestation', *Quarterly Journal of Forestry,* vol. III, 1909.

25   *Punch or The London Charivari,* 27th January 1909.

26   *An Act to give compensation for damage by fires caused by sparks or cinders from railway engines,* 1905, 5 Edw. 7., c.11.

27   *An Act to amend the Railway Fires Act, 1905,* 1923, 13 & 14 Geo. 5, c.27.

28   Anonymous 'Afforestation in the Budget,' *Quarterly Journal of Forestry,* vol. III, 1909.

29   *An Act to promote the economic development of the United Kingdom and the improvement of roads therein,* 1909, 9 Edw. 7, c.47.

30   Anonymous 'Report of Development Commissioners', *Quarterly Journal of Forestry,* vol. VI, 1912.

31   Schlich, W. *Schlich's Manual of Forestry,* vol. III, *Forest Management,* 3rd edn, 1905.

32   Nisbet, J. *The Forester,* vol. II, 1905.

33   Webster, R.J. and Leach, M.H. 'The First British Yield Tables?' *Quarterly Journal of Forestry,* vol. LX, 1966.

34   Maw, P.T. *The Practice of Forestry,* 1909.

35   Hanson, C.O. 'Some Measurements of Larch in the Forest of Dean and Neighbourhood', *Quarterly Journal of Forestry,* vol. V, 1911.

36   Robinson, R.L. 'Form Factors of Various Conifers', *Quarterly Journal of Forestry,* vol. V, 1911.

37   Maw, P.T. *Complete Yield Tables for British Woodlands and the Finance of British Forestry,* 1912.

38   Robinson, R.L. 'Complete Yield Tables for British Woodlands and the Finance of British Forestry', *Quarterly Journal of Forestry,* vol. VI, 1912.

39   *Committee appointed by the Board of Agriculture and Fisheries to advise on matters relating to the Development of Forestry. Reports — July to October 1912,* Cd 6713, 1913.

40   Duchesne, M.C. 'The English Forestry Association', *Quarterly Journal of Forestry,* vol. VII, 1913.

41   Anonymous 'Provision of Technical Advice in Forestry', *Quarterly Journal of Forestry,* vol. VII, 1913.

CHAPTER 10   THE FIRST WORLD WAR AND ITS AFTERMATH

1   Schlich, Sir William 'Forestry and the War', *Quarterly Journal of Forestry,* vol. IX, 1915.

2   Robinson, R.L. 'Forest Policy', *Quarterly Journal of Forestry,* vol. XIV, 1920.

3   Ernle, Lord *English Farming Past and Present,* 4th edn, 1927.

4   Pritchard, H.A. 'The Experience of a Divisional Officer (Timber Supply Department) during the War', *Quarterly Journal of Forestry,* vol. XVI, 1922.

5   Ibid.

6   Forestry Commission *Post-War Forest Policy,* Report by HM Forestry Commissioners, Cmd. 6447, 1943.

7   Pritchard 'Experience of a Divisional Officer'.

8   Ministry of Reconstruction *Reconstruction Committee Forestry Sub-Committee Final Report*, Cd 8881, 1918.

9   Forestry Commission *Post-War Forest Policy*.

10   Robinson 'Forest Policy'.

11   'Letter from the Interim Forest Authority. Report of Council Meeting May 1919', *Quarterly Journal of Forestry*, vol. XIII, 1919.

12   Lloyd George, D. *War Memoirs of David Lloyd George*, 1938.

13   Forbes, A.C. 'Fifty Years of English Forestry', *Quarterly Journal of Forestry*, vol. XXVI, 1932.

14   *Royal Commission on Coast Erosion and Afforestation Volume II (Part I). Second Report (on Afforestation) of the Royal Commission Appointed to inquire into and to report on certain questions affecting Coast Erosion, the Reclamation of Tidal Lands and Afforestation in the United Kingdom*, Cd 4461, 1909.

15   *An Act for establishing a Forestry Commission for the United Kingdom, and promoting afforestation and the production and supply of timber therein, and for purposes in connexion therewith*, 1919, 9 & 10 Geo. 5, c.58.

16   *An Act to provide for the transfer of certain properties to the Forestry Commissioners and to amend the Forestry Act, 1919, and for purposes in connection therewith*, 1923, 13 & 14 Geo. 5, c.21.

17   Anonymous 'British Empire Forestry Conference', *Quarterly Journal of Forestry*, vol. XIV, 1920.

18   Herbert, A.G. Letter from the Forestry Commission, *Quarterly Journal of Forestry*, vol. XV, 1921.

19   Dallimore, W. 'The Empire Timber Exhibition', *Quarterly Journal of Forestry*, vol. XIV, 1920.

20   Forestry Commission Bulletin No. 1, *Collection of Data as to the Rate of Growth of Timber*, 1920.
     Bulletin No. 2 *Survey of Forest Insect Conditions*, 1920.
     Bulletin No. 3 *Rate of Growth of Conifers in the British Isles*, 1920.

21   Forestry Commission *First Annual Report of the Forestry Commissioners Year ending September 30th 1920*.

22   Wood, R.F. *Fifty Years of Forestry Research*, Forestry Commission Bulletin no. 50, 1974.

23   Ryle, G.B. *Forest Service*, 1969.

24   Anonymous 'The Forestry Commission and Unemployment', *Quarterly Journal of Forestry*, vol. XVI, 1922.

25   *Committee on National Expenditure. Second Interim Report*, Cmd 1582, 1922.

26   *An Act to provide for the better government of Ireland*, 1920, 10 & 11 Geo. 5, c.67.

27   *An Act to amend the Railway Fires Act 1905*, 1923, 13 & 14 Geo. 5, c.27.

28   Anonymous 'Imperial Forestry Institute', *Quarterly Journal of Forestry*, vol. XIX, 1925.

29   Mitchell, A.F. and Westall, A.W. *Bedgebury Pinetum and Forest Plots*, Forestry Commission Guide, 4th edn, 1972.

30   Forestry Commission *Sixth Annual Report*, 1925.

31   Rendle, B.J. *Fifty years of timber research*, 1976.

32 *An Act to authorise an increase of the number of Forestry Commissioners; to empower the Commissioners to make byelaws with respect to land vested in them or under their management or control; and for purposes consequential upon the matters aforesaid,* 1927, 17 Geo. 5, c.6.

33 Forestry Commission 'Forestry Grants', *Quarterly Journal of Forestry,* vol. XXI, 1927.

34 Forestry Commission *Tenth Annual Report,* 1929.

35 *Committee on National Expenditure Report,* Cmd. 3920, 1931.

36 Forestry Commission *Twelfth Annual Report,* 1931.

37 *Report on the Census of Woodlands and Census of Production of Home-grown Timber, 1924,* compiled by the Forestry Commission, 1928.

38 Forestry Commission *Forestry Facts and Figures 1977-78.*

39 Forestry Commission *Tenth Annual Report,* 1929.

40 Forestry Commission *Thirteenth Annual Report,* 1932.

41 *Interim Report of the Inter-Departmental Home-grown Timber Committee,* 1933.

42 Forestry Commission *Report on the demand for box and packing-case manufacture in Great Britain,* Utilisation Series no. 1, 1934.
    Report on the demand for timber in coal-mining in England and Wales, Utilisation Series no. 2, 1935.
    Report on the demand for timber in wood-turning in Great Britain, Utilisation Series no. 3, 1936.
    Report on the demand for timber in ship-building and in docks and harbours, Utilisation Series no. 4, 1938.

43 Hiley, W.E. 'Marketing of Home-Grown Timber', *Quarterly Journal of Forestry,* vol. XXVII, 1933.

44 Clinton, the Rt. Hon. the Lord 'Marketing of Home-Grown Timber and other Woodland Products', *Quarterly Journal of Forestry,* vol. XXVIII, 1934.

45 Anonymous 'Native Timber Trade. Deputation to the Government', *Quarterly Journal of Forestry,* vol. XXVIII, 1934.

46 Forestry Commission *Fifteenth Annual Report,* 1934.

47 Hiley, W.E. 'National Home-Grown Timber Council', *Quarterly Journal of Forestry,* vol. XXIX, 1935.

48 Forestry Commission *Sixteenth Annual Report,* 1935.

49 Orde-Powlett, the Hon. Nigel A. 'The Present and Future of Estate Woodlands', *Quarterly Journal of Forestry,* vol. XXXI, 1937.

50 Forestry Commission *Eighteenth Annual Report,* 1937.

51 House, Frank H. *Timber at War,* 1965.

52 Forestry Commission *Eighteenth Annual Report,* 1937.

53 Ryle *Forest Service.*

54 Forestry Commission *Thirtieth Annual Report,* 1949.

55 Hiley, W.E. 'Forestry and the International Crisis', *Quarterly Journal of Forestry,* vol. XXXIII, 1939.

CHAPTER 11   THE SECOND WORLD WAR

  1   Anonymous 'Timber Control', *Quarterly Journal of Forestry*, vol. XXXIII, 1939.
  2   *The Control of Timber (No 1) Order, 1939; The Control of Growing Trees (No 1) Order, 1939; The Control of Trees (No 2) Order, 1939.*
  3   Anonymous 'Timber Control: Changes in the Organisation of Home Timber Production', *Quarterly Journal of Forestry*, vol. XXXV, 1941.
  4   Orde-Powlett, the Hon. N.A. 'Presidential Message', *Quarterly Journal of Forestry*, vol. XXXIV, 1940.
  5   Anonymous 'The War Time Marketing of Timber', *Quarterly Journal of Forestry*, vol. XXXIV, 1940.
  6   Churchill, Sir Winston S. *The Second World War*, vol. III, *The Grand Alliance*, 1950.
  7   House, F.H. *Timber at War*, 1965.
  8   Ibid.
  9   Lenanton, G. 'Home Production of Timber', *Quarterly Journal of Forestry*, vol. XXXVII, 1943.
 10   Meiggs, Russell *Home Timber Production (1939-1945).*
 11   Urquhart, Bruce, in correspondence, 1979.
 12   Meiggs *Home Timber Production.*
 13   Urquhart, Bruce, in correspondence, 1979.
 14   Meiggs *Home Timber Production.*
 15   Ibid.
 16   Ibid.
 17   Ibid.
 18   Ibid.
 19   Ibid.
 20   Hiley, W.E. 'The Future of Estate Forestry', *Quarterly Journal of Forestry*, vol. XXXVIII, 1944.
 21   Forestry Commission *Post-War Forest Policy*, Report by HM Forestry Commissioners, Cmd 6447, 1943.
 22   Forestry Commission *Post-War Forest Policy, Private Woodlands.* Supplementary Report by HM Forestry Commissioners, Cmd 6500, 1944.
 23   Forestry Commission *Dedication of Woodlands. Explanatory Note,* 1946.
 24   *An Act to provide for the dedication of land to forestry purposes; for the deduction from compensation of grants made by the Forestry Commissioners in the event of compulsory purchase of the land in respect of which the grants were made; and for the execution on behalf of the Secretary of State of instruments relating to land placed at the disposal of the Forestry Commissioners,* 1947, 10 & 11 Geo. 6, c.21.
 25   Consultative Committee of the Home Timber Production Department, *Quarterly Journal of Forestry*, vol. XXXVIII, 1944.
 26   *Control of Growing Trees and Home-Grown Round Timber in the Log (No. 1) Order,* 1944.
 27   *The Control of Timber (No. 32) (General Provisions) Order,* 1944; *The Control of Timber (No. 34) (Home-Grown Timber Prices) Order,* 1944; *The Control of*

Timber (No. 35) (Mining Timber Prices) Order, 1944.

28   *An Act to make provision for the reconstitution of the Forestry Commission and as to the exercise of the functions of the Forestry Commissioners, the acquisition of land for forestry purposes and the management, use and disposal of land so acquired; and in connection with the matters aforesaid to amend the Forestry Acts, 1919 to 1927, and certain other enactments relating to the Forestry Commissioners, 1945, 8 & 9 Geo. 6, c.35.*

29   Forestry Commission *Twenty-sixth Annual Report of the Forestry Commissioners for the year ending September 30th, 1945.*

30   Forestry Commission *Thirtieth Annual Report,* 1949.

31   Forestry Commission *Census of Woodlands 1947-1949. Woodlands of Five Acres and over,* Census Report no. 1, 1952.

CHAPTER 12   THE POST-WAR ERA

1   Forestry Commission *Twenty-Seventh Annual Report of the Forestry Commissioners for the year ending September 30th, 1946.*

2   Forestry Commission *Twenty-Ninth Annual Report,* 1948.

3   Forestry Commission *Post-War Forest Policy,* Report by HM Forestry Commissioners, Cmd 6447, 1943.

4   Anonymous 'Report of the Council for the year ending December 31, 1948.' *Quarterly Journal of Forestry,* vol. XLIII, 1949.

5   Forestry Commission *Report of the New Forest Committee 1947,* Cmd 7245.

6   Forestry Commission *Fifty-Fourth Annual Report and Accounts of the Forestry Commission for the year ended 31st March, 1974.*

7   *The Control of Growing Trees and Home-Grown Round Timber in the Log (No. 3) Order,* 1946, Statutory Rules and Orders no. 2209.

8   *Report on the Census of Woodlands and Census of Production of Home-grown Timber, 1924,* compiled by the Forestry Commission, 1928.

9   Forestry Commission Census Report no. 1, *Census of Woodlands 1947-1949. Woodlands of Five Acres and over,* 1952.

10   Forestry Commission Census Report no. 2, *Hedgerow and Park Timber and Woods under Five Acres 1951,* 1953.

11   *An Act to provide for the dedication of land to forestry purposes; for the deduction from compensation of grants made by the Forestry Commissioners in the event of compulsory purchase of the land in respect of which the grants were made; and for the execution on behalf of the Secretary of State of instruments relating to land placed at the disposal of the Forestry Commissioners, 1947, 10 & 11 Geo. 6, c.21.*

12   *An Act to make fresh provision for planning the development and use of land, for the grant of permission to develop land and for other powers of control over the use of land . . . 10 & 11 Geo. 6, c.51.*

13   Merthyr, the Rt Hon. the Lord 'The Dedication Scheme', *Quarterly Journal of Forestry,* vol. XLII, 1948.

14   Merthyr, the Rt Hon. the Lord 'The Dedication Scheme', *Quarterly Journal of Forestry,* vol. XLIV, 1950.

15   Forestry Commission *Thirtieth Annual Report,* 1949.

16 Forestry Commission *Twenty-Ninth Annual Report, 1948.*

17 Wright, H.L. 'Curtailment of Felling', *Quarterly Journal of Forestry,* vol. XLIII, 1949.

18 *Sixteenth Report from the Select Committee on Estimates Session 1948-49. The Forestry Commission.*

19 Anonymous 'Thinning Grant', *Quarterly Journal of Forestry,* vol. XLIII, 1949.

20 Forestry Commission *Thirty-First Annual Report, 1950.*

21 Ibid.

22 Forestry Commission *Thirty-Second Annual Report, 1951.*

23 Forestry Commission *Tenth Annual Report, 1929.*

24 Forestry Commission *Report on Forest Research for the year ending March 1949.*

25 *An Act to provide for the maintenance of reserves of growing trees in Great Britain and to regulate the felling of trees; to amend the procedure applicable to compulsory purchase orders under the Forestry Act, 1945; and for purposes connected with the matters aforesaid,* 1951, 14 & 15 Geo. 6, c.61.

26 *The Forestry (Exceptions from Restriction of Felling) Regulations,* 1951; *The Forestry (Felling of Trees) Regulations,* 1951.

27 Forestry Commission *Thirty-Third Annual Report, 1952.*

28 Ibid.

29 Forestry Commission *Thirty-Fifth Annual Report, 1954.*

30 Forestry Commission *Report of the Committee on Hedgerow and Farm Timber, 1955.*

31 Lewthwaite, Sir William 'Co-operation in Forestry', *Quarterly Journal of Forestry,* vol. XLII, 1948.

32 Lewthwaite, Sir William 'Forest Co-operation', *Quarterly Journal of Forestry,* vol. XLIII, 1949.

33 Forestry Commission *Twenty-Ninth Annual Report, 1948.*

34 Forestry Commission *Thirty-Fourth Annual Report, 1953.*

35 Forestry Commission *Report of the Committee on Marketing of Woodland Produce 1956.*

36 Forestry Commission *Thirty-Eighth Annual Report, 1957.*

37 Southern, H.N. (editor) *The Handbook of British Mammals, 1964.*

38 Anonymous 'Rabbit Clearance Campaign', *Quarterly Journal of Forestry,* vol. LI, 1957.

39 Forestry Commission *Thirty-Eighth Annual Report, 1957.*

40 Bartholomew, C.R. 'Rabbit Clearance Societies', *Quarterly Journal of Forestry,* vol. LIV, 1960.

41 Ministry of Reconstruction *Reconstruction Committee Forestry Sub-Committee Final Report,* Cd 8881, 1918.

42 Forestry Commission *Third Annual Report, 1922.*

43 Forestry Commission *Dedication of Woodlands. Explanatory Note,* Leaflet no. 24, 1946.
   The Dedication of Woodlands. Principles and Procedure, Booklet no. 2, 1948.

44 Ibid.

45 Forestry Commission *Thirty-First Annual Report, 1950.*

46   Forestry Commission *Thirty-Fifth Annual Report*, 1954.

47   Forestry Commission *Thirty-Fourth Annual Report*, 1953.

48   Forestry Commission *Report of the Forest of Dean Committee, 1958*, Cmd 686.

49   Forestry Commission *Thirty-Seventh Annual Report*, 1956.

50   Gibson, V.G. 'Demonstration of Forest Machinery at Hatfield Park', *Quarterly Journal of Forestry*, vol. L, 1956.

51   Forestry Commission *Thirty-Ninth Annual Report*, 1958.

52   Ibid.

53   Forestry Commission *Fortieth Annual Report*, 1959.

54   Ibid.

55   *The Forestry (Exceptions from Restriction of Felling) Regulations*, 1951; *The Forestry (Exceptions from Restriction of Felling) (Amendment) Regulations*, 1959.

56   Anonymous *The Forest Tree Seed Association of England and Wales — Members Handbook*, 1961.

57   Forestry Commission *Forty-Fourth Annual Report*, 1963.

58   Forestry Commission *Seventh Report from the Estimates Committee Session 1963-64*.

59   *An Act to alter the perambulation of the New Forest, to make further provision for the New Forest, to amend the New Forest Acts 1877 to 1949 and for purposes connected with the matters aforesaid*, 1964, Eliz. 2, 1964, c.83.

60   *Ministry of Land and Natural Resources (Dissolution) Order 1967*.

61   Forestry Commission *Forty-Sixth Annual Report*, 1965.

62   *An Act to consolidate the Forestry Acts 1919 to 1963 with corrections and improvements made under the Consolidation of Enactment (Procedure) Act 1949*, 1967, Eliz. 2, 1967, c.10.

63   *An Act to consolidate the Destructive Insects and Pests Acts 1877 to 1927, together with section 11 of the Agriculture (Miscellaneous Provisions) Act 1949*, 1967, Eliz. 2, 1967, c.8.

64   *An Act to . . . make provision with respect to the shape and size of farms and related matters, agriculture and forestry on hill land . . . and other matters connected with agriculture*, 1967, Eliz. 2, 1967, c.22.

65   *An Act to make further provision for . . . the provision and planting of trees . . .*, 1967, Eliz. 2, 1967, c.69.

66   *An Act to enlarge the functions of the Commission established under the National Parks and Access to the Countryside Act 1949 . . . and to amend the law about trees and woodlands . . .*, 1968, Eliz. 2, 1968, c.41.

67   Forestry Commission *Fifty-First Annual Report and Accounts of the Forestry Commission for the year ended 31st March 1971*.

68   Forestry Commission *Census of Woodlands, 1965-67*, 1970.

69   *An Act to amend the law relating to the making of tree preservation orders and the grant of felling licences*, 1970, Eliz. 2, 1970, c.43.

70   Harris, E.M.H. 'Was an Opportunity Lost?' *Quarterly Journal of Forestry*, vol. LXV, 1971.

71   Forestry Commission *Fifty-Second Annual Report*, 1972.

72   Forestry Commission *Fifty-First Annual Report*, 1971.

73 *An Act to abolish certain rights of Her Majesty to wild creatures and certain related rights and franchises; to abrogate the forest law (subject to exceptions); and to repeal enactments relating to those rights and franchises and to forests and the forest law; and for connected purposes,* 1971, Eliz. 2, 1971, c.47.

CHAPTER 13   THE CHANGING SCENE

1 Anonymous *Forestry Policy,* June 1972, HMSO.
2 Anonymous *Forestry in Great Britain. An Interdepartment Cost/Benefit Study,* 1972.
3 Leathart, P.S. 'Forest Policy — 1972', *Quarterly Journal of Forestry,* vol. LXVI, 1972.
4 Garthwaite, P.F. 'Forestry Policy — June 1972. Statement by The Royal Forestry Society of England, Wales and Northern Ireland.' *Quarterly Journal of Forestry,* vol. LXVI, 1972.
5 Anonymous 'A Dark Hour for Private Forestry', *Timber Grower,* no. 45, 1972.
6 Leathart, P.S. 'A Case for Serendipidity, being comments on a report entitled "Some Considerations Regarding Forest Policy in Great Britain" by Professor J.N. Wolfe', *Quarterly Journal of Forestry,* vol. LXVII, 1973.
7 Forestry Commission *Fifty-Third Annual Report and Accounts of the Forestry Commission for the year ended 31st March 1973.*
8 Forestry Commission *Advice for Woodland Owners,* August, 1977.
9 Leathart, P.S. 'The Tree Council', *Quarterly Journal of Forestry,* vol. LXVIII, 1974.
10 *The Report of the National Parks Policies Review Committee,* 1974.
11 Forestry Commission *Fifty-Sixth Annual Report,* 1976.
12 Ibid.
13 Leathart, P.S. 'Interdepartmental Review of Forestry Taxation and Grants', *Quarterly Journal of Forestry,* vol. LXX, 1976.
14 Forestry Commission *Fifty-Fourth Annual Report,* 1974.
15 Wood, R.F. *Fifty Years of Forestry Research,* Forestry Commission Bulletin no. 50, 1974.
16 Forestry Commission *Fiftieth Annual Report,* 1970.
17 Forestry Commission *Progress Reports 1966-72 by the Forestry Commission . . . prepared for the Tenth Commonwealth Forestry Conference,* 1974.
18 Forestry Commission *Fifty-Eighth Annual Report,* 1978.
19 Forestry Commission *Fifty-Second Annual Report,* 1972.
20 Ibid.
21 Aldhous, J.R. 'Aircraft and British Forestry', *Quarterly Journal of Forestry,* vol. LXIII, 1969.
22 Hall, Walter *Barnacle Parp's Chain Saw Guide,* 1977.
23 Anonymous 'Parliamentary Debate on Forestry', *Timber Grower,* no. 67, 1978.
24 Forestry Commission *The Wood Production Outlook in Britain,* 1977.

APPENDICES

A VOCABULARY OF OLD FORESTRY TERMS

This vocabulary contains various terms which were in use between the beginning of the sixteenth and the end of the nineteenth centuries. Where a date appears in or after a definition, this refers to the year in which firm evidence has been found of the use of the word or expression although it may have been in existence for some time previously. Some of the terms included in this vocabulary were still current in 1976 although with the passage of time, their original meaning may have changed.

Aller	An old name for alder (1540) which is still in use in the West of England; the forms *oller* and *orle* also occur.
Alley	A trodden path between the seed beds in a forest nursery (1812).
Aquaticks	Trees, such as alder, which grow and thrive in wet conditions (1670).
Arbeel	Abele or white poplar.
Arrent	To let or farm out land at a rent or to permit the enclosure of forest land or woodland on payment of an annual rent (1600).
Arrentation	The process of arrenting.
Asp	Aspen poplar.

Band	To keep a wood 'in band' was to fence the young growth against deer for four years or against cattle for seven years after felling.
Bark-stripping	In a report on Duffield Frith in 1581 the term *hag* or *hagge* denoted an area of woodland, the felling of which was entrusted to a single woodman, while the total fall which comprised several hags was known as a *flag*. In 1803 W. Nichol stated that a hag varied in extent from 10 to 100 acres and that bark-stripping was carried out by three kinds of workers; *hagmen* who felled the trees, *barkers* who stripped the bark and *carriers* who carried the bark to drying stands known as *horses*. There were two types of hagmen; *hatchet men* who felled the trees and *hookmen* who removed the smaller branches. Bark-stripping was also known as *pilling* (1792), *tan-fluing* (1827) and *flawing* (1882).
Barrelling	Barrelling seed consisted of placing it in moist sand or earth in tubs or barrels during the winter and is referred to by Evelyn in 1670.
Bavins or *bavines*	These were faggots of brushwood which were also known as *house-faggots*. They were bound together with two *weefs* (*q.v.*) and were chiefly used by bakers in their bread ovens. The word bavin occurs in 1670 and probably earlier and was still in use in Kent in 1960.
Beet	To beet, from which the term 'to beat up' originates, is to fill up vacancies or to replace dead or dying trees in young plantations. The actual work of replacing the trees was known as beeting (1803).
Belting	In some parts of the country shelter belts were known as belting or *stripes* (1803).
Billet wood	This consisted of pieces of wood which were usually obtained from the larger branches of a tree and was the equivalent of cordwood. The Act for the Assise of Fuel, 1553, laid down the dimensions of billet wood and these were still in use in 1740.
Binders	Long pliant rods, usually of hazel or willow which were interwoven along the top of a cut-and-laid hedge in order to bind and strengthen it. Laying was originally known as *plashing* (1670). Binders were also known as *edders* (1573), *ethers, etherings, headerings, hethers* and *roders*.
Birk	Birch (1581).

Bole	The main stem or trunk of a standing tree, extending from ground level upwards to the beginning of the crown or head, that is, where the bulk of the branches begin. Other names are *boal, body* or *butt* although the last named usually refers to a felled tree (1670).
Boll	The verb 'to boll' means to remove branches from a tree and has the same meaning as 'to poll' which was still used in Devon in the 1960s with reference to the removal of the side branches of hedgerow trees. The word boll dates from the end of the thirteenth century and also occurs as 'bowl'.
Bottle	A bundle of brushwood or *spray* (*q.v.*) particularly of birch for making besoms (1815).
Bounders	A mark which indicated a boundary and which was often a tree or stone. Such trees were known as bounder trees. Those who marked out the bounds or limits were also known as bounders.
Braid	Also *breadth, brede* or *bredth.* This was a unit of area which was used in Wychwood Forest and probably the surrounding district, when cutting or selling coppice. It measured 1 pole (5½ yards) by 4 poles (22 yards) and 40 braids equalled 1 acre (1677).
Brash	Small branches removed from the boles of young trees when they are usually about 10 years of age depending on the species and rate of growth, the operation being known as brashing. This term is derived from *broche* which was originally the name for the brushwood of a felled tree and dates from the fourteenth century.
Brush	Also referred to as *brushwood,* this was a general term for the small growth on a woodland site which would be cleared before planting (1670).
Canes	Hazel rods, 6 feet in length, which were cleft for making hoops used by coopers and also for building salmon traps. Sometimes known as *smart-hoops* (1832).
Cant	A unit of measurement employed in the south-east of England for dividing areas of coppice into working units.
Charke	The verb 'to charke' which means to char or coke was used in connection with making charcoal while the noun 'charke' was another name for charcoal (1662).
Chasts or *chats*	The winged seed or samara of ash (1611).
Close woods	See *Groves.*
Coal wood	Coal was the original name for charcoal and coal wood

was the kind of wood from which charcoal was made. The first colliers were charcoal burners who had no connection with coal mines (1670).

Cobbing Similar to pollarding (q.v.)

Compass timber Curved pieces of oak used in ship construction to provide knees, futtocks and so on.

Cooper's ware The butt ends of ash poles cut in lengths of 6 to 18 feet which, after cleaving, were used in the coopering trade and for making waggon tilts (1832).

Coppice The system under which broadleaved species are grown on short rotations usually of between 8 and 25 years. After cutting, the stools or stumps produce fresh shoots which grow into the next crop and the operation is then repeated. Many variations of the word coppice occur including the following: copye (1573), coppis, coppse, copps-wood, coppy, copse, cops and copys. The verb 'to coppice' refers to the action of managing an area as coppice and this was also known as coppicing or copsing.

Cord A stack of pieces of wood (usually obtained from the lop and top or branches of a tree) known as *cordwood* and measuring 4 ft high x 4 ft wide x 8 ft long (1670). The dimensions varied according to the district and in 1788 a cord in the Forest of Dean measured 4 ft 4 in high x 2 ft 2 in wide x 8 ft 8 in long.

Corf rods Coppice rods, ½ in to 1 in in diameter, used for making *corves* or large wicker baskets in which coal was brought out of the mines in the north of England (1808).

Crutch A large ash or hazel pole claimed by woodmen in Bedfordshire (in addition to their wages) for every 10 poles (302½ square yards) of underwood which they cut (1815).

Cuffing The sowing of forest seeds in a seed bed with the use of a cuffing rake or board (1812).

Deadwoods Also known as *kiln-faggots,* these were made up of the lowest grade material in a wood such as dead coppice, brambles and other rubbish. Kiln-faggots were used in lime and brick kilns, hence their name (1832).

Disbranching The removal of the branches on a large tree prior to felling it, in order to reduce the risk of damaging the bole when it struck the ground (1670).

Diswooding The conversion of woodland to agricultural land (1817).

Doat To doat is to rot, doating is decaying and doaty is rotten or decayed (1670), all these terms still being in use in

	1976. The word '*dotard*' (*q.v.*) is derived from the same source.
Doles	Hurdle stakes (1827).
Dotard, Dottard or *Dote*	Strictly trees that were beginning to decay (1560) but the name was also used for dead and dying trees. The term *wrangles* was also applied to decayed trees (1550).
Draw	In Berkshire and Gloucestershire, to draw a wood was to thin it while in Rutland drawing referred to draining (1810).
Dressing	This term had two meanings. It could either refer to the reduction of the number of coppice shoots on a stool to one, so as to encourage its development; or to the pruning of a tree in order to improve the quality of its timber (1670).
Encoppice	To enclose a wood or area of coppice after it had been cut so as to protect the young stool shoots. An *encoppice-ment* was an area so treated.
Faggot	A bundle of wood which the Act for the Assise of Fuel 1553, laid down should be 3 ft in length and 2 ft in girth. See also *Taleshides.*
Fallage	A fall or felling of timber (1810).
Fewel-wood	Firewood (1601).
Fir-apples	Cones (1811).
Flake or *fleak*	Sheep hurdles (1815).
Flawing	Bark-stripping.
Foreshortening	Also known as *snagg-pruning,* this was the removal of a branch by severing it some 12 to 24 ins from the bole. The branch was thus foreshortened and the remaining part formed a snagg or projection (1839).
Frow	Tending to decay or crumbling, as applied to timber (1696).
Garble	To thin a wood (1652).
Gash planting	Sometimes referred to as *slit planting* and corresponds to present day notch planting.
Germens or *germins*	Young shoots from a stool or stump but 'lateral germens on the bodies of oaks' (1747) would indicate epicormic or adventitious shoots.
Government of trees	The management of trees or woods and is similar to the term *ordering* (*q.v.*) (1740).
Great trees	See *Standards.*

Groves	In 1796, William Marshall defined these as 'a collection of timber trees only, placed in close order' and also called them *closewoods*. He described coppice as 'stubwood alone without an intermixture of timber trees' and a wood as 'a mixture of timber trees and underwood'. Later, in 1815, he divided woodlands into three classes, 'groves or *springwoods* consisting of trees only; woods consisting of timber trees and underwood and coppices consisting of underwood only'. See also *Springwoods*.
Grub felling	By this method the roots were, for the most part, removed when the tree was felled and this was achieved by cutting all surface roots and then laying in to the main tap root (1787).
Hassill	Hazel (1581).
Head (of a tree)	The crown or mass of branches growing above the bole but the verb 'to head' is to top or pollard a tree (1670).
Heading down	Cutting back to ground level young broadleaved trees whose growth has been checked (1803).
Heithorn	The name for hawthorn which was in use in the 17th and 18th centuries.
Hollyns	Holly (1581).
Holt	A wood.
Hurst	A wood.
Husset	The clippings of holly which were fed to deer, cattle and sheep in winter.
Kept woods	Woods which received regular attention (1811).
Kibbles	Pieces of timber supplied to coopers and wheelwrights (1788).
Kid or *kyd*	A kid was a bundle of brushwood or small material; the verb 'to kid' means to bind up into bundles; while kidwood was the material used (1670). Later a kid became known as a *pimp* or *nicky*.
Laying over	The intentional distortion of trees by deflecting them from the vertical in order to obtain compass timber (*q.v.*).
Loppings	Heavy branch wood similar to lop and top.
Low faggots	See *Sears*.
Mapill	Maple (1581).
Moot	A stump or stool.
Needle wood	A collective name for the silver firs, pines and spruces (1789).

Offal wood	Cord wood or lop and top (1585). See also *Cord.*
Ordering of trees	The management of trees (1679).
Pilcher	See Setts.
Pilling	Bark-stripping.
Pitting	Planting young trees in pits or holes as opposed to gash planting (*q.v.*) (1803).
Pollenger or *pollinger*	Described in a survey of Duffield Frith in 1560 as 'younge timber poles' and also mentioned by Tusser in 1573.
Pollard	A tree, the crown of which had been removed although the term can also be used as a verb 'to pollard'. In 1523 Fitzherbert referred to pollarding as *shredding* but later this term came to mean *pruning* (*q.v.*).
Polling	This could either mean pollarding or the removal of side branches. See also *Bolling.*
Pruning	Other names for this operation were: *dressing, setting up, shredding, shrouding, shrowding, stripping up, under-daging* and, in the west country, *polling.* See also *Fore-shortening.*
Puncheon	A timber support used in mining which was the equivalent of the modern pit-prop.
Quicken tree	The mountain ash, mountain sorb, sorb, rowan, quickbeam or wiggin.
Ram-picked trees	Old trees, usually oaks, which had dead branches in the crown and which are now referred to as stag-headed.
Ramell	This word also occurs as *romell, ramile* and *ramilia* (1762) and it would appear to be derived from the word *rennales* or *rennelles* which was the name for a hollow pollarded tree, the double 'n' having become an 'm' (1540). Rennalles were also known as *rundles.*
Rase knife	A tool used for marking timber and now usually referred to as a timber scribe.
Rifletum	Defined in 1727 as a coppice, thicket, spinney or place of bushes and thorns but in 1892 it was described as an osier bed.
Rind	The bark of a tree.
Rive	To split or rend.
Runting	The removal of old stools or stubs in coppice woods (1717). See also *stock up.*
Sapleyn	A sapling (1556).
Scrogs or *shroges*	An area of rough brushwood or underwood.

Scrubbed trees	Stunted or dwarf trees (1596).
Sears	Also termed *low faggots* these were similar to bavins (*q.v.*) but were longer and bound with three weefs instead of two (1832).
Seminary	Strictly this word applied to a seed bed but it was often used to refer to the nursery as a whole (1670). *Semination* was the sowing of seed and to *seminate* was to sow (1796).
Sett or *set*	The verb 'to sett' means to plant, as is shown in the following extract from a lease of 1665: 'and shall . . . plante or sett . . . seasonable plants of oake, ash or elme'.
Setting stick	Also termed a setting pin, this was similar to a dibber and was used for planting young trees (1803).
Setts	Cuttings used in the propagation of certain species (1670) which were also known as *truncheons* (1670) and *pilchers* (1681). Small cuttings were sometimes referred to as *setlings.*
Shaw	A small wood or spinney but especially a narrow strip of underwood growing along the edge of a field (1577). This term is still in use in the south-eastern counties.
Sherewood	A narrow strip of woodland (1635).
Shredding	See *Pruning.*
Shrowding	See *Pruning.*
Slivery	Ash coppice grown to a large size and then cut into short lengths and cleft into hoop material for coopering (1832).
Smart-hoops	See *Canes.*
Spear oaks	Oaks in the Forest of Essex which were allowed to grow into timber trees and were not pollarded (1715).
Spinney	A small copse; the name being derived from *Spinetum* or underwood of thorns as mentioned in Domesday Book.
Spire or *spyre*	A young upstanding tree, the name probably having the same origin as *spear oaks* (*q.v.*).
Spray	Small material stripped off the branches of coppice and made up into small *coal-wood* (for charcoal making) or bavins (*q.v.*) (1670).
Springs	Shoots growing from the stump of a felled broadleaved tree or from coppice (1483).
Springwood(s)	The term spring wood (in the singular) refers to actual shoots arising from a stool or stump. Spring woods (in the plural) may be high forest grown from selected stool shoots or simple coppice. See also *Groves.*

Stackwood	Similar material to cordwood but a stack measured 3 ft or 3 ft 6 in high x 3 ft 6 in wide x 12 ft long (1670).
Standards	Selected coppice shoots or naturally seeded trees (known as *maidens*) which are allowed to grow on into timber instead of being cut as coppice. In either case these trees ultimately became known as standards (1718) although originally they were termed *great trees*. The younger ones which were not yet large enough to be classed as great trees, although destined for that purpose, were known by the following names, largely according to locality: *black barks, heiriors, heirs, princes, reserves, samplers, staddles, stadles, standells, standils* (1543)*, standrells, storers* (1543)*, stores, tellars, tellors, tellows, tielars, tilars, tillers, tillows, wavers* (1790)*, waverers* and *weavers.*
Starveling or *starvling*	A tree that was not thriving (1670).
Stock up	To grub up trees (1717). This was also known as *stubbing up* and *runting.*
Stole	A young coppice shoot (1832).
Stripping up	The removal of side branches.
Strippings	The branches removed in stripping up or the lop and top (1279).
Stub	The stump of a tree (1585).
Taleshide	A taleshide or *notched faggot* was a bundle of pieces of wood known as *talwood* which were round, half round or cleft. Precise details are given in two Acts dealing with fuel dated 1553 and 1601.
Tan-fluing	Bark-stripping.
Tapping	The cutting of the tap roots of young trees in a nursery which is now known as under-cutting. It was recommended by Marshall in 1796.
Throw	To throw a tree was to fell it.
Truncheons	See *Setts.*
Twaite	An area of woodland which has been grubbed up and converted to arable land.
Tynsell wood	Small firewood which was suitable for use in ovens.
Vomell tree	A decayed tree (1556). This term may possibly be derived from the French *vermoulu,* meaning worm eaten.
Wash	A rack or path which was cut in order to mark out the limits of an area when selling underwood in the south-east of England. The *selling wash* was 3 ft wide and

2½ chains (165 ft) apart while the *little wash* was 1½ ft wide and 75 links (49½ ft) apart, giving an area of 30 square poles. The work of marking out and cutting a wash was known as *washing out* for which *washing money* was paid.

Weeding	Originally weeding was the term for thinning and occurs in the Act for the Preservation of Woods, 1543. It did not refer to cutting surface growth around young trees, as it does today.
Weefs	Pliant shoots of birch, hazel or willow which were used to tie faggots, bavins and spray. They were also known as *withers* and *withes* (pronounced weethes).
Wrassel oaks	Trees which were stagheaded or decayed.
Wrangles	Dotards (q.v.) 1550.

APPENDIX II

STATUTES RELATING TO FORESTS AND FORESTRY
1184 — 1971

This Appendix contains a selection of statutes which are concerned with forests and forestry and were enacted between 1184 and 1971. In deciding which should be included or omitted, the following facts have been taken into account.

In some cases statutes were of a confirmatory nature and in order to avoid repetition, these have been omitted. This particularly applies to the *Charter of the Forest* of 1217, in confirmation of which some 20 Acts were passed. Some Statutes covered several different subjects and only one or two sections were concerned with forestry but where these are thought to be of sufficient interest, they have been included. Certain legislation is more concerned with trees, as such, rather than with forestry and this applies particularly, but not exclusively, to Acts of Parliament that have become law since 1925. Such matters as roadside planting, dangerous or overhanging trees, tree preservation orders and access to the countryside are examples and the majority of those Acts which deal with such matters have been excluded. The dates of the earlier statutes are those which are given in Ruffhead's *The Statutes at Large.*

TWELFTH CENTURY

1184	The Assize of the Forest (also known as the Assize of Woodstock).	30 Hen. 2.

THIRTEENTH CENTURY

1217	The Charter of the Forest.	1 Hen. 3.
1225	The Second Charter of the Forest.	9 Hen. 3.
1277	*Consuetudines et Assisa de Foresta.*	6 Edw. 1.
	The Custom and Assize of the Forest.	
1293	*De Malefactoribus in Parcis.*	21 Edw. 1.
	In what cases the killing of offenders in forests, chases or warrens, is punishable, in what not.	

FOURTEENTH CENTURY

1305	*Ordinatio Forestae.* Ordnance of the Forest. They whose woods are disafforested shall not have common or other easements in the forest.	33 Edw. 1.
1306	*Ordinatio Forestae.* Ordnance of the Forest. This ordnance is divided into six parts which deal with presentation of offences, death of a forester, service of foresters on juries, punishment of forest officers, disafforestation and common rights within the forests.	34 Edw. 1.
1307	*Ne rector prosternat arbores in cemeterio.* In what cases and by when trees may be felled in church yards.	35 Edw. 1.
1327	How every person may use his woods within the forests.	1 Edw. 3, c.2.
1327	How he shall be used that is taken for any offence in the forest. Bailment of him.	1 Edw. 3, c.8.
1350	A Statute of Purveyors.	25 Edw. 3.
	A purveyor shall not take timber in or about any person's house.	c.6.
	Keepers of a forest or chase shall gather nothing without the owner's good will.	c.7.
1369	The King's general pardon to all men of vert and venison saving to the officers of the forest, etc.	43 Edw. 3, c.4.
1383	A Jury for a trespass with the forest shall give their verdict where they received their charge.	7 Rich. 2, c.3.
1383	None shall be taken or imprisoned by the official of the forest without indictment.	7 Rich. 2, c.4.

FIFTEENTH CENTURY

| 1482 | An Act for inclosing of woods in forests, chases and purlieus. | 22 Edw. 4, c.7. |

SIXTEENTH CENTURY

1503	For deer-hays and buck-stalls.	19 Hen. 7, c.11.
1540	An Act concerning the breed of horses of higher stature. (This Act was also known as the 'Drift of the Forests'.)	32 Hen. 8, c.13.
1541	An Act concerning the King's Hundreds of Wimbersley and Alford's How and his Forests of Whittlewood and Sawcey . . .	32 Hen. 8, c.38.
1541	The Erection of the Court of Surveyors of the King's Lands, the names of the officers there and their authority.	32 Hen. 8, c.39.
1543	An Act for the Preservation of Woods.	35 Hen. 8, c.17.
1553	An Act for the Assise of Fuel.	7 Edw. 6, c.7.
1558	An Act that timber shall not be felled to make coals for burning of iron.	1 Eliz. 1, c.15.
1570	An Act for reviving and continuance of certain Statutes. (Sections 18 and 19 refer to the inclosure of woodland after felling as laid down in the Act for the Preservation of Woods 1543.)	13 Eliz. 1, c.25.
1581	An Act touching iron-mills near unto the City of London and the River of Thames. (This Act prohibited the conversion of woods or underwood growing within 22 miles of London, and within certain other limits, into fuel for iron smelting.)	23 Eliz. 1, c.5.
1585	An Act for the preservation of timber in the Weilds of the counties of Sussex, Surrey and Kent and for the amendment of highways decayed by carriages to and from iron-mills.	27 Eliz. 1, c.19.

SEVENTEENTH CENTURY

1601	An Act to avoid and prevent divers misdemeanours in lewd and idle persons. (This Act specifically includes those who 'shall cut or spoil any woods or under-woods, poles or trees standing'.)	43 Eliz. 1, c.7.
1601	An Act concerning the Assizes of Fewel.	43 Eliz. 1, c.14.
1604	An Act concerning tanners, curriers, shoemakers and other artificers occupying the cutting of leather. (Sections 18 to 21 deal with the shortage of bark for tanning and restrict the felling of oak to the period from 1st April to 30th June, where bark is worth two shillings a cart load, with certain exceptions.)	1 Ja. 1, c.22.

1640	An Act for the certainty of forests and of the meets, meers, limits and bounds of the forests.	16 Cha. 1, c.16.
1663	An Act for the punishment of unlawful cutting or stealing or spoiling of wood and under-wood and destroyers of young timber-trees.	15 Cha. 2, c.2.
1664	An Act for confirmation of the inclosure and improvement of Malvern Chase.	16 Cha. 2, c.5.
1668	An Act for the increase and preservation of timber within the Forest of Dean.	20 Cha. 2, c.3.
1670	An Act to prevent the malicious burning of houses, stacks of corn and hay and killing or maiming of cattle. (Section 5 includes those persons who 'shall destroy any plantation of trees or throw down any inclosure'.)	22 Cha. 2, c.7.
1698	An Act for the increase and preservation of timber in the New Forest in the County of Southampton.	9 & 10 Will. 3, c.36.

EIGHTEENTH CENTURY

1710	An Act for making more effectual an Act of the forty-third year of the reign of Queen Elizabeth, intituled *An Act concerning the Assises of Fuel,* so far as it relates to the Assise of Billet.	9 Anne, c.15.
1715	An Act to encourage the planting of timber-trees, fruit trees and other trees for ornament, shelter or profit and for the better presentation of the same and for the preventing the burning of woods.	1 Geo. 1, c.48.
1719	An Act to explain and amend an Act passed in the first year of His Majesty's reign, intituled *An Act to encourage the planting of timber trees . . . and for the preventing the burning of woods,* and for the better preservation of the fences of such woods.	6 Geo. 1, c.16.
1722	An Act for the more effectual punishing wicked and evil-disposed persons going armed in disguise and doing injuries and violences to the persons and properties of His Majesty's subjects, and for the more speedy bringing the offenders to justice. (This Act was primarily directed against the 'Waltham Blacks' who had embarked on an orgy of deer stealing and damage in Waltham Chase near Fareham, Hampshire. It also included the destruction of trees in plantations.)	9 Geo. 1, c.22.
1755	An Act for . . . the preventing the burning or	28 Geo. 2, c.19.

destroying of goss, furze or ferne in forests and chases . . . . (This Act also covers thefts, disorderly houses and the sale of ale without licence; Section 3 deals with fires.)

1756	An Act for inclosing by the mutual consent of the lords and tenants, part of any common for the purpose of planting and preserving trees fit for timber or underwood; and for more effectually preventing the unlawful destruction of trees.	29 Geo. 2, c.36.
1757	An Act to amend and render more effectual an Act passed in the twenty-ninth year of his present Majesty's reign intituled '*An Act for inclosing . . . and for more effectually preventing the unlawful destruction of trees.*	31 Geo. 2, c.41.
1763	An Act to indemnify such persons as have omitted . . . and to prevent the destruction of trees and underwoods growing in forests and chases.	4 Geo. 3, c.31.
1766	An Act for encouraging the cultivation and for the better preservation of trees, roots, plants and shrubs.	6 Geo. 3, c.36.
1766	An Act for the better preservation of timber trees and of woods and underwoods and for the further preservation of roots, shrubs and plants.	6 Geo. 3, c.48.
1769	An Act . . . for the better preservation of hollies, thorns and quicksets in forests, chaces and private grounds and of trees and underwoods in forests and chaces . . . . (This Act deals with several other matters including custom duties. In 1770 an amending Act — 10.Geo.3.c.30 — was passed in order to rectify a mistake in the Act of 1769.)	9 Geo. 3, c.41.
1772	An Act for the more effectually securing a quantity of oak timber for the use of the Royal Navy.	12 Geo. 3, c.54.
1773	An Act to extend the provisions of an Act made in the sixth year of His present Majesty's reign (intituled, *An Act for the better preservation of timber trees . . . shrubs and plants*) to poplar, alder, maple, larch and hornbeam.	13 Geo. 3, c.33.
1786	An Act for appointing commissioners to enquire into the state and condition of the woods, forests and land revenues belonging to the Crown and to sell or alienate fee farm and other unimprovable rents.	16 Geo. 3, c.87.

NINETEENTH CENTURY

1800	An Act for the better preservation of timber in the New Forest, in the County of Southampton and for ascertaining the boundaries of the said Forest and of the lands of the Crown within the same. (An enabling Act — 41 Geo. 3, c.108 — was passed in 1801.)	39 & 40 Geo. 3, c.86.
1801	An Act for dividing, alloting and inclosing the Forest or Chase of Needwood in the County of Stafford.	41 Geo. 3, c.56.
1805	An Act to prevent in Great Britain the illegally carrying away bark, and for amending two Acts passed in the sixth and ninth years of His present Majesty's reign, for the preservation of timber trees, underwoods, roots, shrubs, plants, hollies, thorns and quicksets.	45 Geo. 3, c.66
1806	An Act for the better regulation of the office of Surveyor General of Woods and Forests.	46 Geo. 3, c.142.
1806	An Act for enquiring into the state of Windsor Forest in the County of Berks, and for ascertaining the boundaries of the said Forest and of the lands of the Crown within the same. (Parts of this Act were repealed or amended in 1807 by 47 Geo. 3, c.46.)	46 Geo. 3, c.143.
1808	An Act for the increase and preservation of timber in Dean and New Forests.	48 Geo. 3, c.72.
1808	An Act for alloting and inclosing the Forest or Chase of Charnwood otherwise Charley Forest or Chase and Rothley Plain in the County of Leicester.	48 Geo. 3, c.133.
1810	An Act for uniting the offices of Surveyor General of the Land Revenues of the Crown and Surveyor General of His Majesty's Woods, Forests, Parks and Chases.	50 Geo. 3, c.65.
1810	An Act to extend and amend the term and provisions of an Act of the thirty-ninth and fortieth years of His present Majesty, for the better preservation of timber in the New Forest in the county of Southampton, and for ascertaining the boundaries of the said Forest and of the lands of the Crown within the same. (This Act was extended in 1811 by 51 Geo. 3, c.94.)	50 Geo. 3, c.116.
1810	An Act for disafforesting the Forest of South, otherwise East Bere, otherwise Bier, in the County of Southampton; and for inclosing the open commonable lands within the said forest.	50 Geo. 3, c.218.

1812	An Act for the better cultivation of Navy timber in the Forest of Woolmer, in the county of Southampton.	52 Geo. 3, c.71.
1812	An Act for the better cultivation of Navy timber in the Forest of Alice Holt, in the county of Southampton.	52 Geo. 3, c.72.
1812	An Act for inclosing the Forest of Delamere in the county of Chester.	52 Geo. 3, c.136.
1812	An Act for disafforesting the Forest of Parkhurst in the county of Southampton and for inclosing the open commonable lands within the said Forest.	52 Geo. 3, c.171.
1813	An Act for vesting in His Majesty certain parts of Windsor Forest, in the county of Berks and for inclosing the open commonable lands within the said Forest. (This Act was amended in 1815 by 55 Geo. 3, c.122, and extended in 1816 by 56 Geo. 3, c.132.)	53 Geo. 3, c.158.
1815	An Act for vesting in His Majesty certain parts of the Forest of Exmoor, otherwise Exmore, in the counties of Somerset and Devon; and for inclosing the said Forest.	55 Geo. 3, c.138.
1817	An Act to abolish the offices of the Wardens, Chief Justices and Justices in Eyre, north and south of Trent.	57 Geo. 3, c.61.
1818	An Act for vesting in His Majesty certain parts of the Hayes of Birkland and Bilhagh and of certain commonable lands and open uninclosed grounds in the township of Edwinstowe with the Forest of Sherwood in the county of Nottingham.	59 Geo. 3, c.100.
1824	An Act for dividing, alloting and inclosing that portion of the Forest of Whittlewood called Hasleborough Walk in the Parish of Whitfield and Liberties or Precincts of Silston	5 Geo. 4, c.99.
1825	An Act for dividing, alloting and inclosing the Forest of Salcey in the counties of Northampton and Buckingham	6 Geo. 4, c.132.
1830	An Act for inclosing the Forest of Roach, otherwise Roche, otherwise Neroach, otherwise Neroche in the parishes of Broadway, Bickenhall ... in the county of Somerset.	11 Geo. 4, c.2.
1831	An Act for ascertaining the boundaries of the Forest of Dean and for inquiring into the rights and privileges claimed by Free Miners of the Hundred of St. Briavel's and for other purposes. (This Act was extended in 1833 and 1834 while	1 & 2 Will. 4, c.2.

further Acts dealing with the Forest of Dean
were passed in 1836, 1838, 1842, 1844, 1855,
1861 and 1866 which were chiefly concerned
with administrative aspects.)

1832	An Act for uniting the office of the Surveyor General of His Majesty's Works and Public Buildings with the office of Commissioner of His Majesty's Woods, Forests and Land Revenues and for other purposes relating to Land Revenues. (Other Acts concerned with similar matters were passed in 1851, 1852 and 1866.)	2 Will. 4, c.1.
1849	An Act to authorise Her Majesty to issue a Commission to inquire and report upon rights or claims over the New Forest in the county of Southampton and Waltham Forest in the county of Essex.	12 & 13 Vict., c.81.
1851	An Act for disafforesting the Forest of Hainault in the county of Essex.	14 & 15 Vict., c.43.
1851	An Act to extinguish the right of the Crown to deer in the New Forest and to give compensation in lieu thereof, and for other purposes relating to the said Forest.	14 & 15 Vict., c.74.
1853	An Act for disafforesting the Forest of Wychwood. (This Act was amended in 1856 by 19 & 20 Vict., c.32.)	16 & 17 Vict., c.73.
1853	An Act for disafforesting the Forest of Whittlewood otherwise Whittlebury. (This Act was amended in 1856 by 19 & 20 Vict., c.32.)	16 & 17 Vict., c.42.
1855	An Act for disafforesting the Forest of Woolmer.	18 & 19 Vict., c.46.
1861	An Act to consolidate and amend the statute law of England and Ireland relating to larceny and other similar offences. (Sections 12 and 13 concern the stealing of deer in forests, and Sections 32, 33 and 35 deal with the theft of, or damage to, trees, underwood, saplings and shrubs.)	24 & 25 Vict., c.96.
1861	An Act to consolidate and amend the statute law of England and Ireland relating to malicious injuries to property. (Sections 20, 21 and 22 deal with damage to trees, underwood, saplings and shrubs.)	24 & 25 Vict., c.97.
1871	An Act to amend the Act twelfth and thirteenth Victoria, chapter eighty-one; and to extend the provisions of that Act and The Metropolitan Commons Act 1866, so far as regards that part	34 & 35 Vict., c.93.

of Waltham Forest known as Epping Forest.

| 1872 | An Act to enlarge the powers of the Epping Forest Commissioners; and for other purposes. (This Act was extended in 1873, 1875 and 1876.) | 35 & 36 Vict., c.95. |

| 1877 | An Act to amend the administration of the law relating to the New Forest in the County of Southampton; and for other purposes. | 40 & 41 Vict., c.121. |

| 1879 | An Act to amend the New Forest Act, 1877. | 42 & 43 Vict., c.194. |

TWENTIETH CENTURY

| 1909 | An Act to promote the economic development of the United Kingdom and the improvement of roads therein. (Section 1 deals with forestry research and teaching, planting and the acquisition of land.) | 9 Edw. 7, c.47. |

| 1919 | An Act for establishing a Forestry Commission for the United Kingdom and promoting afforestation and the production and supply of timber, therein, and for purposes in connexion therewith. | 9 & 10 Geo. 5, c.58. |

| 1923 | An Act to provide for the transfer of certain properties to the Forestry Commissioners and to amend the Forestry Act, 1919, and for purposes in connection therewith. | 13 & 14 Geo. 5, c.21. |

| 1927 | An Act to authorise an increase of the number of Forestry Commissioners; to empower the Commissioners to make bye-laws with respect to land vested in them or under their management or control; and for purposes consequent upon the matters aforesaid. | 17 Geo. 5, c.6. |

| 1945 | An Act to make provision for the reconstitution and as to the exercise of the functions of the Forestry Commissioners, the acquisition of land for forestry purposes and the management, use and disposal of land so acquired; and in connection with the matters aforesaid to amend the Forestry Acts, 1919 to 1927 and certain other enactments relating to the Forestry Commissioners. | 8 & 9 Geo. 6, c.35. |

| 1947 | An Act to provide for the dedication of land to forestry purposes; for the deduction from compensation of grants made by the Forestry Commissioners in the event of compulsory purchase of the land in respect of which the | 10 & 11 Geo. 6, c.21. |

grants were made; and for the exception on
behalf of the Secretary of State of instruments
relating to land placed at the disposal of the
Forestry Commissioners.

1949   An Act to make further provision as respects   12 & 13 Geo. 6, c.69.
        the New Forest in the county of Southampton.

1951   An Act to provide for the maintenance of   14 & 15 Geo. 6, c.61.
        reserves of growing trees in Great Britain and to
        regulate the felling of trees; to amend the pro-
        cedure applicable to compulsory purchase
        orders under the Forestry Act, 1945; and for
        purposes connected with the matters aforesaid.

1964   An Act to alter the perambulation of the New
        Forest, to make further provision for the New   Eliz. 2, 1964, c.83.
        Forest, to amend the New Forest Acts 1877 to
        1949 and for purposes connected with the
        matters aforesaid.

1967   An Act to consolidate the Forestry Acts 1919 to   Eliz. 2, 1967, c.10.
        1963 with corrections and improvements made
        under the Consolidation of Enactments (Pro-
        cedure) Act, 1949.

1970   An Act to make further provision for the New   Eliz. 2, 1970, c.21.
        Forest.

1970   An Act to amend the law relating to the making   Eliz. 2, 1970, c.43.
        of tree preservation orders and the grant of
        felling licences.

1971   An Act to abolish certain rights of Her Majesty   Eliz. 2, 1971, c.47.
        to wild creatures and certain related rights and
        franchises; to abrogate the forest law (subject to
        exceptions); and to repeal enactments relating
        to those rights and franchises and to forests and
        the forest law; and for connected purposes.

APPENDIX III

A SELECT BIBLIOGRAPHY
1523 — 1976

This list of publications which is arranged in chronological order by centuries,
is not claimed to be exhaustive although it includes some 216 books or
booklets which have appeared since 1523. However, in selecting these the
following have been omitted:

> *Those relating to ornamental trees and shrubs.*
> *Those concerned with what is now known as arboriculture.*

*Those dealing with timber, as such, its utilization and preservation
and sawmilling practice.*
*Government publications of the twentieth century, including those of
the Forestry Commission which are already well documented.*

Owing to the large number of books which have been written on some of the better known forests, such as the Forest of Dean and the New Forest, the selection has been limited, as far as possible, to one publication for each forest.

During the seventeenth and eighteenth centuries, some books which were written on rural matters such as farming, gardening and landscaping, contained sections concerned with forestry which in those days was generally referred to as 'planting'. In this bibliography, books which contain a substantial part devoted to matters other than forestry, are indicated by an asterisk placed immediately before the title. Until the end of the nineteenth century the word 'arboriculture' was generally used to describe what is now known as forestry and in some instances, this practice continued into the twentieth century. This can be seen in the titles of the Royal Scottish Arboricultural Society and the Royal English Arboricultural Society, in neither of which was the word 'arboricultural' changed to 'forestry' until 1930 and 1931 respectively. By 1930, however, the term 'arboriculture' had come to be used to refer to the growing and management of trees for purposes other than forestry.

In addition to what are commonly regarded as books, several booklets or tracts have been included and where a publication falls within this category, the number of pages, when known, is shown after the title to indicate its length. Although this bibliography is intended, for the most part, to cover publications concerned with English forestry, some Scottish and Irish works which were available in England, have been added. Several forestry books which have been published in this country are translations of those which had previously appeared on the continent particularly in Germany and these have also been included. The translations of J. Nisbet and M.L. Anderson and the last two volumes of *Schlich's Manual of Forestry* are examples of these.

Until the early part of the nineteenth century there was a tendency for the titles of books to be somewhat verbose and to be used to describe the contents rather than provide a short, easily remembered name. Where titles of this kind appear in the bibliography, they are sometimes abbreviated by the insertion of punctuation points or by the addition of the contraction 'etc'. In a few instances books have been published without the date being shown on the title page or elsewhere. In such cases an estimate has been made of the probable date, after taking into account any evidence of the year of publication that may be found in the text. Where this has been done, the date is shown prefixed by the letter *c.* being the abbreviation for *circa*.

SIXTEENTH CENTURY

1523   Fitzherbert, John *Boke of Husbandry.

1565   Taverner, Roger Book of Survey.

1577   Harrison, William *An Historicall Description of the Islande of Britayne . . .
        etc.

1577   Holinshed, Raphael *The firste volume of the Chronicles of England,
        Scotlande and Irelande conteyning the Description and Chronicle of
        England . . .

1584   Taverner, John Book of Survey.

1598   Manwood, John A Treatise and Discourse of the Lawes of the Forrest, 2nd
        edn 1615; 3rd edn 1665; 4th edn 1717; 5th edn 1741. The 3rd edition was
        entitled A Treatise of the Laws of the Forest.

SEVENTEENTH CENTURY

1611   Standish, Arthur The Commons Complaint, pp. x & 34, 2nd edn 1611
        pp. xvi & 40; 3rd edn 1612 pp. 46.

1612   Church, Rocke An Olde Thrift newly Revived Wherein is Declared the
        Manner of Planting, Preserving and Husbanding yong Trees of Divers
        Kindes for Timber and Fuell. . . . Discoursed in a dialogue betweene a
        Surveyour, Woodward, Gentleman and a Farmer. This was published under
        the author's initials of R. Ch. and has been erroneously attributed to
        R. Churton and R. Chambers.

1613   Standish, Arthur New Directions of Experience to the Commons Complaint,
        for the planting of Timber and Firewood, invented by Arthur Standish,
        pp. 48, 2nd edn 1614; 3rd edn 1615.

1615   Standish, Arthur New Directions of Experience for the Increasing of Timber
        and Firewood, pp. 48.

1615   Stow, John *The Annales or Generall Chronicle of England begun first by
        Maister John Stow, and after him continued unto the ende of this present
        yeere 1614 by E. Howes.

1645   Hall, Joseph An Essay on Timber-Trees.

1648   Bently, John A List of Woods, Underwoods, Timber and Trees felled and
        sold out of the King and Queen Their Majesties Forrests, Chases, Parks,
        Manors and Lands in the Counties of Kent, Sussex, Surrey, Hampshire,
        Berkshire and Middlesex for the use and service of Parliament, pp. 6.

1652   Taylor, Silvanus *Common-Good or the Improvements of Commons, Forrests
        and Chases by Inclosure.

1664   Evelyn, John Sylva or a Discourse of Forest-Trees, 2nd edn 1670; 3rd edn
        1679; 4th edn 1706; 5th edn 1729. In the fourth and subsequent editions the
        word 'Sylva' is spelt 'Silva'.

1669   Worlidge, J. *Systema Agriculturae: The Mystery of Husbandry Discovered,
        2nd edn 1675; 3rd edn 1681; 4th edn 1687; 5th edn 1697; 6th edn 1698; 7th
        edn 1716.

1670   Smith, John *England's Improvement Reviv'd: In a Treatise of all Manner of Husbandry and Trade by Land and Sea . . . . Together with the manner of Planting all sorts of Timber-Trees,* re-issued 1673.

1676   Cook, Moses *The Manner of Raising, Ordering and Improving Forest-Trees,* 2nd edn 1717; 3rd edn 1724. 'Another edition' was published in 1679 which included a treatise by Gabriel Plattes on *A Discovery of Subterranean Treasure.*

1677   Yarranton, Andrew *England's Improvement by Sea and Land to out-do the Dutch without fighting, to pay debts without moneys, to set at work all the poor of England with the growth of our own lands.*

1691   Hale, Thomas *An Account of Several New Inventions now necessary for England, relating to building our English Shipping, Planting of Oaken Trees in the Forests.*

1697   Meager, Leonard *The Mystery of Husbandry; or arable, pasture and woodland improved. . . . To which is added the Countryman's Almanack.*

EIGHTEENTH CENTURY

1705   Anonymous *Short treatise of firr-trees.* Considered to be one of the earliest works on planting to be published in Ireland.

1707   Mortimer, Thomas *The Whole Art of Husbandry,* 2nd edn 1708; 3rd edn 1712; 4th edn 1716; 5th edn 1721; 6th edn 1761.

1717   Bradley, Richard *New Improvements of Planting and Gardening,* 2nd edn 1718; 3rd edn 1719; 4th edn 1724; 5th edn 1726; 6th edn 1731; 7th edn 1739.

1726   Bradley, Richard *An Appendix to the New Improvements of Planting and Gardening: Containing the culture of such forest-trees, flowers, etc as were omitted in the former impressions . . . .*

1728   Langley, Batty *A Sure Method of Improving Estates by plantation of oak, elm, ash, beech and other timber-trees, coppice-woods . . . . ,* 2nd edn 1740. The title of the second edition, which differs slightly from the first, begins: *A Sure and Easy Method of Improving Estates . . . .*

1733   Bradley, Richard *The Manner of Making Plantations either for pleasure or profit.*

1736   Hoppus, Edward *Practical Measuring made easy To the Meanest Capacity by A New Set of Tables which upon a Bare Inspection show . . . The Solid or Superficial Content (and consequently the Value) of all kinds of Squared or Round Timber whether it be Standing or Felled. . . .* 2nd edn 1738 which was followed by a further 19 numbered editions, the 21st being dated 1834. In 1837 a 'New' edition was published and thereafter all editions were either described as 'New' or simply dated. Modern copies of these tables, which were widely used until metrication was adopted in about 1972, were frequently undated.

1738   Ellis, William *The Timber-Tree Improved,* 2nd edn 1741; 3rd edn 1742; 4th edn 1745. With the 4th edition is bound a second part which may be dated 1742 or 1747.

1739 De Buffon, M. *A Memorial on Preserving and Repairing Forests*, pp. 25.

1742 De Buffon, M. *Memorial on the Culture of Forests*, pp. 20.

1747 Wheeler, James *The Modern Druid containing instructions . . . for the much better culture of young oaks.*

1753 Watkins, William *A Treatise on Forest-Trees*, pp. viii & 46.

1755 Wade, Edward *A Proposal for improving and adorning the Island of Great Britain; for the maintenance of our Navy and shipping by parochial plantations of timber and other trees.*

1756 Hale, Thomas *The Complete Body of Husbandry*, 2nd edn 1758.

1758 Hanbury, William *An Essay on Planting and a Scheme for making it conducive to the Glory of God and the Advantage of Society.*

1761 Haddington, Earl of *A Treatise on the Manner of Raising Forest Trees.*

1763 Fisher, Roger *Heart of Oak, the British Bulwark showing reasons for paying greater attention to the Propagation of Oak Timber than has hitherto been manifest . . . .*

1766 Anonymous *An Earnest Address to the People of England containing an Enquiry into the cause of the great Scarcity of Timber.*

1770 Hanbury, William *A Complete Body of Planting and Gardening.*

1771 Anonymous *A Report from the Committee appointed. . . to consider how His Majesty's Navy may be better supplied with timber.*

1773 Anonymous *Some hints on Planting, By a Planter*, 2nd edn 1783. The author is thought to be James Fortescue of Ravensdale Park, County Louth, Ireland.

1775 Anderson, James *Essays Relating to Agriculture and Rural Affairs*, 2nd edn 1777; 3rd edn 1779.

1775 Kent, Nathaniel *Hints to Gentlemen of Landed Property*, 2nd edn 1776; 3rd edn 1793.

1775 Boutcher, William *A Treatise on Forest-Trees. . . .*, 2nd edn 1778; 3rd edn 1784; 1st Irish edn 1776.

1776 Kennedy, John *A Treatise on Planting, Gardening and the Management of the Hothouse*, 2nd edn 1777; Irish edn 1784.

1776 Hunter, A. John Evelyn's *Silva or A Discourse of Forest-Trees*, 2nd edn 1786; 3rd edn 1801; 4th edn 1812; 5th edn 1825.

1776 Anonymous *A few minutes advice to Gentlemen of Landed Property and the Admirers of Forest Scenery: With directions for sowing, raising, planting and the management of forest trees . . . .*

1777 Anderson, James ('Agricola') *Miscellaneous Observations on Planting and Training Timber-Trees particularly calculated for the climate of Scotland.*

1778 Forbes, Francis *The Improvement of Waste Lands, and propagating Oak and other Timber upon Wastes . . . .*

1783 Anonymous *An account of the method of raising and planting the Pinus sylvestris, that is, Scotch fir or pine, as now practised in Scotland. Received by the printer from the Right Honourable the Earl of Clanbrassill.*

1785 Marshall William *Planting and Ornamental Gardening.* The second and third editions were published under the title of *Planting and Rural Ornament*, 2nd edn 1796; 3rd edn 1803.

1787 Anonymous *A Dissertation upon the Visible alarming Decrease and Consumption of Naval Timber.*

1789   Emmerich, Andrew *The Culture of Forests.*

1791   Nichols, Thomas *Observations on the Propagation and Management of Oak Trees in General; but more immediately applying to His Majesty's New-forest in Hampshire. . . .*

1791   Gilpin, William *Remarks on Forest Scenery and other Woodland Views,* 2nd edn 1794, 3rd edn 1808. A revised edition edited by Sir Thomas Dick Lauder appeared in two volumes in 1834.

1791   Anonymous *Collection of Acts for encouraging the planting of Timber-Trees.*

1793   Nichols, Thomas **Methods Proposed for Decreasing the Consumption of Timber in the Navy with observations on fastening Ships with Iron Knees.*

1794   Hayes, Samuel *A Practical Treatise on Planting and the Management of Woods and Coppices,* 2nd edn 1822.

1794   Robinson, John **Letter to Sir John Sinclair, Bart. from John Robinson, Esq., Surveyor-General of Woods and Forests,* pp. 71.

1799   Nicol, Walter *The Practical Planter or a Treatise on Forest Planting . . .* 2nd edn 1803.

1799   Rooke, Hayman *Sketch of the Ancient and Present State of Sherwood forest in the County of Nottingham.*

NINETEENTH CENTURY

1800   Pontey, William *The Profitable Planter,* 2nd edn 1808; 3rd edn 1809; 4th edn 1814; 5th edn 1828.

1801   Ramsey, J. *Dissertation on Trees.*

1806   Pontey, William *The Forest Pruner or Timber Owner's Assistant,* 2nd edn 1808; 3rd edn 1810; 4th edn 1826.

1807   Astley, F.J. *Hints to Planters . . . .*

1807   Black, James *Observations on the means of providing Naval Timber.*

1809   Waistell, Charles *The Method of Ascertaining the value of Growing Timber Trees at different and distant periods of time with Observations on the Growth of Timber,* pp. 35.

1810   Blaikie, Francis *The Farmer's Instructor for the Planting and Management of Forest Trees etc,* pp. 42. The 2nd edition, 1814, was published under the title of *A Treatise on the Planting and Management of Forest Trees,* pp. 48.

1811   Haynes, Thomas *An Improved System of Nursery Gardening for Propagating Forest and Hardy Ornamental Trees . . . .*

1811   Lewis, Percival *Historical Inquiries concerning Forests and Forest Laws with Topographical Remarks upon the Ancient and Modern State of the New Forest in the County of Southampton.*

1812   Nicol, Walter *The Planter's Kalendar,* 2nd edn 1920. Nicol died before finishing this book which was completed by Edward Sang.

1818   McWilliam, Robert *Suggestions for the Cultivation of Forest Trees.*

1820   Blaikie, Francis *A Treatise on the Management of Hedges and Hedge-row Timber,* 2nd edn 1820; pp. 52. A 'New' edition, 1828, pp. 60. The treatise first appeared in *Evans and Ruffy's Farmer's Journal* but was subsequently published separately in pamphlet form as the second edition.

1820   Monteath, Robert *The Forester's Guide,* 2nd edn 1824; 3rd edn 1836. In the second and third editions the title was altered to *The Forester's Guide and Profitable Planter.*

1825   Billington, William *A Series of Facts, Hints, Observations and Experiments on the Different Modes of Raising Young Plantations of Oaks. . . .*

1825   Cobbett, William *The Woodlands.*

1826   Withers, William *The Planting and Rearing of Forest-Trees,* 2nd edn 1827.

1827   Monteath, Robert *Miscellaneous Reports on Woods and Plantations.*

1827   Mitchell, J. *Dendrolgia or A Treatise of Forest Trees with Evelyn's Silva Revised, Corrected and Abridged.*

1828   Steuart, Sir Henry *The Planter's Guide or A Practical Essay . . . .* 2nd edn 1828; 3rd edn 1848.

1828   Withers, William *A Letter to Sir Walter Scott, Bart, . . . containing Observations on the Pruning and Thinning of Woods . . . .*

1829   Withers, William *A Letter to Sir Henry Steuart, Bart, on the Improvement in the Quality of Timber . . . of Forest-Trees.*

1830   Billington, William *Facts, Observations etc Being an exposure of the misrepresentation of the Author's treatise on planting contained in Mr Wither's letters to Sir Walter Scott, Baronet, and to Sir Henry Steuart, Baronet; with remarks on Sir Walter Scott's Essay on Planting and on parts of Sir Henry Steuart's Planter's Guide . . . with some additional information, hints, etc.,* pp. 76.

1830   Cruickshank, Thomas *The Practical Planter.*

1831   Matthew, Patrick *On Naval Timber and Arboriculture.*

1832   Anonymous *Useful and Ornamental Planting.* The author was George Sinclair.

1834   Main, James *The Forest Planter and Pruner's Assistant,* 2nd edn ? ; 3rd edn 1839.

1838   Sawyer, James *Growing Gold or a Treatise on the Cultivation of the British Oak,* 2nd edn 1839.

1842   West, J. *Remarks on the Management or rather the Mis-management of Woods, Plantations and Hedge-row Timber.*

1843   Hamerton, J. *Arboriculture,* pp. 40.

1843   Smith, John *Treatise on the Management and Cultivation of Forest Trees.*

1847   Brown, James *The Forester,* 2nd edn 1851; 3rd edn 1861; 4th edn 1871; 5th edn 1882; 6th edn 1894. The sixth edition was edited and enlarged by John Nisbet but it should not be confused with Nisbet's book of 1905 which was also published under the title of *The Forester.*

1851   Anonymous *The British Sylva and Planters and Foresters Manual.*

1851   Cree, G. *Essays on the Scientific Management of Forest Trees.*

1853   Anonymous *English Forests and Forest Trees.*

1854   Billington, William *How the Royal Forests have been ruined; a letter to Alexander Milne, Esq., . . . on the system pursued in the Forest of Dean and the Chopwell Woods,* pp. 43.

1858   Nichols, H.G. *The Forest of Dean: an Historical and Descriptive Account.*

1859   Blenkarn, John *British Timber Trees.* Despite its title, this book is concerned with forestry.

1859   Newton, G.W. *A Treatise on the Growth and Future Management of Timber Trees.*

1860   Mac Intosh, Charles *The Larch Disease and the present condition of larch plantations in Great Britain.*

1866   Craig, R.D. *Legal and Equitable Rights and Liabilities as to Trees and Woods.*

1868   Grigor, John *Arboriculture,* 2nd edn 1881.

1875   Norman, G.W. *Remarks on the Preservation and Improvement of Coppice Woods.*

1879   Rowland, A. *Tree Planting for Ornament and Profit.*

1880   Ablett, W.H. *English Trees and Tree Planting.*

1882   Bagneris, G. *The Elements of Sylviculture,* translated from the French by E.E. Fernandez and A. Smythies.

1882   Michie, C.Y. *The Larch.* Two 'New' editions were dated 1885 and 1895.

1883   MacGregor, J.L.L. *The Organisation and Valuation of Forests on the Continental System in theory and practice.*

1883   Brown, J.C. *The Forests of England and the Management of them in Bye-Gone Times.*

1884   Brown, J.C. *Introduction to the Study of Modern Forest Economy.*

1885   Rattray, J. and Mill, H.R. *Forestry and Forest Products.* A collection of 21 prize essays (seven of which are not concerned with British forestry) written in connection with the Edinburgh International Forestry Exhibition 1884.

1887   Fisher, W.R. *The Forest of Essex: its History, Laws, Administration and Ancient Customs and the Wild Deer which lived in it.*

1888   Bright, Tom *Pole Plantations and Underwoods.*

1888   Michie, C.Y. *The Practice of Forestry.*

c.1888   Curtis, C.E. *Practical Forestry and its bearing on the Improvement of Estates,* 2nd edn 1898; 3rd edn 1908; 4th edn 1920.

1889   Schlich, W. *Schlich's Manual of Forestry.* This work comprised five volumes each of which appeared in different years (with one exception) and ran into a varying number of editions which are given below. Volumes IV and V were translations by W.R. Fisher (not to be confused with the author of *The Forest of Essex* 1887) of two German books by Dr Richard Hess and Dr Karl Gayer, respectively. Vol I: 1st edn 1889; 2nd edn 1896; 3rd edn 1906; 4th edn 1922. Vol II: 1st edn 1891; 2nd edn 1897; 3rd edn 1904; 4th edn 1910. Vol III: 1st edn 1895; 3rd edn 1905; 4th edn 1911; 5th edn 1925. Vol IV: 1st edn 1895; 2nd edn 1907. Vol V: 1st edn 1896; 2nd edn 1908. The absence of a 2nd edition of Volume III is explained by the following note in the 3rd edition: 'Strictly speaking, this is the second edition of Volume III, but as the first edition consisted of a larger number of copies than those of Volume II, and in order to bring this volume into line with Volume II, it has been issued as the third edition'.

1893   Furst, H. *The Protection of Woodlands,* translated from the German by John Nisbet.

1893   Nisbet, John *British Forest Trees and their Sylvicultural Characteristics and Treatment.*

1893   Webster, A.D. *Webster's Practical Forestry,* 2nd edn 1894; 3rd edn ? ; 4th edn 1905; 5th edn 1917.

1894   Hartig, R. *Text-book of the Diseases of Trees,* translated from the German by W. Somerville and H. Marshall Ward.

1894   Nisbet, John *Studies in Forestry.*

TWENTIETH CENTURY

1900   Nisbet, John *Our Forests and Woodlands,* 2nd edn 1909.

1900   Simpson, John *The New Forestry,* 2nd edn 1903.

1901   Turner, G.J. *Select Pleas of the Forest.*

1904   Forbes, A.C. *English Estate Forestry.*

1904   Curtis, C.E. *The Management and Planting of British Woodlands,* pp. 36.

*c.*1904 Schlich, W. *Forestry in the United Kingdom.* This is a reprint of chapter V of volume I of *Schlich's Manual of Forestry.*

1905   Cox, J.C. *The Royal Forests of England.*

1905   Curtis, C.E. *Elementary Forestry.*

1905   Greswell, W.H.P. *The Forests and Deer Parks of the County of Somerset.*

1905   Nisbet, John *The Forester,* 2nd impression: 1925. This book, which was published in two volumes, is based on the sixth edition (1894) of *The Forester* by James Brown (1847) which Nisbet edited. However these two volumes can justifiably be regarded as comprising a separate book and not another edition.

1905   Schwappach, A. *Forestry,* translated from the German by Fraser Story and E.A. Nobbs.

1905   Simpson, John *The Estate Nursery.*

1905   Unwin, A.H. *Future Forest Trees.*

*c.*1905 Hewitt, Sir Harold *An Introduction to the Study of Forestry in Britain,* pp. 30.

1908   Gillanders, A.T. *Forest Entomology.*

1908   Nisbet, John *Sylva, a discourse on Forest Trees by John Evelyn F.R.S. with an essay on the life and Works of the Author.* This is a reprint, in two volumes, of the 4th edition.

1909   Simpson, John *British Woods and their Owners.*

1909   Maw. P.T. *The Practice of Forestry,* 2nd edn 1912.

1910   Forbes, A.C. *The Development of British Forestry.*

1911   Hanson, C.O. *Forestry for Woodmen,* 2nd edn 1921; 3rd edn 1934.

1911   Nisbet, John *The Elements of British Forestry.*

1912   Maw, P.T. *Complete Yield Tables for British Woodlands and the Finance of British Forestry.*

1913   Hudson, W.F.A. *A Handbook of Forestry.*

1914   Adkin, B.W. *The Law of Forestry.*

1916   Stebbing, E.P. *British Forestry.*

1917   Somerville, W. *British Forestry: Past and Future,* pp. ix & 82.

1918 Boyd, John *Afforestation,* pp. 40.

1918 Whellens, W.H. *Forestry Work.*

1919 Beddoes, W.F. *The Management of English Woodlands.*

1919 Henry, Augustine *Forests, Woods and Trees in Relation to Hygiene.*

1919 Hiley, W.E. *The Fungal Diseases of the Common Larch.*

1919 Somerville, W. *Some Problems of Re-afforestation,* pp. 13.

1919 Stebbing, E.P. *Commercial Forestry in Britain.*

1919 Webster, A.D. *National Afforestation.*

1920 Webster, A.D. *A Handbook of Forestry.*

1921 Jackson, H. *A Short Manual of Forest Management.*

1924 Drummie, A.C. *Practical Forestry.*

1926 Albion, R.G. *Forests and Sea Power.*

1928 Stebbing, E.P. *The Forestry Question in Great Britain.*

1928 Thompson, G.W. St C. *The Protection of Woodlands.*

1928 Troup, R.S. *Silvicultural Systems,* 2nd edn 1952 revised by E.W. Jones.

1930 Hiley, W.E. *Economics of Forestry.*

1931 Hiley, W.E. *Improvement of Woodlands.*

1932 Anderson, M.L. *The Natural Woodlands of Britain and Ireland,* pp. 32.

1935 Jerram, M.R.K. *A Textbook on Forest Management,* 2nd impression 1945.

1937 Chrystal, R.N. *Insects of the British Woodlands,* 2nd edn 1948.

1937 Anonymous *Estate Woodlands,* pp. 32. Published by The Royal English Forestry Society.

1938 Thomson, T. and Jerram, M.R.K. *An Outline of Forestry.*

1938 Ackers, C.P. *Practical British Forestry,* 2nd edn 1947.

1938 Coke, Richard *How to make forestry pay,* pp. 24.

1938 Troup, R.S. *Forestry and State Control.*

1939 Jerram, M.R.K. *Elementary Forest Mensuration.*

1941 Rogers, John *The English Woodland.*

1941 Davey, R. *Measurement of Trees.*

1944 Rayner, M.C. and Neilson-Jones, W. *Problems in Tree Nutrition.*

1945 Rayner, M.C. *Trees and Toadstools.*

1945 Ackers, C.P. *Our Woodlands, their sacrifice and renovation,* pp. 30.

1945 Taylor, W.L. *Forests and Forestry in Great Britain.*

1947 Edlin, H.L. *Forestry and Woodland Life.*

1947 Rowe, W.H. *Our Forests.*

1948 James, N.D.G. *Working Plans for Estate Woodlands.*

1949 James, N.D.G. *Notes on Estate Forestry.*

1949 Meiggs, Russell *Home Timber Production (1939-1945).*

1950 Anderson, M.L. *The Selection of Tree Species.*

1951 Harrison, J.L. *Forest Engineering.*

1951 James, N.D.G. *An Experiment in Forestry.*

1951 Taylor, Sir William L. *Estate Forestry.*

1953 Brasnett, N.V. *Planned Management of Forests.*

1953 Edlin, H.L. *The Forester's Handbook.*

1953 Knuchel, H. *Planning and Control in the Managed Forest.*

1953 Petrini, S. *Elements of Forest Economics,* translated from the Swedish by M.L. Anderson.

1954 Champion, H.G. *Forestry.*
1954 Hiley, W.E. *Woodland Management,* 2nd edn 1967 revised by C.W. Scott and R.W.V. Palmer.
1955 Gordon, W.A. *The Law of Forestry.*
1955 James, N.D.G. *The Forester's Companion,* 2nd edn 1966.
1955 Robbie, T.A. *Forestry.*
1956 Bolton, Lord *Profitable Forestry.*
1956 Edlin, H.L. *Trees, Woods and Man,* 2nd edn 1966.
1956 Edlin, H.L. and Nimmo, M. *Tree Injuries, Their causes and their prevention.*
1956 Hiley, W.E. *Economics of Plantations.*
1956 Kostler, J. *Silviculture,* translated from the German by M.L. Anderson.
1956 Larsen, C. Syrach *Genetics in Silviculture,* translated from the Danish by M.L. Anderson.
1958 Edlin, H.L. *England's Forests.*
1958 Huggard, E.R. *Forester's Engineering Handbook.*
1959 Huggard, E.R. and Owen, T.H. *Forest Machinery.*
1962 Ailesbury, the Marquess of, *A History of Savernake Forest.*
1962 Hart, C.E. *Practical Forestry for the Agent and Surveyor.*
1962 Peace, T.R. *Pathology of Trees and Shrubs.*
1964 Hiley, W.E. *A Forestry Venture.*
1967 Johnson, D.R., Grayson, A.J. and Bradley, R.T. *Forest Planning.*
1968 Osmaston, F.C. *The Management of Forests.*
1968 Pettit, P.A.J. *The Royal Forests of Northamptonshire.*
1969 Ryle, G.B. *Forest Service.*
1969 Lorrain-Smith, R. *The Economy of the Private Woodland in Great Britain.*
1974 Deal, Warwick *Growing Trees for Profit.*
1976 Rackham, O. **Trees and Woodland in the British Landscape.*

APPENDIX IV

GOVERNMENT REPORTS ON FORESTS AND FORESTRY 1787–1957

In this Appendix are set out some of the principal reports on forests and forestry which have been prepared by Royal Commissions, Departmental Committees and other similar bodies appointed by the Government from 1787 to 1957.

1787 Reports of the Commissioners appointed to enquire into the State and
to   Condition of the Woods, Forests and Land Revenues of the Crown and other
1793 Unimproveable Rents.

1787	1st Report:	Properties leased from the Crown
1787	2nd Report:	Particulars of Rents
1788	3rd Report:	Forest of Dean
1789	4th Report:	Report on Rents

1789	5th Report:	New Forest
1790	6th Report:	Alice Holt and Woolmer Forests
1790	7th Report:	Salcey Forest
1792	8th Report:	Whittlewood Forest
1792	9th Report:	Rockingham Forest
1792	10th Report:	Whichwood Forest
1792	11th Report:	Naval Timber
1792	12th Report:	Observations on Management
1792	13th Report:	Bere Forest
1793	14th Report:	Sherwood Forest
1793	15th Report:	Waltham Forest
1793	16th Report:	Classification of Rents
1793	17th Report:	The Office of Surveyor General

1812 First Report of the Commissioners of His Majesty's Woods, Forests and Land Revenues.

1816 Second Report of the Commissioners of His Majesty's Woods, Forests and Land Revenues.
Note These two Reports are known as the Second Series.

1848 Report from the Select Committee on the Woods, Forests and Land Revenues of the Crown; together with the Minutes of Evidence.

1849 First Report from the Select Committee on the Woods, Forests and Land Revenues of the Crown; together with the Minutes of Evidence and Appendix.

1850 Report of the Royal New and Waltham Forests Commission.

1854 Report from the Select Committee on Crown Forests; together with the Proceedings of the Committee, Minutes of Evidence, Appendix and Index.

1885 Report from the Select Committee on Forestry together with the Proceedings of the Committee, Minutes of Evidence, and Appendix.

1886 Report from the Select Committee on Forestry together with the Proceedings of the Committee and Minutes of Evidence.

1887 Report from the Select Committee on Forestry together with the Proceedings of the Committee, Minutes of Evidence, and Appendix.

1890 Report from the Select Committee on the Woods, Forests and Land Revenues of the Crown.

1902 Report of the Departmental Committee appointed by the Board of Agriculture to inquire into and report on British Forestry; with copy of the Minute appointing the Committee. (Cd 1319).

1903 Minutes of Evidence taken before the Departmental Committee appointed by the Board of Agriculture to inquire into and report on British Forestry; with Appendices and Index. (Cd 1565).

1909 Second Report (on Afforestation) of the Royal Commission appointed to inquire into and to report on certain questions affecting Coast Erosion, the Reclamation of Tidal Lands, and Afforestation in the United Kingdom. (Cd 4460).

1909 Minutes of Evidence and Appendicies thereto accompanying the Second Report (On Afforestation) of the Royal Commission appointed to inquire into and to report on certain questions affecting Coast Erosion, the Reclamation of Tidal Lands and Afforestation in the United Kingdom. (Cd 4461).

1913   Advisory Committee on Forestry. Committee appointed by the Board of
        Agriculture and Fisheries to advise on matters relating to the Development of
        Forestry. Reports — July to October, 1912. (Cd 6713).

1918   Reconstruction Committee. Forestry Sub-Committee. Final Report. (Cd 8881).
        Note This Report is commonly referred to as 'The Acland Report'.

1943   Post-War Forest Policy. Report by H.M. Forestry Commissioners. (Cmd
        6447).

1944   Post-War Forest Policy. Private Woodlands. Supplementary Report by H.M.
        Forestry Commissioners. (Cmd 6500).

1956   Report of the Committee on Marketing of Woodland Produce.
        Note This Report is also known as 'The Watson Report'.

1955   Report of the Committee on Hedgerow and Farm Timber.

1957   Forestry, Agriculture and Marginal Land. A Report by the Natural Resources
        (Technical) Committee.
        Note This Report is sometimes referred to as 'The Zuckerman Report'.

APPENDIX V

COMMITTEES OF THE FORESTRY COMMISSION
1920—76

The Committees which are included in this Appendix are arranged in chronological
order according to the year in which they were appointed.

CONSULTATIVE COMMITTEES 1920-45

The Forestry Act, 1919, s.6. provided for the establishment of Consultative
Committees for England, Wales, Scotland and Ireland and directed that each of these
Committees should include among its members, representatives of certain bodies
together with persons who had appropriate interests and knowledge. These comprised
the Board of Agriculture and Fisheries (in the case of England); county councils or
other local bodies interested in forestry; societies concerned with afforestation;
woodland owners; representatives of labour and persons who had practical experience
of matters relating to forestry, woodcraft and woodland industries. On the passing of
the Forestry Act 1945, the Consultative Committees were replaced by the National
Committees.

ADVISORY COMMITTEE ON FOREST RESEARCH 1929 TO DATE

This Committee was constituted in December 1929 and the names of the original
members are set out in the 10th Annual Report of the Forestry Commissioners for
1929, although for the first year it was known as the Advisory Committee on Forestry

Research. In February 1960, it was reconstituted 'to cover the wider field now required' and its terms of reference were 'to review the Commissioner's programme of research and advise generally on research problems' (41st Annual Report).

HOME GROWN TIMBER COMMITTEE 1931-33

This Committee was appointed in 1931 in order to 'advise the Commissioners on the subject' i.e., home grown timber, and details of its constitution are given in the 13th Annual Report. An interim report was made in September 1932 and after submitting its final report, the Committee was disbanded in 1933.

HOME GROWN TIMBER ADVISORY COMMITTEE 1939 TO DATE

Set up 'early in 1939', this Committee consisted of 'representatives of the Home Grown Timber Trade, woodland owners, the Board of Trade and the Commission' (30th Annual Report). Under the Forestry Act 1951, s.15, it became a Statutory Committee and was limited to a maximum of 26 members. In 1963, the Committee was reconstituted in view of the recommendations of the Committee on Marketing of Woodland Produce ('The Watson Committee') and three independent members were added, one of whom was appointed chairman (44th Annual Report). In the following year, the constitution of the Committee was again altered by omitting all Forestry Commission members (45th Annual Report).

During 1963 and 1964, two sub-committees were formed within the Advisory Committee as follows (45th Annual Report):

Utilisation Committee

Set up in April 1963, this was previously the Advisory Committee of the Utilisation of Home Grown Timber.

Pitwood Sub-Committee

Appointed in April 1964.

In 1965, the Utilisation Committee was re-formed as the Technical Sub-Committee (47th Annual Report), while in July 1971, the Mechanical Development Committee (q.v.) was transferred to the Technical Sub-Committee (52nd Annual Report).

THE NATIONAL COMMITTEES 1945 TO DATE

These Statutory Committees were appointed under the Forestry Act, 1945, s.3, and replaced the Consultative Committees, one Committee being appointed for England, Wales and Scotland, respectively (26th Annual Report). The Committees held their first meetings in November 1945 and their duties and list of members are given in the 27th Annual Report.

REGIONAL ADVISORY COMMITTEES 1946 TO DATE

These were set up in 1946, one Committee being appointed for each Forestry Commission Conservancy. They were established 'with the primary purpose of providing a close link between the Conservator and all those within the Conservancy who are interested in forestry' (27th Annual Report). Under the Forestry Act 1951, s.15, they became Statutory Committees and their constitution was laid down in the Act. In October 1974, the Committees were reconstituted in order to include representatives of agricultural, local planning and amenity interests as well as forestry (54th Annual Report).

ADVISORY COMMITTEE OF THE UTILISATION OF HOME GROWN TIMBER 1949-62

This Committee was originally established in December 1949 with the following terms of reference: 'to advise the Commissioners on measures designed to promote the utilisation and sale of produce from British woodlands' (31st Annual Report). It was reconstituted with effect from 1st October 1960 (41st Annual Report), but in 1963 the Committee became a sub-committee of the Home Grown Timber Advisory Committee and became known as the Utilisation Committee (45th Annual Report).

MECHANICAL DEVELOPMENT COMMITTEE 1959-71

The 40th Annual Report refers to the appointment of an 'Advisory Committee on Machinery Research' but in the 41st Report it is referred to as the Mechanical Development Committee. In 1971, the Committee was transferred to the Technical Sub-Committee of the Home Grown Timber Advisory Committee (52nd Annual Report). In 1972 the following new terms of reference were given to the Sub-Committee:

> *To advise the Home Grown Timber Advisory Committee on the technical aspects of:*
> *(a) harvesting and other forest operations*
> *(b) transport and utilisation of forest produce*
> *To examine, exchange and disseminate technical information within the forest industry.*
> *(52nd Annual Report).*

MARKETING LIAISON COMMITTEES 1963 TO DATE

Five Marketing Liaison Committees were set up in 1963 which covered the whole of

England and Wales. Their membership, as stated in the 44th Annual Report, comprised representatives of the Timber Growers' Organisation, the Federated Home Timber Associations and the Forestry Commission.

FORESTRY TRAINING COUNCIL 1971 TO DATE

Although this body is not a standing committee it has been included since it is appointed by the Commission. It was formed in 1971 when forestry interests withdrew from the Agricultural, Horticultural and Forestry Industry Training Board (52nd Annual Report).

FORESTRY SAFETY COUNCIL 1974 TO DATE

As in the case of the Forestry Training Council, this is not a standing committee but is appointed by the Commission. It was set up in April 1974 and the 55th Annual Report gives the terms of reference, membership and other details.

APPENDIX VI

SOME NOTABLE DATES IN FOREST HISTORY 1184—1975

1184   The Assize of the Forest (also known as the Assize of Woodstock)
1217   The Charter of the Forest
1482   An Act for inclosing of woods in Forests, Chases and Purlieus
1543   An Act for the Preservation of Woods
1558   An Act that timber shall not be felled to make coals for burning of iron
1598   Publication of *A Treatise and Discourse of the Lawes of the Forrest* by John Manwood
1611   *The Commons Complaint* by Arthur Standish. This was the first work concerned with the planting of trees for timber production
1664   John Evelyn's *Sylva or a Discourse on Forest Trees* published
1668   An Act for the increase and preservation of timber within the Forest of Dean
1676   Publication of *The Manner of Raising, Ordering and Improving Forest-Trees* by Moses Cook
1698   An Act for the increase and preservation of timber in the New Forest in the County of Southampton
1758   The Society of Arts (now the Royal Society of Arts) instituted awards for the establishment of young plantations of exceptional merit
1786   An Act for appointing Commissioners to enquire into the state and condition of the woods, forests. . . .
1809   Yield tables published by Charles Waistell

1847   Publication of *The Forester* by James Brown
1854   The Scottish Arboricultural Society founded (now The Royal Scottish Forestry
       Society)
1882   The English Arboricultural Society founded (now The Royal Forestry Society
       of England, Wales and Northern Ireland)
1884   The International Forestry Exhibition held in Edinburgh
1889   The first volume of *Schlich's Manual of Forestry* published
1893   The Exhibition of Horticulture and Forestry held at Earls Court, London
1897   Working plans drawn up for the Forest of Dean and High Meadow Woods
1903   A Lectureship in Forestry established at Armstrong College, Newcastle-on-
       Tyne
1904   School for woodmen opened at Parkend in the Forest of Dean
       First forestry exhibit staged by the Royal Agricultural Society of England at
       the Royal Show at Willesden, London
1905   The English Arboricultural Society became The Royal English Arboricultural
       Society
       The School of Forestry founded at Oxford
1907   A Readership in Forestry established at Cambridge
       The first technically trained forest officer employed by the Crown (E.P. Popert
       appointed as Superintendent Forester in the Forest of Dean)
       First forestry display exhibited by the Bath and West and Southern Counties
       Society at their show at Newport, Monmouthshire
1909   First competition for forestry plantations held by the Royal Agricultural
       Society of England
1916   Sub-Committee of the Reconstruction Committee ('The Acland Committee')
       appointed
1917   Report of the Acland Committee published
1919   The Forestry Commission established under The Forestry Act 1919
1923   Woods and forests under the management or control of the Commissioners of
       Woods transferred to the Forestry Commissioners under the Forestry (Transfer
       of Woods) Act, 1923
1924   Imperial Forestry Institute (now the Commonwealth Forestry Institute)
       founded at Oxford
       Bedgebury Pinetum established
1925   The Society of Foresters of Great Britain (now the Institute of Foresters)
       formed
       Forest Products Research Laboratory set up
1928   *Report on Census of Woodlands . . . 1924,* issued
1931   The Royal English Arboricultural Society changed its name to the Royal
       English Forestry Society
1934   The Home-Grown Timber Marketing Association formed
1935   The National Home-Grown Timber Council set up and constituted as a limited
       company in 1936
1939   The Timber Control Department of the Ministry of Supply came into operation
       on 3rd September
1942   Women's Timber Corps formed in March

1943   *Report on Post-War Forest Policy* published
1944   *Report on Post-War Forest Policy Private Woodlands* published
1945   Forestry Act 1945
1947   Forestry Act 1947
1948   United Kingdom Forestry Committee set up
1951   Forestry Act 1951
        Central Forestry Examination Board of the United Kingdom established
1952   *Report on Census of Woodlands 1947-1949* issued
1954   Centenary of the Royal Scottish Forestry Society
1955   *Report of the Committee on Hedgerow and Farm Timber* published
1956   One million acres of forest planted by the Forestry Commission in Great
        Britain
        Report of the Committee on Marketing of Woodland Produce ('The Watson
        Committee') published
1957   Report of the Natural Resources (Technical) Committee ('The Zuckerman
        Committee') issued under the title of *Forestry, Agriculture and Marginal Land*
1958   The Timber Growers Organisation Ltd established
1959   The Forest Tree Seed Association of England and Wales formed
        The Forestry Committee of Great Britain replaced the United Kingdom Forestry
        Committee
1960   The Association of Professional Foresters founded
1967   Forestry Act 1967
1969   The Jubilee of the Forestry Commission
1970   Report entitled *Census of Woodlands 1965-67* issued
1971   The Forestry Training Council set up
        Forestry Commission adopted metrication
        The training school for foresters at Parkend which was founded in 1904, was
        closed
1971   The Wild Creatures and Forest Laws Act 1971
1974   The Forestry Safety Council set up
        The headquarters of the Forestry Commission established in Edinburgh
1975   The two millionth acre of forest planted by the Forestry Commission

INDEX

Two points should be noted in connection with this index. First, the names of societies have been given under their current titles and second, the contents of the Appendices have not been included except in the case of Appendix V.